KEEP SWEET

KEEP SWEET

Children of Polygamy

Debbie Palmer • Dave Perrin

To Lorena:
Have a good read.
July 23, 2006

DAVE'S PRESS

Published by Dave's Press Inc.
Box 616, Lister, British Columbia
Canada V0B 1Y0

Library and Archives Canada Cataloguing in Publication

Palmer, Debbie, 1955-
Keep sweet : children of polygamy / Debbie Palmer, David Perrin.

ISBN 0-9687943-3-5

1. Polygamy—British Columbia—Creston Region. 2. United Effort Plan (Mormon Sect) 3. Teenage marriage—British Columbia—Creston Region. 4. Child sexual abuse—Religious aspects—Mormon Church. 5. Collective settlements—British Columbia—Creston Region. I. Perrin, David, 1948- II. Title.
HQ994.P34 2004 306.84'23'0971162 C2004-906370-7

Cover and book design by Warren Clark
Production by Emily Dehaan-Clark
Cover background photograph by Willem Lankhaar
Edited by Dave Perrin
Copyedited by Betsy Brierley
Proofread by Elizabeth McLean

Printed and bound in Canada by Houghton Boston

Grateful acknowledgment is made to the following for permission to reprint previously published material:

Peer International Corporation. Lyric excerpt from "You Are My Sunshine" by Jimmie Davis. Copyright ©1940 by Peer International Corporation. Copyright © renewed. International rights secured. Used by permission. All rights reserved.

Society of Authors, London. "The Highwayman" by Alfred Noyes. Copyright © 1906. Excerpt reprinted with permission of the Society of Authors as the literary representative of the estate of Alfred Noyes.

Norman Gimbel. Lyric excerpt from "The Reverend Mr. Black," words and music by Billy Edd Wheeler, Jerry Leiber, and Mike Stoller. Copyright © 1962. Copyright renewed © 1990, Bexhill Music Corp. Used by permission.

This book is for my eight children—
independent, stubborn souls
who lived through unspeakable horrors
before I brought them out,
and who have worked hard
to build fulfilling,
productive lives.

Authors' Acknowledgments

Debbie Palmer—

I want to recognize all the children who continue to live inside closed polygamous communities throughout North America, children who lack the education to make informed choices, who face traumas every day, and who remain unheard and unseen.

I want to acknowledge Dave Perrin, who challenged me to save my manuscript from the fire and agreed to struggle with me through the tears, the horror, the pain, and hope until my initial rough work became this book.

Thank you to Dr. Gary Deatherage, Beryl Mason, Blaine Munro, Sandra Champion, Aunt Carmon, and Lorna, who helped me come to know how to think, not what to think, and to realize that I would not be destroyed by a vengeful God in the process.

To Jon Krakauer, whose work in *Under the Banner of Heaven* has shone morning light onto communities where secrets and abuses have proliferated in the darkness for decades. To the human rights activists both here and in the United States who are fighting for the education and freedom of children, women, and men who are trapped in the most dangerous and destructive of polygamous groups.

To the child who was my friend "Jeanie" for being there with me in those early years of travail. To my sisters and brothers whose quiet dignity and grace have inspired and helped me in some of my darkest hours—you know who you are.

I here acknowledge indebtedness to my abusers, because even while very often they isolated me from flesh and blood friends, they taught me how to read. And finally, thank you to the Creator for gifting me with the strength and the "unfortunate privilege" to have survived this life with the ability to speak and educate so people who are born "on the outside" will never underestimate the value of their rights and freedom.

Dave Perrin—
My appreciation goes to Debbie Palmer for her courage; to Betsy Brierley for her tireless work in copyediting, research, and permissions; to Warren and Emily Clark for their creative flair; to Elizabeth McLean for proofreading and pertinent advice; and to Billy Edd Wheeler of Swannanoa, North Carolina, for his assistance in obtaining permission to quote from his song, "The Rev. Mr. Black."

I will always remember the encouragement of dear friends and family when the goalposts kept moving and completing this book seemed an impossible task.

Note to the reader

The events in this book are taken from early memories, letters, and journals, and are true as far as the author knows them to be. Most names have been changed to protect people's privacy.

Prologue

My father had six wives and I have forty-seven brothers and sisters. My oldest daughter is my aunt and I am her grandmother. When I was assigned to marry my first husband, I became my own step-grandmother since my father was already married to two daughters of my new husband. According to the eternal laws of the polygamous group I grew up with, I will be a step-grandmother to many of my own brothers and sisters "for time and all eternity."

Several of my stepsons were assigned to marry my sisters, so I also became a sister-in-law to my own stepchildren. After my mother's father was assigned to marry one of my second husband's daughters as a second wife, I became my own great-grandmother. This stepdaughter became my step-grandmother and I her stepmother, so when I gave birth to two sons with her father, my own sons became my great-uncles and I was their great-great-grandmother.

My ancestors were fierce and uncompromising when it came to religion. Once converted and baptized into the Fundamentalist Church of Jesus Christ of Latter Day Saints, they became more entrenched in their beliefs with every hardship and persecution brought on by the "Gentiles," a term which is all-inclusive for people who are non-members. Many members of my family and extended family, including the three men I was assigned to by the prophet of our particular group of Mormon Fundamentalists, were drawn by the teachings of Joseph Smith and plural marriage to one place—the Creston Valley in British Columbia, Canada.

Grandpa Romney, Michael Merrick, and Kelvin Whitmer had been having cottage meetings in Rosemary, Alberta, with curious members of the Church of Jesus Christ of Latter-day Saints since 1945. Uncle Kelvin was related to a man by the name of Owen LeBaron who had been assisting Saint Joseph White Musser to print and distribute pamphlets outlining their beliefs. According to their testimonies, the sacred principle of plural and celestial marriage revealed to Joseph Smith in the early days of the church was the *only* way to get to the highest degree of celestial glory to be kings and queens, gods and goddesses. Owen and his brothers worked tirelessly with Saint Joseph White Musser to publish a set of books called *Truth* to educate as many members of the church as would "answer the call of the elect." This sophisticated collection of stories and mysteriously recovered "revelations" became the main source of information that Owen presented to Kelvin Whitmer and anyone else who would listen.

Uncle Michael was the first one to pray for a testimony. He had a dream about a valley God had created where His chosen people from Canada could live together away from the critical eyes of Gentiles and dissenting relatives in the church. He jumped a train to the East Kootenay region of southern B.C. and got off in the Creston Valley, where he had an aunt. He heard of a piece of land for sale in a part of the valley called Lister, which was only a short walk from the American border. When Uncle Michael set foot on the land in question, he swore it was the place he had seen in his dream.

By 1946 he had moved his wife, Loren, and children to this chosen land where he was determined to raise his children as "calves in a stall," away from the influences of the world. Michael and Loren had both served missions for the church and had been married in the Cardston Temple. As soon as they were settled in their mountain valley, they began searching for someone who had the "priesthood power and authority from God" to perform plural marriages. They prayed with Aunt Loren's sister Pauline from Idaho and decided God meant for the sisters to both be married to Uncle Michael. They traveled to Salt Lake City and met Saint Joseph White Musser, who assured them he had the required priesthood from God to perform the marriage.

Michael held a high profile in Rosemary—as a dairyman, a teacher, and an elder in the LDS Church. With the same missionary zeal he had displayed during his assignment for the church in Eastern Canada, Michael approached his friends and relatives in Alberta, giving everyone the opportunity to join the Lord's "Work" and continue the sacred principle of polygamy. Before he could convince all the people he felt would join him, stories about evil men tempting the good members of "God's only true church" spread like a prairie fire through southern Alberta.

Michael's uncle, Isaac Merrick, was the same age as Michael. Isaac quickly embraced the law of plural marriage and its promise to become a god and govern over people on his own earths. He had just returned from a mission to New Zealand, where he converted and baptized more people in his two years than any other missionary in the church. He bought into Michael's thinking and was determined to convince the rest of his brothers to join them. Although none of them did, the LDS Church looked on them with suspicion for many years.

The oldest Merrick brother, who had been a well-known politician, was excommunicated for refusing to denounce his brother Isaac and his son Michael. Although he was not interested in having more than one wife, he claimed he couldn't denounce his son and nephew because the church still taught the principle of the plurality of wives in the temple ceremonies, and Joseph Smith's revelation had never been repudiated. He maintained that the manifesto given by Wilford Woodruff in 1890 to condemn the practice of polygamy in order to pacify the government of the United States was not a revelation and did not contravene the serious commandment God gave to Joseph Smith to preserve plural marriage.

Uncle Isaac traveled to Salt Lake City to meet with Saint Joseph White Musser and John Y. Barlow, the leaders of God's chosen people. They convinced him that the Church of Jesus Christ of Latter-day Saints no longer held the keys to the priesthood. When he asked if he should gather with the Saints living in Colorado City, the apostles told him that he and the Canadian faithful should remain in their own country, because God needed men with the true power of the priesthood all along the chain of the Rocky Mountains. They prophesied that when the earth was being cleansed in preparation for the Second Coming of Christ, it would only be the powerful "prayer circles" of our elect people from Canada to Mexico that would save the earth from being torn asunder. Although John Y. Barlow was a dying man, he impressed on the minds of these fiery converts that only the very elect, the "heart's core of the heart's core" of men born and raised in the church, could survive the call, make the Work grow, and save the earth. Few men, they were told, would have the courage and "faith of the ancients" to follow the secret teachings. These Canadian converts took it as a special challenge that they and their wives and children could expect to be persecuted, hated, and reviled as soon as they were fully engaged in the true Work of the Lord and living the principle of plural marriage.

When John Y. Barlow died, there was a struggle to determine who the new prophet should be and a resultant three-way split of his followers. The LeBarons took all the people who would follow them and moved to Mexico. Rulon Allred gathered those who considered him to be the prophet and started a community in Montana with a few faithful scattered throughout Utah. The rest of the apostles reformed their Council of Seven with LeRoy Sunderland Johnson as its head and prophet. The Canadian converts decided Uncle LeRoy was the man who held the true keys of the priesthood.

In 1953, Uncle Isaac followed Uncle Michael and Uncle Kelvin to the Creston Valley and experienced another miracle when he was able to purchase a ranch right next to his nephew. Around that time Uncle Kelvin met a man by the name of Harry Manning. As soon as his family converted, the new prophet married Harry's daughters Celia and Enid to Kelvin on the same day. This was an exciting event for the growing group since it was the first marriage performed by a prophet in Canada. The celebration was especially sweet for Uncle LeRoy because the persecution of his people in the community of Short Creek, Arizona, by the American government had been resolved only a few months earlier.

Grandpa Romney finally invited my father, Adam Nilsson, who was courting his daughter Vivien, to learn about the secrets of the kingdom of God. Daddy liked the idea and was anxious to be part of the Work. After several years of study, he decided to leave the church and the prairies behind and join the "Lord's anointed" in Lister.

My story begins when Uncle Michael and his family were building homes for Gentiles and operating a secondhand store in the town of Creston; Uncle Isaac was surviving mainly by hauling hay for farmers in the valley. Uncle Kelvin moved into Creston because he needed work, and there wasn't enough room in their tiny cabin for three wives. Both Uncle Isaac and Uncle Michael said Uncle Kelvin was weak and had a hard time leaving gentile ways—otherwise, the Lord would have opened up a way for him to earn money in the group. Uncle Isaac prophesied every Sunday during our meetings that Uncle Kelvin would "rue the day" he didn't keep his children away from gentile influences.

By this time, Uncle Isaac had three wives: Bettilyn, Naomi, and Lydia. His third wife, Aunt Lena, died when she was having a baby or he would have had four. He had been sealed to his first wife, Bettilyn, in the Mormon temple in Cardston just like Daddy had been sealed to Mother before they joined the Work. Naomi, Uncle Isaac's niece, had gone on a mission for the church and joined the army in the United States before coming back to Canada and marrying her uncle. Aunt Lena was her little sister. Lydia was a sister to Uncle Kelvin's two youngest wives, and all of us little kids were scared of her.

Although Uncle Michael and Uncle Isaac didn't see eye to eye on much beyond the principle of plural marriage, they both agreed that the Hutterites were the best example of how God meant for the United Order to be lived. They both favored the way the Hutterites consecrated their work to the one colony. It made sense to Uncle Isaac and Uncle Michael that no one be rich, but no one should be really poor, either. They were sure this should be the model for the United Effort Plan that our prophet and his council were organizing.

Each man was adamant he should be the "file leader" for the Canadian followers. Because Uncle Michael had arrived in the community four years before Uncle Isaac, the members of Michael's family were determined he had seniority and should be the leader. However, on the ranch where I lived, there was no question who was in charge in Canada.

The Families

Isaac Merrick

His wives:	*Bettilyn's children:*	*Naomi's children:*	*Lydia's children:*	*Deborah's children:*
Bettilyn	Janessa (Jan)	Irene	Thomas	Janessa Dawn (Jan Dawn)
Naomi	Lemuel (Lem)	Aline	Priscilla	
Lydia	Laman	Jonah	Velma	
Emilia	Emilia	Jean (Jeanie)	4 more boys	
Deborah	Martin	Ward	3 more girls	
	James	Katy		
	Nephi	Joab		
	Ophelia	Rhoda		
	Phoebe	Pamela		
	Babette			
	Joseph			
	Nora			
	1 more boy			

Michael Merrick

His wives:	*Loren's children:*	*Pauline's children:*
Loren	Erica	Reeny
Pauline	Lavina	2 boys
	Ralph	2 more girls
	Gilby	
	Art	
	Evan	
	2 more girls	
	1 more boy	

Kelvin Whitmer

His wives:	*Genevieve's children:*	*Enid's children:*	*Celia's children:*
Genevieve	Selena	Liam	Lucia
Enid	Derek	2 girls	Leora
Celia	Lorena		Robert
	Rose		Eugene
	Sidney (Sid)		Isaac
	Grady		1 more girl
	Nuela		5 more boys
	6 more boys		
	1 more girl		

Adam Nilsson

His wives:	*Vivien's children:*	*Jan's children:*	*Irene's children:*	*Elsa's children:*
Vivien	Deb	Lena	Grant	Jarom
Jan	Nettie	Tabitha	Nakita	Natalia
Irene	Brent	Rebecca	5 more girls	5 more girls
Elsa		Nanette	5 more boys	3 more boys
		6 boys		
		4 more girls		

CHAPTER 1

I was having a really bad day. From the moment I woke up and went to Mother for my morning hug, Jan was talking as if she were in church.

"Vivien, I don't know why you waste your time worrying about the lost causes in our Work. I've had to give up all my aunts, uncles, and cousins in Cardston because they won't join the Work. You'll just have to get used to it."

My stomach tied in knots when Daddy's second wife sounded so annoyed, and I went outside to get away from the bad feelings. The moment was haunted by the early morning calls of the killdeer and the howling of coyotes under the rock formation we called the devil's chair. The sun was still hiding, but by nine the mists would clear, and the land would be dry enough so the haying crew could get to the fields.

The moment I closed the cabin door, I heard a lonely wail. At first I wondered if it was one of the wild animals I could hear at night when I was trying to go to sleep. When I stepped onto the little porch where the yellow rose bush was blooming, I could see baby Thomas sitting at the end of the long boardwalk that led to the milking barn. It wasn't as bad today as when I had found him sitting in a puddle, his white-blond hair streaked with the muddy water. Then, he had been wearing nothing but a cloth diaper and a T-shirt, and his body was blue to the lips.

Today he was just dusty. When I called Mother to come see, she ran and scooped him up, not minding the dirt that he got on her clean blouse and skirt. As she rushed him into the cabin she shook her head and muttered, "How on earth does a baby who can barely walk get out of the house without anyone noticing? He's sick so often anyway, it'll be a miracle if he doesn't get pneumonia."

The grown-ups were always saying baby Thomas might die because he was premature and had been born in a gentile hospital. I was terrified for him and watched carefully as Mother warmed him by the cookstove.

Jan's thin braids bounced with righteous energy as she harrumphed and railed on in a high-pitched, impatient tone. "I don't know what you're so worried about—he's bound to be tougher than he looks. If his mother had real faith, she wouldn't have had him in the hospital, and he wouldn't be like this! No one needs doctors or hospitals—especially to have babies. Being sick is just a state of mind."

Mother didn't answer. Her face was sad as she gently bathed Thomas and put him into our baby Brent's clothes to send him back to the big ranch house.

Jan grabbed the baby with a jerk. She was peeved and resentful. "Really, Vivien, it's beyond me why Lydia can't stay home and take care of her own kid instead of flying into one of her insane fits and running to town to complain to her mother. Why is she always leaving him for the rest of us to care for? She's been nothing but a trial ever since she thought she was old enough to marry Daddy...The least she can do is grow up! Momma says all the time Lydia would be lots better off if she just wouldn't let evil spirits possess her."

She made a sharp turn toward Mother, and Thomas's head, too big for his frail body, jerked forward trying to catch up. Jan stomped her foot. "I can't believe I ever thought I was best friends with her. She's such a spoiled brat! No wonder Naomi yells at her—Lydia would be an absolutely impossible sister wife. I don't think even you could be sweet enough to figure her out."

"I know what you're talking about, Janessa...but all the people who are living around us here are supposed to be part of our new priesthood family. If we can't work together and try to stop the malicious gossiping and fault-finding, I don't see how Heavenly Father and the prophet can use us." Even though her voice was quiet, her meaning was clear. Jan stopped complaining.

An uncomfortable silence fell over the room, and I raced to Mother. "Wouldn't today be a good day to stay home and make bread and draw things, Mother? I could play with Brent and Nettie and do finger-plays. We haven't done that for a long time." I spoke all in one rushed breath. Mother hugged me, then told me to go wake Nettie and she would come help us get dressed.

Jan's voice cut through me again as she turned to the door. "You know the way things are done around here, Vivien. It's high time Deb, Nettie, and Brent get used to running with the rest of the kids. They'll never be accepted if they get special treatment." She shot me a look of disgust. "Deb is such a trying child. Why can't she just act her age?" With little Thomas perched on her hip, she hustled from the room, her flour-sack skirt flipping behind her. The walls of the tiny cabin shook when she slammed the door.

Mother looked weary as she gathered me into her lap. Closing her eyes, she murmured, "The principle can be such a beautiful thing. I know we've done the right thing to come here...If people could just see the way the Lord means it to be."

Once Daddy had discovered the "Lord's anointed," our family left the prairies behind and gathered with the Saints here in these mountains. Rosemary, Alberta, where almost everyone who joined our Work had come from, was now only a homesick ache in my four-year-old heart. We lived in a cabin built at the foot of a hill in the middle of Uncle Isaac Merrick's ranch. My daddy, Adam, had two wives now. A little while ago Uncle Isaac's daughter, sixteen-year-old Janessa—from his first wife Bettilyn—was married to Daddy, and he now stood proudly shoulder to shoulder with the rest of the servants of the Lord.

Uncle LeRoy Sunderland Johnson—we called him Uncle Roy—was God's anointed prophet. He told Daddy and Jan in solemn tones, "You have proven your worthiness to enter the high and holy principle of plural marriage and can be sealed with the sanction of the priesthood. You've paid the price and sacrificed your feelings as I instructed you to do. I can now reveal to you the Lord's will, as He has revealed it to me."

His voice trembled with fervor. "Adam, we find among our people in the States that those who have had to sacrifice the most—friends, family, the apostate church—to live the highest redeeming principles of the gospel, are the most faithful. We feel that even though you joined us only recently, you are ready. You have passed the test of separating yourself from the church and your family who will not answer the call. Many men twice your age have not passed this test. Welcome!"

Our holy prophet turned solemnly to Mother. "You will add jewels to your husband's crown by consenting to live the law of Sarah* and give this good sister to your husband to wife."

With a commanding air despite his gray hair and stooped shoulders, Uncle Roy ushered the witnesses into the little bedroom off the kitchen in the white-gabled ranch house. He turned to the group and told them to hold their right hands to the square.**

"Do you all swear to stand before God as witnesses of this ceremony and protect each other and these good people from Satan and his gentile influences that would strike down the actions of the Lord's servant this day?"

---

*Celestial or plural marriage (the law of Sarah) originated as a revelation to Joseph Smith. It refers to Sarah in the Book of Genesis—Sarah was barren and gave her handmaid to Abraham to bear him a child. Section 132 of the Mormon scriptures, The Doctrine and Covenants, is the foundation of Mormon Fundamentalism: "And if he have ten virgins given unto him by this law, he cannot commit adultery, for they belong to him, and they are given unto him; therefore, is he justified...But if one or either of the ten virgins, after she is espoused, shall be with another man, she has committed adultery, and shall be destroyed...And if any man have a wife and he teaches her these things...then shall she believe and administer unto him, or she shall be destroyed, saith the Lord your God; for I will destroy her."

**Putting arms to the square is a ritual of the Church of Jesus Christ of Latter-day Saints and fundamentalist offshoots. It is used by men in meetings and ceremonies that require special powers from God. Putting both arms to the square is usually reserved for occasions when men of the higher priesthood call on God to protect the group or to put a curse on enemies.

They obeyed the directive and solemnly took the oath. One of Uncle Roy's apostles, Uncle Guy Musser, perspiration shining on his smooth head and a triumphant gleam in his eyes, declared the battle cry, "A victory for the side of the principle of plural marriage and the Lord! We're glad to have you on our side, Adam."

Mother's face was wet with tears as she instructed Jan and placed her hand into Daddy's, carefully helping to guide their fingers into the patriarchal grip—the sure sign of the nail.* Mother was in awe. "My heart is full of joy. I'm so grateful to be found worthy to live this holy law." She embraced Jan, saying, "Welcome to our family."

Jan had been at our little cabin with Mother and Daddy a lot over the months before their marriage, and Daddy had spent hours with her in the barn and on walks. Once she turned sixteen and got the inspiration she should marry Daddy, she was anxious to become a plural wife in the Work. Even though Mother was happy about the idea, the prophet told Jan she needed to wait for him to pray and ask the Lord if it was truly His will. He said there had been too many cases of men with lustful hearts who were full of false pride having revelations about beautiful young girls belonging to them.

He told Uncle Isaac that the priesthood brethren were putting a stop to men thinking they could run after young girls at will, and were starting the system of "placement marriage," whereby God would tell the prophet exactly who each young woman promised to marry in the pre-existence. He said too many girls were having revelations about marrying young men who hadn't "proven themselves" to the priesthood.

Jan was upset when he told her that, because there had been at least four plural weddings in Canada in 1957 where the people picked each other. But when she thought about it, she agreed. She

---

*The patriarchal grip is a ritual placing of hands during wedding ceremonies performed in the Mormon Church. The couple clasps right hands, interlocking their little fingers and placing tips of forefingers on the center of the wrist to signify Christ's being nailed to the cross. It is also a handshake of recognition between men—inside the temple or at secret ceremonies of polygamous groups.

said she would be glad to wait a thousand times over if she had a chance at a man as good and handsome as Daddy and a sister wife as generous as Mother. She said she knew of no other woman who could stay as sweet as Mother, even when Daddy and her intended sister wife came back from the barn after visiting with each other.

Patriarch Arlo Whitmer, who was related to Uncle Kelvin Whitmer, had given my mother her blessing when she was just fifteen. Every child in the church and in our Work got to have a patriarchal blessing after they were twelve. A patriarch was ordained and set apart by the prophet to have special inspiration about each child. He would tell them what God wanted them to know about their life in the pre-existence, what God wanted them to do in this life, and what He would do with them in the next. I had known about Patriarch Whitmer since before we left Rosemary, because he told Mother in her blessing that she was so special to God He wasn't going to make her stay on this earth very long. Mother was going to go to the celestial kingdom and do good things to prepare for us and help Heavenly Father. The blessing said she wasn't going to be healthy, and that when life was too painful for her, she could leave. That worried me. I didn't want her body to hurt, but I sure wanted her to stay here with me.

I didn't want to leave her now to join the other kids. She had told me three times I had to go, but I was worried about her. How could I make sure she was okay if I wasn't with her all day? Mother was disappointed in me, and Jan was disgusted—that combination hurt worse than a licking.

Tears welled in Mother's eyes; her face was gaunt and pale. I threw my arms around her neck, begging as panic washed over me, "Please don't cry, Mother, I'll hug you better." I pulled her so tight my arms hurt. I was disappointed when she set me on the floor and handed me a dishtowel to dry the silverware.

She was moving slowly and as she pushed her feet into her saddle-oxford shoes she muttered, "I wish I knew why my feet and hands keep swelling like this. These shoes hurt my feet so much I can hardly stand to be on them...You need to go over your verses, Deb. Nettie has already learned hers."

Mother was determined to keep our minds as busy as our hands and had us practice our verses while we worked. Nettie was always good at doing two things at once, but I either lost my place in my verses or forgot about drying the dishes. Mother helped me with the 23rd Psalm. I was learning it for Grandmother when she came to visit from Rosemary. "The Lord is my shepherd; I shall not want..." I was doing well until I got to "Yea, though I walk through the valley and the shadow of death, I will fear no evil..."

"No, Deb," Mother corrected, "it's the valley *of* the shadow of death. You always get that part wrong. We must be very careful to say the verses from the Bible correctly. Remember the pictures in the Bible storybook I read you? You know how King David killed the lion with his bare hands and slew Goliath with a slingshot and saved the entire Israelite nation from the wicked Philistines. Heavenly Father inspired King David to write this psalm, so saying these words is like speaking God's words. We must know these scriptures to be good disciples of the Lord's Work.

"Once you've memorized it, you'll remember it always and be able to use it to comfort you when you're scared or sad. I say it or sing it with our hymns all the time. Remember to think really hard about the words. It's the valley *of* the shadow of death, not *and*. Okay, Deb...now start from the beginning and try very hard to keep it right."

Mother read to us from her big book of *Children's Bible Stories* so often we knew them off by heart, so getting a word wrong in this sacred psalm was mortifying. I said it to myself dozens of times in an attempt to memorize it, but trying to practice without Mother was difficult since I couldn't read myself. The worst of it was, every time I was sad or scared or worried, I could never remember the beautiful words. I still got stuck on, "Yea, though I walk through the valley and the shadow of death." I could never get to "I will fear no evil."

This valley of Uncle Isaac's must be like the valley King David was writing about, so I felt even worse that I couldn't get the words right. When I said my own prayers, I begged Heavenly Father to help me know why I was so afraid here. The heavy mists and cold fogs blocked the sun for weeks at a time in the winter. Janessa's mother, Bettilyn, said Aunt Lena and baby Elias died right here in this valley. Naomi, Uncle Isaac's second wife, talked about how all the kids were sick for a long time with scarlet fever, how she came in the house from doing chores after dark and looked into the room where the children were sleeping on the floor. It was lit with only a coal oil lamp, but she saw the angel of death hovering. She ran into the room praying and grabbed Emilia up, because somehow she knew, since Emilia was the most frail and couldn't even swallow water, that the angel of death had come for her. Emilia was a special spirit because she'd been born to Gentiles, but God had wanted her to be part of the Work, so he guided the Gentiles to let her be adopted by Uncle Isaac and Bettilyn. Naomi sat up all night watching, and in the morning Emilia opened her eyes and asked for her old dolly and some water. Naomi said she had to bend over real close to Emilia's little mouth to hear her whisper, "I kissed my little heart-sweet on the head-fore."

I asked Heavenly Father to help me remember the sunshine, the yellow roses with the butterflies stuck to them—all the beautiful things of the light. I thanked Him for letting Naomi beat the angel of death and save Emilia, but I couldn't shake the horror in my heart. Every night in my dreams, baby Thomas turned cold and became stuck in the black mud like a white baby statue. He grabbed Mother and pulled her into the mud and the fog until she disappeared. I ran frantically back and forth calling for them, but only a faint echo came back through the fog—like a taunt from the other side of a dark world.

The last chore of the morning was the braiding of our hair. Nettie's dark brown locks made a rope as thick as her arm, and Mother worked it into wonderful smooth braids. I sat down for her to start on mine, but I was in no hurry for her to finish, because as soon as it was done I knew we would have to go play with the other kids. I hated the confusion, the crying of babies, and the fighting that was always a part of it. Staying in the quiet cabin with Mother and just playing with one baby was much more appealing to me. That way, I didn't have to pretend I was as brave and tough as the rest of the kids. It was hard for me to get used to kids calling each other "stupid" and "idiot." I couldn't figure out how they could scream and fight and say they hated each other one minute, and then laugh and play together the next.

I'd get a spanking if I got caught screaming any of those words at anyone—"hate" was a word that you just didn't use around our house. Daddy even cried when Nettie and I had a fight once and I yelled, "I hate you!" to her. Daddy made me apologize and say extra prayers so I wouldn't forget. He said that love and forgiveness and kind words were the only ones acceptable for the people in our Work, and I was supposed to discipline myself to be a "good example" at all times, no matter what. Daddy told us about the "recording angels" who were assigned to each of us to follow us around all day, every day, and write notes about everything we said and did and take them to Heavenly Father every night. These notes would be permanently included on our eternal records, and unless we figured out how to repent and make atonement for our sins, we'd never get to be in heaven.

When I was out with the kids or helping as a kid-tender, I wasn't sure what being a good example meant. If I had tried to stop the kids from fighting and screaming at each other and using mean words, I'd have had to yell at the top of my lungs before they even heard me. Besides, I was just a little kid, and they would look at me like I had lost my marbles. I could just hear James and Jonah if they thought I was trying to boss them around; they'd claim I was acting like a "goody two-shoes." I was sure I would even get tossed into a cow-pie if I told them I was just talking about what the prophet wanted us to be like...and there were plenty of big fresh cow-pies all around where we played.

Mother interrupted my frantic thoughts. "It's time for you to take Nettie out to the rest of the kids. I want you to be good and help her out all you can. Janessa will come back before I go to the big house to help with dinner, and she won't like it if you two aren't out playing." I considered trying to beg again to stay in the cabin, but one look at Mother's weary face changed my mind. With a sigh, I grabbed Nettie by her tiny hand and went to join the noisy swarm outside.

Ophelia was the kid-tender for the day. She was ten years old and one of Uncle Isaac's daughters from Aunt Bettilyn—she was assigned to kid-tending most of the time. Twelve children from four different mothers were her charges this morning—all of us were under seven.

The huge filthy gray buggy groaned under the weight of four white-haired, freckle-faced babies. Baby Thomas was one of them. I always watched over him when no one else was noticing. He looked tired all the time. Today he was slumped over and his head bobbed up and down as the baby carriage bumped over the rocks and ruts of the path. I shivered in spite of the sun that had warmed the valley. The heat had chased away the morning mist, and I carefully stepped around cow patties on the hard-packed trail—sick at the thought of being a baby alone in a cold puddle.

When we made it to the sheep-herder shack under an old wild apple tree, Ophelia pulled a worn patchwork quilt out of the buggy and laid it on the ground. We girls who were already four or five years old carried the babies under the sheep-wire fence and onto the blanket, then passed her the diaper bag, the sandwiches, and the jars of water. Even though we were all supposed to stay with her and the squawking babies, she had to yell at us all the time to keep us close enough to be of any help. I was afraid to stray too far for fear someone might tell on me, but it was hard not to go see what the other guys were doing. Mother wouldn't be happy if she knew I didn't take part in the kid-tending. Jean, Jonah, and James were all Uncle Isaac's children; Naomi was Jean and Jonah's mother, and Bettilyn was mother to James. All three of them were real strong and smart, and no matter how hard I tried, I couldn't get used to their games or be brave enough to go exploring.

Within a few minutes of getting to the tree, the boys shinnied up the trunk to the bigger branches and crawled carefully out till the limbs started to bend. Then they shook apples down for us. All the kids but me and Nettie had pants with pockets to put apples in, so I made a little pouch with my skirt to horde them. Soon I discovered that it was hard to play holding up my skirt, so I found a spot away from everyone else and stacked my apples in a little pile. When I came back, everyone was standing in a circle in serious negotiation.

Jean called me over and draped her little freckled arm over my shoulder. "We got some chunks of cow salt. D'ya want some?"

James and Jonah were already rubbing the tiny green apples with salt and munching away. Just seeing them eating made my mouth water. After considerable haggling, the boys dug into their pockets and sorted through their treasures. In addition to the pieces of salt, there were yards of string, bits of wire, and squished grasshoppers for fishing. James even had a small frog. I winced when Jonah thrust his hand toward me with a piece of salt. I could see clean blue granules on the side that had been chipped off the block, but on the other side tiny bits of yellow straw were stuck down with dark brown stuff that looked a lot like cow manure. Jean grabbed a grungy piece, rubbed her apple, and bit into it.

When she realized I was just staring at my salt, she asked, "What's wrong?"

Mother was always talking about washing our hands a lot. She was constantly sterilizing things in boiling water. I was certain there had to be something wrong with dirty salt. "What do you do to get rid of the germs?" I asked.

Jeanie's stare turned into a look of disbelief as she tossed her short blonde hair and clicked her tongue impatiently. "All you have to do about germs is lick 'em off. Don't ya know anything?"

I played with Jeanie enough to know that when she was annoyed enough to click her tongue, she was thinking you were really stupid. I flushed red with embarrassment. To prove how smart I was, I gave the salt a big lick, then rubbed it off on my dress when no one was looking.

I overheard James whispering to Jonah how lucky they were to get away with that much salt without getting into trouble—that's when I remembered it was against the rules to steal cow salt from the blocks. Before I had given it proper thought, I asked James, "What if I get caught with this salt—am I gonna get a lickin'?"

My companions stopped dead in their tracks. Five-year-old James looked dumbfounded. "Man, are you ever stupid. If ya catch a lickin' for havin' cow salt, it's your own fault for tellin' or gettin' caught. Don't come cryin' to us if you're that dumb!"

I didn't understand. I tried to tell myself it was all right, but I couldn't turn my conscience off. Even though I'd have a sin on my head and have to tell Daddy, I decided not to worry about it until the last minute—I'd eat as much salt and green apples as I could. I made sure to share it with Nettie so she could have some, too, but I didn't worry about her because she was too little to have a sin.

For the rest of the morning we played with a couple of sheep that were dumb enough to stray toward us. The boys even took turns riding them. Some of us made mud patties and set them out in the sun while other kids just lay on the blanket with the babies, sucking their thumbs and twirling their hair until they slept for a while. At noon the big dinner bell sounded. The confusion of a morning spent with Uncle Isaac's children—the ones of us who were too young to be part of the haying crew—came to an end. Three kids were fighting over who got to help push as Ophelia struggled down the rutted road with the heavy load, past the turkey shed and toward the food. By now the summer sun was scorching hot, and we were all ravenous.

As we neared our destination, my steps slowed and I started tugging on one of my long brown braids. My conscience was bothering me—I'd been bad. I lagged far behind the other kids with my lump of salt clenched in my hand. The closer I got to the turkey shed, the more nervous I became. That wasn't good, because every time I got this way, I got itchy—I hated that feeling. Daddy would be eating lunch with the haying crew, and although I was determined to see him, I was sure he'd be able to tell that I did wrong just by looking at me. I couldn't lie to Daddy, and he always said not telling the truth about something you did against the rules was as bad as a lie, especially if someone like your daddy or the prophet had taught you about the rule of confessing your sins so you could be forgiven.

I admired Jean, James, and Jonah, because they were tough and afraid of nothing, but you could catch a real hard licking for stealing cow salt. I didn't think Jean and James knew about the rule of confession, but I knew I couldn't go for dinner unless I got rid of my salt.

The hill to the right was covered with Canada thistles that grew tall and proud despite a lack of water, and in some places, even soil. I struggled a few feet up the hill, stood on my tiptoes, and tried to touch the top of the tallest one. With my arms in a huge arc, I turned to face the mountain. I pretended I was a thistle—a strong, proud thistle with bright purple flowers. A rock at the base of the majestic plant was the perfect place to hide my salt…but I had to mark it. I lined the thistle up with the giant hawthorn bush and tucked the blue lump carefully under the rock.

Mumbling to myself, I continued to the house. I knew I had to tell Daddy. I'd probably get a lickin', but then it would be all right to use the salt for my green apples again, 'cause I paid for it. I finally stopped worrying about my sins long enough to realize I was alone on the road, and I should have been scared. I heard a weird thumping, whirring noise from the direction of the apple tree. The place that was safe only minutes before when we were busy playing now seemed terrifying and dangerous, especially when I let my imagination run away with me. My heart pounded as I flew down the road past the buttercup field, past the grazing sheep, past the spot where the big kids saw a black bear three days ago, and on to the house where the haying crew was eating lunch.

Determined to find Daddy, my lungs bursting, I ran past the circle of children sharing tin plates of food on the lawn. I knew it was against the rules for kids to bother the grown-ups at mealtimes, but if I could make it to Daddy, no one would send me away. I paused at the door to adjust to the dim light. Wrinkling my nose at the smell of the sweaty chaps, I stared up at the rows of fearsome hay hooks that lined the walls and steeled myself for a gauntlet of stern stares from busy, indignant mothers. I continued past the glaring faces, past the massive cookstove, past cupboards laden with loaves of fresh baked bread, roast chicken, gravy, mountains of mashed potatoes, and dozens of pies, past the eating crew, and into my Daddy's strong arms. His thick dark hair was still wet with sweat from a grueling morning in the hayfields. I felt safe.

I peeked around Daddy's arm at the man sitting at the end of the table. Uncle Isaac was dark from long days spent in the sun. He had a hawk nose, broad shoulders, and piercing blue eyes that could either look right through you or pin you to the wall on his whim. The man could pass for a prince, a king, or the devil himself. He always wore the same thing day in, day out—bib overalls, a blue shirt, and special boots built for his injured leg. With one leg shorter than the other, he limped when he walked. He loved telling the gruesome story about how the leg of his coveralls got caught in the power takeoff of his tractor while he was spreading manure back in Cardston during the dead of winter. The wicked machine had spun his leg around until it was broken in many different places, and his foot was dangling from the mangled leg. He was able to swing up and push the lever to shut the tractor off, but not before he was bleeding badly and far from help. Only the subzero temperatures had stopped him from bleeding to death and saved him to be one of the leaders in God's sacred Work.

His limp fascinated me, but his thick dark brows and widow's peak frightened me. His eyes were something else; they absolutely sparkled when anyone let him see he intimidated them. He made me flinch as he spoke in an intense voice, stabbing the air with his fists and spitting out his words. Whether he was manning a crew or expounding on the secrets of the kingdom, he was impossible to ignore.

"Well, Brother Isaac, do you think you can use a greenhorn like me?" Daddy's tone was reverent, almost pleading.

"Now, that's a good question, Adam. We'll soon knock off the soft edges, and when you've toughened up a bit, you'll be fine—just fine."

Uncle Isaac leaned back in his chair, lifted his right leg onto the corner of the table, and looked at Daddy as if he were sizing up a prizefighter. "There's no room for a namby-pamby in this Work. You're either for it or against it. Only a strong man would take the stand you did in coming here. Leaving your family and forsaking the church for the gospel is what's required if you're going to make it. You must sacrifice all things, even suffer the same as Christ did when He was crucified, if you expect to make it to be a god with goddesses and your own earth. Christ won't accept you in His kingdom if you aren't prepared to pay the price." He paused for emphasis and shook his fist. "Believe me, the wolves and the law dogs will howl at your door, but the Lord will fight your battles if you're willing to stand strong. It'll take nerves of steel. Mark my words! Nerves of steel!"

I knew Isaac Merrick (Uncle Isaac, I was supposed to call him) was the file leader of the Lord's true Saints in Canada. He was second only to the prophet, Uncle LeRoy, who came from Colorado City, Arizona, to collect tithing and tell us exactly what the Lord directed him for us to do. Uncle Isaac was mesmerizing when he started to preach, holding all within the sound of his voice captive. Even people who disliked him stopped and listened.

With tears in his eyes, Daddy said respectfully, "I understood these things when we came here. I'll be yours and Aunt Bettilyn's adopted family if you'll have me. My own father has disowned me as a son. He'll never recognize me again unless I reject this Work and return to the church."

Uncle Isaac spoke again with fire in his eyes, his nostrils flaring. "Our people in Arizona have been hounded from pillar to post and our leaders put in jail. Mothers and children have been taken away and put in foster homes. Men that do the work of Lucifer, like Governor Pyle of Arizona and those that support him, will be a hiss and a byword in the last days! The good old LDS church can't see it, but she's sold her birthright for a mess of pottage.* We can't be too careful here in Canada, either, I want you to know...The police would be more than glad to catch any one of us and carry on more of this persecution. Mark my words! That's one of the ways you can tell if you're doing the Lord's will. If you're in harmony with the world and not being persecuted, you're guilty of striking hands with the devil."

Uncle Isaac, his nephew Michael, and Kelvin Whitmer, with their many wives and children, represented God's hope. All the people in the whole world who didn't live in this secluded corner of Lister or with our polygamous groups in the United States or Mexico were Gentiles. Every day I heard talk about how the wicked ones who wouldn't hear the call of our prophet would be burned

*In the Old Testament, Esau, "a man of the field" became faint with hunger and sold his birthright as first-born son to his brother, Jacob, for something to eat. Pottage is stew. The reference here is to the fact that the LDS Church renounced polygamy in order to gain statehood for Utah.

when the earth was cleansed with fire before the Second Coming of Christ. Sometimes I wondered why the Gentiles couldn't see the truth—maybe they *were* just born to be evil.

All the ladies who had stopped clearing tables to listen to Uncle Isaac's mini-sermon now started to hustle up dessert. As Mother passed Daddy with a plate of raisin pie, she paused to give him a quick hug and hurried on to feed another hungry hayer. As if someone had given a secret signal, everyone stopped talking until the last plate had been polished clean.

Uncle Isaac let out a wild war whoop to Naomi and the crew, most of whom were under fifteen. Some were as young as eight. Naomi, who worked by Uncle Isaac's side and was as valuable as any two men, hollered, "Come on, you bunch of renegades! Let's get back to work—we'll do another five hundred bales before chores, and after the milking's done, the rest of the night's free." There was unanimous groaning and moaning from the aching, exhausted crew. Daddy set me down after one more squeeze, and I ran to see if I could find some food.

Jeanie waited for me at the door. She stood on one foot and smiled nervously. She had saved me a piece of bread and some spuds on a large chipped enamel dish.

"How d'ya dare go in there where the big guys eat?" she asked. "Dad would just tell me to get if I did that." I couldn't understand a daddy being like that, but then I couldn't imagine cuddling on Uncle Isaac's lap, either. I liked to look at him from a distance, but touching him would be scary.

I thought for a minute, then put my arm around her. "If you want, I'll take you with me the next time I go see my daddy—then you won't get yelled at." Just for a moment I felt almost as brave as her and James. We meandered to the front of the ranch house and plunked in the shade of the porch next to a maze of giant blue, pink, and purple hollyhocks.

We picked at the food until the plate was bare. Jean slipped her arm around me. Leaning closer, she earnestly confided, "I always wanted a ruly-truly friend, and now I have one. Before, I always had to play with boys, but now I have you."

"A ruly-truly friend." I repeated it slowly. "Am I, really? Thank you, Jeanie!" I set my empty dish down on the ground and we hugged.

Mother came around the corner balancing Brent on her hip and holding Nettie by the hand. "It's time to go home for a nap, Deb. Take your plate back to the kitchen and thank Aunt Bettilyn for the lovely dinner...then come on over to the cabin."

"Oh, Mother," I pleaded, "couldn't I play with Jean just this once, please? I'm a big girl now...Daddy said...and I'll be real good."

"Now, Deb! You do what you're told the first time...without complaining. That's the way to make me happy." Mother turned and walked slowly toward the cabin. "Come along!" she hollered over her shoulder.

I was suddenly overcome with all the guilt of the day. I felt sick as I said goodbye to Jeanie and took my plate back into the house. As I entered the porch, Uncle Isaac was bent over cinching up the laces of his heavy workboots. Just then, he let out a blast. "Come on, you bunch of no-good numbskulls! The sloops are waitin' and if you're not out here right smart, I'll help you with a boot to the rear end. Get a move on!" When I tried to pass him, he let go an ear-shattering whoop, which startled me so much I shrieked and leapt into the air. He released a deep-bellied laugh that shook his whole body as my plate clattered to the floor. That frightened me even worse than his yelling. "Scared you, did I? Serves you right!"

He left the porch, chuckling, and I broke into a run for home. When I crashed into the cabin, Mother put her finger to her lips, shushing me. I wrapped my arms around her legs and held on tight, babbling frantically, "Mother, why does Uncle Isaac say it serves me right when he yells? He scared me...and he laughed."

Mother pulled me up with obvious effort. "It's all right, Daughter, he only teases. You'll get used to him."

"What's a numbskull?" I asked her.

Mother ignored my question. "Come now...hop into bed. We must count our blessings." She stared past me and was silent for a moment. "Nothing else matters if we can count our blessings. I'll sing our song, and then you can sleep." She cradled me in her arms and sang softly.

"You are my sunshine, my only sunshine
You make me happy when skies are gray
You'll never know dear, how much I love you
Please don't take my sunshine away..."

I fell asleep with Uncle Isaac on my mind, sure that he had spied into my very heart and now knew all my sins.

Chapter 2

"Hops are a much valued herb for women's complaints. Aunt Susie Barlow from Colorado City said so before her husband died…He was a prophet for our people, so you know Aunt Susie is really special."

Mother and Jan were in the next room talking in hushed voices. Mother agreed with Jan. "If you trust in the Lord and use His natural pure medicines uncontaminated by the evil designing men of the world, then all illness and weakness will be cured. That's if it's the Lord's will, of course." Mother's voice dropped almost to a whisper, and I could just barely hear her. "If it isn't His will to cure us, then if we are truly faithful we'll accept His hand in all things and recognize that He must need us in heaven." There was an uncomfortable silence before she continued. "We're so blessed to have a wonderful prophet to give us this inspired direction. We don't have to rely on doctors who only have the teachings of man."

"Yes," Jan answered fervently. "To be chosen from all our families to be saved from outer darkness is indeed a humbling thought. Like Daddy quotes from the scriptures, 'Many are called but few are chosen.' And to think we are the ones chosen out of the whole world. It really behooves me, because I know if my faith is strong enough, my baby will be born without the help of Gentiles—and under the covenant.* Isn't it marvelous, Vivien? I will give Adam his first covenant child!"

I slipped out of bed, put on my slippers, and crept to the door. When it was ajar, I could peek through the hinged part without being seen. Mother was sitting at the little yellow table with her daily quart of hop tea in her hands. Jan was standing behind her, pulling Mother's long black hair into braids. Her hair used to be shorter with soft curls around her temples; her face used to be fuller, too. In Rosemary, her skin had been soft and warm like creamy rose petals. I remembered how I would run my hands across her smooth cheeks and turn her face just so, to kiss her. Her hair looked so severe pulled back this way…but if you could get to be a queen in heaven that way, we should just be glad.

Watching them, I thought about Jan's belly and the "covenant baby" they were talking about. I wondered about myself and my sister and brother. Brent was born after we came to this sacred valley, but Nettie and I were born in a gentile hospital, and our mother was the first wife and married legally to Daddy. Maybe we weren't as special as the covenant children. Jeanie was a plural child and I didn't hear anyone making a big fuss about that, and Jonah was Uncle Isaac's first plural son under the covenant and no one said much about that, either. Maybe they'd make a bigger deal about Jonah if he looked more like Uncle Isaac's other sons. He was much darker than they were and had jet-black hair, deep brown eyes, and a sharp nose. Bettilyn's sons were fairer, and James had freckles. Uncle Isaac talked a lot about the Lord needing a "white and delightsome people to be worthy of the highest degree of the celestial kingdom to be gods and goddesses." Was that why they didn't get exited about Jonah—because his skin was darker? I checked my arm and pinched it because in the summer sun my arms turned brown so easily and my skin was not milky, pink-white like Jeanie's or even Jan's. Everyone said I thought too much for my own good, but I decided I should ask Daddy about what I could do to be extra worthy.

---

*The law of plural or celestial marriage.

Mother let out a groan she tried to smother. Grimacing at her bottle of hops, she muttered, "I just wish this stuff wasn't so nasty…but if it will help ease the terrible faintness I feel, then it'll be worth it. Oh dear, I sound like I'm questioning, and I'm really not. I'm so tired of bleeding three weeks out of four and washing those pads…I'm in the saddle more than not, but the brethren said in my last blessing if I follow direction with unquestioning faith I'll be well." She held her nose and downed the last half glass with one swallow and a shudder.

Jan put an elastic on the final braid with an impatient flip. "I, for one, don't have time to be sick…never have. I'm sure you'll be fine, if that's what they said." She took off abruptly, oblivious to Mother's wince of pain. "We better get moving. We're going over to Mom's to help her clean up around the new addition. It'll be wonderful to have a place away from Michael's when the brethren come. We can never get the right spirit over there—his family is always so contentious." She said it was miraculous the way the Lord used a rebellious person like Michael to build the new room to further His work. Uncle Michael was supplying the material and labor, but Jan said he didn't clear it with Uncle Isaac. "Of course, Daddy has no obligation to pay for it. Mother made the deal, but Michael should know by now things must go through Daddy. Maybe this'll teach him a lesson." She moved impatiently across the room. "Since I've been set apart to establish our own school, the big room will be the very thing for classrooms."

The look of pain and sadness on Mother's face sent me flying out from behind the door. I bolted toward her and jumped onto her lap almost in the same movement. My arms clutched her neck and held her so tightly she finally pried them away. I kissed her again and again, desperate to change the expression on her face. Her sadness filled me with a horrible fear that I couldn't explain.

"It's okay, Mother. It's morning, right? And the sun is up today…and I love you."

Mother smiled. "Yes, one more kiss, then you run and get dressed. We have lots of work to do. Grandmother's coming when the priesthood men come. We're very blessed."

I jumped down, all worry forgotten at the thought of Grandmother. "Does she get to stay longer this time? Is Grandpa coming?"

Jan turned and questioned sharply, "When did you find out? You didn't tell me! I always feel so inferior when Isaiah and Selma come…They don't say anything in so many words, but they're so fancy and churchy."

Mother explained patiently, "Adam brought the letter to me when he came to say goodnight last night…and this is the first chance I've had to mention it. Besides, I know you worry about putting on a good impression around them, and I wanted to spare you as long as possible."

Jan's voice trembled and rose to a shriek. "I know what it really is! You're jealous Adam was with me last night instead of you. I knew all this love and gentleness was too good to be true…It always turns out this way!"

I ran to the bedroom. Nettie was awake now and together we crept wide-eyed to the door and crouched on the edge of the bedroom step. We weren't used to angry tones in our home and we were scared.

Mother sighed. Slowly getting to her feet, she put her arms around Jan's stiff, angry shoulders. "We left our home, our family, our whole way of life—everything I've ever known. We came three hundred and fifty miles to live this precious sacred principle of the plurality of wives. I knew what would be required in the sacrifice of sharing my husband, who is now our husband. I love you more than if you were a sister. I was only waiting for the right time to share the news about Mother and Dad."

She told Jan again about Grandmother going through the temple just like Bettilyn did, and they could both do the special washings and anointings for Daddy's first plural child. "Do you realize how special this fulfilling of the covenant is? Our mothers have been set apart by our prophet to do this sacred Work." Mother paused. "Glenna's coming, too. She's a lot of fun. Please forgive me…and let's be friends. Besides, I don't want to have cross words in front of the children. They should never hear us disagree. You know how hard it is on your brothers and sisters when they have those horrible fights at your folks'."

Jan started to cry and hugged Mother back. "You're just too

good to me and I'm sorry. You don't need to tell Adam, do you? I couldn't stand to upset him...and he'd be real cross if he knew."

"No, we won't tell. Now, let's hurry...he'll be in from milking soon, and we don't want him to know we've been fighting."

Mother hurried to get us ready for the day, and Jan finished fixing breakfast.

When we met the rest of the kids for the morning playtime, we gathered at a huge pile of fresh sawdust to play King of the Castle. Some days we got to take turns riding Diamond, a handsome white horse with enough spirit to be a challenge to the big boys, but gentle-natured enough that even the smallest of the children could ride him alone. Jeanie rode him like she was born on his back...I only dared try if I could ride behind a big person.

This morning I longed to escape to the cabin with Mother and her peaceful teachings. Secretly, I hated playing King of the Castle. I didn't like to get dirt in my mouth and ears and up my skirt. I always ended up on the bottom of the hill, under someone. Most times, I stayed on the outside edge and only pretended that I wanted to be king. James and Jonah said I fought like a pantywaist, so I couldn't be on their team. I felt bad but I didn't like to get dirty and it was real hard to win if you didn't.

After my nap Mother said I could go and find Jean and help her put hay in the stanchions during chores. I gave her another one of my tight hugs and flew out the door before she changed her mind. By the time I found Jean in the main corral by the watering trough, I was panting so hard I could scarcely talk.

"Jeanie, guess what! I get to help feed cows."

She didn't look up from trailing her fingers through the cold water. "That's nice, I was hopin' you would. Let's drink and eat apples till Daddy comes. He hasn't even come back on the sloop yet, so we're safe here till he brings the cows home. Then you can bet we have to be out of the corral or get trampled."

Her serious expression didn't change as she gave me one of her green apples. I watched my friend bend over and take a drink, then carefully stepped up on the rough cement ledge that the trough was secured to. Bending at the waist, I pursed my lips to slurp up the mountain spring water. We solemnly took bites of the sour apples, and then sucked the icy water again. Jean heard the rumbling first, grabbed my dress, and pulled me to the corral fence.

"Dad's comin' in! We better head for the high timber, so's we don't get run over."

The rumbling was followed by a wild whoop as Uncle Isaac swooped down the road in a cloud of dust. He stood on the sloop like a captain riding the deck of his ship. His legs spread wide, he leaned back and held the reins of the galloping horses in one hand. He looked simply majestic.

Along with twenty other kids who had scrambled for the fence, we were spitting dust and wiping it from our eyes. Uncle Isaac pulled back on the horses. "Whoa there! Whoa there!" The heaving horses slowed to a quivering, snorting halt, and he sprang from the sloop. Yelling to the boys on the fence, Uncle Isaac headed toward the barn. "Here, you boys…come get these harnesses. And see you hang 'em up straight or I'll tan your hides."

The old green John Deere tractor puttered up the lane and jerked to a halt on the far side of the horses. Jeanie's mother, Naomi, swung in exhaustion from the seat. She'd been helping with the chores and farming for the last ten years with God's people, working like a man while giving birth once a year, every year, for the last seven. All the other women in our Work babbled on about her strength and endurance, but mostly they said they were grateful that they weren't so strong and dependable. Mother found it hard to believe anyone could give birth one day and be back driving the tractor the next.

Naomi walked wearily over to the sweating horses and ruffled the mane of the nearest one. "The rest of the crew'll be here shortly. I'm going in to check on Ward and Katy. I'll come out to help milk later."

Uncle Isaac growled, "They'll be fine…I need you here!" He pulled the harnesses off and added, "We sure put one over on Michael, didn't we? He doesn't understand true brotherhood if he could keep a perfectly good set of harnesses that we needed and he didn't. We just helped him along a bit with supporting the kingdom. That's what I'd call helping him donate to the United Order." He finished with a mirthless chuckle.

At Uncle Isaac's first words, Naomi started to steam. I could see the anger build, and I was suddenly afraid of both of them. I'd never seen such fierce, piercing eyes or heard the kind of towering rage that erupted like a volcano when these two disagreed. They were very much alike and with good reason. After their last yelling fight, Jan told Mother that her dad was really Naomi's uncle, too, because he was Grandma Liza's brother. So Jeanie's dad was really her great-uncle, too. That didn't make sense to me.

Naomi's eyes flashed dark as her voice became sharp and accusing. "You can call it what you want, but it seems an awful lot like stealing to me…And you can be damned, 'cause I've been working since four this morning in your bloody hayfield, and I'm going to find my babies." Her face was a violent red color as she turned on her heel and strode to the house, muttering under her breath. Uncle Isaac turned on the boy nearest him and gave him a boot that sent him flying. The howling boy lit out running and disappeared into the barn.

Jean gripped the rough board fence and ground words between her teeth. "I hate when Mom and Dad fight…it's so loud. We better watch out, because when he's mad, he always brings the cows in fast."

Uncle Isaac disappeared down the lane, swinging his crippled leg in a sort of hop in his agitation. In a few moments thirty-five cows came charging into the corral, their huge udders swinging awkwardly from side to side. One giant Ayrshire cow had milk streaming from teats that were too stretched and engorged to hold it in any longer. The frothy liquid soaked into the hard dried manure pack in the corral, filling the air with the aroma of manure and hot milk. The hunching cows and the pungent sweet smell of cow pee awed me. I was embarrassed that the cows didn't have a private place to relieve themselves. As we watched them, one of the black and white cows jumped on the back of a solid black one.

When I asked Jeanie what they were doing, she answered me patiently, as if explaining to someone who was simple-minded. "Well, sometimes the cows come into heat, and then the bulls jump on 'em and breed 'em so they can have calves, and if the bulls aren't in the pen, then the cows just jump on each other…Gee, Deb, you hardly know a darn thing."

She hopped nimbly to the ground, explaining how each of the cows had a name. This was old Bess, that there was old Wretch, and no one liked milking her…that was Dolly, and there was Pansy. She said I had to learn the names, and she'd teach them to me. I doubted she could—the cows looked different, but there were so many of them I couldn't imagine remembering all their names. I carefully climbed down from the fence board by board until I could place my foot in a halfway dry spot in this sea of manure. We picked our way into the barn, careful to stay out of the way of the big boys and girls who were arriving home from the fields. In the cool room we set up the straining buckets.

Jean proudly showed me how to rinse the big stainless steel buckets and set the round white disks into the strainers to remove foreign bodies from the milk. Finally, I had the privilege of turning on the tap to start the icy mountain water going through the system to cool the milk in the cans for the truck to pick up the next morning.

I looked up with a start when Uncle Isaac came to the door of the milk house. He was rounding up kids and herded Jeanie and me, the two smallest members of his crew, in front of him. "All right, you two, let's see if you're any good." He took us to the front of the mangers and directed us brusquely, "One scoop of grain like this and then a flake of hay. Move slow and don't scare the cows or out you go. We can't afford to have the cows upset, or they won't let their milk down."

He swung toward the big door where I could hear the steel click of the stanchions as the cows were being snapped into their stalls. He looked us up and down. "You two are the perfect size to throw into the wool bags next time we shear the sheep. I'll keep that in mind, and when the boys get too tired, we'll throw you both down there!"

He laughed at the look of horror on Jeanie's face. After he left she told me he wouldn't be able to find her at shearing time, because even the bigger boys hated being stuck in the bottom of the huge bags to compact the wool before sale. She grimaced. "The sheep are so dirty…and remember we showed you those horrible ticks crawlin' all over them? Well, try havin' their wool all cut off and thrown down on top of you. Ya have to stomp fast just to keep from gettin' buried. Just watchin' is bad enough!"

I tried to imagine what she was talking about.

"Don't worry, Deb, I'll help you get out of havin' to stomp wool—but we better hurry or we'll be in trouble."

The windows in the cow stanchions faced the mountains. Thirty-six square panes with white trim filled each hole, giving a total picture of the craggy peaks from whichever one you were tall enough to look through. Fifteen T-shaped milking stools hung on the wall, waiting for the kids who would be balancing on them. As the haying crew filtered in, each boy grabbed his favorite stool and his own big silver bucket. I stared in fascination as the milkers hunched earnestly into the haunches of the cows, racing with each other to see who could fill a bucket the fastest. Strong, steady streams of milk soon sent foam rising to the tops of the buckets. When they were full, they were given to James and Jonah in exchange for empty ones, and the boys trotted back and forth to the milk house.

The steady rhythm of the milking was disturbed by an argument over who was going to milk old Wretch. She could let down four gallons a milking, but kicked like she was possessed of a demon. Laman, Uncle Isaac and Aunt Bettilyn's son, stood in the lane, his jaw stuck out stubbornly, declaring, "I'm not milkin' her tonight! I did it this morning and I can barely walk yet from when she stomped my foot. You have to do it, Sid."

His older brother Lemuel moved to the next cow and gave Laman a brutal punch. "Aw, quit your complaining. You're nothin' but a damn sissy," he said.

Sidney, Uncle Kelvin's adopted son, swung his two-and-a-half-gallon bucket full of foaming milk toward Jonah and traded for an empty one. With a crooked smile he said happily, "I'll milk her, sure enough! But I'm not using the kickers…I trust a rope better. When it's tied the right way, I'll handle her all right. She'll fall over before she can hurt me." He jumped the gutter and swiped a piece of rope off the wall beside the steel kickers. Leaping back to

Wretch, he proceeded to cinch her legs together so her hind legs were like one. I watched in fascination as the quivering cow shuddered and lurched each time she was touched and with each pull on the rope. I thought I knew how she felt. Several of the boys stood back watching Sidney's struggle with the old cow. Staying out of range of her thrashing legs, they hooted their advice.

"Here...here...enough of this lallygaggin'. Get back to work! There'll be lots of time for yappin' when the chores are done." Uncle Isaac moved down the lane with the scoop shovel, cleaning the gutter behind the cows as he went. Stooping to check the rope on Wretch's legs, he grunted his approval. "That's right, nice and tight. Damned cow! She's just like a woman—gives a great bucket of milk, but if you don't keep a tight watch on her, she'll kick it over every time or stick her dungy foot in it. Let that be a lesson to you boys."

The steady rhythm resumed and Jean tugged on my dress to get my attention. She whispered anxiously, "If you don't hurry, Dad's not gonna let you help...and I don't want you booted out." I stopped watching Wretch, took the scoop with great pride, and carefully started to fill it. The grain had a strong smell of malt and molasses and was sticky to pick up and rather itchy to touch. It was also heavy, and I was not tough like Jeanie.

I put both hands in the grain barrel to scoop faster just as Uncle Isaac came up behind me. His voice was gruff and he startled me. "What's the matter with you? You got cookstoves tied to your feet? Get a hustle on there." I jumped and twirled around to look up at the blue denim of his bib overalls. His legs were planted wide apart, and his fists were firm to his hips. I felt a warm blush to my cheeks as I tried to explain. His voice took on a softer tone. With a twinkle in his eye, he said, "You'll do, just don't dawdle." I turned back to the grain bucket and hurriedly doled out the grain without stopping once. I'd do anything to keep him from scowling at me again.

When the last bucket of milk had been carried past our station, Jonah and James were too tired to even talk. The milkers began to wander off. Jeanie and I left the barn together and held hands until we reached the place in the yard where we separated. She headed to the big white farmhouse teeming with children and mothers, and I to the little cabin. The pleasant smells and evening calm of the ranch were heaven. The time passed in a blur, and the last thing I remembered was being carried to bed on Daddy's shoulders. I felt safe.

Chapter 3

The crews had finished all the contracts for hauling first-cut hay, and second cut wouldn't be ready for some time yet. So aside from chores and pulling weeds, it would be easier work for a few weeks. It was Saturday, the day Uncle Isaac went to town to do the shopping for all of us at the ranch. He was taking Lydia with him so she could visit her mother. Lydia now had a big belly like Jan and Naomi, and Uncle Isaac was careful to drop her off before shopping so not too many Gentiles would see her with him—especially pregnant and young like she was.

Aunt Bettilyn gave Uncle Isaac her shopping lists. For hours, everyone had known just how unhappy she was he had taken Lydia instead of her, and we all stayed as far from her as possible. Uncle Isaac almost never took anyone but his legal wife to town with him, so when he took Lydia, Bettilyn would smile sweetly until he left, then huff and puff around, making sarcastic remarks until he got back. Lydia eventually learned what was good for her and would often stay with her mother for a couple of days until her sister wife cooled off.

I was just about to the porch of the big house in search of Jeanie when kids emerged from the playhouse, the haystacks, the granary, and exploded in all directions. I was standing in open-mouthed confusion when Jeanie ran past me. Turning back, she tugged on my arm with a sense of urgency, "It's the cops…We gotta run! Come on!"

Fear was instant and bitter in my stomach. "Where? Show me…where?" I looked frantically up the road toward the hill.

Jean pulled at my dress. "Run! You don't try to see the cops—you just run. Come on!"

My heart was beating wildly as I turned and sprinted after her. We leapt like frightened fawns over the pile of boards on top of the septic tank and fled behind the house to the raspberry patch. Racing down the rows, we came to a place where the bushes loaded with fruit bent over to the ground, forming a secret cave. Jean fell to her knees and crawled in first. I followed.

She hissed fiercely, "Stop breathin' so loud. D'ya want them to hear us?" I swallowed hard and closed my mouth, taking slow, agonizing breaths through my nose. My heart was pounding so hard I was afraid the police would hear that, too. We lay flat, face down in the dirt, with our ears searching like antennae for the slightest sound of danger. After awhile Jean whispered, "If we're real careful to stay in the shadows, we can check for the all clear." With hearts still pounding madly, we sneaked back to the kitchen of Jeanie's house.

Bettilyn was bristling with righteous indignation as she punched furiously at a batch of bread dough. Ranting on to Jan, who was sitting on a stool watching, she emphasized each word with a jab at the dough. "You'd think the cops could find something better to do than check up on a bunch of defenseless women! If we were bothering someone I could see some point, but this is stupid."

Her voice rose several octaves. "Big brave men—you should see the pictures of the way they hauled the women and kids away down in Colorado City. Damn them, anyway. When they get crime stamped out in all the other parts of the country, they can come back here, but not until!" She flipped the bread with one more thud and gave it a resounding whack. "As if we knew anything about Jerry Williams. I, for one, wouldn't tell 'em if I did. Illegal alien, they called him…Nobody's business!"

Jan tossed her thin braids over her shoulders. Giving me a frightful glare, she bragged to her mother. "Well, all I can do is thank the good Lord for Adam. He's the best man on earth except for the prophet and Daddy. Adam told me since I started showing with our baby that he doesn't want me running and hiding from the cops. He says he'll stand up and claim I'm his wife anytime, and I'm not to hide in the trees or in the barns under straw like they do over at Michael's."

She carried on in her best preaching tone. "Why, even Vivien says she'd rather hide and pretend I'm the legal wife just to protect me and our baby and the sacred covenant. And Adam agrees. I'm just very spoiled compared to any other plural wife I've ever heard of, aren't I, Mom?"

Bettilyn grunted and nodded her head. "Of course, Daughter, but we could tell that about Adam from the start. He knows he has a real prize in you. The brethren have been clear what an important role you have to play with our people. I know what you mean, though. I'd like to see the day when I went running to hide like I was guilty of some kind of immoral sin!" She paused her kneading and stared intently at her daughter. "Why would Isaac risk getting the police nosing around by taking Lydia into town like this? I tried to tell him one of the older boys or Adam or even Naomi could take her in so he stays far away from any questions...but do you think he'll listen?"

The conversation was interrupted when the door flew open. Everyone jumped and turned as Naomi stormed into the room. She was returning from the trees at the base of the mountain where she had run to hide. Her stomach was large and swollen; her baby was due in just a month. Harshly, she demanded of Bettilyn, "Well, what did they want this time? I'll be damned if I'm going to hide if they come again—someone else can hide next time! And what were you saying about Lydia?" She glowered as she watched Bettilyn at work. "Just for the record, I don't appreciate being sent like an errand boy after Lydia whenever she has a tantrum. Why the hell doesn't she grow up and take care of her own brat? He doesn't look all there to me; a stiff prairie wind would just blow him to kingdom come. It'd serve her right, too." Naomi poured herself a glass of water. "The only darned thing Lydia seems good for around here is having more kids."

"I think the cops were just snooping around," Bettilyn sighed. "We shouldn't even let 'em on the property. It was bad enough when they poked around here saying Lena died from neglect." Bettilyn had told my mother that Aunt Lena died from something called toxemia, and it just about killed Grandma Merrick.

She hacked a piece from her massive ball of dough and molded it into a buttered pan. "I guess you can hardly expect the police to have any idea about the Lord's will in these things." In silence, she carved off several more pieces of dough and put them into pans, then said, "Well, they're gone for now. I guess if we had enough faith we could just pray 'em away. I'll have to speak to Isaac about that."

She rearranged the pans on the counter in front of her. "I think it's high time Isaac sets Lydia straight again, too—not that you don't do a pretty good job of that yourself, Naomi." She groaned. "Lydia just must be our cross to bear. We can do it, I suppose. It's a good thing the big girls take care of Thomas or he'd only get attention when Vivien was busy rescuing him. She definitely has a different outlook on things—can't quite figure it out. People like Lydia will be taking advantage of her if she isn't careful."

Jan was watching Naomi and Bettilyn closely and broke into the conversation. "You know, Mom, how you and Aunt Lena and Naomi were so good with each other—more like Vivien and I are? If Aunt Lena hadn't died when Little Elias was born, it would be a different story for our whole family. Then Lydia wouldn't be such a trial, I'm sure."

Bettilyn grabbed a couple of sticks of wood from the woodbin and fired them into the stove. She replaced the lid to the firebox with a resounding clatter. Setting the dampers on the stove to adjust the temperature, she continued to fill the pans, crashing and banging everything as she went. Naomi watched silently for a few minutes, and then with a growl she slammed the door and headed to the barn.

Jean and I faded up the stairs to the bedrooms to see what the big girls were doing, hoping to find something fun to play with. I tried not to listen, but I could hear Jan and Bettilyn talking about the trials of sister wives and how righteous and good men were. I realized that in all the terror about the police, I had forgotten to check on Mother for a while. I told Jeanie my mother needed me and flew back to the cabin where she was rocking Brent quietly. Nettie was already lying down for her nap. Mother worried me; her face was so white and sad-looking. Suddenly nothing mattered but her. I stood by the arm of the chair with my arm over her shoulders, watching my little brother as he slept.

Saturday mornings always started with a landslide of lists: haul water, wash towels, change bedding, wash chimneys on lamps, polish Sunday shoes, wash hair and do up in rags. Jan returned to the cabin, and she and Mother talked over the lists. Crews of boys were splitting and hauling wood, while others scraped the stanchions in the barn. All of a sudden, Uncle Isaac let loose with the whoop that he often unleashed when he felt good at the start of a new day. The sound bounced off the mountain behind us and echoed around the hills.

Mother gave me a preoccupied hug. "Hurry along now and get dressed so we can get our work done. We're walking over to Uncle Michael's this afternoon." To Jan she said, "It's so strange to call people aunt and uncle instead of brother and sister, but I guess I'll get used to it."

Jan harrumphed. "It makes so much more sense than hanging onto the old gentile traditions—especially the ones of the church. We can truly get free from the worldly traditions of this life if we learn to live by every word that comes from the mouth of the prophet."

Jan was always saying if we couldn't obey without question in all the little directions, how could we ever expect to come up to the mark and be queens in the highest degree of celestial glory. "Controlling our speech at the direction of the prophet is the least we can do…And by the way, you'll have to find someone else to walk with you to Uncle Michael's. I've decided it'll be too much for me to go that far when I'm this huge." She patted her belly. "Just a few more weeks, and it'll be all over. I hate being over there anyway, when Uncle Michael just won't admit that Dad is the leader."

Mother smiled at Jan. "Of course, you'll be too tired. I'll take all the children with me, so you'll have a better chance to rest after the work is done. If Adam gets back early, maybe he can lie with you for a while. Most of all, don't stress yourself. It's not good for you or our baby."

She gave Jan a quick hug and then called for me. "Deb, it's time to do your hair." Slowly rising from her chair, she carried the kettle to the basin on the counter and motioned me over. I loved getting my hair washed and my scalp massaged, but I hated having my hair done up in rags. I looked at Nettie hoping she'd go first, then reluctantly headed in Mother's direction. I knew I had to look my best for church, and if I was counting my blessings, I should be really happy that we'd get to spend a few hours without Jan's preaching and scolding about something. I didn't make nearly as many mistakes or even stutter when she wasn't around.

About two o'clock we set out on the mile and a half walk to Michael's. We started our journey with just Nettie, Brent, and myself, but before we reached the first bend a dozen more kids ran whooping up the hill begging to come. Mother struggled along with Brent on her hip, moving ever so slowly.

"This hill is just too much for me today," she panted. "Maybe if someone goes back to borrow the buggy, I'll be able to make it just pushing Brent…I don't think I can carry him." I searched Mother's face, looking for reassurance that she was only joking. Her face was white and there was a far-off look in her eyes.

An overwhelming fear sent me racing down the hill in search of the buggy. By the time I found it and started back up, my stomach was churning and my mouth tasted salty from a mixture of tears and sweat. I got the buggy to Mother, and after she got Brent settled we continued on. I stayed under the handle, pushing for all I was worth until we were through the woods and the gravel pit and had crested the hill on the road to Michael's.

Mother stopped to rest, then insisted, "You run ahead now. I'm fine, and you need to play." I hesitated but she told me again, and I stepped away. The buggy sagged as she leaned heavily on the handle. The rest of the kids were way ahead down the gravel pit road so I ran to catch up. I loved the rush of the wind in my ears and the hot smells of summer in my nostrils. Totally distracted by my desire to reach the other kids, I forgot my worries about Mother and took off after them. I found them feasting on heavily laden saskatoon bushes just to the side of the trail.

Mother caught up, and we were off again. We entered a big clearing, and a house with white gables and red trim came into view. To the left of it, sparkling like a jewel in the heat, was a huge pond. We had been told how Uncle Michael and his boys had dammed the creek to create it. Despite the fact that horses, dozens of kids, and even tractors crossed this dam daily, I was terrified the moment I set foot on it. For some reason, I was afraid my forty pounds could send the dam crashing into the crevice below.

Jean, James, Jonah, and I stopped at the sight of the house. The grass on every hill had been nibbled to the dirt, and the musty smell of goats hung heavily. Every once in a while, a breeze blew a cool, welcome taste of fresh air from the mountain over the pond.

James had a worried expression. "I'm not goin' up to the house till the big guys get here, 'cause Aunt Loren's gonna make us drink goat's milk again."

I pulled myself up straight. "That's a good idea, because Mother would never let anyone make us eat something nasty." Jean and James exchanged doubtful glances, and Jonah said that Aunt Loren would have to catch him before she could make him drink the awful stuff.

The four of us kicked rocks and picked flowers until Mother caught up to us again. When we got to the house, Aunt Loren, with her round, smiling face, greeted us at the door. Dressed in long pants and her trademark ankle-length white apron, she herded us into the dark, cool interior.

"It's good to see you all," she exclaimed. "Come in and let's find you something cold to drink...You need to get your strength back after your walk. Pauline and Michael will be sorry they missed you. They're out on that basement job in Canyon...but they'll see you tomorrow."

Before we knew it we were all sitting around with large tin cups of goat's milk in our hands. Mother tried to decline the offering, saying we were fine and would do well simply with water, but all protests fell on deaf ears. I tried to drink mine, but the smell made my stomach lurch. Finally, Jean jabbed me in the ribs. "If you pinch your nose like this and drink real fast, it goes down and you only have to gag once at the end." I watched in amazement as she did that very thing. Gingerly, I grabbed my nose, held on real tight, and managed to swallow half of it before I had to stop. One more try and it was over. We were free to go outside and explore.

Jonah was true to his word. He had disappeared the moment Aunt Loren produced the pitcher of milk. He came out from behind one of the sheds and walked toward us looking very pleased with himself.

With all its hay sheds, goat barns, and storage areas, this place was a kid's adventure haven; you just had to watch out for the goat turds that were everywhere. I was trying to look at a thousand things at once, but the evergreen trees on the edge of the fields puzzled me. I asked, "Why do the branches start so far up the trees? At the ranch they mostly start at the ground."

James was a year older than Jean and I and loved to prove he was tough and had most things figured out. Sticking his thumbs in the sides of his faded, made-over bib overalls, he thrust out his chest and said knowingly, "It's 'cause of the goats, don't ya know? They eat all the grass, so the horses get so hungry they have to eat the leaves and even the pine needles. That's why Daddy says only fools keep goats. Don't ya know anythin'?" He finished with a swagger and a click of his tongue, which in spite of his round baby face, made him sound like a wise old man.

Jonah added to the lesson on goats. "Yeah, and ya know what else? Mom says the reason the goat milk tastes so blamed horrible is 'cause Uncle Michael leaves the billy goats runnin' with the nannies all the time. And they stink worse than pigs almost." We all stopped and stared at Jonah. He didn't usually have so much to say, and we couldn't figure out what he meant.

The moment we left the house, we teamed up with Reeny, Uncle Michael's daughter. She was our age, but because of the problems between Uncle Michael and Uncle Isaac, we hardly ever saw her. We were on her territory now, and I felt far safer to be under her guidance. With fierce billy goats hiding around every corner, I was nervous—they just loved chasing scaredy-cats like me.

It wasn't long before Reeny was telling us all the secrets of the big kids. She even told us where her brothers and sisters hid food, and led us to a derelict shed. "Move real quiet," she whispered. She turned to James with an air of excitement. "Get on your hands and knees so I can climb on your back. Ralph and Art stole some peanuts from a fifty-pound sack and they hid 'em back there." She pointed to a crevice inside the boarded wall. "The boys don't think I know, and we'll get whipped if they catch us, but that makes it more fun." She laughed.

I hesitated. This had to be an even worse sin than stealing salt. "Don't your moms and dad know?" I asked. "Shouldn't we tell them, so they can teach the big kids not to steal?"

All four of them looked at each other in horror, then at me in pity. Reeny snorted. "If we have to worry you're gonna tell somebody all our secrets, then you can't play with us. It's easy to see you never saw fifty pounds of peanuts! It's the hugest thing you ever saw, so if I was big like Ralph and Art I could steal some easy...Are you gonna tell or not? 'Cause if you're gonna tell, then you have to leave."

Jean barged in, "Yeah, Daddy gets 'em for us, too—mostly for Christmas—and then for a day we get to eat all we want before the grownups hide 'em, and we only get little bits after that. They're raw, too. Daddy says that's the best kind so's you get all the vitamins before the Gentiles get a chance to pollute 'em."

I stood dumbfounded, my tongue glued to the roof of my mouth. All eyes were on me. They said I had to spit and double swear I wouldn't tell, and then we could keep playing. I did. James knelt down on the musty straw- and turd-covered floor, and Reeny sprang up on his back. Very carefully, she doled out four handfuls of peanuts. Giggling excitedly, she led us to a small tool shed that was free from goat poop. We huddled behind the closed door, ate the peanuts, and whispered. Once we had finished our store of booty, we joined the rest of the kids, who were laughing and screaming by the pond. It was two hours later that we were stopped in our tracks by the sound of a wild "Halloo!" It was time to go.

Just two weeks later and within three days of each other, there were two new babies. Naomi's baby was a boy they named Joab; Lydia had a girl they named Priscilla. In both cases, it was as if I went to bed and woke up and there was a new baby—except all the kids and mothers were talking when Lydia and Naomi weren't around about how Lydia could scream and carry on having a kid when Naomi didn't make a sound and then got up the next morning to help with chores. I'd heard how tough she was before, but this time I actually saw the brand-new baby, and I saw her with a flat belly the next day, working around the barn and driving the tractor, acting like nothing had happened.

We'd had Sunday meetings at Uncle Michael's before, but the one coming up with two new babies was going to be special because Uncle Isaac and the other priesthood men like Daddy, Uncle Michael, and Uncle Kelvin would gather in a circle and take each baby one at a time and give them a name and a father's blessing. The babies were three weeks old now, and Uncle Isaac said it was high time they were added into the kingdom of God at fast and testimony meeting. Only men who were elders with the holy priesthood of Melchizedek* could stand in the circle, so the blessing was as special as if God Himself were there.

Mother and Jan sat me and Nettie between their legs to tie our hair in curls with the rags for us to look good for Heavenly Father the next day. We hadn't eaten supper as part of the fast, and my tummy was already aching. As they were getting the rags ready, I stood close to Mother so she would be the one putting the rags in my hair. Jan was irritated with me at the best of times, and with the baby so close, she was especially cranky. The last thing I wanted was to be sitting between her legs while she jerked on long pieces of my hair and twisted them into the rags. I was following on Mother's heels when Jan grabbed me by the arm and hauled me

---

*According to Old Testament history, Melchizedek was king and high priest of the city of Salem. The Order of Melchizedek, which comprises three levels, is considered to be the highest priesthood order in the LDS Church and in Mormon Fundamentalist polygamous groups. In order to become a "prophet," a man must be ordained as a high priest apostle in the Melchizedek priesthood.

toward her. There was no use complaining, but by the time she was finished I was certain she was hurting me on purpose. I couldn't sleep most of the night and pulled some hairs right out because they wouldn't stop bothering me. As I tossed and turned with the pain from the hair and an empty stomach, I heard screaming on the hilltop above our cabin. I pulled the covers tighter around my neck, hoping it was a cougar and not Lydia.

I awoke Sunday morning in discomfort. One of the rags was pulling my hair the wrong way; I tugged at it until the tension was relieved. I was thankful I could look pretty for church, but I dreaded the pain I had to endure to accomplish it. These were the times I was envious of Jeanie. Her mother never did anything with her hair except wash it once in a while. She even hacked it off short, telling her that it would grow out longer and thicker next time.

I was excited about attending the sacrament meeting and getting to visit with Michael's children and see the special blessings on the babies. Mother had just finished a new yellow flour-sack dress for me, and I was anxious to wear it for the first time. I could still remember the beautiful Sunday dresses Nettie and I had when we first arrived here from Rosemary. They had red velvet bodices and white nylon skirts with red polka dots. We had matching black shoes that went well with the outfits. Mother had always taken so much pride in dressing us for church. I remembered how upset she was after our first time wearing them here.

Uncle Michael said we looked like fashion plates following after the vain, glorious traditions of the world. He had no sooner left us than Uncle Isaac came over and told Mother she had better make sure we learned how to work because "the Lord doesn't care how we look as long as we can put in a good day's work for the kingdom of God."

The first time Jean saw me, she touched the red velvet very gently. Her round, freckled face crinkled a little as she said, "Daddy says the children of the chosen race should never wear red."

I ran to Mother and asked what my friend meant. She got a worried look on her face and said she'd have to ask Daddy. Jan was absolutely delighted to tell Mother that red was the color of "prostitutes and whores." She looked at Nettie and me with disapproval.

"Now it's come up, I can tell you we learned a couple of years ago how the Lord's chosen ones, like we are supposed to be, should never wear *that color*." I squirmed under her disapproving gaze, feeling strangely unclean. Mother touched the fabric wistfully. We never wore the red velvet dresses again.

Although I loved my new yellow dress and was excited about wearing it for the first time, I secretly liked the pale green of Nettie's better. Mother had spent hours dying the fabric yellow and making sure the dress was beautifully finished, and I was determined to be grateful. After I hugged her a second time, I asked her when we were going to eat breakfast. After all, we were already in our Sunday best—something we had never done before eating until today.

"Remember, dear, today we're giving our bodies a rest from eating," she responded.

My stomach was growling and I held it as I asked plaintively, "Daddy, couldn't we please have just a little bit to eat? Nettie is really hungry, too, and she'll be lots happier if we can just eat a tiny bit."

Daddy chuckled. "You know this Sunday has been called to be a fast and testimony meeting. We need to show the Lord we care about his hungry poor people. Are you sure you're not just worried about Deb's stomach?" I flushed.

Curled, pressed, and hungry, we got into Daddy's truck and rattled over the dirt road to Uncle Michael's. Jan said earnestly with her hands on her big belly, "I hope we can get through this meeting without another of those awful fights on doctrine again. If only Michael's guys would realize that Daddy's the file leader and has a right to direct the people here in Canada. Michael's only right is to follow and be obedient. His kids would be a lot better off if he'd see the light and give in. If he'd be humble, all the problems of our Canadian Work would be solved."

Daddy answered her thoughtfully, "Well, dear, we can always pray for peace and hope that our prayers will be answered. Once people recognize the plan and God's true order, then this contention will disappear. And hopefully with two babies to give name and bless today, everyone will be filled with the spirit of love, peace, and harmony."

"You should have been here two or three years ago," said Jan. "For a while, the fighting almost came to blows in the meetings—I hated it. Us kids had to be told we could leave the meetings as soon as we bore our testimonies. It was never a problem for me because it was easy to see that Daddy was the one to support and people should just accept it. But other people were too blind to be obedient to the proper order of things."

She sat watching the road for a minute. "You're so lucky you discovered the truth before you moved here, or you might have ended up living with Uncle Michael instead of Daddy. Can you imagine? You might have been led astray." She heaved a huge sigh. "I shudder to think what might have happened to me. I guess people like Uncle Michael are put in our path to see if we'll allow ourselves to be deceived." Jan trailed off and a tear trickled down her cheek. "No one is as blessed as I am to have all of you." Mother put her hand on Jan's to comfort her, saying that we were together and all would be well.

We trooped into the big upstairs room of Michael's house and settled into our chairs. It was hot and some of the adults and children were comforting themselves with makeshift fans. I spotted Jean sitting beside her mother. Uncle Michael and Uncle Isaac sat stonily at the front of the room. After the final stragglers had made their way in, Isaac took his place at the homemade pulpit.

"Our righteous and eternal Heavenly Father, we come before you this day in the capacity of a testimony meeting and pray that Thy Spirit rest down upon us to the furtherance of Thy kingdom. We beseech Thee to do away with false pride and the evil, selfish desires of our hearts. We know that we cannot accomplish this glorious work to the honor of Thy kingdom if we do not accept Thy will in all things and bow to the dictates of your chosen prophet. We have come out of the evils and temptations of Babylon and given up our gentile traditions to this chosen place so we could live your gospel in its completeness and purity. Recognizing your hand in all things, we pray in the name of the Lord and Savior, Jesus Christ. Amen."

The look on Uncle Michael's face as Uncle Isaac spoke was frightful. These men were going to give special blessings to babies, but they acted so mad at each other. Everyone in the room seemed worried until Uncle Isaac announced we would now sing "The Spirit of God Like a Fire Is Burning." The stirring words and music resounded from the walls, as children and adults alike sang at the top of their lungs. The vibrations escaped to the surrounding mountains, and when we got to "We'll sing and we'll shout like the armies of heaven," the large wall of square-paned windows at the front and the big ones on the side were rattling. An uncomfortable silence fell over the room as we finished the last verse and the sound of our voices faded.

Uncle Isaac leapt to his feet and strode to Naomi. Taking baby Joab out of her arms, he beckoned to Daddy, Uncle Kelvin, Uncle Harry, and Uncle Michael to come to the front. They stood in a circle with their left arms on the next man's right shoulder and their right arms in the center balancing the baby. Uncle Isaac said the blessing because he was the father. He said grand words about baby Joab's being a great help to prophets and bringing in the new millennium and building the New Jerusalem for Jesus and so much else that I couldn't remember it all. His blessing for Priscilla was very good, too, and after all the men shook hands and congratulated Uncle Isaac on having two children for the holy covenant of plural marriage, everyone sat back down. That was when Uncle Isaac told us to let the Spirit prompt us to bear our testimonies.

I slipped my hand into Mother's. Uncle Isaac loomed at the front with his overpowering presence, then he, too, sat and the silence grew ever more intense. Finally, Jan stood up and professed emphatically that she believed Uncle Roy to be the true prophet of God, and her daddy to be the file leader in Canada. She had no more than taken her seat, when a boy I knew to be one of Uncle Michael's sons stood up and said he was thankful for his dad and for our prophet, Uncle Roy.

One by one the children from the opposing families stood to declare their belief that Uncle Roy was a prophet of God and that their daddy was the file leader in Canada. The tension had built to an almost unbearable level when Isaac's son Laman stood and proclaimed in fervent tones, "*Daddy is set apart to be the file leader, and he must be supported to be in order with the true priesthood!*"

The good feelings from the baby blessings were completely gone now and the room was suffocating. Mother had been squeezing my hand harder and harder with each pronouncement. With Laman's tirade, the pain became unbearable. I reached up to her and whispered, "Mother, my hand is hurting…bad." She relaxed her grip, then turned my hand over and kissed it gently. She had tears in her eyes and she was trembling. My hand started to tingle as blood returned to it, and I prayed that Brent would start to cry so we could take him outside onto the grass.

I fidgeted and pulled impatiently at my new flour-sack skirt. I was itchy and uncomfortable and had almost convinced myself that I could die in this very room. Uncle Michael got up to speak. Like his uncle, he was a big handsome man with a hawk nose and the huge shoulders of a wrestler. There was not an opportunity that passed that he or Uncle Isaac didn't brag about their wrestling matches in their hometown of Cardston. Michael's slow and rambling manner of speech was always difficult for me to follow.

He started into a sermon of the beauties and advantages of raising children "like calves in a stall." He was expounding on keeping them pure and away from the evil temptations of the world when Brent started to cry. I was surprised how hard I had to pinch him to get his attention.

Mother whispered a half-hearted shush to him, then told Nettie and me to come with her. We descended from the fires of hell in the meeting room to the relative cool of a summer morning. Mother settled Brent in the shade on the lawn behind the house—this little patch of green within the white picket fence was one of the few areas out of bounds to the goats. The grass was strewn with the bright yellow of dandelions. Dandelions were one of my favorite flowers because you could pick them for bouquets or eat them till your belly popped.

I turned my face into the breeze that blew cool from the surface of the pond. I danced and twirled, pretending my springy curls were the fluff of a dandelion seed, and that they could lift me up and carry me with the wind into the distant meadow. Except for the occasional tense outburst that escaped through the huge quivering windows upstairs, the meeting was forgotten. The breeze was just right. My curls had caught an updraft, and I was ready to lift off when Mother called softly from where she sat on the grass with Nettie and Brent.

"Come sit, Deb…this is still Sunday, and we must be reverent. Let's study your Articles of Faith for a while and then we'll do finger-plays."

I pretended not to hear her and crouched to pick from the dozens of dandelions within my reach two of the most special. Mother called again. This time, I ran to her quickly and offered the flowers as if they were rare and precious.

She took them, pretended to smell them, and said, "These are lovely, Daughter. Thank you so much for this special gift. Now, let's hear the first article of faith."

"We believe in God our eternal Father and in His Son Jesus Christ and in the Holy Ghost." I finished the verse in one breath and poked Nettie. It was her turn. We went back and forth until I rattled off the thirteenth article. Then we got to pick finger-plays. My favorite was Inky Pinky Spider, and Nettie liked This is the Church House, This is the Steeple. Mother said we could look at the flowers while she nursed Brent. I played for a bit and then needed Mother again, so I ran back and settled my head in her lap.

The meeting was coming to a close with strains of "The Lord Is My Shepherd" drifting out to us on the lawn. I felt a drop on my cheek and looked up with concern. Mother's eyes were closed as she held Brent to her breast, and tears rolled down her face as she sang along.

"The Lord is my Shepherd, no want shall I know.
I feed in green pastures, safe folded I rest.
He leadeth my soul where the still waters flow,
Restores me when wandering,
Redeems when oppressed;
Restores me when wandering,
Redeems when oppressed."

"I'm sorry, Mother. Please stop crying." I threw my arms around her neck, sandwiching Brent's sleeping body between us.

Daddy came out of the meeting with Jan and said we needed to go home now. I could still hear a lot of noise in the big room, but I was glad to escape to the quiet of our cabin. Mother had us rest in our rooms and look at books after we changed from church clothes. We got to eat some meat sandwiches to break our fast, which was strange because we always had an extra nice meal on Sunday or ate at the big house. After a while Mother said I should go play, so I wandered outside. There was a flurry of activity as Uncle Isaac pulled up, and Aunt Pauline and Aunt Loren hopped out. They scurried into the cabin. When I tried to get back inside to see what was happening, Daddy shooed me out the door and told me to go to the big house. Jeanie met me on the wooden sidewalk, and I asked her why I couldn't go back into my own house.

When I told her that Aunt Pauline and Aunt Loren were in there, she nodded wisely. "Yep, that's what I thought. If your mom didn't keep you with her so much, you'd know the answer to that one already. When Mom had Joab and Lydia had Priscilla, the same thing happened. Aunt Pauline and Aunt Loren came over and there was lots of fussin' and some screamin' from Lydia, and then those two go back to Uncle Michael's and we got a new baby. Happened when Katy was born, too."

She grabbed my sleeve and turned me up the walk into the big house. "Let's see if there's any roast beef or somethin' left to eat from dinner. It's Sunday, so we can get food if we want it and stay out of everyone's way. You might as well stay with me. I was goin' down by the bridge at the creek later. When a baby's comin', you can pick dandelions and eat 'em or any crazy thing you want and no one will even notice."

We went into the kitchen, grabbed some bread and a thick slice of meat, then slipped out through the porch. We picked up the trail at the cow pen and followed it over the culvert to the creek at the base of the mountain. I almost never got to just wander like this. Lying on my belly on one side of the heavy plank bridge that spanned the creek, I picked grass and buttercups and threw them into the water. I hung over the edge as far as I dared without falling in and watched them float to the other side, where Jeanie caught them.

A bit later we walked down the trail, where we sat with our legs crossed, watching some deer. They wandered around nibbling on bushes under the poplars by the huge rock on the trail up to the spring. Little kids weren't allowed to walk to the spring by themselves, because there were bears up there sometimes, but I had been there with Mother. There was nothing more beautiful in the world—I knew it—than the spot where that fresh water burst from the rocks in the side of the mountain. How on earth could there be enough water to make this awesome creek? It was just like one of the verses Mother copied for me to learn: "The earth is the Lord's and the fullness thereof." Except that I thought this part belonged to Uncle Isaac—at least I wouldn't argue with anyone about it.

Jean had finished eating her bread and meat, and we hadn't spoken for a long time. Finally, she blurted, "I saw you pinch Brent so you guys could leave church. Didn't think you'd do that…but know what happened on the way home?"

Jeanie was bursting at the seams to tell me that she and James and Jonah just about got on the trail to the gravel pit when they heard yelling. They went real careful through the bushes and saw Lem with Erica and Lavina, Uncle Michael's daughters. "Lem thinks Lavina's real pretty," Jean told me, "so he wouldn't hurt her, but he says to them both real mean that they better quit stickin' up for their stupid dad. He says they gotta quit sayin' he's the file leader. And Erica yells right back at him, what's he gonna do about it. And he says he'll show her, an' he grabs her arm and yanks her around and puts her in one of Dad's wrestlin' holds. Well, Erica's screamin' that her arm's comin' out of the socket, and Lem keeps twistin' it, and she's on the ground when up comes Dad. We didn't see him comin' with all the screamin' and cryin'."

By this time, I was just staring at Jeanie because I never once heard her talk this long before. Maybe it was because right now there was no one around to interrupt. But I couldn't decide if I was hearing her right because Lemuel could be real mean to little brothers and sheep and dogs and say horrible stuff about Naomi, but I didn't think he'd hurt a girl that much.

Jeanie stopped talking. "What the heck you starin' at? Don't ya believe me? Just wait till I tell you what Dad said. He just says to

Lem, 'That's real good, Son, real good! You know what's right with the priesthood, and don't you ever let anyone lead you astray. And others better learn, too, if they know what's good for them.' So Lem lets go of Erica, and Lavina helps her up and here comes Martin runnin' all out of breath tellin' Dad that Jan's havin' her baby and they need Aunt Pauline and Aunt Loren. So Dad runs for the truck and we hear Erica beggin' Lavina not to tell anyone what happened until the baby is born, so no one fights about what Lem did to her."

Jeanie stopped talking and I didn't have any idea what to say. Her story sounded so much like one of the nightmares I had sometimes with people getting hurt all over. I wondered if all this fighting had anything to do with the song we sang about "the Spirit of God like a fire is burning."

For the rest of the afternoon, we sat on the bridge with our backs to the sun and crawled along the edge of the creek trying to catch baby frogs. Someone hollered for supper, and we heard Jeanie's dad bringing the cows in for milking.

At supper, Bettilyn told me I was supposed to sleep with everyone at the big house tonight. At first I was really excited because I always wished I could do this. Then, I had a feeling I had done something bad. We'd been waiting so long for our new sacred covenant baby, and when it finally arrived, they sent me away.

When I woke up the next morning, Jan's anxiously awaited baby was here. After quickly eating a piece of toast for breakfast, we got to go home to the cabin. We were presented to our special, wonderful child, born of God's celestial covenant. Lena was the name of our new baby. She was named after Aunt Lena, who, Jan said, was the only other woman she ever knew who could be as good a sister wife as Mother.

Jan studied *The Motherly Art of Breastfeeding*, a book she got somewhere, and made a really big fuss about feeding our new baby. Nettie and I had never seen anything like Jan nursing baby Lena. All the other mothers who nursed their babies covered their tops with a blanket, sometimes even their whole heads, and you could hear the babies gasping as they suckled. Other women hid away in bedrooms or in bathrooms like they were real ashamed of exposing themselves. Not Jan! She pulled her breasts out of her bra getting ready to nurse, while Nettie, Brent, and I sat in a row watching the baby struggle to get her little mouth around the big nipple as Jan pinched it and stuck her finger in the side of the baby's mouth. Most always, unless Jan decided to lie in the big bed in the corner of the cabin and go to sleep while she nursed, she just sat in the rocking chair with her breasts bare and sometimes pinched her nipples. She explained to anyone in the room this was how you toughened them so they wouldn't crack and bleed while nursing. Although Mother seemed embarrassed, she didn't say anything. Whenever she saw us watching with too much interest, she would send us to sit in our room or tell us to run outside to play.

Jan even fed baby Lena the same way over at the ranch house, declaring, "I have certainly been blessed to be called of the Lord by the prophet to be an example and teach the growing mothers in Israel not to be ashamed of the beauty of procreation and feeding God's elect children the way meant by nature. It really behooves me to help strike down the false pride of people who should be thankful for this blessing!"

Although most everyone but her mother had something to say behind Jan's back, Naomi was the only one who ever said anything to her face. Naomi mostly fed her babies cow's milk out of bottles because there was some reason she couldn't nurse.

One day when she came into the ranch house in the middle of the afternoon to check on Joab, she stopped short at Jan's display and snorted, "You know, you could put those away. What do you think you are—some kind of prize dairy cow or something? If you want to spread yourself out like that, then get back to the cabin! If they're okay with that over there, they're welcome to it." She stomped into the room where Joab lay sleeping in his crib with his bottle hanging out of his mouth, harrumphed, and left the house, banging the door.

Jan's face went red for a minute, and then she just tossed her head and went on more about her calling to teach. Daddy said there was nothing more beautiful than a "mother in Israel" feeding her child, and he was always holding baby Lena and talking to her and telling her stories while he said goodnight to us all.

In a matter of only a few days, Mother was the main tender for baby Lena—all except for the feeding. Mother made sure there were the softest clothes and towels to bathe the baby, and she washed and kissed between every toe. She let us hold the baby's hands so she wouldn't be scared when she was naked and made sure the cookstove was just right so the baby would never catch a chill. When Lena was hungry, Mother would wrap her carefully and go find Jan and have her feed the baby.

Whenever Mother was around the big house, she would try to spot baby Thomas and see if he was all right. At night she worried about him and often said she couldn't understand what was happening with Lydia, because before her new baby was born she hardly spent any time with Thomas, and now it was as if Thomas were a ghost or something. If I was at the ranch house and the babies were in their cribs for naps, I tried to check on him, too. It was hard to tell if he was breathing—you had to watch real hard without blinking. I was worried, though, because sometimes I got to sit beside the bassinet with baby Lena when she was sleeping, and she breathed the same way. I never said anything, because my heart hurt the same way when I saw Mother looking more and more pale each day.

Lydia's baby Thomas got weaker and weaker. Everyone talked about his being the ghost baby because he was so pale and because his hair was as white as snow. Blue veins stuck out on his skin. Lydia hardly ever touched him, and he was constantly hanging off some kid's hip with his head bobbing up and down. Bettilyn and the big kids who cared for him talked about how weird he was and how he seemed like a bum lamb or something.

Toward the end of August, Heavenly Father decided that because no one knew what to do with Thomas, He would take him back. The harsh, misty reality of his life came to an end. I begged Mother to fix things so his frail body wouldn't have to lie in the horrible cold hole they dug in the ground.

There was a little graveyard in the valley on the other side of the hill from where our cabin was. Lena and her baby were buried there. Lena had been Uncle Isaac's third wife and Naomi's sister, and she had died just hours after Little Elias was born in 1953. The police heard about Aunt Lena from some angry sisters who were not in the sacred Work living the principle of plural marriage, and they came and asked a lot of questions. Everybody was real scared Uncle Isaac was going to be put in jail, but Aunt Lena was already buried and the authorities decided they wouldn't dig her up.

Bettilyn was the one who took care of Little Elias day and night after he was born, and when Jan was telling Mother about him, she said he cried practically nonstop. He threw up his milk all the time and looked like a hungry baby bird. They didn't take him to the doctor, and Bettilyn said that Little Elias died because she saw Aunt Lena in a dream, playing her guitar and singing her favorite song about a lonely little robin.

Everyone cried when Bettilyn told that story, except for Naomi. Whenever people talked about her little sister, she got real quiet and went off by herself into the barn or out to the garden or wherever there was work to be done. All the grown-ups said that Aunt Lena was working hard up in heaven preparing a place for any members of her family who died. I was sure she'd be taking care of baby Thomas because he belonged to her eternal family with Uncle Isaac. We all knew she was in the highest part of the celestial kingdom just waiting to be a goddess with Uncle Isaac and all her sister wives someday. Baby Thomas was luckier than he could ever be on earth, because now he would get to play with his brother, Little Elias, and never be cold again.

I watched as they made a box for Thomas. I couldn't stop thinking about the terrible deep hole they would put him in, and the worms, and all that heavy dirt. At the graveside ceremony, Mother held me close to her trembling body. She didn't speak for a long time, but when she did, her voice was filled with tears. "It's all right…really, Deb. His little spirit has gone to be with Heavenly Father. And you know, He must have decided He needed Thomas, just so soon after He sent Priscilla to Lydia and our baby Lena to Jan. He didn't forget about us, and heaven is warm with millions of flowers and waterfalls, like the one up at the spring in the trees. Remember when we walked across the meadow to the mountain, with the sun shining and the warm breeze blowing? Remember the daisies in the swaying grass, and the buttercups and the butterflies? Thomas will never be sick again, and he gets to be with Jesus Christ."

I followed the pictures her words painted, and I was instantly there. We walked across the buttercup-covered meadow, killdeers crying as we went, up the emerald greens of the densely covered deer trail to the spring. Daisies, snapdragons, forget-me-nots, and majestic Scotch and Canada thistles reached out to me from along the creek. I felt the beauty and the peace. If the place Thomas had gone to was this wonderful and warm, then I guessed it was okay for him to go. If he would never be blue with cold again, then I was glad he was gone, but when I looked up into Mother's face and deep into her eyes, she didn't look as happy as she should have if heaven was as wonderful as she said. But I couldn't think about that right now.

Chapter 4

The last two weeks of September were a blur of activity as every member of the group rushed about to make things ready. Everyone whispered in anticipation that the priesthood men were coming on the first of the month, and we had to be prepared. It was as if Christ Himself were expected. As the routine of our life was turned upside down, I felt anxious and lonely even though I was often with dozens of other children. Mother was so preoccupied that she had trouble watching over us. I stuck as close to her as a burr would cling to the back of a sheep.

Today I wanted her to give me a job so I could stay with her. "Mother, what do you need me to do? Let me help with baby Lena and Brent—I don't need to play."

Jan looked up sharply; I knew she was annoyed. "Can't these kids just go off and play with the rest? Momma really needs us to help with painting the new meeting room...and kids are so annoying when we're painting. I think Nettie and Deb should be just fine with the others. I'll go on ahead, and you can bring the baby over for me to nurse when she wakes up. You're so much more patient with her than I am. Then you can work while I feed her."

Mother was tying the last soft tie on Brent's hand-knit sweater. She studied Jan's face for a moment before she nodded wearily. "Yes, I suppose you're right...Deb, you can help best by keeping

Nettie with you and trying to be good." I opened my mouth like a fish gasping for air but was cut off by Mother's admonition. "I'm glad you want to help with our babies, Deb, but that's not your place today. If you can't stop this bad habit of arguing about everything you're asked to do, you will always end up in trouble!"

Defeated, I clamped my jaw shut and nodded. I reluctantly left Mother and the solitude of the little cabin and led Nettie across the yard toward the shrill screeches of children at play. We entered the barn and were quickly surrounded by kids who materialized from the dark corners of the huge white structure.

Bettilyn's son, Martin, and Jeanie's big sister, Aline, and some of the older kids took Nettie away to play princess. Another of Bettilyn's sons, Nephi, was to be prince. Their throne was the inside of an old tractor tire, but the veils and crowns were real nice.

Jean tugged at my arm. "Come on...we need to find eggs. Some of Dad's best hens got away and they're hidin' their eggs. Let's find 'em. James and Jonah are already lookin', but we can find more than they can. We gotta hurry 'cause they got a head start."

Jean and James were always competing—if not against each other, then both of them against someone else. Jean climbed nimbly up the smooth rungs of the worn ladder that started on the safe solid floor of the barn and seemed to go a thousand feet toward the swallow nests on the rafters above. I looked uneasily up to where the sun's rays streamed through tiny square windows at the highest point of the roof. Peering at the tiny flecks of dust that floated in the shafts of light, I moved my hands one more step up the ladder. With my feet still glued to the ground, I looked up at Jean.

Hanging back from the ladder at arm's length, she hollered down, "You're not scared or somethin', are ya? Come on. Hurry up, or they'll beat us for sure!"

At the first mention of the word "scared," I scraped together every ounce of bravado I could muster and pulled myself up. I advanced one rung at a time. My heart was thumping loudly by the time I reached the first level. I resolved that I'd rather fall crashing to my death on the floor below than let Jeanie know how terrified I was. I looked up at my white knuckles on the rung above me and finally pulled myself onto the hardwood section of the top floor of the barn. Still shaking, I wedged myself into a corner of bales and tentatively looked around me.

Since only the first cutting of hay was stacked up in this loft, there was a huge expanse on either side of us and a drop of at least forty feet. It reminded me of a picture of a big circus tent I once saw in a book at Grandmother's. Jean had gotten bored waiting for me and was walking the beams. They were massive rough-sawn two-by-tens that stretched from side to side under the peak of the building, tying the roof together. Jean walked these wooden girders as casually as if she were a cat or a high-wire artist. Her display of bravery and skill left me staring at her with my mouth hanging open. I'd never dare walk the beams. I settled on a bale of hay as I struggled to calm my nerves. My legs were still trembling from my climb up the ladder. "If you fall from there you'll just splat on the ground!" I hollered breathlessly. "Come back. You have to!"

Jeanie laughed wildly, twirled on her toes, and ran the rest of the way across the beam. With a final hop and a jump, she landed on top of me, sending both of us rolling end over end on the straw-covered floor. I laughed. I loved having her for a friend. "Jeanie, you're the bravest person I've seen in my whole life!"

She proudly assured me, "Someday I'll show you how to walk the beams…It's not really so hard." She jumped up and shook the straw from her short white hair. "We gotta hurry now. We're behind, and I saw that old brown hen over in this corner. Let's go look."

I was nervous about this because I knew just how hard setting hens could peck when you tried to steal their eggs. Grandpa always wanted me to help him gather eggs in Rosemary. He laughed and laughed at my look of horror when a hen pecked at me with her sharp beak. He showed me how he sneaked his hand in fast from the side before the hen could get suspicious, but sometimes he got pecked anyway. I followed Jeanie carefully over the irregular surface of bales to a recess in the hay. At the end of a little tunnel, a large brown hen tried unsuccessfully to blend into her surroundings. At our approach, she tucked her head tight to her body and fluffed out her feathers. "Well, I guess James and Jonah won," I mumbled. "This hen really wants her eggs…She'll never give 'em to us."

"You're such a scaredy-cat, Deb." Jeanie gave a blood-curdling screech, threw up her arms, and charged toward the poor bird. The hen squawked and exploded from her nest, then lost her balance and disappeared into the void. Jean waved at the eggs with a look of smug satisfaction. "There you go. I got 'em for you...now you haul 'em in."

She grabbed my skirt by the hems and carefully placed a dozen brown eggs into the hollow of the cloth. I gingerly straightened and took a few hesitant steps. The eggs were heavy and by the time I had shuffled to the edge of the landing, I was looking for other ways of getting our booty safely to the house. How could I possibly make it down this ladder with only one hand? "Maybe we should get a bucket, Jeanie."

She gave me an exasperated look and quickly transferred the eggs from my skirt to her apron. She disappeared down the ladder as I lay flat on the loft floor and slithered my way to the top rung. Jeanie had already run the eggs to the house and was waiting at the bottom for me when I carefully lowered myself down the last long step. She looked in disgust at my skirt and bare legs. "You should have pants like mine, then you can crawl faster on the hay."

I'd have traded my prettiest Sunday dress for a pair, but dismissed her with a toss of my head. "That's all right...Daddy says that girls shouldn't wear boys' apparel. It says so in the Bible."

I scrambled after Jean up the irregular steps of the bales at the entrance to the hay tunnels. She snorted and dove into the dark cavern. I followed her, shuffling like a crab on my hands and toes. We reached a corner and Jean turned to face me. Sitting cross-legged, she motioned me to stop beside her. I pulled my skirt under me to protect my bare legs and settled on the prickly bales.

Jean whispered in my ear, "You know what the big kids like to play in the tunnels?" I felt important when I got to hear these serious secrets about the big kids. Leaning toward her in the gloom, I held my breath and waited.

"Cows and bulls." She said it fast.

"Cows and bulls?" I was mystified. How could kids be cows and bulls? What kind of game was that?

Jean nodded. "I'm too little to get to play...but it's like the bull jumpin' on the cow's back for breedin'." She gave me a poke. "You know." I sat there stupidly trying to imagine exactly how you would play that game.

"Do you think I could play sometime?" I asked hesitantly.

Jean clicked her tongue. "I just said I'm too little, so you are, too, stupid." I sat there, her face just inches from mine, trying to comprehend what she was telling me. Our eyes locked for several moments before she looked away. "I'm hungry. Let's go find somethin' to eat." She abruptly crawled back down the tunnel.

I was grateful that the darkness of this recess hid my painful blushes. It bothered me that I hadn't listened to what Jeanie had to tell me. Obviously, if she was too little to play cows and bulls, so was I. I just knew that for the rest of the day, Jean would be disgusted with me for being so stupid, and she'd only play with the boys.

I woke up filled with the anticipation of a weekend of wonder. The grown-ups had been cleaning, wallpapering, and renovating as if the farm were to be inspected by the Queen of England or God Himself. Daddy said these days of conference would be better than Christmas, better than birthdays, even better than a million dollars. The priesthood brethren and the prophet would be here later in the day, and on top of that, Grandpa, Grandmother, and Aunt Glenna would be coming.

I had heard Mother talk about how much she'd love for Aunt Glenna to marry Daddy, so then her sister would be her sister wife, too. She mused to Jan how much fun they'd all three have if Glenna were one of the mothers in this house. I knew Uncle Michael's youngest brother, Jack, was in love with Aunt Glenna, and he came here often to cry to Daddy about her. Mother was always so quiet, and I wondered what it would be like if Glenna were a permanent part of our family. When she was nervous, she laughed in a high-pitched kind of whinny. I loved the way she laughed, but Uncle Isaac said that any woman who had to "cackle" like an empty-headed hen all the time would be more trouble than she was worth. He said it was worse than any woman he'd ever heard, and that was saying some, and he warned Daddy that it would be hard work training it out of her. The only time I had ever seen Aunt Glenna upset was the last time she and Mother were together. For some reason she'd gotten angry, and Mother was crying when she left.

I jumped out of bed and scurried into the kitchen. On frosty autumn mornings like these it felt so good to cuddle up in front of a warm, crackling cookstove. Mother was putting the finishing touches to the pies she was making, and Jan was briskly setting the bowls on the table for porridge.

"I'll go straight over when we're done here to help Mom finish her baking and clean up after breakfast. The brethren are expected before noon, and everything has to be in order. Poor Mom, she's at her wit's end worrying about Lydia and hoping she doesn't blow off and cause a scene for the brethren. It's only three weeks since Thomas died, and no one can figure out if she's putting on an act about missing her kid or whether she's really grieving. God knows she'll do almost anything for attention…That woman is such a trial."

She scurried around the little kitchen as she fumed. "I'll borrow this big apron of yours to protect my skirt. It would be such a shame to have to change it and not have our outfits match…I've never seen anything as beautiful as the roses you embroidered around these skirts. Who'd ever think flour sacks could look this good?"

Mother smiled and patted Jan on the arm. "And see how slim you look, too…It's only been two months since you had Lena, and you have your figure back already."

Jan beamed as she tied on the apron. "You can bring Lena on over if she wakes up hungry while I'm gone. You're so much better at caring for that child than I am." She gave Mother an extravagant hug and hustled out the door.

Sighing deeply, Mother sank into an old wooden chair in front of the cookstove. Nettie and I ran to her and fell at her feet. "Let's braid your hair," she whispered.

We sat resolutely until Mother had finished our braids, then Nettie and I sang "I'm a Little Teapot" together, practicing the deliberate actions we'd been taught to make with our hands and feet. As Mother sat in solemn judgment, Nettie practiced her special lines from the Truth book we got from Salt Lake City.

"A red glass makes everything red.
A blue glass makes everything blue.
If everything seems selfish and cross,
Be sure that the fault is with you."

As soon as she'd finished, Mother looked to me. I recited the 23rd Psalm. With a final check to make sure we passed inspection, Mother sent us on our way. "You can go over to the ranch house to play with your friends…but stay away from the barn and the creek. Play in the little playhouse that Naomi just built if you want…just be good." Mother gave me a stern look. "You know what's right."

"Please, Mother," I begged her, "I could do lots of things to help you until Grandmother comes, couldn't I? I'm big and I'll help really good. Please let me stay…please." Mother firmly sent us out the door with the assurance that she'd come and find us if we happened to miss Grandmother's arrival.

Nettie and I walked slowly toward the big house. Halfway across the sunlit yard, we stopped in our tracks to see what Uncle Isaac was yelling about. He was directing his attention to the boys standing in a huddle around the barn door. "Here you, Lem, Laman, Sidney, if the barn is cleaned out now, you can have the rest of the day off to do what you want. Just make good'n sure you're back here for the night chores…And another thing, don't forget that all the critters need to be locked up. If I see as much as a chicken runnin' around when the brethren get here, your backsides'll know it. Your mother'll never let me hear the end of it if the company steps in shit!"

Lem, who was sixteen, and Laman, fourteen, were Isaac and Bettilyn's sons, while Sidney, who was fourteen, was the adopted son of Uncle Kelvin Whitmer. Sidney liked the wild, free companionship of Lem and Laman, and they liked his willing cooperation in doing all the chores. The boys encouraged him to run away more and more often from his dad in town. They were constantly coming up with new ways of tantalizing him into staying, including offering him his own horse. Even though Uncle Kelvin kept coming after him, the guys hoped he'd give up, and Sidney could just become another one of the boys.

Nettie and I sat on the edge of the monster tractor tire that was part of her throne when the big kids were playing with her and Nephi. Watching the big boys was almost the most interesting thing you could do, and it would be a real miracle if they managed to gather up all the animals running loose and scoop up all the manure in time.

Lem and Laman actually stood still and leaned on the fence while Sidney was talking and didn't tease him about the funny way his huge ears wiggled when he talked. "You don't know how good you guys have it—there's always food to eat. I hate being hungry. Lots of times I steal cow grain…and get a beating for it." Sidney shook his head sadly and frowned. "The only thing I don't like is when Naomi gets mad at me…I think she hates me. Sometimes while I'm tryin' to figure out what I've done, she takes after me with a two-by-four. That last time she got mad at me for not movin' fast enough and whupped me with those tractor-tire chains. I couldn't move for days."

Sidney shuffled his feet. I'd never heard him say this much at one time without making a weird joke or pulling a strange face. He play-punched Laman in the back before he went on. "It's a good thing you snuck me food after that first day, or I'd still be layin' there in the bunks." He had a forlorn look as he rubbed his hand over his stomach. "I couldn't even keep from pukin'. Damn, I don't want to be in that much pain ever again! But it's worth it to be here, anyway."

Lem nodded at Sidney, proudly puffing out his chest like he was the king in our fairytale picture book. "You'll never go hungry here, you know. When we're in order with Dad we can ride and hunt whenever we want. And who needs a lot of cash? Your dad can work for the Town of Creston all he wants and get cash, but that don't mean a thing. The ones that'll get the reward are the ones that work for the file leader. We got one over on all of 'em. You know how Dad always says some people wouldn't know how to fight their way out of a paper bag, let alone get into the kingdom of God. We all know who he's talking about…"

Lem told Sidney he didn't need to worry about "that old bag, Naomi." He said it was her and probably Lydia, too, his dad was talking about whenever he said some women are just like an old cow who keeps putting her dungy foot in a good bucket of milk. "But he says Naomi's gonna have to bow down to him in the next life whether she likes it or not...so don't worry about it, Sid."

They leaned closer to each other and spoke more quietly. "We have our ways of gettin' back at her. We just have to be careful 'cause Dad says he needs her for a while still. She does a lot of work. If we ran her off, we'd never get to fool around ever."

Sidney ran his fingers through his black curly hair. His serious brown eyes were a stark contrast to Lem's and Laman's blue ones. As if tired of all the grim conversation, he grinned and wiggled first one of his sticky-out ears, then the other. Lem and Laman laughed, and they both punched him at the same time.

"Let's go to the cat-bird seat!" Laman hollered exuberantly. With a yip, the three boys disappeared up the hill in the direction of their tree houses and their "cat-bird club." They spent long hours practicing secret codes and messages for the big girls—sisters, cousins, and friends who got to visit. The code name for the girls was "tweetie birds," unless the boys really liked you, and then you were a "sweetie bird."

I felt sorry for them as they raced for their club. They didn't realize yet that they were out of order with the Lord's will when they spent time with the girls. As I lay in bed last night I could hear the quiet conversation between Daddy, Mother, and Jan. Jan's voice was emphatic. "Daddy and Uncle Roy are trying to teach all the kids that this pairing off between them must stop. We'll be getting into untold horrors if we can't get a handle on this. The new revelation about placement marriage is just in time."

Daddy's voice in reply was reverent. "It's wonderful knowing that the Lord will reveal who we should marry if we are faithful. Imagine God telling the prophet what we wanted for time and all eternity when we were still but spirits in His kingdom. I can envision this principle doing away with all immorality. And think of it...our little girls being given this revelation right from the Lord's prophet. They'll be guaranteed a beautiful life with a good man."

He struggled with tears, overcome with the huge promise that we could all become gods and goddesses just like the God of this earth if we obeyed this commandment. "Just think, all of our beautiful children will have this promise!"

Mother responded with equal emotion. "Uncle Isaac says he knows it'll take a while for this stiff-necked generation to get the gentile traditions out of their blood. But they must start right away. I love the assurance and promise our prophet gives us when he quotes the scripture: 'If you do as I say, I am bound. If you do not as I say, you have no promise.' So we know that we must be willing to sacrifice our feelings and keep sweet in all things and do exactly as the prophet tells us in order to be exalted. It stands to reason that accepting the hand of the Lord in the direction of the marriages has to be one of the most sacred principles of all."

Mother and Daddy were right. I felt so glad to know I'd never have to worry about who the Lord wanted me to marry, because the prophet would tell me who I promised in the spirit world before I was born. I would never have to go on dates with boys and try to figure out the right one, and I would definitely *never* play in any stupid cat-bird club! I listened to the grown-ups talk every chance I got, and whenever Aunt Glenna visited, she told Mother about how she had to sneak around with the boys she wanted to date. Jan made sure Aunt Glenna and Mother knew in no uncertain terms how she felt about Glenna's sneaky, immoral ways and how she should repent and get the prophet to tell her who she should marry—even if it was Daddy or Jack. Aunt Glenna didn't come to visit after that for so long I almost forgot what she looked like. Right now, all I was worried about was taking Nettie to find Jean and Aline.

James and Jonah were struggling to finish their last task of the day before gaining their freedom for the weekend. They were in charge of filling the woodbin in the porch of the big house with sawmill slabs from the giant pile situated close to our cabin. James was busy stacking Jonah's arms as wide and as high as they could go, but the boys were both slowing down. He called to us as Jonah struggled toward the house with his burden. "You guys can come haul some wood, too, ya know. Anybody that hauls wood gets a cinnamon bun." My mouth watered as I conjured up a picture of the sugary, raisin-filled buns that Aunt Bettilyn was famous for. In my mind I was already tasting the buttery frosting they would be smothered in as I dragged Nettie over to the woodpile.

James showed me how to hold my arms out just so. He placed a big bark-covered piece first, and then piled several more on top of it. "Say whoa when it's enough," he said judiciously. I wanted to prove I was as strong as anyone else, so I didn't say whoa when I knew all I could carry was three pieces. James was stacking on the seventh as I gritted my teeth. My arms started to waver.

"I told you to say whoa, stupid." James impatiently took a few pieces off. "They just fall if you have too many." He gave Nettie the two small pieces he had removed from my arms and we headed toward the house. Ophelia was standing by the kitchen door as I staggered up the steps. She stacked the wood off my arms onto the woodpile, and we made our way back. After just two more trips, the box was full. Jonah, James, and Ophelia raced into the kitchen and exploded from the door with cinnamon buns in their clutches.

Nettie and I hesitantly entered the kitchen. The very cupboards seemed to know that the Lord's prophet would be here today. They sat laden with days of baking and new sets of rose-covered china that Bettilyn insisted be bought for serving the Lord's servants. I ran my fingers over the shining surface of the nearest plate. The huge cookstove gleamed from hours of rubbing with blacking. Freshly painted and papered walls in the dining room and living room shouted new, and everything was clean, clean, clean. The kitchen was filled with the aromas of bread and pies on the counters, and roasts and chickens in the oven. A five-gallon bucket of peeled potatoes sat in the corner. This was truly a bountiful paradise, waiting in readiness to serve the Lord's messengers.

I knew I should just grab my cinnamon bun and run like the other kids, but instead I walked in awe around the kitchen and into the living room, taking everything in. The new addition—the meeting room/schoolhouse—opened through a new door in the living room wall, and was strictly out of bounds for children. My grip tightened on Nettie's hand as I prepared to do something forbidden. I stared at the picture of the prophet, Joseph Smith, on the wall; I could feel his accusing eyes glaring down on us. Nettie squirmed relentlessly. "Deb, we not suppose' to go in here. I don't wanna come. Let go…I'm gonna tell."

She pulled back but I tightened my grip and whispered in her ear, "We're just going to peek and then we'll get our cinnamon buns and go straight away. Everyone gets to come in here tomorrow anyway, so I don't see what the big secret is." I dragged her along behind me and carefully twisted the crystal glass doorknob so it didn't make a sound. I inched the door open and peeked through the crack. Nettie pulled her arm from my grip and ran away.

For just a second I considered turning back. That's when I spied the huge "moose chairs" all lined in a row at the front of this special room. I had heard the grownups talk about these chairs and what a find they had been. They stood six feet tall and were made of black walnut. Wine-colored velvet covered the seats and the backs. Even though I knew that Nettie would tell on me, the amazing throne-like chairs drew me like a magnet. It seemed so right that our leaders could sit in fine chairs that were truly fit for royalty. I gently stroked the velvet of the nearest chair.

There was a sharp hiss behind me, and I whirled in panic. I looked up into the furious eyes of Jan. She grabbed me by the arm, shook me roughly, and snapped, "You knew you weren't to come in here. I'm telling your dad! Only the women who are set apart to prepare this sacred room are permitted to come in before the meeting…and you are no woman." Her voice was scornful and caused more pain than the fingers that dug deep into the flesh of my arm.

She shook me again, then ejected me from the room. I flew through the kitchen and out into the sunshine, forgetting completely all my earlier fantasies about a cinnamon bun. My shame was intense; tears streamed down my face. I was sure that everyone who passed me by would know just how wicked I had been. I walked blindly down the boardwalk.

"You're goin' the wrong way!" Jean was standing on one bare foot on the cooler step. "This is where the little kids are supposed to stay. Mom and us're livin' here now, so there's more room in the big house for the visit. Nettie's already here. Where've you been? We even got some goodies over here."

I blinked the tears away quickly before she could see them and ran my sleeve over my face. I just couldn't tell my best friend the horrible thing I had done. "Oh, I'm just thinking and walking around trying to find my daddy." I shrugged. "But I'll come play now."

Jean put her arm around me and shepherded me into the dark moist interior of the converted cooler. It took a few moments for my eyes to adjust to the darkness and the odd sight inside. Rows of wire were strung from nails in the bare beams of the ceiling, and laundry hung on the lines. A large fan in one corner was blowing the laundry at gale force. Shirt arms, blue jean legs, and diapers seemed possessed with a crazy haunted energy that made perfect sense and fit in with the rest of this day. I stared in wonderment around the room. How could Naomi live here with her children with the laundry from three families choking the entire space? Big girls appointed as babysitters were feeding soup to twenty smaller ones from an iron kettle sitting on a long table that had been pushed to the wall to avoid the wet clothing. The aromas of lye soap and woodsmoke battled with the smell of potato soup. My mind reeled at being locked up in this cloistered little room, and I longed for the quiet calm of the cabin. As much as I wanted to escape, I was already in enough trouble for one day.

Jean carefully filled me in on the way these priesthood visit days would go. "We eat here and stay out of the way of the company until we get cleaned up to shake hands with the prophet. Then the big kids are split up to tend us little kids...and we have to do what they say." She ducked through the laundry jungle and came running back with a chicken sandwich in each hand. She passed me one. "We'll have fun," she said.

I was overwhelmed by the agenda and very unsure of myself. I found a place to sit on the smooth cement floor as close to the open door as I could get and ate my chicken sandwich. I stared through the whirling shirts, pants, and diapers to the children attacking the tin plates of sandwiches. The drone of the fan muted their excited voices.

Slowly, one after another, the company started to show up. Some came from the far south in Colorado City, Arizona, in the

United States, and others from three different points in Alberta. The kids exploded from the cooler into the yard, then stopped dead. Shy and awkward around strangers, none of us were sure what to do or say because we were not supposed to talk to grown-ups that much anyway—besides, these were God's special prophet and his apostles.

I moved carefully around the cars and the strangers, made brave by the knowledge that my grandmother must be here somewhere. Fear of the punishment Jan had waiting for me wouldn't go away. I was suddenly worried that Grandmother might not be here, and a feeling of nausea came over me as I realized how much I wanted contact from her world—from the peaceful place we lived before we landed in this noisy, confusing community of God's chosen people.

I spotted her and leapt toward her. No one, not even Jan at her most hateful, could have stopped me. My body was so tightly wound, I could have tackled the tallest king of the castle even with James on top, and won...even if the hill was surrounded by big wet cow patties and all the other kids put together. Grandmother caught me in her familiar strong arms and held me until I had stopped shaking. I was crying quietly with my face nestled into her warm, soft neck. I closed my eyes and breathed in the wonderful Grandmother smell that I missed so badly.

She whispered, "I have a handkerchief for you here in my purse. You have to hold your head up and not let people see you cry...You can cry later if you need to, but not here. We're made of sterner stuff, as your daddy always says." I knew she had the most delicate snowy-white hankies in her purse. I got to use them when I was little and lived across the road from her in Rosemary. Here, Mother tried to keep some hankies and clean rags for our noses. At the ranch house, kids got their slimy noses attacked with dishrags, pieces of skirts, and dirty aprons. Sometimes noses got so sore that they bled and kids cried. Sometimes they got runny ears that smelled real awful, too.

I didn't want to give up the soft bit of cotton and lace until Grandpa reached for me with a chuckle. He was almost shorter than Grandmother, which was strange because men should be taller than women, but you didn't really notice it when you got to know Grandpa because his round face usually had a grin on it. His eyes were always sparkling as if he was about to tell some kind of joke. I ducked my chin as he tried to whisker me, and then he laughed at his own teasing and stood me on the ground. "You little pup! You haven't forgotten, have you? Did ya see how she ducked her head, Selma? Ain't she cute?" He secretively took a peppermint from his coat pocket and slipped it straight into my mouth. I knew he'd give us more later, but he had to be careful because he'd catch hell if he brought treats out in front of all the other kids and didn't share with everyone—he'd have to have brought his car full. I was careful not to look around too much because I didn't want to see Jan, but when I searched for Mother and Daddy, all I could see were her eyes burning a fiery hole through me. To top it off, she had seen Grandpa give me the treat. I prayed she wouldn't cuss at him about it. I'd rather have given my mint to the cows or any other kid than have Grandpa in trouble about me.

Grandmother fussed around Grandpa, dusting his pants and making sure his coat was straight. She first shook her head, then her finger at him, clucking her tongue the whole time. "Now, Isaiah, you don't go and do that first thing when you haven't even seen her for months—you'll put her off. And you have to watch your grammar. You can't be a bad example, you know!" I looked up at Grandpa all worried, but he just grinned and winked. I smiled back, took hold of Grandmother's hand, and hung on tight.

Jan made her way through the crowd until she was close enough to Grandmother to present a tightly wrapped baby bundle to her. Grandmother smiled broadly as she took the baby and with her free arm drew Jan close in a warm hug. She peeked at the tiny face in the blanket and cooed at her before passing her back to Jan. "This is a truly wonderful day, my dear. You've been such a blessing to Adam and Viv to add this covenant child to the family." Grandmother shivered and looked around in search of Grandpa. "Let's all get inside so this wind and bit of chill won't give Lena the colic."

Jan looked pleased with herself as we waded through the people pressing around to say hello to Grandmother and Grandpa.

Once in the privacy of the little cabin, Mother, Grandmother, and Glenna had a teary reunion. Although everyone pretended to be happy, we all were horrified that Glenna was wearing makeup, had her hair permed, and was wearing tight pants.

As Daddy walked through the door into the mix, Grandpa joked, "Well, Adam, how goes the battle?"

Daddy picked up their familiar greeting. "It goes not to the swift but to those that endure to the end. How are you, anyway, you old sagebrush farmer?" He shook Grandpa's hand and hugged him.

"So you've done it, you old son of a gun," Grandpa said, giving him a playful punch on the shoulder. "That's one fine-lookin' baby you added to the family. I guess you're in real deep now...No backin' out!"

"You bet," Daddy chuckled. "They got me hook, line, and sinker, and I wouldn't have it any other way. Would I, Mother?" He hugged first Mother and then Jan, making sure that Grandpa and Grandmother both got a real good look at our new baby.

The banter was so joyful and good, my tensions melted away, and I sneaked between Grandmother and Mother to give them a hug. I sat very quietly, close enough to touch Grandmother's skirt and listen intently to the conversation. Finally, Mother decided we had better recite our parts before it was time for everyone to go to the big house for supper and the meetings. The palms of my hands started sweating, but Grandmother gave me a reassuring hug and a gentle push into the middle of the room.

Nettie and I sang "I'm a Little Teapot" with all the actions, and Grandpa clapped enthusiastically. "Ain't they just the little dickens?" He smiled at Mother. "It's real good, Vivien, real good. Makes an old grandpa proud."

He started to talk some more, but Grandmother shushed him up. "They aren't finished, Isaiah. Just listen."

Nettie stood in the center of the room, as dainty and fine as a miniature angel, with such a look of innocence on her face. She recited her special poem about the red glass and the blue glass. Everyone applauded and Nettie glowed with Aunt Glenna's enthusiastic praise. Aunt Glenna didn't talk—she gushed.

By the time I realized the room was quiet and everyone was

waiting for me I was mortified, afraid they could read my thoughts. My mind leapt back to my wicked intrusion of the special secret meeting room, and I couldn't stop myself from looking straight at Jan. Her fists were clenching and unclenching, and I knew what would happen if she caught me alone anywhere. I was paralyzed when her nostrils flared and she looked down at me, her eyes black with fury. The words to my recitation stuck in my throat; I couldn't stop the tears of shame that welled in my eyes. My body and hands were shaking.

Grandmother smiled, probably thinking I was suffering from a simple case of stage fright. "Come over here. You can do it! Just do it for me…The Lord is My Shepherd, the 23rd Psalm. It's my favorite scripture. Just look straight at me, and no one else…Think of the beautiful words and you'll be all right." She winked at me. "You can do it."

She was right. Even if Jan killed me later, I could recite my part now better than I had ever done before for Grandmother and Mother. I stared straight at Grandmother and took a breath so big that it hurt way down in my stomach. Everyone else in the room faded away completely. I knew this psalm so well I could say it in my sleep. It was a good thing, too, because I could hear myself saying the whole thing from start to finish with perfect elocution and expression. The only problem was that my heart was saying the valley and shadow of death…over and over.

"The Lord is my shepherd; I shall not want. He maketh me to lie down in green pastures: He leadeth me beside the still waters. He restoreth my soul: He leadeth me in the paths of righteousness for His name's sake. Yea, though I walk through the valley of the shadow of death, I will fear no evil: for Thou art with me; Thy rod and Thy staff they comfort me. Thou preparest a table before me in the midst of mine enemies: Thou anointest my head with oil; my cup runneth over. Surely goodness and mercy shall follow me all the days of my life: and I will dwell in the house of the Lord forever."

I was swaying and about to fall flat on my face when I caught myself. I had been standing as stiff as a poker and had forgotten to breathe. I took a deep breath, stuck my chin out, and glared straight into Jan's face. The daggers from her eyes turned to shock at the look on my face. This time she was the one who looked away.

Mother whispered to me, "That's the best you've ever recited your psalm yet, Deb. Thank you." As everyone started milling around to get ready for the evening's activities, she instructed, "Deb, you'll take Nettie over to the cooler for supper." Then she turned to Grandmother. "We must join everyone at the big house. We have a patchwork quilt ready to tie for our Women's Relief Society session while the men are busy…and, of course, you and Bettilyn have your special work, Mom. Glenna, you can come with me to the quilting until Mom is finished and we can all visit back here later."

Daddy gave Mother a stern look and she flushed red to her ears. We all knew she had said too much out loud about the secret ceremonies that were yet to happen this very night.

Grandmother broke the uncomfortable silence. "I really wonder that this women's gathering is allowed to be called the Relief Society. I would have thought a name still used by the church would be too much of a reminder of its downfall and gentile ways."

"Well, Selma," said Daddy, "we haven't heard any different from the prophet yet, so we'll continue on this way until God tells him different. And you know how important it is to keep a sweet, calm spirit in all things, especially when you've been called and set apart for sacred ordinances." Daddy was matter-of-fact with his knowledge. He knew the answers to everything. He also knew how to calm concerns and skeptical questions, but there was an unmistakable warning in his remarks. Grandmother flushed. He suddenly changed the subject and his tone. "Isaiah, are you ready to take the plunge and be re-baptized with the proper authority? You know you can't sit on the fence about this. It's just too blamed important. We really need you on our side permanently."

Glenna started on one of her nervous high-pitched fits of laughter. "Good grief, you guys, you'd think you were talking about taking sides in some kind of war. Like anyone not here might as well disappear for all they'll matter…way too deep for me. You guys are all crazy." She spun around giggling and took off out the door.

Grandpa cleared his throat. He was embarrassed. "You could

talk the hind leg off a goat, Adam," he joked. "I just have to do a bit more studyin'...A guy can't be too sure."

Mother gave him a hug. "Just don't take too long, Dad. The gospel waits for no man. Isn't that what you taught us when you first brought the pamphlets about this group and the Work to us to pray about?"

I interrupted, desperately tugging on Mother's sleeve. I was afraid of all the secrets, and the night was really dark. "Please, Mother, may I stay with you and sit under the quilt? I can play with Brent, and I won't bother a soul. I promise...Please."

Jan cut in with her sharp voice. "I suppose all the mommies should let all their little darlings play under the quilt, and then no one would get anything accomplished...There certainly wouldn't be room for us ladies."

Shocked, Grandmother looked sharply at Jan. Mother turned gray and stammered, "You'll have great fun with the kids in the playhouse."

There was no more time for talking as Grandpa and Daddy took their best white shirts and fine black suits into our little kids' bedroom to change. When they came out, they were so handsome and sacred-looking that I was sure they'd be the men best ready for the secret things they would have to do in that big room with the king chairs.

Nettie and I were dropped off at the cooler, Naomi's new house. We stood outside holding hands for several minutes as we watched the grown-ups disappear into the bright lights of the ranch house. Inside the cooler was total bedlam, with every child shouting loud enough to be heard over the din. All of the big girls, even the ones from Uncle Michael's and Uncle Kelvin's, were there. From the way the boys were acting, many of the girls must have been "sweeties" in the cat-bird club.

The big kids divided all us little kids into three groups except for Lem. He declared, "I ain't gonna be no baby sucker tonight. You fools can get stuck if you want. I've got plans and I'm outta here! You know who you are that can follow me. Adios, you big dummies." Three shadowy shapes on the outside of our circle slipped into the dark, and their voices faded toward the tree line by the creek.

One of the big boys said, "Well, I've got my group and we know where we're goin'. Getty on up, now."

We made a motley procession as we straggled up the hill to the new playhouse with our box of sandwiches and a coal oil lantern. He shooed first the big girls, then us four little ones inside. He entered and carefully turned the strong wooden lock on the door. Like a magician, he produced four small blankets and gave them to the big girls. Very officiously, he addressed them. "You girls are my nurses, and nurses do as they're told without askin' questions." He waved his hand in our direction. "Prepare my little patients for their operations." He turned to us. "I just about forgot to ask for volunteers to go first. We have to have a volunteer and there's a prize."

My hand shot into the air. Maybe this game was one I might be good at. "The doctor" was the one all the big girls whispered about when they got to play with him in the cat-bird seat. Maybe these big girls would like me, too.

The nurses straightened the four blankets and placed us on them with ceremony, as if we were babies to be wrapped up. I wanted to ask if they played these games every time God's prophet came, but no one was talking. The men had secret meetings, the pregnant women got washed up in secret, and maybe the kids were supposed to do these secret things, too. I hated to think of not doing what the doctor wanted. I'd seen him mad when he was milking, and I didn't want him to get mad at me. Last time Jeanie and I helped with milking, he punched his fist into a cow's belly so hard that she just about fell over. She was breathing funny for a long time.

I stared straight up at the ceiling and listened to the sounds of activity as the nurses settled the other patients. The dim light from the coal oil lantern danced eerily over the walls and ceiling in the cabin, chasing the shadows into the corners over the spots where my little friends were lying. I was a bit concerned that they were focusing on someone else when I had volunteered to be first. I heard a whimper, then a smack. "If you want to play this secret game with us big guys, you have to shut up! Remember what the prophet says about Christ on the cross. You have to suffer like Him. I'm just teachin' you—so thank me."

There was a long pause as the doctor concentrated on his work. "And you better keep the secret or you'll be no good to the Work. And if you're no good to the Work, you might as well be dead." His voice was a low hissing whisper. I tried to see if my other little friends were all right, but one of the nurses was gripping my head firmly so I could only stare at the rafters. The other nurse lifted my skirt and folded it right up to my neck. She then pulled down my panties and forced my legs up and out. When the doctor brought the lantern, he stood right between my spread-eagled legs and stared at my nakedness. I could feel the heat from the lantern on my naked body, and I struggled to cover myself. He yelled sternly at his nurses to hold my hands out of the way. His voice sounded strange, and he was breathing like the cow he had punched. I wanted so much to get my hands free to cover my red face.

But this had to be all right. All my other friends were just lying there. And this night was special with secrets. Daddy said it would be better than Christmas. He and the other men were in their secret meeting in that room with the king chairs, and Jan was doing secret stuff with Grandmother and Bettilyn, so the doctor had to be right. The big kids were tending me in our safe valley, and we were all part of the chosen race for the true church. Only a few people in the whole world were privileged to experience the secrets of our special group.

While the doctor was staring at my naked parts, my mind slipped into the 23rd Psalm. The verses were comforting, but I got stuck again at "the valley and shadow of death," and I hated that. As hard as I tried, I couldn't force my mind to think of the rest. One of the older girls handed the doctor a big round stick. He took it and jabbed it into a jar. I remembered the smell of the cream from the cow barn as something Uncle Isaac rubbed on the cows' teats. With a nurse helping him, the doctor intently set about his task. Someone held me open down there, and I felt the stick being pushed into me. As I squirmed, he drove it deeper, twirling it around and sawing it back and forth. It felt like they were scraping my innards out. I didn't dare try to stop them. I held my breath and clamped my eyes tight shut but tears trickled out. Even though there was no more pushing, I felt pain all the way past my belly button—if this was suffering like Christ, I could do it as good as anyone.

In spite of my passionate vow to suffer like Uncle Isaac said, my hands escaped from the nurse's grip and flew downwards. I made a frantic lunge for the stick but I was too slow, and the doctor grabbed my hands in an iron grip. He held my arms wide to the side, brought his lips next to my ear, and ground out another whisper. "You were the first one with your hand up, so you better enjoy it...And *remember* what happens to people who can't keep the secrets of the kingdom!"

He beckoned impatiently for one of his nurses, who scooted to his side and helped him straighten my legs and pull up my panties. He rested one of his hands on the front of my belly and slid the other down to my privates and that infernal stick. He touched my belly button...I hated that. He touched the fabric covering the stick and rubbed it back and forth. Settling on an upside-down tin boiler, he picked me up in his arms, spread his legs, and slid me down between them. Only my panties separated my bum from the tin, and the cold sent a shiver up my spine. He pushed at the stick again and again and again. The whole time I was reciting "the valley and shadow of death." I was finding it hard to breathe, and the pain grew more and more intense. I lay still with my eyes shut, repeating my prayer.

I couldn't look at his face. Finally, his breathing calmed and he put me back on the blanket. He told me I was real brave and that I was a big kid now. He nodded to the nurses, who removed the stick and wiped the cow salve from my privates.

I could hear the doctor move the big silver tin boiler over to the next patient. He was talking real low and breathing strange again. Except for the occasional whimper from one of the girls and a brief question from a nurse who wanted a turn placing the stick, everything proceeded in silence.

Every time I moved, pain jabbed straight up to my belly button. I had a wet, strange feeling down there and wanted to be wiped again...but there weren't enough rags in the world to wipe away the pain. I was sure I hurt more than the dying cow did with the calf sticking out of her that Uncle Isaac shot while she was bellowing. My insides felt full and raw and I was sure that if I peed, the stick would still be in the way. I wondered what would happen if I could never pee again.

One of the nurses came back to me and wiped some blood away. That worried me, then I thought blood had to be all right because Jesus' blood was shed to save us, and Gentiles murdered Joseph Smith, and his blood sealed his testimony forever. So this pain must be nothing.

At a knock on the door and a wild halloo, the game was over. The doctor and the nurses grabbed everything quickly and shooed us out. I tried to run away fast but I could only shuffle. I focused on the lights of the cabin only a few hundred feet away and walked carefully toward them as if I were walking the beam in the barn afraid to fall off. I maneuvered around the rose bush, across the porch, and into Grandmother's arms.

I was so happy to see her here. I was so happy to see all of them here. For some reason, I was afraid that somehow, in the entire secret goings-on, they might have been swallowed up by the black of the night. Grandmother smelled of something different, and I asked her what it was. She explained it was olive oil, that Christ had anointed his most pure and sacred people to protect them from evil and heal them. I could smell it on Jan and on Daddy's hands as well. I wondered if I should ask for some to put on my private parts. Maybe if I did that, the pain would disappear—especially if I believed really, really hard. But if I questioned the pain and our secrets in the playhouse, I wouldn't be doing my part in this sacred Work.

The next morning Nettie and I woke to sunlight shining in our window. I kept my legs together and moved them ever so carefully over the side of the bed. I needed to concentrate on moving across the floor to the pot. I was afraid to pee last night so I held it till this morning. I was glad there was already stuff in the pot in case there was more blood; they wouldn't be able to see it in the foul soup there. I managed to squat and when the pee came, the sting was so painful I couldn't breathe. Instead of screaming out like I wanted to, I sucked my breath in. I could cry without making a sound if I had to. Nettie looked at me when she heard my gasp. She flew across the floor and held my head in her tiny arms. "Oh Deb, what's wrong? I'll get Mother. Please don't cry. Jan is happy today—we have to keep her that way."

There was no more pee in me. I looked to see if there was a stick in the pot. I couldn't see one, but there was a small pool of blood and a faint red stain on my panties. I wished I had some udder ointment—that would probably help—but the doctor said last night we had to suffer like Christ, and that was for three days at least. If this was still hurting in three days, I'd sneak into the barn, find the cow salve, and rub it on.

Nettie helped me get dressed so we wouldn't get into trouble. She didn't ask me again what was wrong but helped me down the step into the kitchen. After that I had to walk and sit carefully so that no one noticed. I didn't need to worry because everyone was flying in and out of the little cabin getting ready for more festivities. I could hear Aunt Glenna laughing as she hurried with a pot of food over to the ranch house. Daddy was pacing and telling Mother and Jan that he *would not* be late to present us to the prophet.

"We have learned that if we brethren can't teach our wives to be as sweet and obedient as we are expected to be, we will find ourselves trying to knock at the door of the kingdom, and we will be turned away for even being two minutes late...So hurry!"

One last flurry of activity, and we were standing in a row outside the room set up for prophet Uncle LeRoy to receive all of his Canadian followers. "Well, President Johnson, here's my little family," said Daddy, carrying baby Lena. He presented her reverently. "We want to show you this beautiful new baby—our first child born under this covenant. We are so humble to be accepted into this great Work. We want you to know we're ready for your direction. Is there anything you need, great or small? We will do anything—just give us the word!" Daddy's voice trembled with passion.

Uncle Roy held the baby in his arms. After examining the tiny, fragile body, he nodded his approval and passed her back. His voice was solemn as he addressed Daddy. "Good job, Adam, I can see you're the kind of man we need to carry the kingdom off." One by one, we filed by and shook the hand of the frail, balding man.

When it was Jan's turn, she threw herself forward and wrapped her arms around his neck. It looked as if her skirts and bosom had totally swallowed up the little man. "I can't be so formal. If I can be so bold, I just have to hug you, Uncle Roy, and thank you for the wonderful blessing of Adam and Viv. I'm eternally grateful."

The prophet chuckled and patted her on the back. "You'll do. You'll do."

I was very impressed by Jan's boldness and decided to watch closely and learn what to do so someday the prophet would say the same to me. For a second I wondered if I should run back to him and tell him about the blood sacrifice I had made with the big kids in the playhouse. Then I realized that since God talked to Uncle Roy all the time, he probably already knew.

We filed into the same room that was forbidden yesterday. The only thing that looked at all the same was the big velvet chair at the front. The shadows, tables, trays of sweets, and the wine bottle and glasses were all gone. The curtains were pulled back to let the sunshine in, and lots of chairs for ordinary people were in rows facing the pulpit that Uncle Michael had made by hand. I spotted Grandmother in the room and got to her as quickly as I could manage. I grabbed onto her hand and clutched it as if it was all that was keeping me from drowning. The priesthood brethren filed to the front, and Uncle Isaac took his place on the right-hand side of the prophet. Daddy also sat at the front because he had been set aside to designate all the songs for us to sing. Uncle Michael sat with Aunt Loren and Aunt Pauline in the audience. He looked very stern. When I spotted Naomi for the first time, I had to look twice to believe my eyes, because she was wearing a dress. It was made of a soft plaid with shades of purple, pink, and blue. I had never seen her look this pretty, and I whispered it in Grandmother's ear. After a quick glance in Naomi's direction, she whispered back that I shouldn't stare, then she stroked my hand. I kissed hers.

Uncle Isaac stepped grandly up to the pulpit and turned the time over to Daddy. His pick for the opening song was "Up Awake Ye Defenders of Zion." Uncle Isaac seemed very pleased and his enthusiasm was contagious. In spite of being slightly off-key, he belted out the tune with such gusto that we all sang louder and louder until the last crashing stanza.

When the song died down, Uncle Isaac limped to the pulpit again, then stood erect with eyes blazing. "My brothers and sisters," he boomed, "it's good to be here in the capacity of a conference. We are a blessed and sanctified people to have the truth and light revealed to us in this last dispensation of the fullness of times. All peoples, Jew or Gentile, who don't seek out and come under the sound revelation of our prophet and revelator, LeRoy Sunderland Johnson, are in darkness at noonday, and the great destroyer, yea, even Lucifer, son of the morning, will take them and drag them down into eternal damnation in the last day, and they will be burned as stubble from off the face of the earth! We can't pussyfoot and lallygag around anymore!"

He fixed his piercing stare on Grandpa and Grandmother, and everyone in the room turned to follow his eyes. "We must make a stand and the Lord must know it." He looked around the room and then his eyes returned to Grandpa. "Who is on the Lord's side? Who?" He paused for effect. "One third of the hosts of heaven chose to follow Christ. One third followed Lucifer, the great deceiver, the son of the morning...and the other third sat on the fence waiting like cowards to see which side would win!" Uncle Isaac was trembling with a rage I didn't understand, and his voice had reached a pitch that I was afraid would lift the roof off.

"The Lord cursed these fence-sitters, our brothers and sisters who waited with us in the spirit world while God created this earth, and then their cowardly despicable spirits got the best of them. They got their reward, all right. They were cursed with black skins and became the descendants of Cain and beasts of burden. We will suffer the same fate if we don't take this chance to accept the only man God speaks to on this entire earth." Uncle Isaac turned sideways and stabbed his finger toward the prophet. "I testify to you, brothers and sisters, that this man right here is that man, and anyone who will not accept his revelation will rue the day!"

Beads of sweat stood out on Uncle Isaac's face, and he was

pounding the pulpit with his clenched fists. "I beg you, brothers and sisters, to consider this Work in all its glory and *repent!* We must be found blameless before God in the last day when we will have to pass before this prophet right here to even get to see the face of Joseph Smith, let alone Christ. I humbly turn the time over to him."

Everyone let out a breath at once, as if no one had dared to breathe while Isaac was speaking, and a thrill of excitement swept the audience as the prophet took his place behind the pulpit. His voice was calm and so much quieter than Uncle Isaac's that we had to strain to hear him.

"We have traveled far to be with you this day, my dear brothers and sisters, and the Lord says to let His spirit rest upon you this day. The Lord says, 'My people hear my voice and a stranger they will not follow,' so I know from the spirit of inspiration I feel from you here today and from Brother Merrick's inspiring sermon that you are all ready and waiting for the revelations of God. You have answered the call of the Spirit already, or you would not be here today and all that is needed to complete the test is for everyone here to go forth and root out the wicked traditions and idolatries of the gentile world. We must give up our ornaments and trinkets that some of you worship as if they were idols of Satan's gods.

"We are a chosen people and can only be saved upon strict obedience to the ordinance and revelations as they come directly from God Himself to you. Do you know how many people on this earth have this privilege? Only those of our people who are under the sound of my voice here in Canada, our people in Salt Lake City, and in Colorado City in Arizona will be given the privilege of this revelation to be saved and usher in the millennium in the great and terrible day of the Lord. There is a small, struggling band of people in Mexico that the Lord has us continue to work with, and we need all your prayers and tithings to help support our Work.

"We are told there will be two working in a field, and one will be lifted up and the other burned. Two will be working in a mill, and one will be lifted up and the other burned." He pointed a knurled and twisted finger at the sixty people gathered, and for the first time his voice became stronger. "Which will you be? The old mother church, the Church of Jesus Christ of Latter-day Saints, was put under condemnation by God only one short year after it was first organized by Joseph Smith for taking lightly the things revealed to the people by that great prophet. So since 1832 the priesthood has struggled to find a people who could help purify the earth and rule it with Christ after the Refiner's fire has purified all things. Any brethren who question the right of the prophet to direct them in all things spiritual and temporal for the good of the Lord's Work are stubble on the fields of the wicked.

"We are the only people who have pure authority from the Lord since the church has sold her birthright to be popular with the world. In other words, she, the great mother church who would not listen to the Father, the priesthood, and the prophet sold her birthright for a mess of pottage, just like Esau gave his birthright up to Jacob for a bowl of soup. The church has supported Governor Pyle in Arizona in his evil campaign to stamp out the principle of plural marriage or polygamy. She has therefore sealed her covenant with death, hell, and the grave, and all that choose to join her or stay under her skirts once they have a chance to hear the fullness of the gospel will die the final death, with no redemption. This is the day of repentance and we are given the chance to 'Come out of her, O ye my people, and be not partakers of her sins.' "

Grandmother was gripping my hand tighter now, and I realized that something had to be done to save Grandmother and Grandpa once and for all. My heart swelled with worry until the burning and pain in my private parts was nothing compared to it. I could never stand it if I was saved and Grandmother wasn't. There had to be a way to get her and Grandpa baptized with God's chosen people right away. Thinking about getting whisked up to glory while Grandmother remained behind to writhe in the devil's leaping flames until she was like the black wheat stubble was really terrifying. My anxiety grew until tears fell from my eyes onto Grandmother's hand. She reached into her shiny black patent purse with the rainbow mother-of-pearl trim and found me another hanky.

Laying my head on her lap, she stroked my hair and smoothed my face until the exhortations of Uncle Isaac and the prophet faded away. I'd have to figure out how to save Grandmother and Grandpa after the meeting because I couldn't do anything right now. I became vaguely aware that I had to change the way I was sitting on the chair because a fresh set of pains shot up from my private parts into my stomach.

I woke up to an especially loud outburst from President Guy Musser. Grandpa said that this man was responsible for collecting and recording most of our tithings and his father was Saint Joseph White Musser, so we must listen carefully to his history of how the priesthood was taken away from the mother church and given to these special men. Saint Joseph White Musser had many revelations for the Work, and he even wrote pamphlets full of the true gospel and twenty-four whole volumes of books called *Truth* that were published on the priesthood press in Salt Lake City. Saint Musser had written all about the evil government raiding our people in the States, so we were afraid all the time of the police, and every Truth book had hundreds of stories and sermons for every man, woman, and child like Uncle Isaac said. I knew this because Daddy had been carefully saving money for the whole set, and Uncle Isaac already had a copy and so did Grandpa. I never heard yet if Uncle Michael had his, but since he was such a troublemaker like Jan said, then probably not. Uncle Kelvin couldn't possibly live in town and have such sacred books. No one could understand the mission of our chosen people and the holy Work without finding fault if they didn't study them.

I shook myself. Grandmother bent down and cupped her hand to my ear and whispered gently, "You must try to listen. The brethren have come hundreds of miles to teach us, and the least we can do is listen and learn."

President Guy Musser, or Uncle Guy as the rest of the kids called him, was gripping the sides of the pulpit as if he were afraid it would sprout legs and run away. The light from the bulbs above him were causing his shiny, bald head to glow. His face was an angry red color. His weird, mesmerizing voice sounded as if it were being dragged through a wringer—it was so measured and even. I found myself afraid of it, which was really strange because I wasn't even this afraid of Uncle Isaac's yelling. Uncle Guy was saying,

"The Lord's people must be a tried and tested people. Anyone who has not been tried and tested to the very core will not stand the test, for only out of the heart's core of the heart's core that have come out of the wicked old mother church will make it. *There will be a test! A test! A test! And who will be able to stand?*"

Purple veins stood out on Uncle Guy's forehead from the strain of his passion. "The Lord's displeasure is manifest, and the condemnation is great and terrible of the people who want to be known by His name and cannot keep the secrets of the kingdom. The very least sacrifice would be the sacrifice of a broken heart and a contrite spirit. Anyone who will not subjugate themselves and sacrifice their very being and every member of their family on the altar of the Lord's Work under the direction of the Lord's servants without question will be *damned!* They will die the second death and nothing will save them worlds without end, and they will *never* be allowed into the holy protected places of the most high."

I shut my eyes and started to shake, remembering the terrible transgression of sneaking into this very room before the secret meeting. Grandmother looked at me with a puzzled expression and put her fingers to her lips to shush me. I prayed silently: Dear Heavenly Father, please forgive me for sneaking where I shouldn't and please help me to keep sweet and obedient so I don't cause trouble between Jan and Mother, so I won't cause our whole family to burn.

The shadows and shameful pain of the playhouse flickered into my mind but faded into the mysteries and confusion of "...the kingdom and holy covenants, and you must prove to the Lord that you can keep a secret."

The meeting came to an end with a resounding deliverance of our song, "We Thank Thee, O God, for a Prophet." Uncle Isaac hopped to the pulpit again and explained, "We have a meal prepared for all to partake of, and would like to bless this bounteous feast. If you will all come to order I will do just that. Our righteous and eternal Heavenly Father, we want to thank you for the spiritual feast and the guidance and direction you have rained down upon us this day through your holy prophet and his apostles. We are truly grateful you have seen fit to overlook our weaknesses and imperfections and give us this plan of salvation uncontaminated by the evil designing plans of the destroyer. We thank you for this land of plenty that you have led us to, for it is truly a land flowing with milk and honey. We also ask that you guide and protect those returning to their homes this day, in the name of our Lord and Savior, Jesus Christ, Amen."

I saw "the doctor" filing out with some of the other big kids. He ignored me and walked past me the same as he would have on any other day. I followed Grandmother like a baby possum, knowing if I stayed close to her no one would dare shoo me back out to the cooler with the rest of the little kids. All the grown-ups still wanted to impress Grandmother, so I was sure they'd let me stay with her if she said so. She was socializing with everyone and stopped by Aunt Pauline and Aunt Loren. "Rosemary just isn't the same since you all left. You surely have great faith to leave all you had there and come here to be part of this great Work." Grandmother knelt down and said to me, "You know, Deb, Loren and Pauline and I are cousins, so you are related to them, too. Grandpa Norton always said that blood is thicker than water." She looked up into their faces. "We'll never forget our younger days, will we?"

I watched in amazement as Grandmother hugged them both, and all three of them started to cry. I didn't think Aunt Loren and Aunt Pauline could cry if their life depended on it. They seemed a lot like Naomi.

I didn't understand much of what happened this whole sacred weekend…but maybe I was just thinking too much and not having enough faith. We had worked our way to the table when Jan stepped quickly up to Grandmother and addressed her in a brisk no-nonsense tone. "They have places for the kids to eat in the cooler. Deb should run along and not be a bother here so you can visit easier, Selma." My hand tightened in Grandmother's desperately. Grandmother replied in a tone I had never heard her use before. "That's fine, Janessa, it's good of you to be concerned, but Deb is never any bother to me. I'll just let her eat with me, and we'll share a plate so we won't be an extra burden. I know how exhausting this much company can be." Jan opened her mouth and looked as if she might try to argue, but something in Grandmother's eye made her snap it shut like a turtle catching a fly. She stared at Grandmother for what seemed to me an eternity, then turned wordlessly and left the room.

"Thank you so much, Grandmother," I whispered. My voice was shaking and tears were running down my cheeks. Grandmother calmly grabbed a bun, broke it in half, and shared it with me.

Mother, Daddy, Aunt Glenna, Grandmother, and Grandpa all assembled in the cabin for our farewells. I steeled myself to be brave. If Jan saw me cry she'd be so mad she'd go on about it to Mother for days after the company had gone. Grandmother held Mother's hands in hers and spoke with concern in her voice. "You know, Vivien, I've heard that cough too often since we've been here, and your color's not at all good. I want you to find a good doctor in town and see him about what might be wrong. This can't go on for much longer. You weren't well when we were here last time, either. Promise me!" They both had tears in their eyes.

"Oh, Mother, I've had another blessing for my health this conference, and the prophet feels that I'm getting better. I just must have stronger faith. Janessa is always saying my faith must be weak since I've been sick so long...but I still manage to get my share of the work done. I won't be a drone and a burden on God's Work."

They held each other, and through Grandmother's tears I saw her jaw set. "I think the Lord would understand your getting a checkup at least. And if you don't see about it or get someone to help you, I will be taking you myself when I return. But, Viv, don't wait the six months it'll take me to get back. You know we can't travel once winter settles in."

"Come on, Selma," Daddy broke in, "you need to learn your place better. You shouldn't question the prophet's word. You've heard these words before: When the prophet speaks, the thinking's been done. You have seen a few miracles in your day, and this can be one, too."

Grandmother's chin went higher and she bristled. "Yes, indeed, Adam, but I've learned a thing or two on this planet, and I've worked with many a sick and dying woman, as you know. I expect that the Lord just might have had something to do with the inspiration and learning that these doctors have. I *don't* believe that the Lord meant for people to suffer. You'd take her to the doctor if she broke her leg, wouldn't you? Whatever happened to the scripture: The Lord helps those that help themselves?"

Aunt Glenna, who had been standing on one foot looking bored, broke in with her laugh. "Man, are you guys ever a drag. You won't be able to pay me enough to come back here again. Good grief, I'm going out to see if I can find Lem or Jack or some of the kids that are more fun." She grabbed her bag and flounced out of the cabin, banging the door behind her.

Grandpa's round face was shadowed with pain. "There, there now, Selma, we have a long drive ahead of us and there's no tellin' what them boys will have done with the cows and sheep while we've been gone." He attempted some humor. "I won't be surprised if we get back there and find all the cows dry, the sheep rolled into the sloughs, and the hens stopped layin'. We'll be in a terrible fix then—a bunch of no-good rascals, those boys."

My attempts at bravery were fading fast. I dissolved into tears and ran into my room. Grandmother found me there and comforted me with hugs and assurances that she would come back. She told me she had left a present. It would be a wonderful surprise for my birthday in a couple of days, and there was one for Nettie when her birthday came around in three weeks. She said the present would help me remember how much she loved me and how good and kind I must be.

Words spilled out of a stubborn blackness that made me want to bite my tongue off. "I don't want the stupid present—I just want you to stay. It's going to be a million, zillion years before you come back, and Mother is sick and I want you to stay. I'm scared!"

Daddy stepped up into the little room. He was very firm. "Deb, stop your bawling! You're made of tougher stuff than this, and you just need to say your prayers more and be sweeter. Selma, you need to pull yourself together and work on your faith, too. I've got this all under control here... You can trust me. Besides, we're living with God's special people now, and we're protected from the evil things of the world. No children on earth are more blessed than Deb,

Nettie, and Brent, and our new baby Lena just born—born under the covenant."

Grandmother stood up very tall and straight. She stepped down into the room and helped collect the suitcases. Jan had come over from the ranch house just in time to see my crying fit. She had an I-told-you-so look on her face, but she spoke sweetly to Grandmother and made a huge fuss over hugging Grandpa and telling him he was the cutest man she had ever seen.

Grandmother finally lost her control for a minute when she tried to say goodbye to Mother the last time. Grandpa dragged her away and settled her into their vehicle. I didn't cry again, but Grandmother had to pry my fingers one at a time from hers before she could shut the car door. They slowly pulled away and disappeared up the curve in the hill.

The magic and the mystery of the weekend disappeared with the car, and even the magnificent golds and reds of the maple and poplar trees that lined the roads and climbed halfway up the mountain to the shale looked dusty and old. Over by the barn the sheep were wandering around and following their trails out into the yard. I stood inside the porch looking at the barn, wondering if I dared try to get over there to find the udder balm for the throbbing pain I still felt inside. Mother called me—I had hesitated too long. I knew Jan would have told Daddy by now what I had done.

Chapter 5

The present Grandmother left me was a doll with real blue glass eyes, shiny brown hair, and a princess dress. She was beautiful, but every time I looked at her I missed Grandmother, and when I held the doll, I imagined that I could smell her. The only thing that spoiled the fun of this store-bought doll was that Jeanie's doll had matted hair, one eye, and pen scribbles all over her face.

When Jeanie first saw my doll she gasped and clamped her hand over her mouth. She stared with wide eyes for the longest time, then gave a shrug. "I don't care. I don't need a stupid doll like yours anyway—it's worldly. Her mouth is too red."

But then she wouldn't play with me. She played with her one-eyed doll and the boys, until one day I decided I would give my doll to her. Nettie was standing nearby when I did it, and she immediately ran to tell. "Mother! Mother, Deb gave her dolly away! She's not grateful and Grandmother's going to be sad!" I tried desperately to explain, and although Mother understood my motives, she said that I couldn't give this special present away. The doll was settled in the corner of my bed, and I was told I would have to ask to play with it. Mother and Jan decided upon a solution—they would have to find a nicer doll for Jeanie.

It was about three weeks after conference. Mother had just put

Nettie and me down for our afternoon nap when a knock came at the door. Mother answered it. I could detect surprise in her voice as she greeted the person. “Lydia? It’s good to see you…Will you come on in and sit down? We never get to visit.” There was no way I could drift off to sleep after hearing Lydia’s voice. By experimentation, I found that if I moved to just the right spot on my bed and sat cross-legged, I could peek from my little dark room through the crack in the wooden door to watch this woman that everyone said was so bad. Mother might not even be safe with her.

Lydia hesitated at the door. “Aren’t you afraid people will see us together? I can’t think you could really want to be my friend when you and Bettilyn have so much in common—being first wives and all. I couldn’t imagine why you were kind to me sometimes at the house. Don’t you know that’s not a popular thing to do?”

Her voice was ragged with bitterness and pain. Even though I’d seen this woman at the big house, I was totally sure that I didn’t want to know her. The image of Thomas—blue with cold sitting in the puddle—was in my mind and I would never forget it.

Lydia was a pretty woman with cornflower-blue eyes, an eighteen-inch waist, and well-endowed bosoms, as Jan called them. The kids all claimed she was a witch. Bettilyn said that she sometimes howled outside on the hill at night. Since we moved here, I had heard wailing and crying in the trees above the cabin when I was trying to sleep. I didn’t know how to tell if it was a coyote, a cougar, wolves, or a rabbit screaming. The coyotes and wolves howled and yipped in the early mornings all the time, but at night in the misty blackness, how would I know? And why would a mother like Lydia want to run through the trees like a wild animal with tears freezing on her face? She could be wrapping her new baby Priscilla in a soft blanket and rocking her like Mother rocked our baby. Maybe Lydia just needed someone to teach her some lullabies to sing and that would help her feel peaceful inside like Mother said it was with her and baby Lena.

I heard Naomi tell my mother that Lydia could benefit from a good hiding. In fact, she informed Mother that she had done just that one night about midnight when Lydia was sitting outside at the bottom of the stairs closest to Uncle Isaac’s bedroom window wailing and bashing her head against the wall. "I just upped her across my knee and gave her a few hard ones, right where it would do the most good," Naomi declared. "You can bet she stopped her wailing then."

Lydia was talking again. Her voice was still shaking. As I stared from my dark corner, this witch-woman started to cry. "I needed someone to talk to so much," she whimpered. "I didn't get a chance to thank you for getting Thomas out of the rain when I was in town that time. I think Bettilyn hates me, and I never know how to handle her. I'm always doing the wrong thing. Isaac can't see it. I've told him I'll never take another woman's leavings, but he comes to me only when Bettilyn feels fine about it. I know celestial marriage is a true principle and could never turn against it, but if people would only understand it correctly the way you and Adam and Jan do!"

She hunched over in the chair and her tears turned into sobs. Mother stood back a second, as if not knowing what to do. Finally, she stepped forward with a sympathetic croon and put her arms around Lydia. "Of course you needed to come see me. And I don't care what anyone thinks...if you need a friend. We have to forgive people. I know that Bettilyn cared for Thomas just like she must love Priscilla now. At least she's always saying things like that around me—and she must believe in the principle, too, or she wouldn't have performed the law of Sarah when the brethren married you to Isaac. You must remember that. And I'm grateful that I was able to help Thomas in any way I could—I only wish I could have done more." Mother was crying now, too, and for a second I wondered if maybe Lydia was just a really sad, scared girl and not evil and possessed of demons like everyone said.

Mother was struggling to be strong like Daddy said all the time. "Adam always tells us that we must not question the Lord's will, that we need to accept His hand in all things. I've been weak, but now I think that I could have tried harder—that I should have been able to do something to save Thomas. I know how hard it is for you, Bettilyn, and Naomi all in the same house over there—and all so different. You're all good in your own separate ways. If only it wasn't so hard for you three to see eye to eye on things and try to work together. I don't know what to say, Lydia...except Heavenly Father took baby Thomas just like He took the other baby I was expecting when I was pregnant with Brent. Remember how we all thought I wasn't going to have a baby anymore, but then Brent was born? What a miracle! And you have Priscilla now, and she seems healthy and strong in ways that Thomas never was. So we can still count our blessings every day. Adam has us practice that sometimes, you know." Mother laughed, embarrassed to tell someone outside our family about the blessing counts Daddy helped us do if we were complaining or fighting.

Lydia's shoulders shook with heart-wrenching sobs. "I know you're right, Vivien, but I feel so guilty when I let myself think about Thomas. It's like I knew he would never be strong, and I tried to take good care of him at first in spite of everything. Then I got a black feeling I couldn't shake, like somehow I knew he was going to die, no matter what I did—that he would never be strong like Isaac's other sons, that he would just be a burden and not fit in. And no one ever said what you say about baby Lena. You and Jan and Adam are always bragging about how she's your special child, born of the covenant, the chosen race of Israel. I know Thomas was, too, but you talk about Lena like she's your own pride and joy, not another woman's baby...let alone Jan's. I used to think Jan was my best friend until I was married to her precious mother's husband! Now she talks to me like I'm a retard, and I hate the way she takes you for granted...Don't think people around here don't notice that. And I'd like to know why you just let her treat you like that."

Her face was contorted and dark now. "God help me, Vivien, I know what they're all saying about me, but the last few months before Thomas finally died, I could hardly make myself touch him. It hurt too much...I could feel death just waiting, and Priscilla was getting big inside me. And then Isaac just got cold toward me. I get so confused, Vivien...What can I do?"

Although Mother's eyes were misty, her voice was calm and reaffirming as she embraced her. "Lydia, if we ask Heavenly Father for peace in our spirits, He will help us overcome all the trials and tests of our faith." Mother held her and in a few minutes Lydia seemed to relax. When she spoke again, her tone was so assertive that she was almost preaching—it was as if she were a totally different person. When anyone else cried that hard, it took a long time for them to feel this much better.

"Well, Isaac is always telling me how happy he is that he has me...that I have a natural understanding of the gospel." She lowered her voice as if confiding a secret. "I have to stay away from Naomi, though. When I asked for a special blessing when the brethren were here, they told me that she would try to kill me if I wasn't careful. The other thing is I'm just blessed that I don't have a problem like Bettilyn. She's so jealous that she sleeps across Isaac's bedroom door. It's impossible to get to him privately without stepping over her!" She laughed a strange, hollow laugh. "I guess when you think about it, I could learn from Naomi," Lydia went on. "Do you know what she does when Bettilyn sleeps across Isaac's door like that?" She didn't wait for Mother to answer but plunged on, telling the private family secrets. "She actually talked to me the other day and said how stupid Bettilyn was to do that. She said there was no way anybody'd stop her from getting to Isaac if she needed to be there. She just stepped over her and shut the door real hard. There's no nonsense with her, I tell you. Sometimes I wish I could be her friend, but that'll never happen. I'm scared of her."

Mother looked very uncomfortable with Lydia's confidences and turned away from her, talking about Jesus and love and forgiving seventy times seven, and how it was up to God to forgive whom He would. Mother started pacing back and forth between the sink and the stove, fussing about making supper and trying to change the subject. Lydia was facing her with her back to our bedroom.

There wasn't a hope of my sleeping now. I was thinking about so many things at once that my head started to hurt. All I could think about was holding my doll. I wrapped her in her flannelette blanket, tiptoed from my bed into the kitchen, and slipped through the open door out into the warm autumn afternoon. Pulling Grandmother's gift to my breast, I wandered out into the back yard in my bare feet, scuffing the tops of the chamomile that grew abundantly. Holding my doll in one arm, I bent to pick one of the healthiest-looking plants so I could chew off its top. I looked nervously around me to make sure no one was watching. To start with, I'd be in big trouble for sneaking away from my nap with my doll. On top of that, I could just hear what the other kids would say if I got caught eating weeds and flowers again. They already thought I was weird.

Although I often wondered why they didn't eat dandelions, yarrow leaves, and rose petals like I did, I wasn't sure why I craved them. The only thing I hadn't figured out yet was how to eat the blossoms of the Scottish thistles. I had finally learned how to pick them so I could take a bouquet to Mother. I found that if I put my fingers just right to miss the thorns and held on real tight and found a branch with a big flower on it, I could pull down real hard and fast with my other hand, and the flower branch would come right off. Then I'd lay it on the ground and go back for three or four more. Mother always thanked me so much for these bouquets. But Jan just shook her head in disgust and told Mother that anyone with any sense at all would know that weeds were weeds and had to be killed, not put on display in a cup on the cupboard.

I realized I'd been daydreaming again when I arrived at the huge stack of cut slab wood that had been dumped beside the cabin. Slipping around to the back of the pile, I climbed partway up the mound and settled onto the smoothest white slab I could find. I cuddled my doll and braced my feet as some of the pieces shifted. Every time I squeezed her, that wonderful new, store-bought smell slipped out of her to remind me that Grandmother loved me. I still hadn't thought of a name for her yet, and I apologized to her for that. Nettie had got her doll just two days before and named her right off. She was a whole year and twenty-two days younger than me, too. Mary was such a lovely name. I didn't know why I couldn't have thought of a name like that for my doll. Maybe I'd have to call her the doll with no name. I chuckled to myself at how weird that would sound.

I'd have to do something about where my imagination went. Usually it worked really well—too well sometimes, according to Daddy. I kept thinking about Lydia and how she had changed into a different person right in front of my eyes. Could one person have two people inside her? That was bothering me. That's when I thought about Brent. Mother said there were two babies in her when Brent was conceived. That was after we came here to the sacred Work, too. That must have meant there was a baby brother with no name that didn't even breathe. I wondered what they did with him. I didn't remember a box like Thomas's or a funeral. Could Lydia have been born with a sister who died, and they both lived inside her now? Could Brent turn out to be just like Lydia with two people living in him?

I squeezed my doll with no name close to my breast and sang over and over the "sunshine" song that wouldn't leave my mind.

I heard the sound of Lydia's voice. "Thanks for talking, Viv, it's really helped." I peeked around the corner of the woodpile at the cabin. Lydia stepped out onto the porch. "I suppose it's a good idea to find ways to see Isaac where it won't upset Bettilyn. It'll be my secret mission. Things will work out if I have faith...You're so right. See you tomorrow." She stepped lightly across the yard to the big house.

I tensed as I tried to decide how to get back inside and into my bed without being seen. There was only one entrance to the cabin, and Mother wasn't busy with Lydia anymore. I braced myself. Mother came to the door and anxiously called my name. I knew I had waited too long and my whole body suddenly went all prickly. I slid to the bottom of the pile and carefully buried the doll under the shiny white pine slabs. Arranging a big one with bark on both sides to mark the spot, I ran to the house. I'd come back for her later and slip her into the house when no one was watching.

Mother looked relieved when she saw me running toward her. Although I was expecting the worst, she just spoke softly to me. "Daughter, you mustn't scare me like that. I thought you were asleep and when I couldn't find you, I was worried sick...Please be more obedient." I could hear tears in her throat, and I could tell she was still thinking about fighting and dead babies. She looked so weary and gray that I would have almost felt better if she'd spanked me. "Don't you understand that if something had happened to you, I wouldn't have even checked for you because I thought you were safe here in the bedroom."

I threw my arms around Mother's neck as she was tucking me

back into bed, disturbing the covers she had just finished smoothing down. "I'm sorry, Mother, I won't do it again. You love me, right?"

"Why would you ask that? You know I love you. You are my beautiful little daughter. Everything is all right, it really is." A tired, unearthly calm flowed from her body into mine, and I allowed her to pry my arms from her neck. Everything would be all right. Mother said it would be, so it couldn't be otherwise. I felt guilty about my doll resting alone in the woodpile, but I'd get her back as soon as I woke up and then I'd never touch her again without permission. Mother would never have to know that I disobeyed even worse than she thought, and I'd make sure she would never be disappointed in me again.

The events of the last month drifted through my mind as my tired body settled into sleep. The excitement of the brethren coming, the joy of seeing Grandmother, the shadows and confused pain of playing house, the secrets, Grandmother going, and my birthday.

I woke with a start to the smell of supper cooking and the sounds of Nettie and Brent playing together. I sat up, brushed the sleep out of my eyes, and ran to the kitchen to ask Mother if I could haul a bit of wood. She seemed puzzled but gave me permission. I left the house at a run but stopped dead just off the porch. The woodpile was very different! My heart gave a sick lurch as I ran around to where I left my doll. The pile had taken on the shape of a giant doll-eating monster.

I was pulling frantically at the wood, flinging it this way and that, when a gruff voice barked, "Here! Here! Cut that out unless you want to restack the whole pile. You're acting crazy. Get on out of here before I boot you into next week!"

Uncle Isaac stepped down from the huge dump truck that had just finished spewing its load on top of the other pile. The big steel gate on the truck was still swinging slowly back and forth as he came up behind me. He stopped with his legs spread wide and his hands clenched on his hips. His striped coveralls and leather gloves were covered with sawdust. He had yelled at me before, but he had never, ever, said he'd boot me like he booted James and Jonah. I could see that he was really, really mad at me. I knew that since he worked with the prophet all the time as the file leader, he must know exactly what I did wrong. He was here to witness my shame. Of an instant, I burst into tears, spun on my bare heel, and bolted back to the cabin.

I stood silently trembling just inside the door. Mother stepped to my side. "Deb, what's the matter?" When I didn't answer, she gave me a shake. "Deb, you look as if you've seen a ghost."

"It's disappeared," I blurted. "I was bad, and now it's gone 'cause I took it outside...The woodpile has it. Please help me!" I was screaming hysterically.

Mother shook me again, a little harder this time. "What's gone? Calm down...I can't make any sense out of this."

"My doll! Grandmother's beautiful present!"

Mother held me firmly by both shoulders and smacked me sharply on the cheek. I gasped and stood there shuddering. My screams had finally stopped.

"It'll be all right. We'll find the doll, but you must hush. Janessa is resting and baby Lena is sleeping."

We went outside and Mother and Nettie and I sifted through the woodpile from one end to the other. Even though we searched until dark, we could find no trace of my doll. My only hope was that Daddy could think of some way of finding her before she had to spend the night outside all alone. I was disappointed. He was tired after a long day at work. "We'll look again in the morning but you mustn't set your heart on worldly things, Deb. Besides, if you had been obedient, and if you could ever be sweet, you wouldn't be in this fix!" I knew that he was right. I cried and begged him to forgive me. He shook his head in admonition, then took me in his arms to comfort me.

In the morning I rushed outside with Daddy in hopes that a miracle would deliver my doll back to me. My face dropped the moment Daddy opened the door. The first snow of winter had settled six inches deep that night over our secluded mountain valley and the woodpile. Any further attempts to search for my lonely, cold doll were now abandoned. I kept hoping that her blanket would keep her warm and protect her at least a little bit. Every time I passed the woodpile I remembered her, my moment of rebellious disobedience, and the terrible consequences. When Nettie was playing with her new doll, all I could do was open the yellow hope chest Daddy had made for me. I would fold and refold the baby blankets, nightgowns, and sweaters that people gave me on gift days. Jeanie didn't have a hope chest but would sometimes bring her cardboard box of baby clothes over to the cabin, and we would talk about when we got to dress our own real babies and not dumb dolls.

The winter settled in hard and our little valley was filled with a damp fog that threatened to choke all of us. Mother's cough was worse, and Nettie, Brent, and I all got whooping cough. The hacking that went on day and night was more exhausting than pulling weeds or hauling wood without stopping for an entire day. Mother's favorite remedy was Mentholatum on a cold, wet washcloth secured by a prickly woolen sock wrapped around our necks many times.

Baby Lena didn't get the croup like the rest of us did, but Mother was always anxious about the possibility. Although the baby never really got sick, she didn't seem to be growing very fast, either. Sometimes us kids were allowed to hold her if we sat down first and held her head just right. If Mother was busy doing something else, she made sure we were watching the baby sleep.

Jan was busy with starting the new school. She had to have help with the organization because all major decisions needed to be made by the priesthood men. It was a big job setting up a schedule and gathering money for books from Daddy and Uncle Isaac and Uncle Michael. Jan got really upset with Uncle Michael one day and she rushed into the cabin, banging the door so hard it rattled the walls. Baby Lena was startled; her little face wrinkled and her tiny blue hands curled into cat claws.

Mother vaulted from her chair, scooped up Lena, and began cooing to her. Nettie, Brent, and I huddled together and moved toward our bedroom. Mother slid the baby into the bassinet. In seconds she had crossed the floor and thrown her arms around Jan. "I know they chose the right person in you to start God's school, and you have my full support," she said. "Please calm down, Janessa.

Lena seems so listless today, and we don't want to stress her further." But Jan paid no heed to Mother and her attempts to settle Lena.

Mother wasn't sleeping much at night either, because when I got up to pee, she was always in the chair by the baby. When she spotted me, she put her finger to her lips and held out her other arm for my midnight hug. I would have told her that it hurt me to pee, but I could see she was already worried enough with Lena, and I didn't want to tell her about the playhouse and the stick. I wondered how to fix a peeing problem—I could maybe have tried drinking hops tea like Mother. I sneaked a sip of it but it tasted yucky, and I decided to try some sacred olive oil instead. It was really tricky to get to the bottle, though, because it was special and hidden away in the dresser drawer where kids were not supposed to go. I saw Daddy and Grandpa consecrate it during conference by holding the bottle with the cap off and praying a blessing over it. Daddy said that the priesthood gave him and Grandpa the power to act in God's name. I was sure that just a bit of this special oil would take away the burning so I didn't feel like I had to pee all the time.

Earlier in the day I got a lid from an empty bottle of lotion that Mother had thrown away. When everyone was over at the big house, I poured a tiny bit out of the special bottle into the lid and hid it in a corner in the bedroom. That night after Daddy was done listening to our prayers, I got my lid full of oil and put it on my private parts. While I rubbed it in, I prayed for healing and comfort, just like I saw Daddy do when he gave Mother and Jan blessings on their heads. The only thing I knew for sure was that the oil warmed things up right away. That made me think that I had it in the right place. I felt comforted and had big hopes that when I woke up the pain would be less, because right now it didn't hurt so much at all.

During the night Daddy came into the bedroom weeping and pulled me out of my sleep into his arms. "Our beautiful baby is gone to heaven. She will be with Thomas, Little Elias, and Aunt Lena…It will be little Lena and big Lena in heaven together. I guess Heavenly Father only loaned her to us for a little while."

In the morning I wondered if I had just had a terrible dream, but when I got to the little bassinet in search of Lena, it was empty. I stood by the crib for a long time thinking that she couldn't really be gone.

The grown-ups talked about "crib death" and the police came. They took Jan into their car and talked to her for hours. They took Daddy into town and talked to him even longer. The prophet and Uncle Isaac were all concerned that Daddy should try to remain anonymous. Daddy said that meant Jan would have to say she was an unwed mother with a dead baby. He said he wouldn't do that because he was proud to admit that he was Lena's father. Although the police finally decided that the baby's death was an act of God, they wouldn't give permission for her to be buried in the little cemetery on our land.

Even though we were forced to bury our baby in a gentile cemetery in Creston, we could still protect her precious body with the special priesthood blessing that Uncle Isaac consecrated the gravesite with. He held both his arms to the square when he said the prayer so that God would be watching extra careful. Lena's tiny, perfect body was dressed in white satin and laid in a coffin that was designed and handmade by Daddy. Nettie, Brent, and I got to kiss her cheek and touch her tiny fingers one last time before they put the lid on her box. Daddy stood with his arms around us. His voice was almost a whisper and he was on the verge of tears. "She's really just sleeping. We are so blessed that we're part of God's chosen people here. She's an innocent, perfect child and will surely be in heaven in the highest degree of glory forever." We were only consoled by the fact that our tiny sister would be playing in heaven with Thomas, Aunt Lena, and Little Elias. We were sure that they were happy and warm.

After baby Lena died, Mother cried constantly for weeks. One afternoon after she had been crying all day, Daddy came to our room. Mother was sobbing on the floor by my bed. My eyes were closed and I was trying to sleep, but I could hear her pain and it was huge. I was glad that Daddy was here now because I couldn't seem to help Mother in any way, and I was afraid. Daddy knelt down on the floor beside Mother, held her, and rocked her in his arms.

"Viv, tell me why you're so sad. I can't bear to see you this way." His voice cracked and soon he was crying, too.

A flood of words burst from Mother. "Oh, Adam, I should have checked her again! That I'll never have any more of my own made me want to watch over her even more. But this time, I missed watching, and I don't know what to do with myself."

She sobbed some more and caught her breath. "I'm tired and my chest hurts all the time. I'm sick of bleeding, almost all month. Sometimes I think my lifeblood will drain completely away. I don't know what to do anymore about all the fighting at Uncle Isaac's. Bettilyn tells me one thing about Lydia…and Lydia says something else about Bettilyn…and they all scream and fight and say that Naomi hates everybody most of the time. None of them even try to be civil, let alone sweet. And the kids over there—I worry about them all the time. And who is right between Uncle Isaac and Uncle Michael? I don't know anymore and I can't even think about it. I know Heavenly Father will take care of things. He has to…this can't go on forever." She shuddered in Daddy's arms and her breathing slowed down. "Most of all I hate to complain. I know that complaining is the spirit of the devil, and that I can be strong. Please forgive me, Adam. I am so grateful to be here where at least we know that we're getting the pure gospel. We can't blame the shortcomings of the people on the gospel, can we?" She gave Daddy a crooked teary smile, and he held her closer.

He spoke in a low voice, but there was hope in his tone. "I know that all of the fighting and contention is hard for you. I didn't want to tell you until I thought it could work, but Uncle Isaac and the brethren feel that we should buy property in Canyon. There isn't enough cash around here to keep two families going, so they recommended that I find work. It'll be a bit tough for a while, but we can do it. You'll love it, Viv…it's so quiet and private down there by the river, and we'll still be close to Brother Isaac and his family, so we can help the Work grow. I'll take that mechanics job they offered me at the tractor dealership. That means I'll have to work with the Gentiles, but it's the only way we'll be able to get the money we need to work things out." He paused. "I'm sorry I couldn't do more for you all, but things have been tight here on the ranch—there are a lot of mouths to feed. We'll have to find if a doctor can help you. The Lord will help us, especially since we have direction for our move from the prophet."

I was lulled to sleep by Daddy's soft, coaxing voice as he poured out reassuring words to Mother. But his words didn't reach into my nightmare, where baby Lena turned into a moldy, cold, blind dolly buried under a woodpile. Almost every night after Mother and Daddy tucked me in, I would lie awake listening to the sounds in the dark, fearing the sleep I knew must come. Night after night baby Lena came to me. One moment, I'd be holding her like I did when she was with us, making sure that her head was supported carefully against my tummy. The next moment, she would turn into a wet, cold doll. Terror filled me as I stared down at her, part of me wanting to be rid of the wretched thing, part of me afraid I might hurt her neck if I moved too quickly. It was her blind eyes that scared me most, and the mold. How could poor baby Lena do other than rot and mold when buried in that cold, damp ground? But why were the white satin of her dress and the sweet-smelling cedar of the coffin just as beautiful as when Mother had sewn the cloth together and Daddy had placed the final nail?

The bone-penetrating fog, the dirty gray of the sky, and the big brown barnyard puddles of winter gave way to warmer days, tender purple violets, and bursts of green all over the valley. Jan was going to have another baby. All over the ranch, lambs and calves were being born. It was almost possible to forget the winter had been so long and hard. Except for her usual faintness, Mother seemed to gain strength. It was as if the sun had brought with it a miracle.

During the long winter, the woodpile that buried my doll had been used down until now it was fast disappearing. One evening after chores, there came a knock at the door. I answered it to find James standing silently on the porch with Jonah a step behind him. Neither of them talked even after Mother came to the door. With a shy, crooked smile, James held before him my doll. The winter had not treated her kindly—her glass eyes were blind and her hair was matted and dull. She was stained with dirt and muddy water. I recognized her as the very same doll as the one in my nightmares. I reached my hand out and accepted James's offering, and he left without saying a word. I washed her and dressed her in the soft flannel nightgown that Grandmother had left for her. Somehow, I loved her even more now than I did before I lost her. That night I lay awake until everyone else in the house was asleep. When everything had been quiet for a long time, I made my way to Mother's chair. Holding my doll with no name tight to my breast, I rocked her gently back and forth. Baby Lena never came to me in a nightmare again.

Uncle Isaac selected a piece of ground beside the creek and plowed it for a garden. While the mothers and older girls were planting, we little kids ran like wild things through the rich, black dirt and splashed into the ice-cold waters of the creek. Jeanie and James rolled their pants up to their knees and found slippery, silvery clay in the bank of the creek to make figures out of. Before long they were smoothing it up their arms and legs. The hot sun, the clean, cold water, and the smooth clay were all just parts of what Uncle Isaac called our heaven on earth.

To make this spring perfect, Grandpa and Grandmother decided to be baptized and join this group that we were living and breathing for. The celebration and joy at this time filled the valley and spilled over onto Uncle Michael's place. After Grandpa and Grandmother had gone back to their prairie home, Daddy took us out of Uncle Isaac's secluded valley in Lister to see the new land that the prophet had directed Daddy to buy.

It was a lonely feeling to leave the familiar boundaries of the ranch and the mountains and travel six miles down unfamiliar roads, but we had looked forward to this adventure for weeks. Daddy said we were like pioneers in the olden days. It became very clear that he was not exaggerating as we slowly circled down the bright, cornflower-lined dirt road with its hairpin corners. It was an old logging road that wound its way to the riverbed where loggers had come years before to remove giant cedar trees. We entered a tiny clearing to find apple, pear, plum, and apricot trees stretching to the farthest edges of the property on all sides. The trees were gnarled and overgrown—they must have been planted many, many years ago. Tall, graceful cedar trees stood at the end of the road.

Daddy looked in eager anticipation for the reaction from his women. "Well, here we are. The weeds have taken over, the orchard needs pruning, and the house needs some fixing up, but we can do it. I can hardly wait...What about you?"

Mother and Jan looked at one another. "It's really lovely here, Adam," Mother said.

"Let's see the house!" Jan shouted excitedly.

The house was nestled in the grove of cedar trees. It looked sturdy enough even though Daddy said it was built in the 1920s. It was covered with hand-split cedar shakes. Although they were weathered by decades of rain and hot sun, each piece still had a personality all its own. The foundation and basement were built with river rocks that were about eight to twelve inches across. Each of them was different in color and shape but roughly the same size. The floor joists were smooth-peeled cedar logs that were strong enough, but definitely not on the square. If you took a marble and set it on one end of the living room floor, it would roll all the way to the other end. The walls were covered with bright flowery paper that was brittle with age. The colors were faded, but the flowers themselves were very detailed and fascinating. The screen door at the front entrance was hanging from one hinge, and the windows were all broken in the once glassed-in sun porch.

Eager anticipation gave way to dismay as we walked through the old home. Vandals had stripped the walls in some places and broken almost all the windows. Ashes and charred wood remained from fires that had been built on the cement floor of the porch. Everywhere we looked, something had to be fixed before this house could be lived in. As we stood in a circle deciding what to say and where to start, Daddy explained, "You know, this is a bit of history. I found out it was built by a woman and her two daughters. She must have had some help—there's no woman I know that could even think of building a place half this size, except for maybe Naomi. She was the one who found this place. She was going to try to buy it to get away from the trouble at the ranch, but Isaac talked her out of it. He told her the prophet wanted her closer there for the sake of her kids being together with the rest. I think the thing that really made up her mind to let it go was when I talked to her and told her how much we needed it."

Mother tried to protest that if Naomi found it first it wasn't really fair for her not to get it, but Daddy hushed her. "Don't bother worrying about Naomi. Her and Isaac have worked out a deal where she can start building a house on the other side of the hill right on the ranch property." He winked and said almost apologetically, "You don't think Isaac would lose a workhorse like Naomi that easy, do you? And they need to work it out—it's not really our business. Remember, we can't keep sweet like we need to if we don't mind our own business." His voice was gentle but Mother couldn't miss the reproof. Jan had a smug look on her face just like I thought she would about Naomi.

Daddy tried to brighten the mood. "You girls can work in here, and I'll go down to the pond and check out the spring. I hear it's boxed in and all we have to do is put the pump in and we'll have running water. That way, we won't have to send Deb running to get it for us." He winked at me and everyone laughed.

In August Mother, Daddy, and Jan went to Colorado City to visit the Saints. We were left behind to be tended by the mothers and the big girls at the ranch house. I was determined to keep Nettie and Brent close to me until Mother got back—I hated being without her, and I felt responsible for looking after her charges. The days dragged on forever while they were gone, and the big girls, like Ophelia and Emilia, thought I was strange to worry so much about Nettie and Brent.

One hot day after the work was all done, I left them with the mothers and went with the big kids to Uncle Michael's to swim. Mother had never allowed me to go over there before, and I knew nothing about swimming or about playing near water for that matter. Daddy disagreed with Uncle Isaac as to standards of dress. None of the other kids at the ranch ever wore shoes during the summer, but Daddy always made us wear them at home, so my feet were not very tough. We walked past the pond—it was too deep for us—across the field to the mud hole where Uncle Michael's kids were playing. The field was just dirt because of the goats, and the only thing more plentiful than the turds were the thistles. The worst part was that these thistles weren't pretty; they were shriveled and had at least a hundred times more thorns on them than the ones at the ranch. Jeanie and James tromped right on top of them without even flinching, and I was left in the dust gingerly stepping this way and that to find a place for my feet. I had new appreciation for shoes and for that matter, for Daddy's rules.

The big kids, including Jean, ran like crazy and hurtled themselves into the mud hole. Loud whoops echoed through the valley, and the murky water splashed high into the air. I approached with caution and waited until the other kids were in the heat of a water fight on the other side of the slough to slowly edge myself in. I decided that swimming didn't look so hard and started to work my way farther into the water. Jean was just on the other side, and I thought I could walk all the way to her. I got in deeper and deeper until the filthy brown water was up to my neck. I tried to stop but couldn't catch my balance to turn back. I sank down and down until I was entirely submerged. Only for a second was there some pain and a sense of panic as I realized that water had filled my nose and mouth. When I struggled to gasp for air, the pain was gone and I was no longer afraid.

The next thing I knew I was lying on the side of the mud hole and the big boys were crouching over me. I was coughing, spitting water from my mouth and blowing it from my nose. I wished for a minute they had left me there, because breathing did hurt now. One of the big girls had run to get Aunt Pauline and she rushed across the field, muttering all the way about dumb kids who couldn't swim. I tried to shrink as small as I could into the tall stand of milkweeds that were growing behind where I sat shaking and hugging my knees to my chest.

Aunt Pauline gave me an exasperated look and planted her hands on her hips. "Well, aren't you a pitiful mudball with eyes! I plan on having a word with your mother when she gets back. What on earth is she thinking? Imagine a child your age not able to swim yet...and you expecting to be living right next to a river. Some people love ignorance!"

For a moment I feared that she would throw me back in. She stood there just looking down on me, then took pity and tromped back to the big white house, shaking her head.

Reeny whispered to me in wonder, "You're real lucky. When Evan almost drowned, Momma Pauline threw him back into the pond so many times we were afraid he was goin' to die. You can bet he can swim now, though!"

The night before Mother and Daddy arrived home I got to bathe with the girls. This was a new experience for me, as at home things were much simpler. Mother would heat up some water on top of the stove and fill the galvanized tub on the kitchen floor. Nettie and I would get scrubbed up first and when we were done, Brent would have his turn. Mother was very particular about getting us wrapped up the moment we got out so that no one could see our naked bodies. Over at Uncle Isaac's, Saturday night bath time was a much bigger production. Seeing as Jeanie's Mom wasn't living in the cooler anymore—Uncle Isaac kept moving her from house to house—it had been converted into a laundry. It didn't matter if we got things wet, so it was a perfect place for bath night. After all fifteen of us girls were assembled, we closed the door and excitedly started preparations. We pulled the two large tubs to the center of the room and filled them to the brim with warm water. We were all laughing and giggling as we stripped naked. Our long dresses and petticoats were hanging from nails on the wall and slung over clotheslines.

Reeny and Aline each grabbed a bar of pink carbolic soap and jumped into the tubs. Sudsing themselves up, they sprang from the water to be replaced by Jean and Emilia. Before long, the entire floor was wet and soapy with one girl after the other making a running jump and landing with a wild splash in the water. The room echoed with shrieks and squeals as bodies slid this way and that. I jumped in a tub as soon as one was empty and started rubbing myself with a bar of soap. Within seconds I was bowled over by a flying body and went sliding on my bum across the soapy floor. Pretty soon, naked bodies were slipping this way and that. Emilia, Irene, and Ophelia were twelve and thirteen with budding breasts. Every time they ran past the windows, we could hear a chorus of hoots from the boys outside. From the start, we knew they were there sneaking around in the dark and peeking in at us. It wasn't at all difficult for them to see us since it was light in the cooler and there were so many places around the outside of the cooler to hide. For a moment I wondered why the girls or the mothers didn't hang some towels over the windows, but then I just forgot about it and joined in with the fun.

Chapter 6

God's own school started in 1959 in the big new room at the ranch house, and Jan began teaching every day. One morning shortly after the fall session began, she confided her concerns to Mother over breakfast. "It's so much responsibility to be given a calling like this." She paused while she took a mouthful of porridge. "Just imagine, the whole future of the Work in Canada rests in my hands. I can teach and train these kids according to the Lord's plan. The brethren told me I'll be a great influence to train their minds in the ways of the prophet, so they'll be putty in his hands."

She ate another spoonful of her breakfast. "But you know, Viv, even teaching them to read is so hard...I wish I had the chance to graduate myself before I had the full responsibility of the Lord's school." She finished her glass of milk and sighed heavily. "Well, you know I can't question the wisdom of the Lord. So many of the people who have answered His call were the uneducated—so Uncle Guy Musser tells me. He says that people who go out and get higher training are too lifted up in the ways of the world to be prompted by the Lord."

Jan always seemed to be fighting with Uncle Michael about who had the best way of teaching. One day she burst into the cabin at suppertime. She was upset and ranting. "You'd think Michael would get the hint and get off his high and mighty horse. Just because he went to some fancy school to be a teacher, he brags about how he could teach kids to be smart enough to go to university. Like Daddy says, that doesn't mean one tinker's damn. He might be the bad apple that spoils the whole barrel. It's time he accepted that I have been called by God's prophet to be the teacher for his Canadian children."

Jan banged her books ferociously on the table. "Michael won't teach kids right...He'll just teach them out of his stupid worldly philosophy books. What good are the kids if they question proper authority? He pretends he would raise children up for the Work and the prophet like calves in the stall. He talks about it all the time from the pulpit, but he doesn't have a clue how to really do it. How can he when he sets the worst possible example all the time? The prophet said it doesn't matter to the Lord one bit that I've only finished grade ten—that God will inspire me to teach everything the children from His chosen race could possibly need to know...didn't he, Viv?" She pounded on the cupboard.

Mother threw her arms around Jan's stiff shoulders. "Yes, Janessa, you're right. That's exactly what the prophet said. You're exhausted with starting the school, but you're doing what the Lord told the prophet for you to do, and you can have peace in that. You must rest, though—the baby you carry is very important. Adam will be home soon, and he'll know how to help us. If Michael is giving you a bad time, we know that the prophet and God will handle him."

Jan turned her head into Mother's shoulder and started to cry with boo-hoos so loud that I was sure the cows in the barn could hear her. Then I was ashamed for the unkind thought. Sometimes people cried and screamed, but when Jan boo-hooed like that everyone came running and said they'd make sure people paid attention and fixed things right away.

Daddy spent a long time comforting Jan after supper. He promised he'd have Uncle Isaac take the problem up with the prophet, who'd take it up with the Lord. That'd surely fix things, but in the meantime he wanted us all to make sure we were in the line of our calling and keeping good and sweet and kind, which was the only way we could offer ourselves up as "the right kind of clay in the hands of the Master Potter." I wasn't sure the way Daddy was talking if the master potter was Uncle Isaac or the prophet or God. The only thing I was perfectly clear on was that it wasn't Uncle Michael. I listened real carefully because I wanted to make sure I understood it right.

In the midst of the school opening, we moved to our home in Canyon. Although I missed Jeanie and my other friends a lot, I loved to spend days alone with Mother, Nettie, and Brent. Mother had some beautiful books that she brought with her from Rosemary, and in the quiet of the afternoons she read to us. Long after Nettie and Brent tired of listening, I begged her to read just a little longer. I especially enjoyed her big picture book of Bible stories written for children. I knew them off by heart, and sometimes when Mother didn't have time to read, she just let me look at her books. I was careful not to tear them. I knew they were precious and impossible for her to replace. Daddy brought home a piano, too, and Mother spent hours singing and playing hymns. She decided I must learn to play and started teaching me.

One Sunday afternoon Daddy and Uncle Isaac dedicated our new home. We all sat as if we were in a temple, and Uncle Isaac put his arms up and told the Lord to send his angels to look over this home and protect it. He asked Him to keep all evil influences away. He told us that as long as we stayed in this dedicated home under the direction of the priesthood, we would never come to harm unless it was the Lord's will. Mother and Daddy thanked him humbly, and we all felt safe.

Jan's new baby, Tabitha, was born shortly after my fifth birthday. Mother was so happy to have a baby to care for again. Bathing her was her special delight, and I looked on in awe as she carefully washed, dried, and powdered between each toe. After she was finished caring for Tabitha, she would take her cooing to Jan, who spent every spare moment working on correspondence courses from Victoria, determined to get her grade twelve as soon as possible.

Soon after we moved into the house, Mother sat Nettie, Brent, and I down. "You can play on the back stairs, in the basement, and in the cedar trees close to the house. You must not go down the road to the river, or to the pond, or over to the cow pasture without me." She was looking right at me when she said, "You'll get a licking if you do!"

For about a week the newness of all the permitted places was enough for me. But as the autumn rolled on, I started spending a lot of time on the bank of the pond, straining to see the forget-me-nots and watercress that were visible when I stood on tiptoe and peered over the top of the thimbleberry bushes.

Nettie was four now and was always warning me to obey the rules. Strangely, her advice usually had the opposite effect. One day she could see I was looking longingly down the bank toward the pond. She came up behind me. "Deb, you'll get a spanking if you go down there." Her face grew red and the pitch of her voice higher as she dared me to transgress. "You just better not do it…I'll tell if you do!"

"You don't know anything!" My chin thrust out as I challenged her. "Mother won't spank me. I'm going to slide down the bank real slow…I know she won't care." I sat down, pulled my skirt tight under my bottom, and started to slide while humming a little song. I didn't let on that the sharp sticks and rocks hidden under the long crabgrass were hurting me.

As I disappeared over the edge, Nettie tore up the back stairs yelling, "Deb's gone and done it! She's goin' to the pond. Mother…Mother!"

The moment I heard the back door slam, my bravado vanished. I turned onto my knees and scrambled up the bank as fast as I could go. I was walking up the old river-stone steps very slowly when Mother came out the back door. Nettie and Brent were sitting together under the elderberry bushes, waiting for me to get my just desserts. Mother looked very tired and very sad. I wanted to turn into an angleworm without eyes so I wouldn't have to see her pained expression and know that I had put it there. With her hands on her hips, Mother said with determination, "When I was a little girl and disobeyed Grandmother, she made me find my own switch for a licking. That's what you can do now." I stood hesitantly with tear-filled eyes, and for just a second I thought she might relent. Finally, she declared, "Hurry up, or it'll go harder on you!"

Near the base of the overgrown lilac bushes were hundreds of pieces of shingles that Daddy had ripped off the roof when he fixed it. I decided that one of those old shingles would be the best thing to use since they looked like they would break easily. I carefully selected the thinnest one I could find and took it to Mother. I found her waiting in the kitchen on one of the bright yellow chairs.

Calmly she said, "Give it to me now, Deb. You know I don't want to do this, but you have to learn."

I started to cry. "But why, Mother? Why couldn't I see the pond? It's so pretty down there. You don't want to hurt me, do you?"

She took the shingle, put me over her knees, and pulled my hands away from trying to protect my bottom. After ten stinging swats with the stick, she stopped and gathered me into her arms. Her voice was shaking. "Deb, you just have to learn to do what you're told without asking why. I won't be here forever, and you'll be in hot water all the time if you can't break this habit. I thought you understood that I was afraid you'd drown if I wasn't with you at the pond. The seaweed and watercress are so thick you would disappear forever. I couldn't stand that." She stroked my hair and my tear-streaked face and held me tightly to her. She was crying now, too. My sobs slowed and we sat in silence as the shadows in the kitchen lengthened. Mother turned me to face her and smiled. "I love you always—it really hurts me to hurt you. Now give me a kiss and a hug and we'll sing our song." I wiped my face and started mouthing the words. Slowly our voices blended as we softly sang the verses of our sunshine song.

The days took on a quiet pattern. Mother had a big scribbler with rough textured gray pages, which she gave to me. I got to do numbers and letters in it, and Mother seemed proud of each symbol. If I had trouble with a letter, she took my hand and gently traced it over and over until I could do it.

With the onset of another winter, Mother's cough came back worse than ever before. Being far away from the ranch and still so weak made her feel isolated. Our new home was not as easy for her to care for as the little cabin, and it was always cold and drafty. She struggled to keep the potbellied stove in the living room and the old McClary cookstove burning really hot, and we huddled around them for warmth.

Daddy came up with a great invention for keeping the house warm. He decided that although we had to live for the time being with the old windows and no insulation, he could come up with a better way to make more heat. Always ingenious and constantly on the lookout for deals, he found an old coal burner that had been removed from one of the downtown businesses. Uncle Michael brought his crew over on Daddy's days off from work, and they poured a cement pad in the basement. Dad built a huge hopper to fill with sawdust and set the furnace up for continuous burning. The problem was the hopper had to be filled with a five-gallon bucket. That was heavy work for Daddy and Jan—for Mother it was almost impossible. As hard as she tried, the best she could do was to fill the hopper a gallon at a time with a little bucket.

It was exciting for us the first few times the big truck came from the mill to bring us sawdust. We hid around the corner of the house so the Gentile couldn't get us and watched as he dumped his load.

Sometimes if Daddy wasn't too busy he would shovel lots of the sawdust through the basement window nearest the burner so it could dry, but other times the pile would freeze outside too soon. Stocking the furnace became a new chore for Mother. Every morning she had to go outside to this mammoth pile and shovel sawdust into the furnace room through the window. One morning it was exceptionally cold. The house was already chilly, and the sawdust was disappearing from the hopper faster than Mother could keep up with it. She hated to let the fire die right down as it was extremely difficult to restart, so she shoveled frantically to get enough material in to fill the hopper. The sawdust in the pile was frozen and each shovelful was a struggle. Mother would chip away until she got a bit through the window, then she would rest. Her breaths were coming in short gasps, and her mouth looked like the stack of a steam engine discharging smoke into the cold morning air. The moment she got a shovelful into the basement she would have to stop and rest. I found an old square-mouth shovel in the shed, but the relic was almost as heavy as I was. Frantic to help, I chipped madly at the frozen sawdust. Mother started to cry as her shovel clunked against the hard mound. She leaned heavily on the handle, gripping it as if she might soon collapse in a heap.

I tried to take the shovel away from her. A terrible fear was driving me. "Please, Mother, don't work anymore. I'm real strong. I'll do it. I need this shovel, you just go rest, please!" My tears made my face sting like fire in the cold.

Mother put the shovel down and leaned on me. Her voice was heavy and slow. "I have to stop now, Deb...but please don't cry anymore. I can't stand it." Her head was hanging and her nose was dripping. As she staggered to the house, she said, "I'm hardly any good anymore." I worked furiously, attacking the sawdust while trying to think where I could find someone to help. I had to save Mother. I knew I could if I just tried a little harder, but each stab of the shovel moved only a pitiful little bit. I hit the frozen crust one last time and didn't move a single flake. My arms and back were like jelly, and my lungs were hurting from dragging in the bitterly cold air. My heart was pounding so hard I was afraid it would fall out of my body and get lost in the horrible cold sawdust. I realized I had failed and forced myself to go into the house.

In the spring Grandmother came, but the joy of her arrival was short-lived. She took Mother to the doctor, and he told us she had a diseased heart. It had gotten so big to make up for her chronic anemia that it couldn't pump properly anymore. That was why her chest hurt all the time and her breaths came in hard, short gasps. The quarts and quarts of hops she'd been drinking had not cured her.

After Grandmother told us that Mother was dying, I watched her more closely than ever. Sometimes on Sundays when Daddy and Jan were having a nap together, Mother would disappear down the river road. She didn't want to be noticed but I watched her anyway. I let her go but would patiently sit on the back stairs and wait for her to return. It was important for me to be there because she was usually so exhausted by the time she got back that she couldn't make it up the last few steps. Sometimes she was crying, and I could hug her and let her lean on me.

One Sunday afternoon I was in my place on the stairs waiting for her when Daddy came to the door. "Where's Mother?" he asked anxiously. I pointed down the rock-strewn hill. Daddy ran down the road toward her. "Viv, you know I don't want you to go off all alone."

Mother calmly replied, "This is the last time I'll see my special place. I rest and feel closer to Heavenly Father on the river bottom than I do anywhere else. It's a great comfort to me. I feel like I'm in a holy place alone underneath the cottonwood trees. I was fine. I had to say goodbye."

Daddy pulled her into his arms and started to cry. "Don't talk like that, Viv…I don't want you to leave me. I always ask the Lord to spare your life. I don't think I can make it without you." They stood like that for a long while. I sat not feeling the cold breeze that was blowing up from the river, not realizing my tears were soaking the front of my dress.

Mother held Daddy from her. "Adam, I'm in pain all the time. Sometimes I don't think I can stand it another second. I can hardly do anything anymore, and there isn't time for me to be sick—there's so much work to do. If I can just hang on till school is out, then you can find some help with the children for next year. Help me to the house now." I ran sobbing up the stairs to my bed.

Mother had been slightly overweight but was now losing weight rapidly. She grew weaker each day. Most of the time she was bedridden. Jan was caring for us, and we were forbidden to run into Mother's bedroom anytime we wanted. I was sure that wasn't her idea—I knew she needed me.

Nettie and Brent slipped around like waif-shadows, always together, holding hands in the dark corners of the house. I couldn't even think of playing with them. It was my duty to wait close to the door in hope of a glimpse of Mother. I knew if she saw me she would want me to come to her, and if she said so, no one could make me go away. Once, the door was left slightly ajar. I saw Jan help Mother sit on the tall commode that was kept under the bed. She looked up and saw me. "Is it Deb?"

Jan glanced at me and said with exasperation, "Yes, she just won't stay away from the door. She can go play. She doesn't need to bother you." She shot me a warning look but I refused to flee.

Mother held out her arms. "Come see me, Deb. I'm going to the hospital tomorrow, so you need to come hug me." I ran to her gladly, thankful that the days of waiting at the door had paid off. It was good to be in Mother's arms again, but scary. Her flesh was gaunt and the sour, rotten smell of the commode destroyed the Mother smell that I was longing for. I held on tightly as if my strength could make this nightmare go away, and Mother would get up out of this horrible, dark, stinking room and take me by the hand. We would dance across the meadow through the buttercups, with the killdeer and butterflies flying all around us. We would find the deer path and walk up the first hill to the spring and sit beside the water and take strength from the mountain, and she would hold me.

Mother reached a bony hand up to my arm. "You're hurting me, Deb, please don't hold on so tight. I have to lie down now, I'm just so tired. Before I go in the morning I want you to say the 23rd Psalm for me. And remember our song."

Jan grabbed me by the arm fiercely and propeled me out the door, muttering, "I'll speak to you later, young lady!" I spent the rest of the day trying to be as invisible as possible, hoping Jan would forget her threat.

The sun was shining the next morning, but it was a dark day for me. I was told to come to Mother's room, where she was dressed and waiting on the bed. She held her hands out to me. "Come close to me, my Deb, and let me hold you. Say the Lord is my shepherd for me." I felt numb but I repeated the psalm, staring at the lines in the hardwood floor. When I looked up at the end of my recital there were tears in Mother's eyes, but she was smiling. "Kiss me and give me a big hug. You're getting to be a big girl now and I'm very proud of you. You must be obedient and very brave. Take care of Daddy...He's going to need you." Her voice cracked, "Go play now, Deb. I love you."

"When will I see you again, Mother? Please tell me! Who's going to tend us? I don't want anyone but you!" My panic escalated, but when she started to cry, too, I calmed down and said as bravely as I could, "I'll be real good, Mother...I will. You get better and come home soon." I quickly kissed both of her pale cheeks and ran from the room. I couldn't bear to watch them put her in the car and take her from me. I heard the car start, pull away, and go slowly up the hill. My heart was stone. Why couldn't I cry?

Grandmother came again to Creston—not to our house, but to the hospital to be with Mother. I was so lonely, even when we went to the ranch house for meetings with the prophet. I got to visit with Grandmother and Grandpa for a few minutes when they drove us kids to the conference services. Over and over on the way back home they said how inspiring the sermons were. The one I remembered the best was Uncle Guy Musser's. He stated emphatically that if you had the strength and faith necessary to be exalted, then the destroying angel would pass you by. It had something to do with the faith of a mustard seed, and the fact that we were a part of the Lord's chosen people—the only people on earth who had a right to the Lord's fully restored gospel. I thought he meant that we wouldn't die if we had faith. When we got home I prayed for hours, concentrating on having faith and saving Mother.

After Daddy said goodnight, I got back out of my bed and knelt on the wooden floor with my hands clenched as hard as I could. "Dear Heavenly Father, please let Mother come home. Your servants say if we have strong faith, all we have to do is ask. I am trying so hard to be good and righteous, and Jan hardly got mad at me at all last week, but I need my mother so bad." I was just about to return to my bed when I was struck with the fear that I was sounding too selfish. Daddy said God didn't like people to be selfish. Folding my hands again, I added, "So do Nettie and Brent. Please heal her for us. Please! In the name of Jesus Christ, Amen."

The next morning we knelt in a little circle around Daddy and concentrated our whole emotional energy in pleading with the Lord for Mother's life. With a shaking voice, Daddy prayed, "Dear Father in Heaven, we present ourselves this morning on our knees to beg for your mercy and love for Vivien. We know you can perform miracles and heal the sick. We have searched and found the group of people here on this earth that are striving to live the fullness of the gospel, and we are trying with all of our strength and might to help the Work along. Please look down upon us with your mercy and spare Mother's life. We pray in the name of Jesus Christ, Amen."

Mother had been in the hospital for six weeks, and we hadn't been allowed to go in to see her. Once, we stood on the grass outside, but her room was too far up and the shutters didn't open enough. It was so hard to be that close and not be able to touch her. I wanted to run to her, but I didn't know how to find the door to get into the hospital, and I was terrified of being in the Gentiles' town. I knew it wasn't a holy place, so I was constantly worried for our safety.

One evening when Daddy came home from work he was very happy. He gathered us around to tell us that the Lord was answering our prayers, and the doctor was going to let Mother come home to visit. He told us to be ready at noon the next day and he would bring her home himself.

Everyone was overjoyed. We worked very hard cleaning and polishing, until every single corner was shining. The side hill above the yard was still covered with sweet williams. Mother loved them. We gathered bouquets and put them in large jars all over the house. I found a swallowtail butterfly that had been caught in the branches of the bush and had died there. The butterfly was so perfect that I had to watch how I breathed because maybe it would come back to life and fly away. I carefully unhooked it and carried it in cupped hands to the house.

I was very excited and took it to Jan. "I found a beautiful butterfly for Mother. She's really going to love it. I'll put it on the flowers for her."

Jan's face twisted in disgust. "Deb, what is the matter with your head? How can you think she'll like a dead butterfly? We can't have her looking at dead things! Take it back outside." I suddenly felt so stupid—of course Mother wouldn't like to see something dead.

The minutes dragged into hours, and noon came and went without a sign of Mother. I paced the house, telling Nettie and Brent I couldn't play with them. Finally, at Daddy's usual time to get off work, I heard him coming down the road. I was disappointed when I realized he was the only one in the car. He just sat there, his head in his hands. I ran and opened the passenger door. Peering around inside, I hoped that I had somehow missed her.

"Where is she, Daddy? You said she'd be home today!"

He put his arms around me and held me close. He was crying. "Her heart was hurting worse today, and the doctor wouldn't let her come. I'm sorry Deb...I'm really sorry." When Daddy was crying I decided I had to be tough. I would do this for Mother. I stopped crying and hugged him.

When school started in the fall, I was old enough to attend classes. Since Nettie, Brent, and Tabitha all had to stay home, we needed someone to tend them. Uncle Isaac, with the cooperation of Uncle Michael, decided that Lavina, Michael's second oldest daughter, would be called upon to help until the Lord had something else in mind.

The anxiously awaited and prayed-for return of the leaders from the States came to pass one more time. Mother was apparently getting weaker by the day. When Grandmother came to visit again, it was decided she would stay in Creston and spend every single minute that she could in the hospital so Mother wouldn't be alone.

School started at eight o'clock, so we had to get up very early to get there in time. Jan organized us with lists, because she needed to call us at six and then go back to bed with the baby to feed her for a while. My list sounded simple enough, but by the time I made my bed, brushed my teeth, said my prayers, and finished the breakfast chores, it was seven-thirty and I was so tired I wanted to go back to sleep. When Daddy drove us to school, we traveled a circuitous route into Creston for Kelvin Whitmer's children and back to Lister. Uncle Kelvin wanted his kids to go to the priesthood school, but he couldn't drive them every day, so Daddy was called to help out. Daddy dropped us off and then went to work. After school there was a long wait for him to pick us up and tell us how Mother was. I got to play with my friends and practice letters and numbers.

There was a family called the Hortons who had joined the group, and the mother in the family was named Anita. She had very dark skin but didn't look like the pictures of Negroes in the schoolbooks. When I asked Daddy why her skin was the color it was, he said they came from South Africa and she was East Indian. When I told Jean and Aline, they were as relieved as I was that she wasn't a

Negro, because we knew they were cursed with a dark skin by God because their first father on this earth, Cain, killed his brother Abel. Some of the Hortons' children were dark-skinned like their mother and others were light-skinned like their father. They had a retarded son named Gordie, who was seven and still only in grade one. We had never seen a retarded person either and didn't know how to talk to him, but we felt guilty because no one would be nice to him.

Jean and I worried about Gordie. One recess we ran to our secret place under a grove of saskatoon bushes on the hill beside the ranch house to talk about him. Jean was determined. "You know, Deb, I just don't think it's fair the way James and Jonah treat Gordie. He's only a little bit retarded, and they treat him real mean. I think if we are special nice to him, it'll help him learn faster. Don't you think so?"

I shrugged. Since I was living in Canyon, I didn't know the Hortons very well, but Jean was usually right about things, so I nodded my head in agreement with her.

She had it all planned. "At noon hour we'll ask him if he wants to come up on the hill with us and we'll be his friends." We were pleased with our plan, and at lunchtime we took Gordie by the hand and escorted him up the hill. After making him sit down, we shared our lunches with him, then we sat staring at each other not sure what to do. Certainly we should have done something more. Jean and I crawled behind his back and whispered to one another.

"We gotta do something else!" Jeanie said emphatically.

I suggested, "I think we should kiss him."

"That's what we'll do," Jeanie agreed. "You kiss him first."

"No, you."

"No, you."

Finally, I said, "Let's do it together."

We got Gordie to stand up, and at the count of three we kissed him at the same time. Then we ran as fast as we could down the hill to the schoolroom. We never talked about it again.

I was feeling strangely happy when Daddy picked us up after school that night—a bit like a saint for bringing even a moment of happiness into someone else's life. I could see Daddy wasn't happy.

When we got home, he told us that the prophet had told him to stop praying for Mother's recovery. Daddy said Mother's heart was getting bigger and bigger, and that she was in terrible pain. He said she was suffocating because her heart was pressing on her lungs. I ran to my room when he told us the prophet wanted us to pray for God to take her home. How could I do that? God could heal anything and anyone, and who was more worthy of saving than Mother?

I lay on my bed until my pillow was wet from tears. Even though Mother had continued to worsen, I had never for one moment doubted that she would get better. How could I now ask God to take away the most precious thing in my life? I got on my knees and prepared myself. The words I had readied got tangled in my throat, and I pitched forward on the bed, lost in tears. Again and again I tried and failed. At last, I managed to tell Him if He really, really thought He needed her, I guess it would be all right for Him to take her...but I would much rather He fixed up a miracle that let her come home to me. "Whatever you do, Lord, please take away her pain."

One week later in the afternoon, Daddy came to the schoolroom at the ranch to let us know that Mother was gone. He and Jan stood quietly together just outside the door at the front of the class with tears streaming down their faces, then they shuffled off in the direction of Daddy's truck. Lots of kids were crying openly, clustered by the door, but all I could do was sit frozen in my desk and stare at Daddy's retreating figure. Jan came back and announced that the school day was finished early. For a fleeting moment my heart gave a strange thump, and I thought maybe she had come back to get me. But she left again without looking at me. I wondered vaguely if someone had found Nettie and Brent to tell them—I should have been with them when they found out. What if they needed me? My head was hurting, and I thought I should cry, but couldn't.

Jean came back into the classroom and stood wordlessly on one foot. In unspoken recognition, I followed her out onto the hill where Aline waited. I felt that time was standing still as we wandered across the carpet of tiny flowers that still persisted on the rocky ground. I walked with my eyes downcast, taking in the pinks and blues of the dainty little baby nipples. Each tiny flower was begging me to reach down, pick it, and brush it with my lips. The popberries* and rose bushes were alive with chickadees that hopped crazy and free and sang us their uplifting songs.

I stumbled as tears blinded my eyes. Aline and Jean linked my arms with theirs and held me upright. We walked like little windup toys around and around the top of the hill until the sun was gone and we were getting cold. When they started to talk, I joined in, talking about a little girl and her sad little sister and brother whose mother had died. It wasn't me—not Deb. "How terrible it is that she died on Nettie's birthday," the little girl was saying. "Nettie's five today, you know—for your mother to die on your birthday is just the worst thing."

I don't remember how I ended up at home. I kept telling myself that Mother had been at the hospital a long time but she would be home in a day or two. It was late when Daddy finally came and talked to me. The tiny room was so dark that there were no shadows. I was curled up in a tight ball in my bed trying to sleep, but my mind kept swirling. I lay like a frozen doll on his chest as he gathered me into his arms. There were tears in his voice.

"Mother's free from the pain of her mortal body now. She will help God carry on His important work and organize things in heaven. We'll just have to be brave and carry on without her. We can do it, can't we, Deb? She'll be with baby Lena and Thomas, and she'll watch over us from there until we see her again. You can understand that?" He was crying again, and I was, too. He said Mother was helping baby Lena, and it would be selfish not to be happy about that.

I wanted to scream, "No, baby Lena already has Aunt Lena and baby Thomas!"

My brain reeled with words I couldn't say out loud. Did God

---

* Snowberries are called "popberries" because of the snapping sound they make when squeezed or stepped on.

really need her more than I did? I bet if I went downstairs, she'd be sitting in the yellow chair in the kitchen, or coming up the river road, and I could run to her and she'd hold me. She could even spank me or do anything she wanted. I would even stop asking why so much, and never forget to do what I was told. Please, God...please let her come back!

Daddy went out to the kitchen. In the light of the coal oil lamp, he talked to Jan in low tones. "We'll have to call the relatives in Alberta...they have to know."

Jan answered in anguish, "I know you have to Adam, but it's so horrible. They treat me like I'm invisible. They just don't think I'm good enough for you, and I can't stand that."

I heard Daddy's chair slide across the floor. He sounded very tired when he answered. "Don't be like that. I'm sure they don't mean anything by it." He sighed. "You have to admit, we are different...but that's as it should be, according to the gospel and the Work we're engaged in."

In a few days all kinds of people came to our house. Although some of them seemed familiar, I wasn't sure who they were. I watched carefully to see how these fancy people, especially the ladies with their pantsuits and poofy hair, would treat us. Aunt Rita, Daddy's worldly sister from California, came late one night to talk to Daddy. They all half sat in their chairs as if poised for flight, and Jan settled on the chesterfield across the room. Aunt Rita was hesitant as she addressed her brother. "Now, Adam, we don't know what your plans are, but Larry and I are prepared to take the children to live with us. I really loved Viv and would make sure that they were raised according to the things she cared most about." Jan drew in her breath with a sharp hiss. I was suddenly glad I wasn't sitting in the room with her—that hiss always meant somebody was about to get a beating.

Daddy's voice was stiff and cold as he answered. "I think we'll manage all right. I've got Jan to help me raise the children...and we're fine." He was barely polite as he went on, "I'm sure you mean well, but you don't need to worry about us."

My mind was awhirl as I went to bed. If this gentile aunt were to take me, I wouldn't be a burden to the peace in the family, and I wouldn't have to think about getting Jan to like me. As scared as I was of her, I was even more worried about the gentile relatives. The ladies wore pants and they painted their faces with the vain things of the world. Who would protect me from that, and who would tell me what God was telling our prophet for us to do? I hugged my blind doll with no name and rocked myself back and forth. Daddy said that Mother had died for the Work, and death would be better than living with Gentiles for any reason. I just had to do my best to make things work with Jan.

The day for the funeral was hazy gray and cold. Although my body was there, a part of me was not—just like Mother. Her body was there in her coffin at the funeral chapel in Creston, but where was the rest of her? The coffin was beautiful—Uncle Michael had made it by hand. His wives said he cried while he put it together. He was such a big gruff-looking man that I was glad I didn't see his tears. Grandmother and Bettilyn's lining and padding of the coffin with heavenly white satin brocade was a labor of love. They dressed her, too, and curled her hair. I wondered why they made her look like she did before she came to God's sacred Work. With her wedding dress and her black hair soft and full around her face, she looked just like her pictures when Daddy married her in the apostate church. Daddy lifted me up so I could touch her hand. He said she wasn't in her body anymore, but her spirit was here with us—she was free.

They sat Nettie, Brent, and I in the front row beside Jan. There were men from our group standing on both sides of the coffin as if to keep the gentile relatives from grabbing Mother, coffin and all, and taking her to their worldly hell. There were so many other people there that I didn't recognize. Most of the Gentiles didn't look very friendly, but one old lady came over and hugged me, sobbing bitterly. "She's just like my little Viv," she said. "See this, Selma? She's just like Viv." The weeping woman was soft and strong like Grandmother, but I wasn't sure who she was. Grandmother told me that she was her mother—Great-grandmother Norton. I looked around, trying to decide if Mother was truly there. I sat up straight, looking as reverent as I could: if she was there, I wanted her to be proud of me.

Suddenly the need to see Mother's face one more time overwhelmed me. I walked straight to the coffin and pulled myself up by the edges until I could touch her face and hands. Everyone gasped. I looked up at Mother's brother, Nick, standing behind the pulpit. His face was flushed red; he was stammering as if he didn't know what to do. I could hear a heavy sigh and a bustle from where Jan was sitting, and I gripped the coffin as if I were clinging to my own life. She grabbed me by the arms and pulled. "If you make a scene in front of all these relatives, you'll be sorry," she hissed. "Now let go!" I let go, shrugged her hands off me, and went back to my chair. I couldn't cry right then, but I was only a little bit sorry for looking at Mother.

Uncle Nick conducted the service. I didn't remember seeing him before. I remembered Uncle Peter, who had a glass eye and skated with Nettie, Brent, and I in a wheelbarrow on the ice of the irrigation canals by Grandmother's house in Rosemary. But Uncle Nick was different from Uncle Peter—he seemed angry. When we arrived at the funeral chapel, I heard him yell at Daddy about how he could let Mother die at the age of twenty-three. He said it was all the heavy labor the crazy Merricks expected from their women that killed his sister—that and Daddy's not getting her to a doctor soon enough.

Daddy fought back tears and patted him on the shoulder. "There, there, old boy, we all loved Viv. Don't you think if there were something I could do to bring her back healthy and strong, I would do it? You know her patriarchal blessing said she wasn't long for this earth, and who are we to argue with God?" Uncle Nick mumbled that he didn't think God meant we should hurry things along by not getting proper medical attention, but he would drop it for now and get on with the service.

I couldn't understand why Uncle Isaac wasn't doing the talking. He loved Mother and was the file leader for all of Canada, so he should really have been the one in charge of the meeting. But he hated hospitals and death and gentile women, so he sat at the back of the room, not talking and not singing. I felt terrible that Daddy would let an apostate send my mother to heaven. I decided no matter what happened, I had to be brave. I held back my tears.

There were talks. Our prophet and apostles spoke and told us that this woman was perfect. She had made the supreme sacrifice, and her calling and election* were made sure. Daddy spoke through a thousand tears, saying, "I'm eternally grateful that Vivien has been my partner this long on earth and that I will have the opportunity to be with her into the eternities if I only follow the teachings of the restored gospel and the words of my prophet. She was a mother in Israel and had unquestioning faith in the things the Lord wanted her to do. I want to challenge all women to follow her example." Daddy looked in our direction for a brief second. "The most I want for my daughters is for them to follow in her footsteps."

As they sang "Unanswered Yet" they lowered the lid of the coffin, and a great procession of people left the funeral chapel. They put Mother in a long black car, and a sad-looking man led us in our cars along the highway and up a hill to the cemetery. They put the coffin on ropes on top of a really deep black hole and then dedicated the spot. As they started to lower Mother into the ground, I grabbed Grandmother's hand and held on tight. Mother wasn't in there...not really. My mother just wouldn't leave us little kids—even for God.

---

* In the LDS Church and Mormon fundamentalist polygamous groups, "calling and election" signifies acceptance by God as a god or goddess in the highest degree of celestial glory. Calling and election are attained when one has achieved the required level of sacrifice and righteousness.

Chapter 7

As I worked at my Saturday job of washing and shining the coal oil lamp chimneys, I remembered how Mother would hold up each one for inspection. I could just see her look of pride as she told me how they sparkled like diamonds. That was when I thought how black it must be for her down there in that box beneath all the dirt. I wished I could have put one of my shiniest lights inside her coffin to burn forever—I hated that she was in the dark.

I was convinced she was watching over me sometimes. I guess it was only when Heavenly Father didn't need her too much and she had the time. It was too bad He wouldn't let us talk like we were on a telephone, because sometimes I just didn't understand what she was trying to tell me, and I was terrified I would forget the way she wanted me to be. Sometimes I wondered if I could be any use at all. Jan seemed to be upset with me most of the time, and I sure didn't know what to do about that. Once she got mad, there was no reasoning with her. It was too bad Mother couldn't just tell me what to do, or talk to Jan and soften her heart a little bit.

I was having lots of trouble with my reading and couldn't seem to learn some of the words in the Dick and Jane reader. Jan always got so impatient. She was way too busy and didn't have time for anything, let alone a slow reader. Daddy bought a jeep so she could drive us back and forth to school. Almost every day, the moment we got in and started up the hill, she would tell me to get the reader out of my little pink lunch box. I would read all right for a while, but when I got to "Come, Dick," my brain would freeze.

Jan scolded me. "We learned that yesterday! Say it quick." But I just couldn't say it. Every single time, she leaned over to my seat and hollered, "C!" and thumped me on the head. "O!"—thump. "M!"—thump. "E!"—thump. "Come!" she yelled again, thumping again with her knuckles. "Do you get it?"

Pretty soon my head was aching and my ears were burning. Why couldn't I remember a simple word like "come?" Maybe I was stupid, or my brain was full of cotton batting, like Jan said. I would flinch every time she shifted the gears and was grateful when we got to Uncle Kelvin's to pick up their children. Then Jan spoke in a happy voice, and she wouldn't hit me anymore. Sometimes I had to hide my face inside my coat and not talk if I'd been crying, because I didn't want Selena and all of Uncle Kelvin's kids to know how stupid I was.

That winter seemed so much colder than other ones I could remember. Maybe it was because Mother wasn't there to give me hugs and make me forget the cold, but maybe it was partly because I stayed as far from Jan as possible, and she was often near the heaters. One crisp, cold day, a yellow and brown cat showed up on the back porch. She was really friendly and loved it when I paid attention to her. Every time I ran my fingers over her bony back I could feel her purr. She stretched out for a hug and rubbed up against my legs for more attention. I fed her warm porridge every morning for a week, and after school I would sit in my coat on the back steps and hug her for as long as I could take the cold. The minute I saw her I called her Susie, and then I felt guilty because I still hadn't come up with a name for my blind doll.

One day some of the porridge from the morning was frozen in her bowl. I called and called before she finally came. She moved very slowly and tottered back and forth as she crossed the porch. When I picked her up, she was shivering and twitching instead of purring, and she only lapped a bit of the milk I put out for her. All of a sudden she would lie right still, then she would twitch again. It was the coldest night of all, and I was afraid she'd freeze to death if I left her alone. I decided to put her in a box and take her into the basement. When I asked Jan if it was all right, she said she wouldn't have a smelly cat in her house. "Get it outside…now!" I took Susie back outside all right, and I walked real fast. One look at my "big crocodile tears" would have her clenching her fists and in a menacing voice she'd say, "Stop your bawling." The next thing I knew, she'd be hitting me.

I wrapped Susie up in an old coat I found in the basement and laid her in a cardboard box. She lay there so quietly—she just looked at me and blinked. I decided that at least she wouldn't jump out of the coat if she were lying that still. I checked her again before bedtime, and she was still there. When I put my cheek close to her fluffy face, I heard a faint sigh. I stroked under her chin to get her to purr; only her whiskers twitched. I prayed hard about Susie that night, but the next morning after I finished my chores and Jan finally said I could go outside, I found her frozen stiff.

I tried to convince myself she didn't matter—she really was just a stupid cat. Jan said I had to do something with her body, that she didn't want dead things lying around. I got a shovel and tried digging, but the dirt was frozen solid. I held Susie for a few minutes with her beautiful golden fur pressed to my cheek. Then I took her, still wrapped in the old coat, and threw her as far as I could over the bank, where the swamp flowers bloomed in the spring. I didn't cry, I just stood looking down, wondering if the coat was still wrapped around her.

I asked Daddy if God took care of dead cats. He sat in his big chair and said absently that he doubted it; he didn't really know what God would be doing with cats these days. That night after I talked to Heavenly Father, I asked Mother to keep her eyes open in heaven to see if she could find Susie. I hoped she was up there.

Lavina's older sister Erica, who had been assigned to marry Uncle Freddie Russell, was tending us now. Lavina said it was too dark and lonely down at our house in all the cedar trees, and she wanted to go back home to Uncle Michael's. I could kind of understand what she meant. It hadn't been too dark last winter when I was a little girl and Mother was there, but it was darker this year. It seemed that the sun almost never came out anymore. Maybe spring would be better. Erica was really kind. She helped us little kids with the dishes a lot, and she and Jan laughed and talked. Things were always a lot better for everyone when Jan laughed.

I knew something was bothering Erica, because although she tried to be cheerful and happy most of the time, sometimes her eyes were red and I'd catch her wiping away tears. When I caught her like that one day and asked what was the matter, she said it was none of my business. That worried me even more, because Erica never talked to anyone like that. Later that week when I was sitting in the library room looking at pictures in Mother's big Bible storybook, I heard her crying. She was talking to Jan about Uncle Freddie and how she was angry and sad at the same time, because he didn't want the children from his first wife, Elizabeth, to know he'd married her. I was horrified to find out a man could be assigned a wife by our prophet and not let his children know about their other mother. Erica couldn't stop sobbing. She said Uncle Freddie acted like a scalded cat around her, and when she asked him to let her be part of the family he told her she was trying to be the tail wagging the dog. How could any man be so cruel to a new celestial wife?

She told Jan how horrified she was when the prophet told her who she was supposed to marry. After the ceremony Uncle Freddie literally ran for the door, leapt into his car, and took off back to his home in Cardston. She said she didn't know what to do with herself after that except to work as hard as she could whenever anyone needed her. I decided to take a good look at Uncle Freddie the next time I saw him to see if I could understand what made him treat Erica this way. I figured someone should tell the prophet and Daddy so they could fix him up. You would never treat "a jewel in your crown" the way Uncle Freddie was treating Erica.

One day just before Christmas, we got home from school to find Erica agitated. She cornered Jan in the kitchen before she could even get her coat off. "I don't know what's wrong with these kids, but Brent gives me the creeps! Him and Nettie go to the basement to play, and Brent comes back up and tells me, 'My mother's down in the basement.' Well, I tell him she's not, and he says, 'Yes, she is too!' I want to shake him and then he says he can smell her down there." Erica shook her head. "Someone has to talk to him. I can't handle this."

Jan looked concerned. "I'm sure he'll get over it…I guess it'll take some time." She studied Erica's anxious face. "I suppose we can't worry about it too much. It'll likely be best for them not to play downstairs for a while. He'll get used to Viv not being around. He isn't quite four yet, and it soon won't matter—he'll forget." With that, Jan went off to work on her grade twelve correspondence course. She hollered over her shoulder to Erica how she sure appreciated her good cooking and cleaning and kid-tending.

I went down to the basement and sat on the stairs. Closing my eyes, I drew in a deep breath. I had almost convinced myself that I could tell what Brent had smelled when the door to the sawdust room squeaked. I jumped. It was as if I were wishing for Mother so hard that she made the door move to say hello. When Erica called me for supper, I ran up to the kitchen to set the table still thinking about the message from Mother. After supper Jan got Mother's book of nursery songs out, and we sang some we had learned when I was little. I sang, too, but my bones were aching and I wasn't feeling well. I couldn't sleep that night. All I could think about was how much I wanted Mother back, how much I wanted her to hold me and make this terrible pain go away.

When Jan called us to get ready for school, my head was burning hot. I tried to struggle into my dress, but even lifting my arm exhausted me. Nettie had put on all her carefully laid-out clothes before she realized I had sagged back onto the bed. She pulled at me, "Deb…Deb, you look really dumb with only one arm in your dress." She tugged more frantically. "Do you want Jan to get mad at you again? Please, Deb, come on!" I struggled to get up so the desperation in her voice would stop, but everything went black.

When I woke up, Daddy was leaning over me and I was under my covers again. "Well, I guess you won't be going to school today. You just do what Erica says, drink lots, and Heavenly Father will have you well in no time." I tried to tell him I was sorry for being so much trouble, but the words were a jumble. For the next while my fever was so high that Erica had to change my blankets every day. Jan and Daddy discussed my symptoms with Uncle Isaac, and they decided I had rheumatic fever.

Daddy came to give me the news. "Well, kiddo, with all the pain in your bones and the fever, we've decided you have the same sickness Lemuel just got out of the hospital for. Isaac feels we're well capable of doing as much for you at home as they did for Lem at the hospital, so we'll just follow his direction and have faith. You can do this, Deb."

All I knew was that the hospital was where Mother died, so if I could have faith and stay out of there, then I better do it. I really wished my legs didn't feel like melting wax every time I tried to stand, though. For weeks Erica helped me onto a pot in my bed because when I tried to get to the floor to sit on the big white one with the lid, I just crumpled. Not even babies sat on pots inside their beds, so this was mortifying. I was so glad it was Erica helping me, though, because I was not scared with her arm around my back. Uncle Isaac told Daddy that all I needed to cure my illness was a big spoonful of blackstrap molasses three times a day, Mentholatum on my swollen joints, and a bit of carbolic salve for my cracked lips. The last part of my cure was four cups of alfalfa tea mixed with milk and honey taken throughout the day.

I guess Uncle Isaac was truly inspired, because I was only unable to move until Brent's birthday on the first of February. After that, Daddy decided I better get up a bit every day and help Erica with the kids. The first while, I could only walk by holding onto the walls and furniture; a two-year-old could have done better. The only good part about being sick was that I got to use the indoor pot, since it was cold and the snow was so deep. As soon as my temperature was down and I could get out of bed, Jan declared I was well enough to go to the outhouse again. She chastised Erica for spoiling me, insisting that I would start to enjoy poor health if I was coddled too much. When I had to pee, I held it until I couldn't tell which hurt worse, my bladder or my bones. Only after I couldn't stand it for one more second would I hobble down to the outhouse. Sometimes I couldn't make it all the way, and if it was dark outside I would crouch down and pee in the snow. I worried about not being ladylike—I knew how Mother hated people being rude. I hoped anyone seeing the yellow stain in the snow would think a dog made it.

Jan told me that my mind could make me well, and I'm sure she was right, but the cold air made my bones ache for hours after I went outside, and my joints were as stiff as a frozen doll. Some of my classmates sent notes home with Jan saying they missed me. I liked Jeanie's and was real surprised at the one from James. One of the Whitmer boys sent a card that said "Dear Ded" instead of "Deb." I knew what he meant, but the moment I saw it I started to cry like someone had opened the doors of a big dam behind my eyes. I had been so hot and dry for so long and I hurt so bad I thought I might really die. I wasn't sure if I was crying because my get-well card said "Ded" or because being really dead couldn't possibly hurt as much as rheumatic fever. At least then I could be with Mother. I was surprised and sad when Jan told Daddy she yelled at the boy for his mistake. I wish she hadn't, because he was such a nice, quiet boy and had never once tried to hurt me at school. He sent me a package the next week and inside was a beautiful white ivory comb and brush set. Even though it hurt like the dickens to comb my hair, I tried the brush out right away.

I really hated missing school—from before Christmas to Valentine's Day—because I had to work hard to keep up with Jean and James in my lessons at the best of times. We had a party on Valentine's Day. Aunt Bettilyn helped us make heart-shaped cookies, and we each got to decorate our own. When I sat at my desk at lunchtime and looked out the windows, the chickadees were back on the saskatoon and popberry bushes. I thought of Mother whenever I saw them busily jumping from one branch to the next. I was so glad spring was coming. I remembered how Mother always started to feel better this time of year—maybe the sunshine would make my bones stop hurting all the time.

Bettilyn had started to come to school to help teach. She and Jan decided to have a bazaar to raise money for more supplies and books. There were huge cookies, giant popcorn balls, and lots of other interesting things for people to buy. Daddy gave me ten cents, and I had to decide what to spend it on. It was hard because I wanted everything, but after fifteen minutes of looking I narrowed it down to either a popcorn ball or a compact. The popcorn balls had lots of peanuts in them and were coated with brown sugar caramel. The compact was powder blue with a smooth, hard finish, and when you opened it there was a mirror just like Grandmother's. When you shut it, it snapped with a tight little click. My longing for the sweet crunch of the popcorn ball overpowered me, so I parted with my precious dime. I slowly ate the sweet treat, savoring the taste of each peanut. As it disappeared, I became more and more upset that the compact would never be mine.

I went back to look at it, opening and closing it, and imagining myself combing my hair in the mirror. I gathered my courage and marched right up to Jan to ask her for another dime. She said, "Absolutely not! Your dad works real hard for his money, so we aren't going to waste it."

I was ashamed of myself—wanting extra things was so selfish. I went back into the classroom and sat alone looking out the window. I watched a flock of redheaded birds with parrot beaks flit from branch to branch, harvesting the rose hips from the bushes. I loved those birds and didn't think about my disappointment until Theresa, one of the Horton kids, came in clutching the compact. She was in grade three and her East Indian mother still had a lot of worldly things, like compacts and rouge. Some days we were sure Theresa even wore makeup to school. She put the coveted prize into the corner of her desk and skipped back outside.

I gripped the desk until my knuckles were white. I wanted that compact more than anything I could think of. I went to Theresa's desk and held the compact in my hand, just feeling its smooth surface. On a terrible impulse, I took it to my desk and put it in my lunch box and then ran outside. Involving myself in all the activities, I almost forgot about what I had done.

The bell rang and we all went back to class. Everyone was laughing and chattering and showing off the interesting things they had bought. I sat there knowing I was the wickedest girl in the world. I kept hoping that Mother was busy with God right then, because I would have died if she knew what I had done. Theresa was talking to one of her friends. She looked in her desk for several minutes before she let out a piercing shriek. "It's stolen! Some evil person took my compact." Except for her screaming, there was dead silence.

My cheeks were flaming red and tears of shame were threatening to spill out of my eyes. I sat like a rock, wishing the ground would open up and swallow me like Uncle Isaac preached would happen to the dogs, the hypocrites, and the vain people of the world.

Jan glared at the class. "This is something you would expect in the public schools, where people have never heard of our Work and our prophet. We have the light and the truth, yet someone in this room has stolen. We are not doing another thing until the guilty party comes forward." I sat frozen. My dad was in charge of the school, and my other mother was the teacher. I had brought shame on both them and the leaders of our group.

Theresa still sobbed in her desk. Jan was looking as if any minute she would erupt, and my stomach filled with bitter, sick dread. Suddenly, she slapped her hands down on her desk, hard. Everyone jumped. She leapt up and growled, "If no one is going to do the right thing, I'm going to search all the desks if it takes all day!" She rummaged through one desk after the other in search of the damning evidence.

I clenched my hands tighter and tighter as she got closer to me. My head started to hurt. She sorted through the contents of my desk without finding anything. I thought she was going to move on when she grabbed my lunch box and opened it. She drew in her breath in a shocked gasp when she found the compact.

She pounced on me and shook me. "How could you do such a horrible, shameful thing? You are in detention! Go out on the porch and wait for further word from me." All of the thirty kids in the school witnessed my bitter shame: Jeanie, James, Jonah, Aline, and even Lem, Laman, Sidney, Emilia, Ophelia, Irene, and Uncle Michael's kids.

I walked outside as straight as I could to await my fate. I looked across the yard to the big white barn and the cabin that I remembered from long ago when I was little and we lived there. Back then when there was trouble, I could run to Mother. But she wasn't there anymore—Lydia lived there now. I watched Uncle Isaac limp across the yard toward the barn. He swung to the side once, and I was sure he had seen me. I was betting that God had already told him about my sin.

When Jan came out on the porch with the ruler, I gladly held out my hand for my punishment. She said I had to tell Daddy. When I did, he cried. After many moments of holding his head in his hands, he told me how the desire for worldly things was the downfall of all God's people. I hung my head, not knowing how to respond. I was hoping that Mother was still busy with God's work.

The spring was melting my heart and my stiff body with its enchantment. The cottonwood trees burst into bud, and the final mounds of ice were melting from the edges of the river. I felt delirious with the wind blowing strong and warm in my face. For the first time since I got sick, I couldn't feel pain in my legs. Dancing onto an open stretch of grass, I twirled around and around and leapt into the air. Today, I felt like I could fly. When I tired, I collapsed to the ground and opened my book.

I could read now. When alone, I would read almost anything I could get my hands on, although it was still difficult when Jan was looking over my shoulder. When she was there yelling at me or hitting me or pinching my arms, it was as if a switch turned off somewhere deep inside my brain. I loved to slip away into the library room at school every time there was a spare minute and travel to places in my mind where Jan couldn't find me.

Here at home, with the magic of spring and my books, I could escape more easily from the confusion, pain, and constant disappointment I caused for Daddy. Out here, I could lose myself in the majesty that was all around me. Butterflies were coming alive again and flitting like the fairies from the books through the corners of my life. The blossoms of cherry, apple, pear, and apricot trees transformed our place into an enchanted fairy kingdom. Heaven could smell no better.

Robins and killdeer had returned for the season, bringing

flashes of color and their special music. After my list of jobs was finished for the day, I often lay on my back and watched as robins hopped from limb to limb above me. I would sit by the cedar tree closest to what used to be Mother's bedroom window and watch the squirrel that lived there dart toward me, then run back up the tree. Sometimes he would come within inches, and we would talk to each other with our eyes.

Spring conference was almost here, and Grandmother, Grandpa, and the prophet were coming. It was time to clean and get ready for the company. Sometimes, after I finished washing the floors and baseboards, my knees hurt really bad, and I couldn't straighten them because of the rheumatic fever. Uncle Michael found a special deal on some battleship linoleum, and Daddy got a piece from him. It was exciting to cover the wooden floors with it because then we could sweep and mop more easily. Daddy found us a rag mop with a handle, too, which made the job even easier. We washed the floor, waxed it, and then skated all over it with our wool socks to polish it. It looked real shiny and smelled so good.

Jan was all right with us shining the floor as long as we stopped the second she thought our fun had gone on enough. If we tried to carry on longer, she would be furious. "You will rue the day that you wasted so many precious moments in frivolous play. There's too much to do to waste time this way!" She was nervous about the house being clean enough for Grandmother and Grandpa's visit. She was afraid they'd think she didn't work as hard as Mother.

It seemed like a zillion years since they had been here for Mother's funeral. I was sure Grandmother would notice I had grown a lot but Nettie was still tiny. Although she worried almost as much as I did about pleasing Jan, she was much better at making her happy. She didn't do as many bad things to get Jan mad. The only thing was that she was wetting her pants, and Jan didn't like that much.

I didn't know why it was so hard for me to pay attention when Jan talked to me. Sometimes when she got mad, my head started to hurt and then things went fuzzy so I couldn't remember what she wanted me to do. That made her flex her fingers and look really cross and then the pains got worse, and I'd get scared and duck.

When I did, she really got mad and would hit me for sure. She said I looked at her with cow eyes. Sometimes I went over to the barn at Uncle Isaac's and watched the cows eat. I was never sure what I did with my eyes to make mine look like theirs. I prayed for Heavenly Father to help me please Jan.

When Grandmother got to our house, Jan was much happier. I wished Grandmother could come every week because for two whole days Jan was good to me. She didn't hit me once, and she only looked daggers twice. It just went to show how special it was when God's servants came to Canada. Nettie and I got to ride over to church in Grandpa's car, and then sit with Grandmother for the whole meeting. We shook Uncle Roy's hand and gave him our tithing. For sure we got our names in the Lamb's book of life now, and we wouldn't get burned with the wicked. Grandmother whispered to me that President Johnson's sermon was "so inspired."

He talked a lot about Mother and prophesied that blood would run down the streets of Creston, and "the One Mighty and Strong will set His house in order before there will be one more death in this group of God's people in Canada!" He said, "I do not know a man, woman, or child, but what if they will repent, I want to see them in the morning of the first resurrection. But, if some will not repent, I do not want to look at them anymore because they have been given a chance. It is God's work we want established. We must learn to render service to those who fill the office of a prophet and thus render service to God. The church of Jesus Christ of Latter-day Saints chose to support the state of Arizona in persecuting God's holy law of plural marriage in the raid of 1953, and I ask you if this tells you if the church has taken hands with the evil destroyer or not. The easiest way to grieve the Spirit of God is to complain. And then it's hard to get it back again. Let us get the Spirit of God and keep it so we will have some protection against the evils of the world. The judgments of God have already started in our land, and it is going to get worse to prepare the way for the ten tribes. If you older people can't be persuaded to throw off the yoke of unrighteousness, your children will have to take your place and carry off the kingdom. And remember, no one, old or young, rich or poor, will be found worthy unless they are willing to offer up as a sacrifice a broken heart and a contrite spirit, keeping sweet while obeying every direction from the Lord. Go to your homes and speak no evil to anyone. I ask the Lord to bless you in the name of Jesus Christ, Amen."

They even asked Daddy to talk. He told the meeting that he was so humble and unworthy he couldn't believe the Lord's prophet would have him speak. He mentioned Mother and said he would sacrifice everything required of him to be with her for the eternities. He said the sacrifice of a broken heart and contrite spirit was the least he could do.

I wasn't surprised about the broken heart, because I knew Mother died of something broken in her heart, and everyone said she went straight to the highest degree of the celestial kingdom forever. I still needed to figure out what a contrite spirit was—I had to remember to ask Daddy.

Grandmother and I were real brave until she had to go. Then she took me aside and held me. "I know you miss your mother." Tears were in her eyes, and my throat was hurting. "But you are doing really well and need to help look out after Nettie and Brent. Help Nettie remember to go to the bathroom so she doesn't wet her pants—Jan's been saying how she's wet all the time. Always heed the things that Mother wanted...and do what Jan says. Remember the talks today." She laughed nervously. "If us old folks don't make it, it'll be up to you...so you can't let us down."

I was horrified. "I could never ever be as good as you, Grandmother!" I hid my face in her neck until Grandpa said they had to go. He gave me a white mint and a hug. These special visits were so good, but so sad, too. One minute you could hug someone you loved so much, and the next minute they were gone. I was glad I felt Mother's spirit here sometimes. After Grandmother and Grandpa left and I went to bed, I felt all right inside.

We started fixing up the yard. I got tired as we raked and hauled rocks and buckets of dirt, but whenever we slowed down Jan told us how much Mother had wanted a nice yard, and I could work real hard again. I didn't know why I was such a wicked, stubborn girl. I wished I could be more like Nettie. She did all the things

Mother had wanted us to do—hurrying real fast and never asking why—and she almost never got in trouble.

One Saturday after we finished our cleaning, Jan sat the three of us down. She had a real serious look on her face. "It's been almost a year since your mother died, and I know we all miss her, but I was talking to your daddy, and we've decided it will help us to feel closer if you all call me Mother or Momma instead of Jan. I want you all to call me Mother now."

We all stared at her until the silence was horrible. When she insisted we answer, we all three looked at each other and then shook our heads. Jan jumped to her feet. "No? You all say no…after all I do for you! Well, you can think about it until after lunch. Maybe you'll realize I'm really your mother once you're hungry!"

Tabitha had been standing quietly in the corner staring at us with wide eyes. Jan swept her into her arms. In a flurry of activity, she slammed the dishes and pots around in the sink. Finally, she settled with her back to us while she fed the baby a bowl of soup.

We looked at each other dumbly. Nettie's delicate body trembled as she tried to hold herself straight. "What should we do, Deb? She won't stop until we do what she says! I'm so hungry and I know you'll get beat again. Just do what she wants. I hate it when you get beat." Tears rolled out of her eyes, and Brent's little round worried face was flushed.

"I'm sorry, Nettie, but I can't call her Mother…I won't. She'll just have to beat me, and if she won't give me food, I'll starve to death!" My body was rigid with fury. Nettie's body sagged. Brent took her hand and together they went outside.

I walked up the road alone, past the orchard. When I got to my deep thicket of thimbleberry bushes, I fought my way to the center and nestled down. I sat hugging my knees and swatting mosquitoes. I could see the house from my hiding spot. In a while Nettie and Brent walked back through the grove of cedar trees. I knew they would make peace with Jan and get to eat. I knew Nettie was right, but I couldn't do it.

Later when the shadows were growing longer and longer, I heard Jan calling, angry first, and then with a sweeter tone that only made me more determined to stay in this safe place until

Daddy came home. My gnawing stomach became a diversion from the throbbing of my head. I didn't want Daddy to find out I had been bad again, so I finally decided I better try to apologize to Jan. I found Nettie and Brent eating in the kitchen. My stomach growled as I smelled the soup.

"Do I get to have some?" I asked Nettie.

"You better ask Mother."

"She isn't Mother!" I responded quickly. "She's Jan…How could you call her Mother?" I suddenly wasn't hungry anymore.

"It doesn't do any good to fight, and we were hungry." Nettie looked resolutely into her bowl of soup, then up at me. "We think you should call her Mother, too. You know how Daddy says we should keep the peace, and Mother always said the same thing."

Jan came into the kitchen. "Well, have you made up your mind?"

I kept my eyes down so their look wouldn't infuriate her right to start with. "I'm sorry I didn't talk to you. I didn't mean to be rude, but I can't call you Mother."

"*Won't,* you mean!" Jan glared at me. "You'll just have to talk about it with your dad when he comes home…Wait in your room."

I lay on my bed and tried to bring Mother's face into this pitch-black room—not the gaunt, pale Mother but the beautiful, rose-colored, soft-skinned Mother I would always remember. "I'm sorry, Mother. I know I promised to make life easier for Daddy, but I can't do this. She isn't my mother, she just isn't you! I tried to call her Mother a couple of times, but it stuck in my throat. Please forgive me."

I pulled my doll with no name from the place I hid her beside the bed and curled up with her under my chin. When I finally heard Daddy's truck coming down the hill, my heart pounded with anticipation. I hid under the covers. Within a few minutes, Jan came to the bedroom door with Daddy in tow. She was explaining to him. "Deb refuses to call me Mother. I could just give up with her. I've tried absolutely everything, and still she defies me. You'll have to talk to her. How can one six-year-old child be so stubborn and infuriate me so much!"

"Just leave it with me." Daddy spoke calmly as he pulled back the curtain and sat down on the bed. He pulled at the covers. "You must be under here somewhere…Come on out, Deb. What's all this I hear about the trouble today? Can't you just call Janessa Mother? She tries so hard to be good to you guys. What would we do without her?"

I wrapped my arms around his neck and hung on tightly. "I can't do it, Daddy! Please forgive me. I'll starve if I have to. I tried to do it…I really did." Daddy patted my back and smoothed my hair.

"If it's really that hard, I'll fix it up with Jan." He ran his fingers through my hair. "I just wish you could control your feelings better, Daughter. The most important thing in life is to be a peacemaker." He held me, smoothed my straggly hair out of the way, and led me by the hand to the kitchen where he poured me some soup.

Jan never insisted that I call her Mother again, but talking to her from then on was more difficult. I knew for a certainty she would hate me forever. Nettie said she wished I would just do as Jan asked, that she was sure Mother wouldn't mind…but I just couldn't. Jan said lots of "honeys" and "dears" to Nettie and Brent, but never to me. That was all right. I just wished I could stop disappointing Daddy.

Daddy, Jan, Uncle Isaac, and Bettilyn had been worrying a lot about a girl from outside our group who came to stay at the ranch just after we moved to Canyon. Bettilyn's brother, who was in and out of jail and wasn't in our Work, had a daughter who had lived in foster homes in Vancouver. Elsa was barely thirteen years old when she came but looked lots older because she wore makeup and had permed hair. Daddy said the stories she told about her family would make your skin crawl, so it was no wonder she didn't know how to be a proper priesthood girl. Bettilyn kept Elsa in her sight because most of the big boys wanted to have her for their sweetiebird, and she couldn't make up her mind which one to pick. She got caught a couple of times sitting on a boy's knee in a corner, where everyone thought they were up to no good.

Uncle Isaac talked about the cat-bird club in church, which really surprised the big boys because they were sure they'd been careful enough that the grown-ups wouldn't know. Our file leader indicated how disgusting and evil "necking and petting" were. He left no doubt in my mind that hellfire and brimstone awaited any young priesthood person guilty of the sin. Elsa didn't seem to understand his message though, because she still had to be carefully watched so she wouldn't cause the boys to go astray. It seemed she learned a lot about how to tempt them living among the Gentiles.

When the prophet was made aware of the situation, he was concerned as well and said he'd talk to the Lord about her. Everyone was waiting with great interest to see what God would decide was the right calling for this wild, worldly creature. I felt so fortunate to be born to parents who protected me and didn't let me suffer the way other kids did out in the world. When I asked Daddy why some people had so many trials, he explained, "You and other spirits born into our family were spirits who were especially valiant and good in the war in heaven. Because of your righteous choices, your spirits were saved by God to be born in this last dispensation for the specific purpose to help this Work grow. Because Elsa has ended up here with us, we'll just have to help Uncle Isaac work with her and hope for the best. Maybe her spirit can be redeemed if she'll accept the gospel and be baptized—that should help control her worldly ways."

Just when Erica found out that Uncle Freddie wanted her to go to Cardston for the summer and she might not be back to help us with school in the fall, the prophet decided Daddy could help Elsa better if she were married to him. She was fourteen by then and was certain she was very grown-up. Although she was really nice to us kids most of the time, I was sad because Erica wouldn't be tending us anymore. I really missed her.

Elsa knew how to make all kinds of interesting food—like raisin pudding and scalloped potatoes. Nettie, Brent, and I loved the raisin pudding, but Tabitha hated it. When they tried to feed it to her, she cried and gagged. Elsa whispered under her breath to us that Tabitha was just a spoiled little boob anyway. When Jan heard that comment, she flew at Tabitha and beat on her the way she always did me. While she was stuffing the pudding into the baby's mouth with her hands, she was screaming at Elsa, "I hope this satisfies you! I hope this satisfies you!" The raisin sauce and cake ran all over Tabitha's face and down her dress until finally she threw up.

We sat there, trying not to look or cry. I had bile rising in my throat, and now I knew how hard it was for Nettie whenever Jan beat on me. After the tantrum died down, Nettie and I decided the next time Elsa made this pudding we would find a way to eat Tabitha's bowl before the mothers knew what was happening. We just couldn't stand to watch such a thing again.

Jan seemed glad to have Elsa around most of the time, but she was convinced her new sister wife was wasteful and appallingly messy. She was always saying, "Some women could throw more out the window with a teaspoon than most men could bring in the front door with a scoop shovel."

Except for the times right after a big fight when Elsa worked really hard all day to keep the house clean, it was a mess when we got home from school. Those days Jan would have us start from the beginning and work and work. She constantly bawled and wrung her hands in frustration. Again and again she said the same thing, "I just can't do it all!"

As the weeks passed, Jan and Elsa were having more and more difficulty getting along. Daddy seemed weary when he showed up to kiss me goodnight, and I was worried about him. Jan was determined to organize us better to cut down on her workload. She spent long hours writing lists for each of us. The lists for Elsa were very detailed and included directions on how to fold the dishcloth after the dishes were washed—how it must be placed carefully on the corner of the sink.

Even though she was only fourteen, Elsa felt she was grown-up because the prophet had married her to Daddy. She wondered who Jan thought she was to boss her around so much. She was sure Jan shouldn't get away with the way she was treating her, even if she was the legal wife now. Elsa thought she was every bit as special since she was going to have Daddy's baby.

One night Jan was crying to Daddy, "I'm trying to follow Vivien's example of how she treated me, but Elsa's just like another kid in the house. All she wants to do is read, and when I get home at night I have to clean up after her, too." Daddy calmly told her he would take care of it, and everything would be fine. He said that the Lord would open up the way, and at least there was someone here to look after Brent and Tabitha, so we could be grateful.

So Jan was really grateful and said, "Oh Adam, you're just so patient and sweet and good. You're such a wonderful example to all of us."

I couldn't decide who to feel the sorrier for, Jan or Elsa. I wished I could be more help, but instead my head just started to ache.

One night we had a beautiful program at our house, and the entire group came to watch it. There were sheet curtains for the stage, and everything was so perfect. All the big kids had starring roles. One of the plays was *The Sword and the Dragon* and the other was *Darby and Joan*. Laman was the valiant knight, and Sidney was the town fool and the dragon. Sidney was so funny. He kept wiggling his big ears and pulling his face into different shapes that made him look like a clown without a mask. Everyone just about died laughing at his antics.

After the sword fight in the last scene, the dragon died with a lot of agonizing moans and groans. When they pulled its mask off, the townspeople realized their horrible mistake. It wasn't really a dragon they had killed—it was the fool they all loved who lay dead at their feet. The music and singing went on until little kids were falling asleep all over the floor. When Daddy closed the program with a prayer, he told Heavenly Father how grateful he was we could have such a good time without needing gentile help to entertain us. I couldn't wait until I was big enough to act in a play like this.

Soon after that, Jan had a special meeting at the school and asked one of the big boys to come tend us kids. He was strong and handsome. He had never paid attention to me before, but he was especially nice this day. He invited me to get into the old blue and white car Daddy had abandoned in the grove of cedar trees. Nettie and Brent were playing together in the creek and Tabitha was down for her nap, so we were alone. He showed me how to shift the gears and things.

He smiled at me really nice and held out his hand. He asked me if I had ever steered a car before and I told him no. He said it was time I learned and helped me to climb onto his lap. I felt so special to have him talk to me like I was one of the big kids. He started making car noises and bouncing up and down. I was flying into the air and landing with a plop. I was worried I'd hurt him, because my bottom was coming down really hard on his legs.

That's when he slowed down and said it would be more fun if I turned around to face him. When I did, he smiled at me and rubbed his fingers up and down my arms. He said I was a really beautiful girl and that I looked just like my mother. He told me how special I was. I smiled timidly at him—maybe I wasn't so stupid after all. He smoothed his hands down my arms again and kissed my lips, then he squirmed underneath me and told me he needed to fix his pants. When he pushed his hands between us, his fingers slipped inside my panties and rubbed right into my private parts. I started to feel kind of funny as I remembered the stick in the playhouse, but this wasn't hurting like that did. His fingers were round and smooth and his touch was gentle. He looked into my eyes and asked me if I wanted to feel him, then took my hand and pushed it onto something hard and long and hot pushing up against my privates.

He told me to move back a little bit and maybe it would work better. He pushed his stomach out and up, and I realized the hard thing was his penis trying to get inside me like the stick. He held me still and pushed me down, but my hands were stuck to him, and when it started to hurt me bad he bounced me up again until I got my hands free. He was breathing hard and moving funny. I asked him if he was okay, but he just kept staring at me strangely. I was scared now because he was jerking around and making the same strange noise the doctor had made in the playhouse.

I told him I should maybe go into the house. He said I could, and he'd be there in a minute. Then he asked if I knew how to keep a secret. I remembered the playhouse and nodded my head. I didn't tell Daddy or anyone—I knew how to keep secrets. I hoped Uncle Guy Musser would be glad, and when I grew up I'd be able to learn more secrets of the kingdom. I felt strangely better about things even though my private parts hurt every day for a while again. Someone besides Mother, Daddy, and Jeanie liked me. I was really lucky. I was also tired, and my head was hurting.

Nettie started coming to school now, too. She seemed so little to be in grade one—she only weighed thirty-two pounds—and she was still wetting her pants. I couldn't help her, because she got worried if Jan saw us together too much. At first that bothered me, but then I realized she was right. I was used to playing with my squirrels and imaginary friends at home, anyway. At school I played with Jean if she wasn't mad at me.

One day at the beginning of a new week, Jeanie told me that the big kids had played cows and bulls in the barn on the weekend. She said that she got to play, too, for the first time, but she didn't like it very much. I wondered if cows and bulls might be special if you really understood it. I didn't tell Jean about my secret—I knew she wouldn't understand. I just asked her if I could play now. She and Aline talked to one of the big boys. They thought he would be good to learn from because he was older than me and knew lots. Jeanie told me I was to climb into the attic of the big ranch house after school, and he would be there to show me how to play the game.

When Jan dismissed the class for the day, Jeanie smiled at me; several other kids turned and snickered as I lingered at my desk. I was almost hoping the boy wouldn't show up. There was lots of time before Daddy would arrive, and Jan had plenty of papers to grade from today's lessons. I was worried. Mother's voice echoed through my mind: "You know what's right, Deb." I did know what was right, but just because I lived six miles away from Uncle Isaac's kids was no reason I shouldn't get to play the games that they did.

I slipped out of the schoolroom and into the main part of the house, keeping a wary eye out for Jan. I sneaked carefully past the picture of the prophet on the wall, around the corner, and up the stairs into the room with the ladder to the attic. I climbed the ladder until the top part of my body was in the hot darkness. I couldn't see a thing. The attic air was stale and tasted dry and dusty. After a few moments my eyes grew accustomed to the darkness.

"Hurry and get up here," came a whisper from the dark recess.

"Where are you?" I searched the gloom. "I don't know what to do."

"Just get off the dumb ladder and get over here so I can show you," he hissed.

I crawled toward his voice over the expanse of wood chips. When I reached him, he turned me around with my face to the corner. I was still on my hands and knees with slivers jabbing into me. He mounted me the same way I had seen the bull jump on the cows in the corral. He humped and humped with his legs thumping against my bum. My hands and bare knees were grinding into the wood chips, and shortly after he started I'd had enough. It was certainly not fun. I kept thinking it would probably be even worse in the hay tunnels on all those prickly bales. I wanted this game to be over but didn't want to say so, and I was relieved when he stopped humping and disappeared down the hole without a word.

I sat in the darkness staring at the light that shone up from the entry port. I was confused about this game. It had turned out to be just as disappointing as King of the Castle. What was wrong with me? Everyone else thought the games were great. I cautiously made my way to the trap door and down the ladder. By the time Daddy arrived, I had already done two pages of adds and take-aways.

CHAPTER 8

Jeanie was living with her mom and brothers and sisters in a house that Naomi built herself. She had had a big fight with Uncle Isaac about what was fair and what wasn't. She was sick of working twenty hours a day on the ranch for nothing and being moved from the big house to the cooler that had no proper bathroom and then back again at Isaac's whim. She was tired of Lemuel and Laman growing to be men and still not working as hard as she was. She hated that they were getting horses and guns and every fun thing they wanted, while she had to argue to get even a new handle for the scraper in the barn. It bothered her, too, that all the while, the boys were getting bolder about making fun of her and mocking her behind her back.

She said Bettilyn might have been her best friend in Cardston before they moved to live the Work in this valley, but a best friend who was also your sister wife wouldn't just take your family allowance and all the money you helped your husband earn, and spend it without ever letting you get a few things you needed. Most of all, Naomi hated the waste of remodeling the ranch house every time the prophet came to Canada. She said Bettilyn was always making too much food for the occasion and wasting it when sometimes her own kids didn't have enough. She hated waste and laziness of any kind, and she was really sick of Lydia.

Uncle Isaac yelled at her. "What the hell is a damned woman supposed to know about this stuff? If you'd mind your own business and stay in your place, things would be a lot better around here."

Naomi told him he didn't have to worry. She would definitely mind her own business and make her own way and never bother him and his precious sons ever again. When he thought she might leave with all her children, Uncle Isaac gave her a rocky piece of ground down by Aunt Lena's grave. Jeanie said Uncle Michael helped her build the house. That only made Isaac madder because it meant Naomi wouldn't have to crawl back to him. She was putting shingles on the roof when she was about to have a baby. Jeanie was real upset because she said Lydia came by and told her mom she hoped she'd fall off and break her fool neck. I thought about Mother and how she would feel bad about the cruel way people were talking to each other now.

Jan scanned the day's lists to make sure she hadn't missed anything. She frowned at us with her hands on her hips. "Well, it's a fine day. If you want any time to get out there and enjoy it, you have a lot to get done first." She turned to Elsa, who was doing her best to keep from looking bored. "Elsa, the kids can take the laundry downstairs before they do the breakfast dishes, but make sure they hurry!" She headed out the front door into the sunshine. "Make sure you kids get all the dishes put away properly after you wash them."

Elsa watched as Jan disappeared from sight in the direction of the orchard, then went into her room and shut the door.

Nettie, Brent, and I looked at each other with mischievous sparkles in our eyes. We knew Elsa was reading in her room again. I picked up an armload of laundry from the massive pile in the hall. I had a great idea. "Let's throw all these clothes down the stairs. We can slide down on them like the kids do at Aunt Bettilyn's. It looked like fun—and no one will care."

I threw my load of laundry down the stairs and ran back for another. Nettie and Brent squealed with delight as they did the same. By the time I grabbed the last dress from a chair in Jan's room, Brent had already made the first trip down the slide. Each step was covered with clothing. Diapers, sheets, underwear, and dresses were all intermingled. Some sat in a jumble at the bottom; a few hung crazily from the wire lines strung in the basement. With happy whoops, we grabbed towels to slide on or just bump-bump-bumped down the stairs on our bums, dragging the rest of the clothes with us.

I was beginning my third trip down when I saw some legs, and my stomach went sick. I looked all the way up and there was Jan hovering like a furious cloud. After that everything was a painful blur. She was yelling and hitting and bawling. Even though her flying fists made contact with my back half a dozen times, I couldn't feel the pain. I jumped from the third step all the way down to the cement and headed for the far end of the basement. Nettie was already hiding behind some boxes in the corner.

Elsa came flying out of her bedroom and Jan shrieked, "Every time I turn my back, everyone stops working. I can't stand it! There's so much to do, and no one cares!" She kicked dirty clothes out of her way as she hurried down the steps. Halfway down she ran into Brent, who was cowering in terror. She picked him up by the back of the shirt with one hand and beat on him with the other. He screamed. Jan dropped him like a sack of flour. My brother bounced down the remaining stairs and collapsed in a heap at the bottom. His head hit a five-gallon honey bucket, then landed with a sickening thud on the cement. He went limp and lay real still. Jan was all the way down now and spied me. Yelling at the top of her lungs, she jerked me out of the corner and beat me up and down my back until I couldn't breathe. I pulled away from her and she turned on Elsa. They hurled the most unkind words at each other, and then Jan started chasing Elsa—out the bottom door, up the back stairs, through the kitchen, and down the basement stairs, again and again.

I crouched behind the honey bucket, and each time they disappeared I tried to see if Brent was all right. I was so afraid he was dead! Finally, they stopped the circle chase, and I could hear their voices way off in the distance.

Nettie came out from behind her boxes and together we helped

Brent sit up. He was moaning and his face was white. Nettie and I were both crying. Nettie's skirt was wet from urine. She moaned over and over in a soft little voice, "I don't know why she does that. I don't know why she does that." She hugged me and we both hugged Brent. Our wet cheeks pressed together, mingling our collective grief. Brent was beginning to look better. The blue color was leaving his lips and life was returning to his eyes. We helped him stand.

I put his arms over Nettie's shoulder and whispered, "I'm running away. Maybe things will be better if I'm not here."

"No, don't," Nettie pleaded anxiously. "It won't matter...She'll still get mad, no matter what." Together, she and Brent hobbled from the cool darkness of the basement. I was on pins and needles, sitting in a corner and listening intently. I had to be careful. If Jan caught me running away, there was no telling what she'd do to me. But I had to—I was always the one who made her the maddest. Nettie and Brent wouldn't get beat near as often if I wasn't around. I stood up, then winced as a sharp pain sliced through my back. I cried out—just breathing hurt, and crying made it unbearable.

Peering out the door, I looked carefully in both directions, then scurried along the cement pad. I slipped across the road to the big cherry tree and slid out of sight down the bank. I gathered my courage. My heart was pounding as I crouched and ran along the bank until it gave way to the side road. I followed the edge of the gutter, staying well back in the protection of the thimbleberry bushes. When I reached the top road, I looked back. Nettie and Brent were over in the cow pasture, walking together like Hansel and Gretel. Elsa and Jan were sitting beside the house. It looked like they were making up. That was how it always went. They'd be nice to each other all the rest of the day, and their voices would be like sticky honey...but I wouldn't be here.

My sobs were sporadic now, and I became more and more conscious of pain. My ribs were sore and my feet were bare and hurting from dead sticks that poked at them from under the thimbleberry bushes. I took one last look at the house, wondering if I dared go back for my shoes.

Bowing my head, I knelt in the prickly underbrush. "Dear

Heavenly Father, I was bad again and made Jan real mad. Please forgive me. I guess if I run away to Jeanie's house I could be their girl. It would be the best thing. I'd miss Daddy a lot, but he wouldn't have to hear about the bad stuff I do. I'm thankful for my blessings, but I don't know how to make her happy, so please don't think I'm being ungrateful or anything. Please watch over me while I'm on the devil's ground, and help me so I don't get lost. In the name of Jesus Christ, Amen."

I stood up, my shoulders squared to face the road, the Gentiles, and what I must do. I was sure I knew the way, but leaving our dedicated property scared me a lot. Daddy was always telling us that the Lord couldn't protect us if we went on the devil's ground.

My bare feet carefully sought the smooth-packed clay spots of the road, and I ran until the sound of my heart was pounding in my ears and my breath came in gasps. I concentrated on the ground as it flew beneath my feet, and soon I had made it past the hairpin turn at the top of the steep hill to the first of the gentile houses. I warily examined the landscape for Gentiles and devils and moved like a frightened deer to the side of the road. The shoulder was strewn with rocks that dug into my feet. I longed to walk in the middle, where the traffic had kicked the rocks into the weeds. The ditches were overgrown with shoulder-high blue-flowered chicory and grass, and my plan of escape from any Gentiles was to dart quick as a mouse down into the grass and lie still—like we hid from the police—until they were gone.

The heat waves that rose from the long stretch of paved road in front of me made me dizzy, and I tried not to look ahead. My throat was dry; all I could think about was finding water. I hugged the ditch and sneaked past gentile homes where sprinklers were soaking down the lawns. How I wanted to just wet my tongue.

The road came to the top of the longest steep hill I had ever walked on, and I could see the mountain. I knew what the one above Uncle Isaac's ranch looked like because of the devil's chair in the rocks just about at the top. I searched until I was sure I could tell where it was. It seemed a thousand miles away, and I suddenly felt confused. Since Daddy brought me to this valley, I was at home or at school or at Jeanie's, but I was never in the middle of a dangerous gentile road, my feet bleeding, and so thirsty I couldn't think. I just knew that I was here and I was hot and I was scared. I heard the rumble of a car coming and made a mad scramble for the bottom of the ditch. My knees and elbows hit hard on some rocks, but I lay very still, listening to my heart throb in my ears and whispering "The Lord is my shepherd" over and over. The gentile car rattled past me and faded into the distance. All I could hear was the hot summer whirring of grasshoppers. Nursing new wounds, I pulled myself out of the ditch, picked the sticks out of my petticoat, and continued my journey.

I kept thinking about the story of *Pilgrim's Progress* that Mother used to read to me. I focused on all the pain those poor saints had suffered. I prayed that somehow the pain I was enduring now would help me get to the highest degree of the celestial kingdom. Uncle Isaac was always telling us we would all have to suffer the way Jesus suffered to ever hope to get to heaven to be with him. Jesus did have a lot of bleeding and pain before he died. I had read the stories and seen the pictures in Mother's book of Bible stories.

I reached the long straight road above the Lister store, and a white horse came galloping full tilt up the road. I stared intently until I was certain it was Diamond...and that was Emilia riding him. I was suddenly excited and certain I had been delivered from the devil's clutches. Emilia would help me. She would give me a ride.

I tried to call out but the words wouldn't come. I broke into a run. I didn't care about the rocks and sticks. The only thing that mattered was getting Emilia's attention and returning to dedicated property. A helpless wail came from deep in my stomach. Tears flooded my eyes and I was running blindly. I tripped and sprawled into the rocks. When I lifted my head and wiped the mud and gravel from my eyes, Diamond was disappearing around the corner. All that remained was the dust he had kicked up.

I sat up sobbing and praying. "Dear Heavenly Father, I need you to help me...I guess I did something real wrong, and I'm sorry, but please help me get to Jeanie's. I want to be good...Please forgive me." My mind went fuzzy with the thirst and the pain and the worry, and I couldn't even remember what I was trying to tell God. I waited until I quit breathing hard, then pulled myself onto my bleeding feet. My dress was torn and bloody. I limped along, mindlessly mumbling, "The Lord is my shepherd, I shall not want. Yea, though I walk through the valley and the shadow of death…Yea, though I walk through the valley and the shadow of death." I knew it wasn't quite right, but I couldn't remember what came next. The words were stuck in my mind, and they just came out the same, over and over.

I trudged on until I reached Ivany Farms. I knew their farm because I had worked there with the stick-picking crew. In the distance was Helme's hill. Naomi's house was straight across these huge fields as the crow flies…but I wasn't a crow. I looked down the last long straight road and turned into a second-cut hayfield. I would walk across it and save my feet from the constant jabs of the gravel. After ten minutes I longed to be back on the road. The dry green-brown stubble attacked me every time I set my foot down. Soon I was leaving a trail of blood behind me. It took me two hours to cross this field of torture.

I struggled up from a gully, looked across the road, and I was there. I staggered the remaining distance and sank to the grass by Jeanie's place. I cried and I cried. Jean came out of the house. "What're you doin' here?" She looked all around in disbelief. "How'd ya get here?" I just shook my head. She ran over and put her arms around me. "Come and we'll find Mom. She'll know what to do."

"Jan just beat us and beat us. I had to come here. I'm never going back!" I was sobbing so hard I could hardly be understood. She helped me up and let me lean on her. Jean's sister, Irene, was the only big person in the house. When I finally told her why I ran away, she said she would help me stay away forever, and if she was one of my moms she'd make sure I never got beat again. She said Naomi would help, too.

When Naomi got home and saw me, she was real mad. I wondered at first if she was mad at me; her eyes were fierce. She started swinging her head and stormed, "What in the sam hell do they think they're doing? People should be reported for this kind of goings-on. I'm having a talk with your dad about this…You can bet your life on that!"

I didn't know what to say, and I was suddenly worried. I started to sob again. "It wasn't Daddy's fault. We were sliding on clothes and being bad and Jan was busy!"

Naomi told me not to worry about the clothes, that they weren't important now. She disappeared up the trail with a shovel to continue digging the ditch she needed to get water from the spring on the mountain to her house. It was a huge job—over a mile of rocks and roots and very steep hills. The task would have daunted any man with a backhoe, let alone a woman with an old shovel. But Naomi was stubborn and very determined.

I spent the rest of the day in a tired haze following Jean around and resting in the quiet, cool interior of her house. As the sun was setting, Daddy's truck rattled over Helme's hill. I stood by the stuccoed wall until he stopped. Naomi came out of the house drying her hands on a towel and told us kids to get back inside. I waited just inside the door and Naomi started to yell.

Daddy remained calm, and I heard him say, "I realize things aren't good for the kids sometimes. I try the best I can to work with people to get them to do the right thing, but sometimes these things are slow to change. I appreciate your concern, and I'll do the best I can to make sure it doesn't happen again."

Naomi sternly continued, "You're damned right you better, and I intend writing Selma about this."

Daddy looked miserable and changed the subject. "I need to take Deb home now. Can you get her to come? I really miss her mother and I need my Deb." Daddy spoke thickly now, through tears.

I flew out of the house and up to the open door of the truck. "I'm sorry I ran away, Daddy. I want to come with you now. It'll be just fine."

He drove me home slowly with one arm around me and the other managing the steering wheel. We were silent most of the way. As we turned down our road he begged, "Please don't ever run away again, Deb…Please don't. I lost Mother and I couldn't bear to lose you, too. We'll work things out together; you know we can. We just need to pray and the Lord will help us endure everything." He looked at me through his tears. "Jan wants me to use the belt on you for running away, but I'm not going to. It can be our secret."

I would rather he had spanked me instead of crying. I promised him I'd never run away again. We pulled up to our house and got out. My whole body was aching and I was unspeakably tired. Jan stood at the door glaring at me. She stepped back as we approached, went into her room, and closed the door. Daddy sat me on my bed and said, "I'll take care of things, Daughter."

When he left, I removed my soiled dress and crawled into bed. My feet throbbed and my back and ribs hurt with every breath. All I could think about was my mother's arms wrapped around me, my face pressed into her soft neck. I pulled the covers up to my chin and lay there crying and shivering. As warm as it was in the house, I just couldn't stop my body from vibrating. Every time I closed my eyes, a different picture popped into my mind. One moment Jan's fists were flailing against my back, the next I was picking myself up from the ditch and watching Diamond disappear into the distance.

I prayed, "Dear Heavenly Father, I don't see how you think you need my mother more than I do—especially tonight! I want her. Maybe you could think about it and change your mind. I know Grandmother and Daddy say all this experience is good for me to learn to keep sweet, but I can't see how. I know I'm wicked to complain, but I just don't understand. The prophets in the Bible talked to you and you helped them. I feel Mother close to me sometimes, but I can't see her, and I can't touch her. I need her to hold me so I can stop shaking. Please, help me! In the name of Jesus Christ, Amen."

Hugging my old blind doll to my breast, I sang softly, "You are my sunshine..." When I got to the part about waking up and being mistaken, the tears choked me and I couldn't think anymore. I quit trying to remember the words and hummed the melody over and over again as I faded into blessed sleep.

•

Elsa's baby came almost eight weeks early, and we were real scared he wouldn't be all right. He was so tiny. Aunt Susie from Colorado City was here for the birth, and everyone said it was such a good thing or Jarom might have died. She was famous down in Arizona for delivering polygamist children. She had been the wife of John

Y. Barlow when he was the prophet. Our prophet, Uncle Roy, would care for her for John Y. Barlow until she died, and then she'd be with him in the eternities. Daddy said it was the most humble privilege to have her in our home. He said she had the faith of the ancients and God really listened to her. Aunt Susie sat by the cookstove with the oven door open, and every time our baby went blue she breathed into his mouth and spanked him until he started breathing again.

I was so grateful. At least he was living. I knew Mother was up in heaven with baby Lena and would look after Jarom, too, if he went up there, but I just thought he should stay on earth for a while.

Grandpa and Grandmother came for the conference and the happy display of Daddy's first plural son. Grandpa slapped Daddy on the back. "Well, it looks like you did it, you old son of a gun!"

Daddy replied humbly, "It's such an honor to be allowed to bring these special covenant children to the earth. I just pray that I can be worthy of it."

Grandmother had tears in her eyes when she hugged Elsa. "Vivien would have been so proud and grateful."

Elsa blossomed under the admiration and acceptance, and the smile didn't leave her face for the rest of the weekend. Grandmother was fascinated with the patriarchal blessing Uncle Guy gave to Elsa, prophesying that "prophets and priestesses will be born through her loins." Grandmother thought it was quite likely that Jarom would be a prophet. I grew nervous that Grandmother would be so busy with all of her women's ordinances and visits that she wouldn't have time for us, but when we left for the priesthood meetings, I was sitting very happily by her side in Grandpa's new car.

Jan had started a new program for us to order books from the library branch in Victoria, and I had been saving a wonderful book about Blaze, the horse, to show Grandmother and Grandpa how well I could read. I was reading fast because I knew this was the only time I would have to be private with Grandmother. The road was dusty and winding, and my stomach was rolling. I tried to tell Grandpa I wasn't feeling well, but when I opened my mouth, my breakfast came gushing out in one horrible stream. It ended up all over my lacy dress, all over Grandpa's new car, and all over Grandmother's skirt. I wanted to die. I was so glad Jan wasn't there, or I would have really been in for it.

I was worried Grandmother might not love me anymore. She just said, "Too bad, too bad," and helped me off with my dress. She used her carefully folded white handkerchief to wipe my face, and then she even kissed me. When we got to the ranch, she wrapped her jacket around my shoulders and rushed me into the house where Aunt Bettilyn found me a dress to wear. I said I was sorry a hundred times.

After Grandmother had me all washed and changed, I went out onto the boardwalk to let the wind blow the smell of vomit out of my hair. I was standing straight as a poker with my dress and hair blowing backwards when Sidney tried to pass me. He was Lem and Laman's friend even though he was a Whitmer. He didn't live at home anymore, and he always said hi to me. He stopped with a grin and said, "What are you doin' out here in the wind? Did you hear I'm goin' on a Work mission for our prophet in Colorado City?" He paused and looked very serious. "I really miss your mom, you know. I loved her. She always fixed me an egg in the mornings before I had to do the chores, and she told me to always brush my teeth. I do, too. Even if I don't have a toothbrush, I use a rag and soap—and see how white my teeth are!" He forced a huge smile and his teeth gleamed white at me. "I'm headin' south with the prophet when he goes back home. I'm only seventeen and I'm goin' to be gone a long time, so you can wait for me and marry me when I get back."

"Sure I will!" I said with a smile. I would marry anyone who could remember my mother and love her, but immediately I felt guilty because the prophet didn't want us to like anybody or talk married unless he said. We both went into the meeting.

The talks this day were inspiring—especially Uncle Guy's. He rose to his full height and spoke in his most intense manner. "The time has come to put away all of the gentile traditions and stop clinging to the ways of the world! To begin with, we have a problem with some of the women clinging to worldly ornaments and trinkets, to the point of worshiping them. This was displeasing to the Lord in the times of Moses, and it is displeasing to Him now. Any of you women who want to prove to the Lord that you are ready to make the sacrifices and stand up to the line can prove it by going home and sacrificing your idols. When the Lord asks you to do a thing, you must not question it, and you must do it now.

"We want to cling to the ways of the old church when they have given up all of the saving principles of the gospel. The institution of the Relief Society was got up by a bunch of women who were trying to control their husbands and the priesthood, and the Lord was displeased with this. The women must learn to be more obedient to the priesthood and their husbands. We will have no more gatherings of the women in the organized capacity of the so-called Relief Society. We have found that when women get together in this way without a priesthood man in their presence, they tend to take upon themselves the spirit of fault-finding and complaining, and the Spirit of the Lord is sorely displeased. We must be more humble and take upon ourselves the job to get out from under the condemnation the Lord placed on the church, so He will find us worthy to come into the glory of the exaltation of the principle of plural marriage, where we can rise as kings and queens.

"If we will take upon ourselves these directions from our prophet, the Lord will be able to work with us and save us from the destroying angels, while the rest of the world will be destroyed. I prophesy to you that you will live to see the day when the yellow hordes will come in a flood over these mountains that surround your valley, and it will only be through the power of the priesthood and your prophet that you will be saved. In fact, the prayer circles will be called from Canada to Mexico, and by the power of the obedient in our priesthood gatherings, the whole world will be saved from utter destruction. The waves of the devil's destroyers will be halted as long as these trained and righteous men and women stay faithful to the call of the prophet. The people who do not hear the voice of our prophet, LeRoy Sunderland Johnson, are as whited sepulchers, and even though they may live lives that seem to be acceptable to the sectarian teachers of the earth, they will all be destroyed until not so much as a yellow dog will be left to wag his tail!"

Everyone in the room was in awe. When he sat down, I was praying I could be humble enough to be found worthy before the Lord for this great calling. I could see the horrible yellow Chinese and Japanese people come screaming over the mountains trying to take over God's holy country, and we would pray and pray and pray…We could save the world! I knew we could!

Uncle Michael was really popular today because he was answering the call of the prophet to move with his family to Colorado City. He was going to help build new homes for the Saints. He stood to speak and in his slow, deliberate way said, "I am glad to answer the call of the prophet and go on to the greater furtherance of the priesthood—to help build up the kingdom in Colorado City. I have had a difficulty with the principle of placement marriage but have come to realize that the pure and holy race of Israel can only come into this world under the direction and inspiration of the prophet. The rebellious and evil strains of the gentile worlds must be bred out of a people before the Lord can use them in the redemption of Zion. You young people can thank the Lord every day that this principle of the covenant has been revealed to save you from the contamination of an evil mate. And thus the children born to these unions of the covenant will be born and raised as calves in the stall. Then and only then can we rid ourselves of the wicked and vain traditions of the gentile world."

Grandmother whispered to me, "We can be so grateful the Lord cares about us this much that we are learning these wonderful secrets of the kingdom."

"Oh yes, Grandmother, oh yes!" I replied.

Uncle Roy took the stand and told us in gentle, loving tones that the Lord truly loved us, and so did he. He said we were a chosen and elect people and that the Lord cared about us very much, and then he called the Lord's blessings down upon us and closed the meeting.

The people were much quieter after this meeting, and we quickly said our goodbyes and went home. I was saddened by the smell of my vomit in Grandpa's new car, and I was happy when we got home and I could get away from the reminder that I had sinned.

When we settled in the living room, Grandmother sat in

silence. Finally, she got up, stood toe to toe with Daddy and said, "Adam, I want you to explain something to me. I feel that the Lord was speaking to us today, but I'm confused. I was the president of the Relief Society in our ward in Rosemary for ten years, and we worked hard to help the poor and the sick and gather food for the storehouse. None of us were perfect and we did gossip a bit, but we had wonderful spiritual times and studied and learned about Christ. It's hard for me to face what the brethren said about it today. How could anything that accomplished so much good be an evil and unworthy thing in the eyes of the Lord? And my glass ornaments and statues are so beautiful and perfect; I have a hard time thinking that the Lord is displeased with them. It isn't as if I worship them, but I always thought the Lord loved beauty." Her voice was trembling with passion. "I know I shouldn't be questioning this direction, but I guess it's hard to teach an old dog new tricks."

Daddy patted her on the arm. "Now, Selma, you do have this problem with thinking you can steer the ship sometimes, but you're a good old girl and I'm sure you'll realize it is all for the best."

Jan interjected with fervent admonition. "Yes! I'm eternally grateful for the chance to prove I can be grateful for the Lord's interest in us as a people, without questioning the Lord's servants! It's proved time and time again that the Lord knows what He's doing. Take for example calling Uncle Michael down to the States. I'm sure he thinks he's big and important now, but it's really a blessing that he's leaving. He's been nothing but a trial for years and refuses to give Daddy the support that he should have for the Work to progress here in Canada. I, for one, resent being held back by such contention. Also I would say, Selma, that your saying you can't teach an old dog new tricks is just an excuse!"

"I'm sure you're right. I will get better and better, if the Lord will just be patient with me." Grandmother sighed and took me off to talk by ourselves.

"Naomi has told me about you running away. I feel badly things seem so hard for you, but I've talked to Jan and I believe she has your best interests at heart. Promise me you won't run away again, no matter what. A little girl like you could get into terrible trouble out on the devil's ground." She had tears in her eyes. "Losing your mother was hard enough."

I looked into her eyes until I couldn't stand her pain anymore, then dove into her dress and hid my face. "I never will. I never will again! But why do you have to go? You come and then you go again so fast."

And suddenly, they were gone, as if they had never come. All of the special treats, kind words, and considerations from Jan disappeared with Grandmother.

In the next week Jan threw away all of Mother's beautiful ornaments. I asked if I could have them because they were Mother's, but she said I needed to let the worldly things go. I guess I understood you couldn't do anything halfway and expect to get anywhere with the Lord. After I thought about it awhile, I was pretty ashamed and remembered all of the times Mother told me that we shouldn't question the Lord.

CHAPTER 9

The police came and took Elsa and her baby away. We were terrified and were all praying real hard. Elsa's horrible gentile mother was the one who told on Daddy. I always wondered if Gentiles could really be so evil—now I knew. Daddy and our prophet were always right.

This wicked woman came to our house with a tall black man and the police. I couldn't believe it. This man was all black—his face, his hands, his hair. I thought he must be the devil. Our prophet and God's teachings said that black men were sons of Cain and fence-sitters, and if any of the pure children of Israel like us mixed our seed with these black people, then we would be instantly condemned to the second death. The police said Daddy was unlawfully cohabitating with a minor, and Social Services was going to see about it. That's when they took our little brother, Jarom, and Elsa away.

Jan explained it all to us kids that night while Daddy was over at Uncle Isaac's trying to get the word of the Lord on what to do about this persecution. They even called the prophet to ask him if God had told him what to do. That way, no matter what happened, all the condemnation would be on the heads of Elsa's mother, the black man, and the police, because Daddy, Uncle Isaac, and the prophet had talked to God.

Jan was trying not to cry. "I need to explain to you children that Daddy might go to jail, because the devil works especially hard to stop the Lord's work—especially plural marriage. You can tell you're doing a good job if you're getting persecuted, because that's just the way it works. We need to pray really hard that the Lord will protect Daddy, and we can all be back together soon. It's really ironic someone like Elsa's mother could get us in trouble with the law when she's living with a nigger and isn't even married at all! I guess the devil protects worldly sin, so it's just as well we're being tried."

When I went to bed, I spent a long time talking to Heavenly Father and Mother, asking them to help Daddy in his time of need.

Everything was very quiet in the morning—no laughing or talking. After the work was done, Daddy told us we needed to go over to the ranch for a little while. He looked serious and very sad when he put his elbows on the piano and gazed at Mother's picture. He cried and cried. I hugged him with all my strength. Mother must have known something like this would happen, and I knew I had to be brave for Daddy now. "I've been praying really hard. I know God will send the police and the Gentiles away so they can't hurt us anymore. Jarom is our brother, so the bad guys can't have him. We won't let them!"

Daddy shooed me out to the truck. I heard him tell Jan he was expecting the police at two o'clock, and he would bake the bread while we were away. I was so afraid he might be gone when we got back home and we would never see him again.

Jan got in on the driver's side and said, "It's going to be fine...you'll see." Nettie, Brent, Tabitha, and I sat in a worried little row as we rattled and bumped over the six-mile road to the ranch. Jeanie and James walked with me and we talked about the police and our dads and how, if we were big, we'd sure fix the Gentiles...and somehow we needed to save Jarom.

All unscheduled, the prophet came again, bringing a couple of his best apostles. Grandpa came from Rosemary, too, to be part of this special meeting. Daddy was reverently humble and very grateful as he explained to him, "The brethren have come back to Canada on a special mission to petition the Lord on our behalf to revoke the evil designs of the world. You know, Isaiah, you just can't go anywhere else on the earth and find a servant of God ready to use his power this way. It really behooves us."

Grandpa was shaking his head wisely, his round prairie-worn face beaming as he talked. "Ain't it amazing! Ain't it amazing!"

The prophet called a special prayer meeting to bind Elsa and Jarom up against Satan. There was a hushed, expectant feeling as we bowed our heads and Uncle Guy Musser stood and put both arms to the square.

"Our righteous, eternal, all-powerful Lord and Savior! We stand before you this day in all the robes of the power of our calling and dispensation. We call down your judgments on the heads of the people who are working with the adversary in this evil hour. We hereby revoke their power and strength and render them useless in their intent. We will here state that they will be thwarted in whatsoever they desire to do, and your covenant child will be returned to your work and your glory!" Beads of sweat were shining on Uncle Guy's bald head, and his arms were trembling. I knew because I was peeking. I shouldn't have been looking, but I just had to see how apostles prayed to revoke the adversary. Uncle Guy looked transparent, as if God were standing in his face that very moment.

After he was finished praying, he lowered his arms and shouted, "Hosanna! Hosanna! Hosanna!" He raised his arms again with every shout and called on the prophets each by name and all the generations of Saints that had ever been on the earth. He charged them to rally behind the special Canadian Saints and bind up the government of all nations to be helpless against the mighty purposes of the priesthood and the sacred Work of plural marriage and the United Order, the governing body of the sacred Work. Every adult was crying, even the men. We sang "The Spirit of God Like a Fire Is Burning."

When we got home, Grandpa gave us a peppermint and told us all with awe in his voice, "You have to know that it's a rare privilege to hear the holy shout of hosanna. The Lord has only ever directed his holy servants to use it when they mean business, and then God Himself is bound to step in and do whatever the apostles ask of Him. It only happens once in a lifetime. We have certainly been fed spiritually tonight and left with no doubt that the power of God rests with this group of His people."

Just as the Lord brought the mothers and children home after the government raid in Short Creek, Arizona, Elsa and Jarom got to come back home in just a few weeks. I felt so sorry for anyone who didn't get to have plural brothers and sisters and God's truest servant to shout hosanna and make the law dogs and politicians bend to their will.

On the day of my baptism I wrote a letter to Mother.

Dearest Mother, I'm eight now. You would be so happy about that. I remember you telling me about when I would be old enough to get baptized—and now I am. Uncle Isaac had a baptism over at the ranch for Jean and James in the summer, but Daddy said he wasn't going to bend the rules and baptize me before my birthday. He said in little meeting if you had enough faith, the water would be warm even in October. I didn't want anyone to watch, so Daddy and I walked down to the river alone. It was so nice, Mother. The leaves crunched under our feet. The gold and brown and green of the cottonwoods was everywhere—as if King Midas had gone crazy down here in this Canadian jungle. Joint grass and watercress lined the edges of every stream and boggy corner. The smell of skunk cabbages was mixed with the first wintery smells of moss and the rushing water. I was alert to the squirrels and chipmunks, and near where the old bridge used to be a white-tailed deer jumped out of a stand of new cottonwoods. Last year the snow in the mountains was especially heavy, and the spring thaw roared down the Goat River, ripping and tearing our ancient cottonwoods up from their roots and changing the riverbed as you knew it. We were surrounded by these dead giants, which settled in huge logjams. My grip on Daddy's hand tightened when we stopped at the edge of my secret baptism hole.*

Daddy turned me to him, put both hands on my shoulders, and said, "Daughter, you are about to enter the waters of baptism and become a

---

*Common horsetail is called "joint grass" because the segments making up the stem can be easily separated as the plant matures.

member of the kingdom of God, and all of your sins will be gone. Mother will be here with us and so will the angels if we think about heavenly things. I'm really proud of you." I thought of my sins—all the times I talked back to Jan, and the compact I stole, and I was almost certain that cows and bulls was a sin. I was really happy to hear I wouldn't need to ever worry about any of that old bad stuff again after Daddy said the words.

"Sister Deborah Ann Nilsson, having been commissioned by the Church of Jesus Christ of Latter-day Saints, I baptize you in the name of the Father, the Son, and the Holy Ghost." He lowered me into the water, and I came up filled with an incredible feeling of oneness with the angels and with you, Mother. You died for this Work, and now I am an official member.

Daddy wrapped a towel around me. As we walked back up the hill, I asked, "Daddy, why am I baptized a member of the Church of Jesus Christ of Latter-day Saints when the prophet always says the church has lost the priesthood and is against the truth? I don't understand."

Daddy explained it to me patiently. "When the church gave up plural marriage, it was against the commandments of the Lord, so He took the priesthood away from them and gave the keys to President Johnson, so we are really the Church of Jesus Christ of Latter-day Saints, and they just think they are. You have to understand that we are pretty special for the Lord to think enough of us to lead us to the truth and see that we aren't deluded like the rest of the world." I was so impressed and thought about poor Aunt Rita and my skinny cousins in California who thought they were living the truth but were really being led far away. We finished the walk home in a special glow.

Elsa made raisin pudding for supper and told me it was especially for me since I was baptized now. Later we went to Jeanie's house where Uncle Isaac was staying the night, and Daddy and Uncle Isaac put their hands on my head and confirmed me. Daddy said in the blessing that in any time of terrible need the Lord would let you come to me.

Oh Mother, it was all so wonderful today. I am really a part of God's chosen people now, and I'm determined not to fight with Jan anymore. I know I can do it. I sure don't want any more sins to come back on my head, so I'll use all of my strength to listen very carefully and do what she wants. Ever since I ran away, we've sort of been friends. She lets me brush her hair out at night when she's doing her correspondence, and sometimes she reads me the interesting stuff she's learning. If I brush her hair just right she even gives me a hug after, and at bedtime we kiss. She started reading amazing adventures about pirates and kings and queens and things. We all gather around the lamp and she reads and reads. I could listen forever, really. Goodnight, Mother, I love you.

The weeks had been long since Grandma went back home after Jarom was born, and so much had happened. Uncle Michael and most of his family had gone to Colorado City, where the prophet lived. Lavina was looking after her brothers and sisters—Uncle Michael's kids who were still here in Canada—and she was having problems with Uncle Isaac. He had moved Lydia and her into the house the Hortons had lived in on Uncle Michael's land. He also got up in church and told everyone he was in charge of Uncle Michael's property, and it would be called the priesthood property from now on. He explained how the prophet had a special calling for the property because it had been turned over to the United Effort Plan and dedicated to the Lord.

He told Lavina in no uncertain terms to either get rid of the goats or lock them up, which was impossible because she had no hay to feed them. She had no transportation to get to town to sell the goats, and anyway, she needed them for the milk and meat since there wasn't much money for food. Just as Lavina was getting so scared she didn't know what to do next, Uncle Freddie let Erica come back to help her. Erica calmed her sisters and brothers, telling them she was sick of the fighting and would talk to Uncle Isaac. She asked him to please wait a little while and both the goats and her family would all be gone, and then he could do what he wanted.

Naomi wasn't happy with the situation at all. She wrote a letter to Uncle Michael asking if he knew his property in Canada belonged to a "United Effort Trust Corporation" and Uncle Isaac was bossing everyone around like he owned the place. Uncle Michael was more surprised than anyone because the prophet and apostles had told him they were turning his farm into a dude ranch for tourists to help give jobs for God's people—and he would have shares in the company. He was angry that he'd been tricked and that his children were being treated like lepers. Naomi talked to Daddy. She said she didn't know why Uncle Michael should be so surprised, what with the bad blood between him and Isaac for so many years. She was frustrated and more angry than ever with Isaac. "What kind of stupid logic started their ridiculous fight over the right to rule? Do they both think they're already gods?" Daddy had a hard time calming her down.

Naomi told him about a showdown Isaac had with Michael over who the file leader was and why. The three of them had been talking in Michael's kitchen, and Isaac was trying to tell him all the reasons *his* prophet had decided Isaac was in charge in Canada. She said Michael just sat there and wouldn't argue about anything. Naomi's usual tough demeanor was shaken with the memory.

"Isaac wrenched an axe from the chopping block and held it over Michael's head. I'll never forget how Michael just folded his arms and calm as you please said, 'Go ahead and swing it, you know you want to. You can end it here and now!' I think Isaac would have done it, but I grabbed his arm and told him to stop being such a bloody fool!"

She glared at Daddy and his look of disbelief. "I don't care if you don't believe me. At that moment I could see one thing clearer than anything I'd ever known in my life, and I told Isaac, too—Michael had the best of him, no matter what else Isaac thought he had won! I took the axe out of his hand and told him he'd be a murderer. Well, you should have seen the look on his face. He even cried and begged Michael to forgive him. He said their oath and covenant of brotherhood was more sacred than brothers born of the same mother."

Naomi told Daddy that Michael agreed and shook hands. Then on the way back to the ranch, Isaac started hopping along on his leg the way he always did when he was so mad he couldn't think straight. "After all his sanctimonious tears, he went back on his vow. I heard him swearing to the skies and all that was holy that Michael would have to bow down to him someday...What a wonderful priesthood man!"

Daddy winced. He didn't dare call Naomi a liar or defend Uncle Isaac to her face, so he just mumbled something about peacemakers. He wouldn't allow himself to find fault with the file leader—that would have been as bad as finding fault with the prophet. Now it was up to Erica to get Uncle Isaac to leave her brothers and sisters alone long enough for them to get down to the States.

Everyone in the group was happy when the last of the goats was sold. Michael's children all went south and Erica went back to Uncle Freddie in Cardston. Although everyone else was congratulating themselves that the priesthood property was finally free from contention, Daddy said there was reason for much sorrow, because from that day on Uncle Michael was on the road to becoming an apostate—he would be someone we had to guard ourselves against.

Elsa had a terrible second pregnancy, and even after her delivery had to stay in bed most of the time. That made it really hard for Jan to keep up with things. Daddy asked Uncle Freddie if Erica could come back to help us out. Having her in the house that winter was like having an old friend back. Uncle Freddie never had much to do with her even though she was pregnant with his baby. After her son was born in the Creston Valley Hospital, Uncle Freddie came to visit her for a day. He told her the baby was to be called Lyle, and then he went back to Alberta.

Erica was really weak after the birth because she lost a lot of blood. It was hard to get used to her lying around all day because she was usually the first one to bounce out of bed and cook something. One morning I went to tell her breakfast was ready, because I knew she'd let me hold the baby. When I knocked, the bedroom door swung open. Erica was standing there giggling, with both hands in the basket. Her face looked strange. I told her to come, but she acted as if she hadn't heard me. She started to sway, and to my horror, she fell down in slow motion. The baby rolled out of the basket and hit the floor at the same time. I leapt for him and scooped him up, praying as hard as I could that Erica wouldn't be dead. I screamed for Jan, who rushed down the hall and sent me to the kitchen. Erica was all right, but for weeks every time I closed my eyes I could see her falling.

Emilia came to visit us in Canyon and asked Jan if I could stay at the ranch overnight. I knew better than to ask because she always said no to me, but this time she said yes to Emilia.

Uncle Isaac had a black and white television now; I had never seen one before. I couldn't imagine it—cows and horses and singing and dancing, all in a little box. Jan said television was a skilful tool of the devil and could bring all kinds of evil into your house without your even knowing it.

After he had milked the cows and the mothers had fed the last hungry kid, Uncle Isaac got out his copy of *The Fate of the Persecutors*. "Gather round here, kids," he called in his huge voice, "and I'll tell you what happens to anyone who persecutes the Lord's servants and his faithful followers!" We collected from all parts of the house, and he read horrendous stories of evil men who tormented and killed the early members of the Latter-day Saints. In one story, wicked men painted their faces black and shot little children and cut up an old man with a corn cutter. These evil persecutors took ill and started to rot; their flesh fell off their bones. The man who shot the prophet, Joseph Smith, died screaming in agony and praying for someone to kill him as worms crawled out of his eyes.

Uncle Isaac expounded, "People just don't know what will happen if they turn away from the Lord's anointed. In this day, people who torment the Lord's Work will come under the same condemnation as the men in this book. I want you kids to remember that. *Mark my words!*"

I could scarcely tear my eyes from him, until the image of wicked black men with worms crawling and flesh falling off became too much for me. After this gruesome rendition of God's judgment, Uncle Isaac watched *Rawhide* on television. Then he sang some Maori songs, which he had learned in New Zealand when he was on his mission for the Church of Jesus Christ of Latter-day Saints. Back then, he thought the true priesthood was really with that wicked church...That was before he found the proper authority. The songs were native war and love songs, and he was magnificent. The war song was accompanied with the wild stomping and fierce emotion of the battle, and the final blood-curdling, tongue-lashing yell sent all of us kids into excited screaming.

Then he played his mouth organ. He threw his white head back, closed his eyes, and started to tap his sore foot. The music soared, one moment laughing, the next crying. He told us he used to play the mouth organ when his brothers sent him out onto the prairie in Cardston to gather up the cows. I had seen the prairies when we went to conference at Grandmother's, and this music sounded just like the wind blowing up the coolies, tossing the sagebrush over the fences, whipping the grass into waves, and tickling the fields of shooting stars. Sometimes the songs sounded as if a lonely angel was trying to get someone to listen.

After Uncle Isaac put his mouth organ away, all of the kids sitting around begged him to recite "The Highwayman." He stood up with a flourish and ripped into the story with a fierceness that set my spine tingling until the last syllable.

"Back, he spurred like a madman, shrieking a curse to the sky,
With the white road smoking behind him, and his rapier brandished high!
Blood-red were his spurs in the golden noon; wine-red was his velvet coat,
When they shot him down on the highway, Down like a dog on the highway,
And he lay in his blood on the highway, with the bunch of lace at his throat."

Uncle Isaac's eyes flashed and his voice first rose with fury, then fell with tenderness. He was a lover and a villain and a posse of the army all in five minutes. It was better than *Rawhide*, better than anything. I was mesmerized.

We reluctantly went upstairs to bed. I was sleeping with Emilia, and she was reading her book. The upstairs rooms were all for kids now since Lydia and Naomi were both in their own homes. A bunch of boys slept in the big room that faced out to the white barn and the front of the house. Laman had painted one whole wall full of jungle animals. I saw the picture he copied out of a textbook, and his picture was better. Palm trees with monkeys swinging from them reached from floor to ceiling. Ferns and vines were interspersed with flowers and exotic parrots. In the very center was a huge orange and black tiger leaping right out at you with a ferocious snarl. I wanted to peek at this picture in the moonlight. I had forgotten my nightgown, so I was wearing my panties like Emilia. She was wearing her bra, too, since she was almost grown-up. I got out of bed and sneaked around the corner to the boys' room. Moonlight flooded in the window; the tiger snarled in the eerie dark shadows. The boys were whispering to each other, and one of them spotted me. "Come all the way in, we dare you! We double dare you! Are you scared?"

The chant was taken up by the other boys until I was caught up in the rhythm. "Dare" and "scared" were like red flags to me, so I ran light as a deer into the middle of the room. My lithe body flashed white in the moonlight. Hands reached out of the shadows and grabbed at my panties. Twisting and turning, I leapt and twirled into the corners, dancing back into the center. All on my toes I was a night-sprite or a fairy down by the pond at home. I spun faster and faster. My long thick dark hair pulled loose from the heavy braids on my head and cascaded around my body, mixing with the moonbeams, covering my little breasts. I stopped to catch my breath, reveling in the boys' hooting. I leapt across the hall and sprang back into Emilia's bed, covering my shaking body. I fell into an exhausted sleep, afraid to think about what I had just done, not wanting to decide if I had committed another sin. I didn't even remember my prayers.

The morning mountain air was shattered by Uncle Isaac's wild "Halloo!" to the world in general. The wake-up call echoed around the mountains, and when the last reverberation sounded, the boys' feet hit the floor. Emilia sprang out of bed, jumped into her jeans, and was gone before my eyes had scarcely opened. It was chore time and cows needed to be milked. When I poked my nose out, the air was so cold that I hurriedly pulled the covers over my head and went back to sleep. I awoke to the smell of hot pancakes and fried eggs. I dressed and went downstairs, where Aunt Bettilyn greeted me with a smile.

"If you'd put these plates around, it would help me out a lot." I did as I was asked with eager energy, and when Emilia came back from the barn I told her what was on my mind. "I'd like to go over the hill to Jeanie's house to see her later, if it's all right."

Emilia shook her head impatiently. "Naomi is fighting against Daddy, and we stay away. If the kids want to come over here, they do sometimes if we aren't working…but we don't go over there. Besides, you came here to stay, and if you don't like it here you can just go home." My cheeks turned red, and I hurriedly assured her I didn't really want to see Jean that bad.

I decided it was better at home where I didn't have to worry about all the trouble at the ranch. I was especially worried about Jeanie. I hoped her mother would try harder to obey the priesthood so she didn't go astray and have to be destroyed and burned in the stubble.

Chapter 10

I was trying hard not to complain, but my legs were hurting again, and my back, too. Some nights I couldn't sleep; sometimes my face got hot, and I would feel like throwing up. I tried to tell Daddy I was sick, but Jan and Elsa said I was nothing but a hypochondriac. I wasn't sure what that was, but it couldn't be anything very good because Jan got that hot look in her eyes and her lips curled and I felt like something filthy. When I went to the bathroom my private parts burned and hurt, and I wondered if it had anything to do with the stick from long ago, but I couldn't tell Daddy that. Every once in a while I started feeling all right again, but then it would get worse. Daddy suggested to the mothers that maybe I should go see the doctor.

Jan heaved a huge sigh and said in a sour voice, "I can just see it all now. We'll get that started and what will she do for attention next." Daddy didn't say anything more about it to her and told me to pray. He was sure I'd be fine, and I believed him. If I had the faith to be healed, I just knew I would be.

Daddy wanted all the rocks picked off the top field. The summer schedule started at five o'clock so we could do most of the work in the cool of the day. The sun had barely broken over the cedar trees on the big hill when Nettie, Brent, and I sleepwalked up the road. I loved the look of the field when it was clean and ready to plant, but my legs and hips hurt so badly when I bent over. The cut grass was wet and cold; Nettie's and my skirts were soon soaked through. I hated the way the ankle-length garments caught the grass and made it tear at our legs. It gave me a painful rash with thousands of little bloody spots. I asked Jan if we could just wear pants to work. She was furious. "Yes! I suppose *we* can do anything *we* want, if *we* want to question the priesthood. I know I'm not big enough to do it, but maybe you are!"

The next morning when she called me and I didn't get up right away, she came flying into my bedroom with a jar of cold water and threw it on me. She dragged me out of bed, hollering and pounding my body in the process. I listened really careful after that, no matter how tired I was. Mother had been so brave when she was in pain. I knew I could be, too.

Four books came for me in the mail from the library in Victoria, and I spent all Sunday afternoon and all the nights I couldn't sleep reading them. They were spellbinding. The last one was about unicorns that came out of the ocean every night and danced and played in the mists with magical boys and girls beside a magnificent castle. When I was pulling weeds or picking rocks, the unicorns were there to play with me—I was on their backs springing over the grass. The rocks were carrots and sugar to throw to them. The unicorns would toss their heads and dance toward me, and I would put my arms around their necks and away we would fly. I was light and free! I was beautiful and nothing hurt. I was going to go back into the ocean with the unicorns when it was daylight and stay there forever.

I heard Nettie's anxious, impatient voice through the mist. "Deb, Deb! You're dreaming again. You better hurry up or Mother will be pounding on you for not getting enough done. You love getting in trouble, don't you?"

The unicorns disappeared at the sound of her voice, and with a disgruntled sob, I came back to my wet skirt and aching shoulders.

Fighting between Jan and Elsa was getting worse every week, so Daddy decided to fix the bottom part of the house under the kitchen into an apartment for Elsa to live in. This was a great sorrow for him, because he was trying hard to get the mothers to live with broken hearts and contrite spirits and forgive each other seventy times seven. The ideal way to be sister wives was to share everything and live under the same roof, as Daddy was always saying in church. "Some women want to divide men up so one woman has his arms and another his head, and so on, until a man is all chopped to bits. Women will never experience the true beauty and joy of celestial marriage if they don't live together." But he finally realized Elsa just needed her own space.

He put boards and linoleum over the grease pit Uncle Michael had helped him make out of cement, and before you knew it there was a little kitchen, a bedroom, and a spot for Jarom and the new baby Elsa was going to have. Jan was mortally offended when Elsa took a sewing course and spent hours making a tiny sampler of fine stitching. She let everyone know it was a waste of time. She had problems with sharing the food, too. Sometimes Elsa cooked Daddy nicer meals than we had upstairs, and we could smell the fine food they were eating. She also baked cookies and squares. Jan kept telling us that Mother wouldn't want us to have such rich treats, but we sneaked away and knocked on Elsa's door to see if she happened to be feeling generous. She'd usually share a cookie with us, but she was careful—if we got caught with a treat, we'd be in trouble and so would she.

Elsa had a heck of a time keeping her house from getting messy, but that was the least of her worries. It didn't seem as if Heavenly Father wanted her to bring spirits into our Work. After Jarom was born, she lost two babies in a row. One was a little boy who was born too soon and only lived a few minutes, and the other was a little girl. We were praying with all our might for the baby she was expecting now to be born healthy. She had to rest in bed a lot, so maybe having her own little apartment was the best thing.

Uncle Isaac came to visit on a Sunday afternoon. He sat down at the kitchen table with Daddy. Leaning back on his chair after dinner, he hollered to Jan, "Bring me some of that good Alberta honey, Daughter! And a little of that peanut butter so I can lick it up."

Jan hurried over to him with both of the required treats, and he proceeded to dip a butter knife into the peanut butter and then into the honey. Licking off the knife, he repeated the procedure again and again. Nettie, Brent, and I sat on our bench and watched in amazement as his long, fascinating tongue repeatedly lashed out to wipe the blade clean. Several times his tongue reached clear to the tip of his nose.

Uncle Isaac looked real serious when he got down to the important business at hand. "Well, Adam, we always knew it wouldn't be easy, but Naomi is getting more rebellious by the day. Anyone who can't be worked with is no damned good to the priesthood. I fear that she'll leave someday and take the children with her. We have to get as many of them as possible away from her before she does. President Johnson tells me in these cases, you most often lose the girls...The boys always stay with the fathers. I'm taking Emilia and Ophelia down to Colorado City Academy to be with our people in the States this year, and I'll take Irene, too, but my feeling is she'll be too homesick. Naomi's threatening to put her in public school if she stays, and she'll be destroyed if that happens. Irene likes you a lot. If she comes back, I want you to befriend her...If you can get her to marry you, you can have her."

Daddy looked at Uncle Isaac for a long time, then told us impatiently to go play. Nettie and Brent ran outside, but I dallied. Daddy said to Uncle Isaac, "If there's anything at all I can do, you know I'll do it. It'll work real well for me to befriend her without getting Naomi suspicious since President Johnson has told us to live in Michael's old place this winter and hold school there, too. The icy road is too much for Jan, and since there's enough room, we might just as well live there if you'll give your stamp of approval for the move. You know I want only to be found in the line of my duty. We're so blessed that the priesthood has added the management of this property to your file leadership authority from God. Zion is truly growing. If it suits you, I'll proceed with the move. There's nothing too big to sacrifice for the Work. I'll be honored to take on the responsibility of saving Irene...I'm sure I can have great success working with her."

This revelation about Naomi was terrible news for me, and I spent the rest of the day worrying about Jeanie...I had to save her.

Naomi was scary, but I couldn't believe she was prepared to go to the devil and take her children with her. That night after I prayed to Heavenly Father, I spent a long time talking to Mother. I said if she could just talk to God about this, I bet He would make Naomi see that she needed to repent. I told Mother I didn't know what I'd do without Jeanie. Other than Daddy, she was the only real friend I had on this earth.

When all this trouble happened, my other pains hardly mattered, although I found something that seemed to help. When I went to bed and lay real still, my back didn't hurt. A long time ago I found out if I touched my tender private parts when my mind and heart were cold, I would warm up and I could sleep.

Uncle Michael's moving his family to Colorado City was good for everyone. We had room in his big house to have classrooms for all of our people and for two families to live at the same time. Erica and Lyle had moved over there earlier in the summer, and it was great to be back with them. I loved the white picket fences and the tires full of flowers that Aunt Loren and Aunt Pauline had planted.

Nettie and I started piano lessons with a lady who lived not far away from the ranch. She was a Gentile, but Daddy said it was all right to see Gentiles if you needed to learn something from them and didn't let worldly stuff rub off. I liked her house, and she had an amazing book about a type of dancing called ballet. I asked her if I could borrow it, then hid it with all my music books. In the morning before I played the piano, I practiced first position, second position, and pliés. I could turn my feet totally out like the pictures, and my arms looked really graceful in the mirror. There was a school for ballet in the book, but it was in a town called Paris, France, and I guessed that must be a gentile place, too, because of the weird clothes they wore. Daddy would never let me learn ballet if I had to take off my dress in front of a teacher to practice. I wished I could get over my worldly desires, but they just seemed to keep happening.

I was learning to play some nice songs, but practicing was a problem because I was so slow at my jobs at night. Jan said I must have a cookstove tied to each foot, and sometimes she tried to beat them off me. It was often very late before I got started on my homework, and then when I finally got to bed I had to read my library book so I could relax. Sometimes it was after midnight before my brain slowed down enough so I could sleep. Getting up to practice the piano at five was hard, but Daddy told me that Mother would be so proud of me.

When Uncle Freddie came to visit Erica, it made everyone edgy. He was such a serious man and talked and talked to Daddy about the secrets of our Work. He kept going on about how "natural man is an enemy to God!" He said that ordinary men didn't understand this because it was the meat of the gospel, and most people were only ready for milk. His huge Roman nose flared when he said this and Daddy instantly replied, "I see what you mean, Freddie...I see what you mean."

I asked Daddy what it meant, and he said he didn't really know, but he didn't see any sense in telling Uncle Freddie that.

Erica cried every single time he came to visit. I just didn't understand how he could make her so unhappy. Daddy said in church all the time that if a woman tried hard enough to do the will of a good priesthood man, she would be happy, and if you married who the Lord wanted you to marry, then you'd be married to a good man. I couldn't imagine what Erica's problem could possibly be since the Lord told the prophet she was supposed to marry Uncle Freddie. I decided she'd just have to get a better testimony.

Daddy was trying really hard to save Irene, and it seemed to be working. She didn't want to stay at Colorado City with our people there at all. She said she hated the Miller girls and that was where Emilia and Ophelia were staying. The Miller girls sang songs like famous people from Rodgers and Hammerstein or Walt Disney movies, and they all wore costumes as beautiful as any from the finished productions and danced in beautiful lines. Daddy said it wasn't worldly if the workmanship was of your own hands and you could teach yourselves the dances without being puffed up in vanity. Uncle Stanley Miller knew how to live plural marriage the very best. All of his wives had girls the same age who did everything together and wore the same kinds of dresses made out of the same colors of cloth. I hadn't seen them yet, but Irene said we wouldn't like them. She said no one should be that fancy.

Daddy kept picking Irene up on the road and driving her to school in town. Uncle Isaac and Lem sometimes passed her by. One day when it was raining, they drove so fast she got splashed with the muddy water. Irene didn't know this was all part of the plan—that her dad and brother left her so when Daddy picked her up, she was even more grateful.

Sometimes Daddy arranged to meet Irene at our school, and Aline walked her down the long road from Naomi's place. Then Daddy and Irene would sit in the dark classrooms, and he would tell her how everything was going to be really fine. He hugged her a lot.

It really upset everybody that Irene was going to public school. Jan sat at the front of our class one day and said, "I have been set apart to work in this school and teach you kids the truth. I want you to know that the wages of sin are death! Anyone who deliberately turns away from the chance the priesthood offers them to go to this private school will suffer the *fate*. When we study the Truth books, we learn that Brigham Young said any woman who fights the principle of plural marriage and rejects the counsels of the Lord's anointed will walk the streets as a common harlot. It is my responsibility to make sure you kids are taught, and I intend to do it. You will not be able to get up at the judgment bar and say you didn't know, because I am teaching you."

She looked directly at Jean and Aline and continued with renewed fervor, "We all know that women who think they have a right to fight the priesthood and don't teach their daughters the right way will be eternally sorry!"

Aline had grown a lot lately; she was almost thirteen with waist-long thick black curly hair and green eyes. Before Jan was finished talking, Aline's eyes were flashing fire and she exploded, "I'm sick of you preaching about my mother! I know you're talking about her, and so does everyone else. If you'd been decent to Irene, she wouldn't have wanted to go to public school, and I'm glad she did. My mother can work harder and is a better person than any other woman in this entire group. You'll never hold a candle to her!" Her voice was trembling as she glared at Jan. The glowering match continued for several long moments, and the classroom was in total silence. Finally Aline burst into tears and ran from the room.

Jean and I consoled each other about our confusion. I knew Daddy was right about the gospel, and I told Jeanie she could love her mother but it would be better to be dead than to question the Work and the priesthood school. Jean nodded solemnly, a worried frown on her face.

I was praying nightly that Daddy would be able to save Irene. I thought it would be great if she was one of our mothers, and then Daddy would be able to help Aline be happier, too, and see that her mother was just being rebellious and ruining all the good work of the prophet.

One morning the stove in the house part of the school got stoked too high, and the shavings around the chimney caught fire. Erica leapt onto the ladder and climbed into the smoke-filled attic. She started kicking shavings around and hollering for water. All of us kids ran for the pond with buckets and were back so fast it was a miracle. We had the fire out in a hurry, then all we had to do was mop up. Someone had called Daddy, and he made the fifteen-minute trip from town in no time. We were all shaking and grateful for each other for the rest of the day.

With Emilia and Ophelia gone to Colorado City for school, I was almost the oldest girl at church except for Irene and Aline and some of Uncle Kelvin's kids. Some of his kids went to town school, so Uncle Isaac told everyone again that they better get more concerned about their salvation, because anyone who knew what was good for them would never live in town. Uncle Kelvin's second wife, Celia, lived in an old building by our school with twelve kids. Everyone said she had to be greatly admired for standing out against a weak husband. Daddy said she would definitely get her reward. I really hoped she would, because she didn't have any running water all last winter because her pipes froze, and there wasn't a bathroom anywhere close to their house. Toward the end of the winter, she was huge with child. I couldn't see how she made it up the steep icy hill from the creek with the water for her wash.

They didn't have a lot of food to eat, either, and even though Jan said it was because "some women" wasted more than they ever ate, I still felt bad when we had lots of cream and baked potatoes and corn from our garden. I didn't think Uncle Kelvin liked Celia living in Lister very much, because he hardly ever came out to see her.

Uncle Isaac started teaching our Sunday school class. He told exciting stories about growing up on the prairie in Alberta and taught parables like Jesus did, only his parables were about horses and sagebrush. He told us how he and his brothers rounded up runaway cattle, and how his horse bolted and tore through some brambles and thorn bushes. He said it was just like the gospel, where temptations and trials came along and tried to scrub you off the back of the truth. He said the Lord's true way would never be easy, so we had to prepare for the trials and tribulations, and never waiver.

Uncle Isaac told us he had to make sure he was teaching us the most important principles of the gospel, since it was his responsibility as file leader. He had us memorize all of the early history of our church. He said we didn't need to worry about any of the history after 1890, since that was when the LDS church joined hands with the devil. He gave us tests on the lessons and handed out peanuts if we passed with good marks.

The memorizing all started with Joseph Smith's story, and although I knew the story already, I hadn't memorized it like Uncle Isaac wanted. When I was done, I knew it real well and could stand up and spout, "I was born in the year of our Lord one thousand eight hundred and five, on the twenty-third day of December in the town of Sharon, Windsor County, State of Vermont. My father, Joseph Smith Senior, left the state of Vermont..." On it went until verse five, where all the worldly churches were saying "Lo" here and "Lo" there, and the Lord told Joseph Smith that all the churches had strayed away from the true spirit of his gospel, and that He was displeased with them all.

Joseph Smith was only fourteen when he went into a sacred grove to pray. God appeared to him with Jesus Christ. The devil tried to kill Joseph Smith, but the Lord saved him and told him that he had a special mission. The Lord gave him some golden plates and a Urim and Thummim* to translate them. When Joseph was all done it was called The Book of Mormon and is the only true history of the early American Indians and how Jesus Christ came to America after he was crucified and resurrected on the third day. Uncle Isaac told us to go home and read it, and he would have a prize for the first one finished. I was the third one finished. He told us to pray about what we read, and Heavenly Father would tell us if it was true or not.

I went down to the river and knelt in the leaves and moss close to the base of a giant cottonwood tree and prayed and prayed. The next time I read the Book, I knew it was true. Whenever I started praying and thinking about Uncle Isaac's exciting voice and the way he looked at me with his cobalt blue eyes, I knew I was real special—so special I could be a queen in Israel, a goddess of the eternal worlds. I knew everything he said was true, and I would remember his teaching for eternity.

The LDS church was officially organized in 1830. That was when they started to send missionaries around the world to tell everyone about The Book of Mormon and Joseph Smith's being a latter-day prophet. Only a few good men had a true understanding of the things the Lord wanted them to do, and the Lord told Joseph Smith to organize a camp to train men to do his work. They called it Zion's camp and God promised Joseph Smith if he could get the men to be faithful, then He would redeem Zion.

Uncle Isaac said there were only about ten men in the whole Mormon Church who would be obedient enough. He said that was when the Lord first put the church under condemnation. Uncle Isaac got real wild when he started telling us about the weak-minded, lily-livered men who would not sacrifice their all for the Lord's true Work. He told us we were the generation that would get to walk to Jackson County, Missouri, to build the New Jerusalem

---

*Urim and Thummim, two stones fastened to a breastplate with bows of silver metal, were considered to be seer stones given to Joseph Smith by God to translate the golden plates. According to Mormon teachings, the golden plates contained a history of the Native American people and their origins. In the story, Christ came to North America after the crucifixion to visit these people.

for the Christ to bring in the millennium. Uncle Isaac said we would get to rule the world then. He got real mad when he talked about the Church of Latter-day Saints being the whore of all the earth because she sold her birthright for popularity and a mess of pottage. That's why we were so special, because we would be more obedient than Zion's camp, and we would fight the world and give up everything—even suffer like the Savior suffered.

Uncle Isaac told us how some of the leaders of the LDS church were so worried about the riches of the world that they made Wilford Woodruff sign the manifesto that destroyed the principle of plural marriage. That was when he lost the keys to be a prophet and the leaders of our Work took over. John Woolley was the first prophet of our group, and then Lorin C. Woolley, J. Leslie Broadbent, John Y. Barlow, Joseph Musser, Charles Zitting, and LeRoy Johnson.

We memorized all this in church and in school, too. Jan pledged she was going to teach us why we were different or die trying. That's how important it was, she said. She told us all the time that except for a few of God's chosen people in the States and Mexico, we were the only ones who got to know the correct line of authority from God. I could say this line of authority in my sleep, and I always got good grades in our tests. Jan told us we were the blessed of all young people—that we would never have to worry about worldly things like if we were marrying the right people or not, because God would tell the prophet who we were promised to in the pre-existence, and we wouldn't have to make any mistakes by courting. If we could be faithful in all these things, then our calling and election would be made sure. In fact, just by entering into the principle of plural marriage under the direction of our prophet, we were guaranteed the highest exaltation in the highest degree of the celestial kingdom.

Jan passed us each some pamphlets that Uncle Guy Musser had printed up. "The Lord has seen fit for us to have these wonderful copies of the 1886 revelation. I want all of you people to read through these and memorize the actual revelation. I will read through the minutes of the eight-hour meeting, and you will have a clearer picture of the importance of this whole thing. Open up the first page and listen carefully. 'My son, John, inasmuch as you have asked me regarding the new and everlasting covenant of marriage, I say unto you, it shall never be taken away or given to another people, and I will fight your battles.' " Jan's voice rose fervently. "Lorin C. Woolley wrote this account in 1929, and it has been preserved and handed down for us from that generation to this. John Taylor died swearing to never give in to the law and the demands of the weak and greedy money-hungry men of the world.

"John Taylor's words were very plain when he said, 'Sign that document, never! I would suffer my right hand to be severed from my body first. Sanction it…never. I would suffer my tongue to be torn from my mouth before I would sanction it!'

"This account is more important for your life and salvation than the study of any other history or worldly information," said Jan. "The signing of the manifesto in 1890 was part of a conspiracy by the church to become popular with the wicked world, and the power of God left the church and went to John Woolley and down the line to Uncle LeRoy Johnson, who is the prophet of our time. We are truly blessed." She closed the pamphlet with reverence.

Jan always ended our regular classes with: "The gospel is so simple and pure; it's usually too uncomplicated for the gentile world. We must prepare to welcome the lost tribes of Israel back from the North Country and set an example before the world. We must also remember that we should never cast the pearls of the gospel before the swine of this earth or they will destroy us."

I was very proud to hear Jan talk about the lost tribes of Israel coming back from the North Country, because Patriarch Arlo Whitmer had given Grandmother and Daddy blessings, telling them they would live to help feed the ten tribes when Christ sent for them to help usher in the millennium. Not too many people had a promise from God as important as keeping enough food and supplies on hand to feed the lost tribes of Israel. Grandmother even checked with our prophet to make sure her calling was true, and she was told Arlo Whitmer was a good man with the true priesthood so she better be prepared to fulfill this prophecy.

School days with Jan were often very long, but it was sure wonderful that Heavenly Father had given us this private priesthood school so we could learn about the Work away from the Gentiles. Daddy said we could never learn about the secrets of the kingdom in public schools. We would never even get to say the Lord's Prayer, and all kinds of wicked people taught school in the world so we were doubly blessed here to have only the finest.

We were settling into a daily routine living at the school. It was great having Erica around—she was always telling us fun stories or playing dress-up, and she had a way of making all of us kids feel safe and good. Once she recovered from her hard delivery, she was right back to her energetic self. She amazed me. She was the first person to offer help to anyone in need no matter who they were, and the only person I knew who was friends with just about all the grown-ups in the group at the same time, including Lydia and Bettilyn. It was absolute magic the way she managed to keep from getting in the middle of some horrible fight. Naomi even liked her, so I thought it would be great if she stayed with our family forever—especially since Uncle Freddie didn't seem to want her at all. Erica never talked much about Uncle Freddie, but nothing got her more upset than to find out he was keeping secrets from her. She was furious when she heard he had bought a nice little farm in the center of Lister without telling her about it.

Sometimes on Saturday or Sunday afternoons she'd take us for a walk up the hill where Gentiles from the Creston Valley dumped their garbage over a bank. It wasn't an organized dump; I didn't know there was such a thing until the regional district decided to put one right in the gravel pit we loved to play in. Going to the dump was just about as exciting as gift day, because you could never tell what good stuff the Gentiles would throw away. Erica always made the best finds—sometimes she picked out shoes, sweaters, and other clothes, but one time she found a toaster and a strong solid toilet seat. One afternoon after a snow, when I was picking through garbage bags, I tipped one over to see a big old-fashioned book. It had lovely verses with hand-painted pictures of babies on each page. The pages were so soft to the touch that they were more like cloth—the only thing wrong was the book had no cover on one side.

Most times we would all rummage around until everyone had found some sort of treasure, then we would trek happily home. We were lucky we didn't really *need* to dig in the dump—we had food and plenty of homemade clothes. I was sad when Lucia told me a secret. She said sometimes her brothers had to go to the dump to find clothes *and* food. If Uncle Kelvin didn't bring them food for a while, her mother was humiliated and too proud to tell anyone when they were really hungry. Naomi took her bags of potatoes when she thought things were tough, and we took her milk most of the time, but when we moved back to Canyon in the summers, Celia often found herself in dire straits. Where she lived, there wasn't even a good place to grow a garden. After a while they got a cow, but finding food for her was tricky, too.

With so many new kids in our classes, Aunt Bettilyn was looking after the younger grades. She was good at teaching the proper handwriting techniques she learned when she was young. As the winter wore on, it was getting harder for her to teach every day. She was pregnant with her thirteenth child and due to deliver in February. Her youngest son, Joseph, was only four and too young to bring to school. Even though Naomi didn't have much to do with us now, she'd help if she was needed. Since she had Rhoda to look after, she said she'd watch Joseph at the same time so Bettilyn would be able to teach.

The only thing a bit nerve-wracking about Bettilyn being at the school all the time was Lydia. She lived so close by that if something went wrong, or someone was mean to her or one of her kids, she'd charge into the classrooms and give whoever she was mad at a fierce talking to. Of course, the person she was mad at the most was Bettilyn. Then, all us kids would go around feeling sorry for Bettilyn and wishing "some women" could just get rid of their evil spirits and repent. I knew I'd never cause such terrible grief and embarrassment to my sister wives or my husband.

One afternoon there was just half an hour left in the school day when two trucks came roaring around the corner and skidded to a stop. People ran in hollering that the big ranch house was on fire. The two little kids had gotten away from Naomi and started the fire while she was cutting wood to stoke the furnace in her house. The older kids jumped into the trucks, which then roared back to the ranch house. Naomi got the kids out safely, and Erica managed to smash a window on the far side of the building. She threw out clothes and everything else she could find. Before she would quit, people on the outside had to threaten to drag her out.

When I finally saw the charred mess, I was most upset about the huge jungle mural on the wall upstairs. I kept thinking it was a shame they couldn't just move what was left of it somewhere safe. Bettilyn was devastated by the loss of the house. She had great plans for the new baby and had just recently fixed the room above the cooler with the most lovely carpet, bed, and fine bathroom for the prophet and his apostles to stay in on their visits to Canada. She had also just purchased beautiful new curtains for the whole main floor of the house. Now she had nothing—she even needed clothes for the new baby. All the people in our group helped out, but most surprising was all the clothing and household things that came from the Gentiles who knew Uncle Isaac and his big family.

Erica decided that Freddie's farmhouse couldn't sit empty while there was a family in such need, so she called him and told him of the disaster. He made a deal with Uncle Isaac for the use of the house. Even though the family moved in, Uncle Isaac didn't like living in someone else's place, and he hurriedly organized his outbuildings and the cabin so he could move his family back to the ranch. He and Bettilyn took over the cabin and the boys jammed into the bunkhouse. After lots of figuring, he decided to turn the turkey shed into a home. No matter what he did to try to make it nice, though, nothing could ever be as good as the ranch house had been. The turkey shed was much too small for everyone who needed to live there, so he built another bunkhouse on top of the new building where he'd put the bulk tank for the dairy.

When Bettilyn's baby Nora was born, everyone said how sad it was she wouldn't get to grow up in the house that the rest of the kids had enjoyed.

Chapter 11

Having school classes inside the same huge house we lived in was hard because long after the other kids went home, teachers were still working in the classrooms. After my chores were done, I would take my books from room to room, looking for a quiet place to do my homework. One night I came across Jan and Bettilyn crying in each other's arms. Jan was moaning that history was about to repeat itself, that Elsa was a big enough trial without sending her another, especially one of Naomi's daughters who could be as hard to get along with as Naomi. She told her mother if it weren't for Erica helping her out, she could never carry the terrible burden of God's school.

Bettilyn tried to comfort Jan, saying at least she had Daddy to support her, and he seemed to have a way with troublesome people. As I passed out of earshot, Jan was berating herself for her lack of faith and the sin of ingratitude. "I'm only a weak shadow of the example I must be to keep a sister from going to Satan in a public school."

A couple of weeks later, Daddy went to conference in Colorado City with Uncle Isaac, Uncle Kelvin, and some of the big kids—Irene was one of them. When they came back, Daddy walked in the door with our presents and Irene on his arm and announced we had a new mother for our house. Irene's face was red. I felt sorry for her, because she wasn't sure where to put her hands or where to sit or even where to look. She awkwardly moved from one foot to the other, and then asked Daddy if she could go see her mom now.

Daddy looked worried. "Well, dear, I guess we could if you really want to. I suppose Naomi will have to know sooner or later. She'll be as ornery as an old ma bear in early spring, since we've sort of sprung this on her."

Irene stood in silence and in a few minutes they left. When they came back, she ran straight to the room Jan and Erica had fixed for her and shut the door. I hovered outside for a few minutes, then knocked. Her voice trembled when she told me to come in. I walked partway into the room and stood with my hands behind my back. "I'm glad you're married to Daddy now. I think we'll have a good time. Please don't cry so hard." I walked closer and held my hands out to her. She seemed so small and helpless in her pain.

Irene wouldn't look up and just sobbed harder. "How could you know anything? You're only ten years old and I'm sixteen. My mom just told me I can never go crying back to her if things don't work out here, since I got married behind her back. She said I made my bed now, and I have to lie in it...I don't understand anything!"

Daddy was determined to get the worldly stuff out of Irene's mind. He had her throw away her jeans and got Jan to make her some proper dresses. He had her stop going to the public school and come back to our sacred private school. He insisted she get rid of her record player and her collection of Elvis Presley records. Irene would let go of all the other worldly things but got down on her knees and begged Daddy to let her keep her records. He finally relented and told her if it was so important to her, she could keep them for a while longer.

It was good to see that Uncle Isaac's plan to save Irene from her rebellious mother had worked, and all the good group stuff was happening for her. It was a huge relief for Jeanie, and I was happy we didn't have to worry about the wicked worldly influences Irene had been soaking up in public school—maybe the rest of her sisters would be safe now.

There was still one serious problem: Irene hated the priesthood school with a passion. When Jan spoke in assembly on the evils of Elvis Presley and modern music, we all knew Irene was the subject of her lecture, and we tried to look anywhere but to her corner of the room. Her desk became the personal hell where she hunched, biting her nails and crying as Jan ranted. Sewing period was even worse. Naomi wasn't big on womanly things, and Irene hadn't learned how to sew. She had a hard time putting in zippers or making a flat feld seam that was good enough to suit Jan. After she started picking on Irene, she showed no sign of letting up.

One afternoon she said, "You people need to realize that when a girl gets married, she should try to know some of the skills she'll need to be a blessing to her husband and his family. Some girls when they're married have to be spoon-fed and coddled until they're no earthly good to their families...That just leaves the poor man with another baby to take care of." Irene's face burned red as she fought back tears of shame. All the rest of us struggled to keep from looking at her. You just didn't look at a person in trouble, whether it was a friend, a sister wife, or a mother—especially right when it was happening. And nobody better catch you trying to make them feel better.

Sewing class later in the day was torture for all of us. Irene and Jan sent barbed retorts back and forth to each other until finally Irene jumped from her desk and ran downstairs to her room. To complete her rebellious day, she went to milk the cow and wore a pair of jeans she had hidden in the bottom of her drawer. When Daddy caught her with them on, out in the cow pasture, he turned her over his knee and spanked her.

I watched him give her a bunch of whacks, then he hugged her, wiped her tears, and told her, "You know I only chastise you because I love you. You need to make sure you're always found in the line of your wifely duties. If you're going to be a queen in heaven someday, you must act like it now." He held her at arm's length and looked into her tear-stained face. "You know, my Deb and Nettie are watching your example."

Irene apologized over and over, and each time she said she was sorry, she told him she loved him. All the pain and humiliation of the last week of school spilled out of her. She stormed, "I hate Jan.

I hate that she embarrasses me and never says a kind word to me in front of anyone. I wish I never had to see her and her smug, self-righteous ways again!" She sobbed, "I love you so much, Adam. I'm sorry, but I don't think it's fair at all...and I hate it when Elsa comes over on the weekends. Her and Erica are such good pals, and Jan does what she does, and I don't have anyone."

With that final explosion of anguish, Irene was spent. Throwing herself on Daddy's shoulder, she wept. Daddy said patiently, "I know you can do better than this, Irene. I know you can forgive and forget. Remember, you're supposed to forgive seventy times seven. Your hate hurts only you. I work with Jan and Elsa all the time, and they know they can improve, too, but you have to know you need to be good to them because they are part of me...You can do it for me...Please, Irene?" Irene melted and promised to try just a little bit harder.

January came around again and I was eleven. Watching the struggles that Daddy had with his wives, I was certain I knew the things I would never do when I got to be part of the kingdom of my husband. I even wrote lists titled Things I Will Never Do When I Become a Sister Wife. Irène was still struggling with Jan, and Daddy was helping her make some New Year's resolutions about both Jan and Elsa. Irene took in everything Daddy had to say and then spoke in a sweet voice to everyone for the rest of the day. In the evening she went into her room and listened to Elvis crooning "Are You Lonesome Tonight" and Dottie West singing about people with aching hearts.

Jan flew off the handle the moment she heard the first notes. "How can a full-grown woman possibly listen to such whining drivel? The Mormon Tabernacle Choir record with its uplifting hymns, or just about anything else, would be better than that. It's little wonder some people have such a hard time getting the spirit of the celestial law of placement marriage with their minds in such mire!"

"Now, Mother," Daddy said, "just give it a little time, and she'll come around."

I tried to talk Irene into giving up the music, but the more I heard it, the more I was getting to like it, too. The music got inside me; I could capture the twang, and it was fun to sing.

After two weeks of being perfectly sweet as she'd promised Daddy, Irene snapped. It happened on a Sunday—the very worst day to go back on a promise. The day hadn't started well. Daddy mentioned to Irene over breakfast that he was going to visit Elsa in Canyon and spend the rest of the day with her. Irene didn't like it one bit. As if that wasn't bad enough, Jan caught me humming and doing the twist with a soapy plate while I was washing breakfast dishes. My stupid daydreaming set off another horrible argument where Jan issued ultimatums and Daddy argued with Irene and told her he was going to have to get tough with her and make her get rid of her records and destroy the devil's influence.

Irene turned on Jan in a way that shocked everyone. "If I get rid of my records, are you going to make your precious brother get rid of all his music? I guess Monopoly and all your books are all *righteous*. You make me sick! You think Deb and Nettie won't hear any music from the radio? You guys are all hypocrites!"

Daddy stepped back with a look of shock I had never seen before, his shoulders slumped, and he went upstairs to the big room, which had been prepared for church. With tears streaming down her face, Irene locked herself in her room and refused to go to the services. She played her records softly all morning until Daddy went in to see her on his round of goodbye kisses before he went to be with Elsa. He didn't even try to talk her into forgiving seventy times seven and being a better person with a broken heart and a contrite spirit. I was worried about Daddy and Irene both now; they weren't acting like themselves at all. A short while later she came out, put on her coat, and headed outside. Her cheeks were flushed and she had a frantic look in her eyes. Nettie, Brent, and I trailed along behind as she left the school grounds and headed straight for the half-frozen pond. I screamed her name until my lungs hurt in the cold wind. She wouldn't answer. I felt as helpless and afraid as when Mother died.

Right in the middle of a mountain-splitting scream, Irene stopped and turned on me. "Shut up, Deb, you're always trying to fix everything, but you're always in trouble yourself. You can't talk me out of this…so don't try!" With tears in her eyes she told us she was going to jump into the pond and drown herself. We begged her not to but didn't know what we could do to stop her. There was no way of contacting Daddy at our other house.

We followed Irene across the dam to where the diving board stood ten feet above the ice-cold water. Laughing giddily, she clambered up the ladder and walked to the end of the board. She said that her watchword as she jumped would be, "Be kind to Jan and Elsa!" We were supposed to tell the world that those were her dying words. We were all crying by then, and Nettie and I were both screaming at her to come down. She bounced crazily on the end of the diving board with her long skirt and layers of petticoats flapping in the winter wind. She stopped for a few minutes and stood in complete silence. Just when I thought she had come to her senses, she jumped hard twice and sprang from the end of the board. Her wild words were carried away by the wind. With a sickening splash, Irene disappeared beneath the thin ice on the pond. I held my breath for an eternity until her head finally popped to the surface. She slipped back beneath the water, and when she came up again we all yelled at her to swim.

In slow motion, she paddled her way to the jagged, ice-covered edge. We scrambled to grab what we could—a sleeve, an icy hand, a long black braid—anything to pull her to safety. She lay exhausted on the edge of the pond for what seemed like forever. Nettie and I were weeping hopelessly, thinking she was going to die. When we heard her sobs, we realized she would live, for now. We helped her up and supported her all the way back to the house. When we got her to her room, she curled into a dripping wet ball on her bed and refused to move. I piled a mountain of blankets on her, but she told me to go away and kept pulling them off.

I watched from the upstairs window for Daddy, and the moment I saw his truck, I raced to tell him what had happened. I was terrified that the cold clothes would still make Irene die. I begged him to please make her change and please stop telling her she had to be good to Jan and Elsa. Daddy looked grim and told me people just had to learn to sacrifice their feelings. He strode into Irene's room and stayed there for a long time. When they came out, Irene's face was still white, but she was smiling and talking sweetly again.

For the next few days, our home and school dripped with sticky loving phrases and apologies. It was as if Irene and Jan were locked in a desperate battle for the title of sweetest Nilsson wife. Jan made Irene pretty maternity outfits to celebrate another plural celestial child—one smock with little blue and pink kittens on it, others more ordinary, and a fine blue one for church. When Irene was modeling them for us, she told us she was going to have Daddy's baby, and that she was happier than she'd ever been before. She constantly called Daddy "darling" and "sweetheart." Jan winced every time Irene said the words—maybe that was because Jan was going to have another of Daddy's babies, too.

In the spring Daddy took Irene to Canyon to live by herself in the top of the house. Once when he took me down to stay with her for a weekend, she told me of a wicked secret dream she'd had in which she was Daddy's only wife. Living there was the closest thing she had to her dream, because before her baby was born the whole family moved back home for the summer, and Irene had to work hard on being sweet again. I constantly wondered what Mother would have done if she were still there. I was sure she would have kept Irene happier and more able to see the great calling of the Work.

I loved to read and lose myself in an imaginary world. I read dictionaries and encyclopedias; I read all the old *National Geographic* magazines that were stacked on the bookshelves in our classroom. When the rest of the kids were out playing Red Rover on the dandelion-covered lawn, I took my book to a quiet corner and roamed the world.

One day over the lunch break, I was swimming in the warm tropical sea among coral reefs with a little black native boy. Wearing only a sheath for a knife, he was diving deep into the Indian Ocean and bringing up clams with pearls in them. He had the knife to protect himself from the hammerhead sharks living in the cove. The sand was white and sparkling with fool's gold in the tropical sun. My white silk petticoat ruffled against my body in the hot wind until I galloped across the sand and hurled myself into the sea. I was free and weightless; the water caressed me like Mother's arms. But the clanging of the cowbell shattered my vision and brought me solidly back to the heat of the large schoolroom. The pain from the knuckles descending on my head while I was trying to get my books ready was insignificant to the flaming shame I would have felt had someone seen my wicked adventure. I don't know what Daddy would have done had he known I wasn't wearing my dress to swim, and that my body looked naked as my wet petticoat clung to me.

I wondered absently as Jan started the afternoon lecture if God loved the little native children. I guessed maybe not, since they didn't know the leader of our Work, and they never wore clothes. Worse even than that, they had black skin like all the cursed infidels in the Bible and the Book of Mormon.

As Jan lectured about working hard to become a king or queen in heaven, I realized I wouldn't have time to worry about places of worldly beauty. Daddy was probably right when he said that heaven was so much more beautiful than the most fantastic places on earth, and I didn't need to worry about anything but being good and doing what the prophet said here, so I'd be sure to get there.

At the spring conference, Apostle Uncle Marion Hammond had a special message for all young women. "You girls need to get down on your knees and give thanks daily when you are married to older men—especially when you're given men who have the stamp of approval by the prophet. These older men can take you by the hand and teach you the principle of the plurality of wives and take you to the highest degree of the celestial kingdom where you will be queens and priestesses. You will not have to endure a young man who hasn't made his way over fool's hill yet. You mothers, teach your daughters to be grateful for that call, so when the priesthood places them, they'll be prepared." He was truly magnificent up at the pulpit, and his flashing blue eyes pierced my very soul. There was no question in my mind that he was speaking the truth.

After Uncle Marion finished speaking, Uncle Guy Musser got up and gave us the history of our group again with a list of all the true prophets after the LDS church signed the covenant with death, hell, and the grave. He stopped for an ominous moment, and then his whole body shook as if he were coming out of a trance after talking with heavenly beings. The top of his bald head glistened with sweat; heavy blue veins bulged on his flushed forehead. He glared around the room, stabbing each one of us with his eyes.

When he spoke again, his voice was heavy, suffocating. "We, as a priesthood people, are losing the battle to put away the gentile habits and traditions. We are not training our daughters the proper way to cleave unto their husbands when they are married. How can a man have oneness in his kingdom if his wives each cling to the worldly traditions of their fathers?" His voice was shaking now, and his hands trembled as he pulled out a snow-white handkerchief and attempted to wipe away the perspiration on his brow. "When the Lord has assigned young wives to me, I take them into my bedroom, remove their clothing, fold it piece by piece on top of their hope chests, and pull the pins from their hair. Within the hour they are dressed in clothes I had prepared for them, and I send everything back along with the trunks and hope chests their mother and father presumed to send with them. These young wives know without a shadow of a doubt that they belong to me for all the eternities and no longer have any connection with their fathers and mothers." He had curled his fist and was hammering the pulpit; spittle was spraying like venom from his mouth with every word. Tears streamed down his face. "It takes *major surgery* to get rid of the traditions of our evil gentile fathers. We must be as new clay in the hands of the Potter! Will we...will *you* subject *your* will to it?"

For the first time, I was truly afraid of one of our apostles. I wouldn't want to ever be in a room alone with this man and have him touch my body, my hair, or my precious hope-chest things. For a moment I feared I would vomit right there in the middle of the sacred meeting. I forced the bile down in my throat and held the edges of my seat with all my strength to keep from crying. Panic was rising in my body, and I didn't know why. I wished Mother were here—she would help me make some sense of it.

I forced myself to listen again. He was still shaking, and one of the other apostles from the States ran forward with a handkerchief and blotted his forehead as if he were an honored surgeon. "*Only* those who will bend to the teachings of the prophet, LeRoy Sunderland Johnson, will make the cut in that last day. Out of the heart's core of the heart's core will the people be chosen, and the sifting process has already begun. You fathers and mothers must teach your daughters and sons that *they do not belong to you!* The only right a father has from the second his daughter is born is to teach her that she belongs only to the prophet and the man the prophet will give her to. Write this in your little books. Write this on your brains and teach your daughters...they must be willing to enter into the kingdom of their husband the same way they entered this earth from the Lord—naked! I say this in the name of the Father, and of his Son Jesus Christ, and the Holy Ghost."

Uncle Guy was swaying at the pulpit. Just when I thought he was going to fall backwards and smack his head on the heavy oak arm of the velvet moose chair, he caught himself and said, "The Lord has just instructed me to deliver the hosanna shout." He steadied himself, reached both arms into the air at the square, and yelled, "*Hosanna! Hosanna! Hosanna to the highest! In the name of God the Father, his Son Jesus Christ, the Holy Ghost, Father Abraham, Isaac, and Jacob, and all the sons of the priesthood and the prophets from the earliest time till now. Amen! Amen and amen!*"

He was shaking so hard two apostles leapt to their feet and helped him back to his chair. I was filled with revulsion for this man, and the image of him stripping young girls and depriving them of all their worldly things just wouldn't go away. Would they never get to see any of their brothers and sisters again? Would their mothers and fathers have to forget them? I thought the Doctrine and Covenants said Jesus Christ came to bring families together forever in one long chain. If Christ meant for the gospel to seal families together forever, then how could what Uncle Guy just said make sense? I shivered—I'd have to figure it out later.

After Uncle Guy's speech, Grandpa got up and gave his humble talk. Earlier, before the conference services began, he'd been married to Uncle Frederick's nineteen-year-old daughter, Noreen, by the prophet and Uncle Guy. Grandpa was red in the face when he stood in front of everyone and told us how humble he was to have been found worthy to be called to live the new and everlasting covenant of marriage. He thanked the prophet for his insight in selecting his new wife and Uncle Frederick for raising such a fine daughter. After thanking Grandmother for supporting him in living the law of Sarah and telling everyone how grateful he was to have a special woman like her by his side all these years, he sat down.

When the service was over and everyone was crowding around Grandpa, Daddy slapped him on the back and joked, "So they roped you in, eh, old timer? Baptism by fire is what it's called…no turning back now."

Grandmother said it was an answer to her prayers to be able to perform the law of Sarah, and everyone congratulated her that she finally had a sister wife. I'd only seen Noreen from a distance before, and I wanted to let her know I felt Mother would have been happy for her—happy that she was my other grandmother and Mother's other mother, even though she would have been a lot younger than Mother. When I asked Daddy about it, he said age was irrelevant to Heavenly Father because one of his days was a thousand of ours. It just wasn't important if a husband was forty years older than a wife—or even older.

I was still upset from Uncle Guy's talk so I got my food and sat alone in my favorite corner behind an overstuffed armchair. Uncle Kelvin came along with his plate and sat in the chair in front of me, and Uncle Freddie took the chair next to him.

They kept their voices low, as if they didn't want anyone else to hear their conversation. "You know, Freddie, I was sure Noreen was meant to be my wife when we discussed the problem with the prophet last year. How could this have happened? I knew Isaiah back in Rosemary when we all lived there. He's stayed out there all this time and refused to break his family ties—and he gets Noreen? You know I would have treasured her beyond description, Freddie. This is hard for me to take without questioning somebody about it…I hope my son never finds out why he was sent to the States. He tells his mother he's very unhappy on the Work missions—he's thinking about running away."

Uncle Frederick answered Uncle Kelvin in a stern voice, as if he were talking to a little boy or one of his wives or something. "You know, Kelvin, I thought you were being stricter with that girl of mine when I let her stay with your daughter. I needed her to have a friend in the Work here since she was finishing her high school in Cardston with all the gentile temptations. Here we found out you were allowing Grady to spend time alone with her. If that boy doesn't get some gumption and learn to be obedient, he'll be done for...He certainly doesn't have much of a testimony, and I couldn't have that for my daughter, anyway." He snorted in the back of his throat, and I jumped. His voice was rising in his criticism of Uncle Kelvin's lax care of Noreen. "Grady definitely needed to be sent down where their missionary president could work all the immoral ideas out of his silly head. I thought the brethren were going to give Noreen to you, too, but you won't catch me questioning the prophet. If I was, don't you think I'd have more to say about the trials they put on me with that big daughter of Michael's? You've got to know how hard Erica is to deal with!"

Uncle Kelvin shifted in the chair. When he spoke it was with a heavy sigh. "Well, I guess I know better what you mean when you say Peck's bad boy.* That must be what I am, since I haven't been added upon and blessed with any more wives since I got Enid and Celia twelve years ago. With Isaac and Adam's interference, my attempts to school and train them the way I need them to be fails all the time. But we better talk about this later somewhere else—we're being watched. If that boy gets the idea we're having a problem, he'll cause no end of trouble!"

Frederick replied, "He's one I'd like to see sent someplace. Talk about a spoiled boy who'll stay permanently stuck on fool's hill. People think I don't know things, but I know how he's been at your daughters and any others he can get to. You know that's why they wouldn't let him stay in Colorado City. He got at so many of the young girls who were meant for the apostles that Marion Hammond would have none of it. They said they didn't need to import another troublemaker." Both men got out of their chairs

---

*Peck's bad boy was a fictional character created by George W. Peck in the late 1800s.

and walked away. I waited a few more minutes before I dared stretch out my aching legs and escape from my corner.

When it was time for Noreen to go home to Rosemary, her dad asked Grandpa what he wanted her to have and what he didn't. Grandpa stumbled over his words, trying to be as stern and grand as Uncle Marion had suggested he be. Finally he shrugged and with a red face said, "I guess we might as well get everything she wants, and what you'll let her take. President Hammond couldn't want us to be too tough all at once."

Freddie's eyebrows rose and with a look of disdain, he answered, "'They could see, yet they saw not…They could hear, yet they heard not'—I guess she's yours now, and I suppose you know what you're doing."

Grandpa covered his hurt and embarrassment by bustling around and gathering everyone to leave. I was sorry for him.

Irene had her first child, Grant, on Dominion Day. It was Canada's 100th birthday, and her plural child got a golden medallion from the government. And then the most exciting thing I could imagine happened. Daddy decided that Nettie, Brent, and I could go to Rosemary and stay at Grandmother's for a week. Jan was upset the moment he announced it. She was worrying about our manners and saying she just knew all of her inadequacies were going to be on display for the relatives in Alberta. The moment she started harping on the topic, we knew she was likely to start beating on us, so we were extra careful to stay out of her way.

It was great to be with Grandmother with only the three of us there. I couldn't get over how neat and quiet meals were with no babies or little kids around. Nettie and Brent followed Grandpa most of the time while I bothered Grandmother with questions about Mother.

The second day we were there, Grandmother invited Noreen to her house for a visit. Noreen was living in one of Grandpa's other houses on the farm. It seemed funny to think she was my grandmother and yet wasn't much taller than I was. She came into the house while Grandmother stayed out in the yard talking to Grandpa. She boosted herself up on a tall kitchen stool, and we grinned at each other like idiots. "How do you like being married to Grandpa?" I asked.

Noreen laughed and forced herself to say the right words in a haughty manner. "I'm very happy to be married to your grandpa and I'm the queen of the castle…This is my throne." She gave the stool a silly little twirl with her arms in the air. We both whirled in surprise as Grandmother walked into the kitchen. Noreen slid to the floor and with a nervous gulp asked, "Is there something I can do to help…I might as well, since I'm here for dinner."

Grandmother nodded brusquely and set a task for each of us. Before long we sat down to a meal of chop suey and buns. The dessert was angel food cake and strawberries smothered with thick whipped cream.

Grandmother arranged visits with Great-grandmother and Great-grandfather Norton, and her sister, Great-aunt Marg. I didn't remember ever seeing Aunt Marg before, but Grandmother told me she had a child die about the same time I was born. Sometimes when she was talking to me, she called me Viv, which was wonderful since more than anything I wanted to be like Mother. The next day Grandmother made sure we were dressed very neatly and drove us from the farm into the town of Rosemary. I didn't know how to look or where to put my hands as Grandmother Norton kissed me again and again and cried over and over, "You're just like Vivien, you're just like my little Vivien. Just look at her, Selma! Isn't she just like Viv?" We all stood crying in Grandmother Norton's porch. They must have really loved Mother.

While we visited, I kept trying to think of something grown-up to say. We sang some children's hymns we had been memorizing, and then Grandmother drove us to Aunt Marg's. On the way I thought about how much I loved the attention Grandmother and Grandfather Norton had showered on us. We arrived at Aunt Marg's place, a farm similar to Grandmother and Grandpa's. They didn't have a sister wife there, and I felt sorry for them—it must really have been an empty life. Aunt Marg was like Grandmother but a lot softer and slower moving. She greeted us with the same hugs and tears and the same mention of Vivien.

She soon pulled a big plastic bag from a hall closet. "Here are some clothes that used to be Maisie's. I'm sure these children could use them." She beckoned to me. "Here, come go through these things." I loved bags of clothes, and these had belonged to a cousin I'd never met. Every time I pulled something out, there was a promise of excitement and surprise—strapless prom dresses, little suits, lacy tops, and a couple of circle skirts. The fabric was fine and filmy and the colors were brilliant. Grandmother and Aunt Marg reminisced about the parties, school days, and dreams that Maisie and my Aunt Glenna had shared. It sounded as if these two girls had been inseparable. We bundled the clothes into the car and headed for home.

Grandmother seemed concerned. "You know, Deb, your dad won't likely let you keep any of these things. It'll be just as well for you to leave them with me. I'll do something with them. I couldn't tell Marg you'd never be allowed to wear them. She wouldn't understand, and I couldn't upset her." The happy aura that had surrounded me as I listened to the stories of girls from another world faded. I tried to convince myself that Grandmother was wrong but ended up berating myself for not saying it first—for not shunning the very appearance of evil.

After supper I kept drifting over to the bag of clothes and smoothing the crisp taffeta of a wine-colored evening gown covered with pink roses. I argued fiercely with myself until I lost, then I begged Grandmother to let me try it on. When she gave me permission, I disappeared into the bathroom and stripped off my long-sleeved, high-necked dress and my long petticoat. I worried that I should have kept my petticoat on, but it would have shown above the gown. The mirrors in Grandmother's bathroom were lower than any bathroom mirrors I had ever seen before. I turned sideways and pulled my stomach way in. Already, I was growing small breasts. I slipped the dress over my head and reached behind to zip it up. I turned toward the mirror with my eyes shut, and then opened them quickly. My shoulders were creamy olive and the low shawl-like neck of the dress made my breasts seem larger. I looked fourteen instead of eleven.

I was determined to have a night in this dress, but I had

nothing to cover my shoulders, and Nettie and Brent were out there. With shaking fingers, I took the elastics out of my hair and undid my braids. I groomed my hair with Grandmother's gold-handled brush until the plaits were cascades of dark brown waves, then borrowed two of her bobby pins and pulled the hair up on the sides. I stepped out into the living room.

Grandpa and his son, my Uncle Giles, stood there with their mouths open for a while until Grandpa shook his head and said, "Well, I never…I never…how old are you?"

Giles sat on the couch beside me as we watched *Rin Tin Tin* on television. When he got up to go to the bathroom, Nettie and Brent both whispered, "What do you think you're doin'? We're telling when we get home."

Fear gripped me at the thought of Jan's reaction, and I begged them not to tell. As soon as Giles came back, I went to change into my nightgown. In bed I tossed and turned. I finally drifted off, only to have a terrible nightmare. I was running away from a woman who screamed at me like a blue jay, a screech owl, and a cougar all in one. I ran and ran until she just about caught me. I hid under a big square washtub, and then Babar the elephant came out of nowhere and did tricks on top of my tub while the woman ran screaming up the hill.

I woke up exhausted and Grandmother asked me if I was sick. I started to cry and begged her, "Please let me stay here. I can't go back home. I always frustrate Jan so much. She beats me and usually one or two of the other kids, and it's my fault. It would be easier on Daddy, too, if I was gone, because Jan wouldn't always have to cuss him about how slow and stupid I am!" I was ranting hysterically. Grandmother wrapped her arms around me and cried softly as she rocked, just like Mother used to.

After a while, she stopped and shook herself. "You know you can't stay here, Deb. Your dad needs you. It was hard enough on him to lose your mother. The gospel is clear—one shouldn't interfere in another man's kingdom. It'll get better…Jan always tells me how much she loves raising you kids for Viv." I was still panic-stricken, and I begged her to see if Grandfather Norton or anyone else would have me.

Grandmother suddenly looked stern. "You know how much the gospel and plural marriage meant to your mother. You're too important to the Work to do anything else. I know you have a testimony. You wouldn't be able to grow up and live the principle anywhere else."

Her words pulled me out of my frenzy as well as a slap would have. I couldn't imagine what got into me. "I hope you can forgive me, Grandmother...I hope Heavenly Father will, too. The worldly dress just went to my head."

Two days later Uncle Giles took us home to Canyon; the dress and the churchy relatives faded into a dreamlike memory. Jan didn't seem all that glad to see us back but didn't waste any time getting us weeding. The first time she got mad at me, she snarled, "You don't need to walk around with your head in the clouds like you're still in Rosemary. This is reality. This is day-to-day slugging it out. Too bad you have to do as you're told—Grandmother's not here to protect you." With that, she would twist my braid or pinch my arm until I was bruised.

The raspberry patch we planted really paid off that year. We picked the berries into crates to sell as many as possible and froze the extra. Some of the gentile relatives from Cardston came and picked for a couple of days. Daddy said their money was as good as anyone's, as long as we didn't let any of their bad ideas take root. Nettie, Brent, and I picked quietly and listened to them as they worked. After a few hours I could sure see how blessed we were to be protected from constant worldly influences. It shocked me how the men were so mouselike, while the women bossed them around with loud voices. I had heard Uncle Isaac say the women of the apostate church had castrated their men. Now I understood what he meant.

I'd seen him castrating calves and baby pigs in the barn with a knife and had a hard time imagining a man holding still for that sort of treatment. The boys in our group had to be careful something like that didn't happen to them, though. When Uncle Isaac's kids were here picking raspberries one day, they told us some of the big boys had put bobby pins in the end of their peters, and one of them almost got one stuck. It wouldn't be very nice if Uncle Isaac had to use his knife to cut it out.

Uncle Kelvin's wives, Celia and Enid, took turns staying for the summer at the little log cabin in our other orchard up the hill from the Canyon house. Although the Whitmers were part of our group, they were very different in our eyes. The children, and even the mothers, wore short sleeves sometimes, and they left empty cans from store-bought food lying around. Jan was horrified at the waste and declared, "If I was as poor as the Whitmers pretend to be, I wouldn't be eating out of a can. It's little wonder they all have pasty white skin and lily-limp fingers!"

I was embarrassed all summer because, since Daddy took us to live in Canyon, it was hard enough to be accepted and feel like we could be as good as Uncle Isaac's kids. They did more exciting things because their dad was the file leader—way more exciting than our dad, who was just a mechanic. Even though no one actually dared say it since Daddy was married to two Merrick women now, he was working for a gentile boss at the tractor dealership just like Uncle Kelvin was working for the Town of Creston. What if all of Uncle Isaac's kids decided they could make fun of us just because Daddy was letting the Whitmers stay with us all summer? My heart sank when I thought about this. If this made going back to school worse, I'd just die.

One afternoon when Jan decided to go to town and left Elsa babysitting us, Elsa disappeared with her book, and the Whitmer kids came down from their cabin. One of the first wife's kids, Nuela, was with them. She was a five-foot-two, dark-haired, brown-eyed spitfire. Before Laman went south on his mission, she was his tweetie bird, and he always had chocolates for her and the sweetest sayings ever, and since he'd been gone, she had as many boyfriends as she wanted.

Nuela sat in the middle of a circle of a dozen kids, telling ghost stories. I had never heard about such things as bloody heads in breadboxes. Even the violent murders and wars in the Bible stories and Greek and Roman myths I had practically memorized didn't seem as gross as this. Maybe it bothered me more because these stories were about real kids like us, and I didn't like thinking about the real horrors of the world.

Watching the intense faces, listening to the ghoulish humor, I got a sense of what it was like to belong to an exclusive Whitmer world that Merricks and Nilssons didn't enter. None of the Whitmer kids seemed to realize they were pasty-faced, lily-fingered milksops. I even thought I might get to like the girls who were my age if I could know them a little better and they learned to dress properly. They didn't seem to realize it was evil to wear worldly bathing suits to swim in the river, even though they watched us being righteous and swimming in clothes the way the prophet wanted us to. I sort of thought, too, they should have been more grateful to us for getting to stay at our place.

Later in the summer Daddy and Uncle Isaac called a baptism under the direction of the prophet. Daddy tramped around the river bottom for hours looking for the most beautiful spot to dedicate the water for the sacred ordinance. There were six kids to be baptized that year, and by the time Uncle Isaac and all his wives and children, Uncle Kelvin and all his wives and children, and Daddy with all of us got there, it made quite a crowd. The baptism was over and we were starting to head home when two of Uncle Kelvin's little girls, Lucia and Leora, asked why the beautiful ladies in white dresses with flowers on the skirts didn't come across the river to sing with us. The mothers were alarmed, but Uncle Kelvin and Uncle Isaac decided that the women, visible only to the children, had been angels.

I was so ashamed that I hadn't seen the angels. I thought Mother might have been one of them and felt terrible not to recognize her. I wondered why Heavenly Father would let girls who wore bathing suits and ate white bread see angels when there were so many other people around—especially Uncle Isaac and his family, with his being the file leader and all.

Daddy came back from the 1968 April conference in Colorado City with hepatitis; all the men said they picked it up from eating food at a gentile restaurant. He was yellow for weeks. When he finally got better, I got sick. This wasn't a good time for me to be sick because Jan was having frequent gall bladder attacks and sure didn't want to deal with me. She was pregnant for the second time in two years, and the doctor said she couldn't have an operation for the gall bladder until the baby was born.

It was one of the worst times I could remember since Mother died. I'd been hoping that with the onset of summer, the pain and stiffness from the rheumatic fever would lessen, and I would start to feel better. But by June my skin and the whites of my eyes were a ghastly orange-yellow. Sometimes the diarrhea was so bad I soiled myself and then threw up. I couldn't decide which end to take care of first, and no matter how hard I washed I couldn't seem to get away from the stench. Dragging myself to the bathtub was a major undertaking, but it was my only salvation. Sometimes a whole day went by with no one checking on me. Nettie, Brent, and the rest of the kids wouldn't come around because they couldn't stand the horrible smell. Besides, Daddy told the family I was contagious and we couldn't have everyone laid up and puking or we wouldn't be able to get the summer work done to have food canned for the winter.

Daddy would usually come to check on me for a bit each night when he got home from work. He would hold me and make sure my water jug was full. He told me to remember to drink every time I thought of it, because the doctor told him the worst part of hepatitis was the fear of dehydration and hurting your liver permanently. Daddy said he was sorry things were so rough, but he knew I'd be okay because I was made of "tough stuff." When I moaned about how much I hated being sick and washing out my own soiled underwear, he told me I should be grateful and keep sweet because some of Celia's kids got hepatitis from Uncle Kelvin, and they didn't even have running water. They had no beautiful white porcelain flushing toilet and no bathtub to wash in where you could just drain the water. Daddy warned me to make sure I used a few drops of Dettol to clean up after myself when I washed my soiled clothes or puked in the toilet. I was also supposed to rinse the tub in Dettol when I was finished. He said he had brought it home especially for me so I would get better faster, and so none of my brothers and sisters would get infected. We just didn't have the time to have more sick kids during the busy summer months.

As I started to get better, the smell of food cooking made me feel hungry instead of sick to my stomach. I was still not allowed to mix with everyone else, so I'd sneak into the kitchen to find food when all was quiet. Too often, the soup or macaroni—Irene's favorite things to cook—was gone. With the sores in my mouth, it hurt too much to chew bread, so I'd open a jar of tomatoes or pears. The tomatoes bit my sores, but they were soft enough for me to get them down. After I started to feel stronger, I walked around the house a bit and out to the elderberry bushes along the pond. The elderberry fruit was good that summer, and I ate them until I thought I would turn purple.

One afternoon while I was foraging, I came upon Irene and Emilia sitting together. Emilia was crying. She knew the prophet wanted her to marry Uncle Isaac. It was common knowledge in the group that she was in love with one of Uncle Isaac's brother's sons and wanted to marry him. Leonard was a great horseman and magnificent in the saddle, which was very attractive to Emilia—she lived for her horses, too. Leonard and his wife Brandy had come from Winnipeg where she had been a rodeo queen. For the first time, Emilia had a reason to be happy she was adopted, because it made her blood different from the rest of the Merricks, so it didn't matter if she and Leonard were first cousins. Brandy seemed glad enough Emilia might be her sister wife, but Jan and Bettilyn felt just terrible that she wasn't taking direction about placement marriage properly.

Leonard had taught us math in school that winter, and there was no doubt his way was different. All of us kids weren't sure what Leonard stole or from whom, but all of a sudden police were asking questions, and Leonard and Brandy and their kids were gone in the night to the States. Everyone heaved a huge sigh that Emilia was saved. Uncle Isaac said she had a really special mission to perform to be saved out of the gentile world when he and Bettilyn were inspired to adopt her like that. I saw him and Daddy and the prophet talking about it and shaking their heads and saying, "Marvelous how the Lord works—just marvelous." It had been several months now since Leonard crossed the border into the States. Emilia was here on the grass at our house in Canyon and wouldn't go home to the ranch and Uncle Isaac.

I sat quietly beside Emilia and Irene while they talked. Emilia's face was haggard. "Ophelia is so hateful," she said. "She thinks it would be the most wonderful thing to be married to Daddy. She told me she wished she'd been adopted so the prophet could have placed her with Daddy instead of Sidney. She's been crying ever since Sidney came back from his Work mission and the prophet assigned her to him. Sidney told me she won't even take off her clothes to go to bed. She puts on more clothes and more underwear. She loved one of the Williams boys in the States, but why can't she just try to like Sidney?"

Emilia told Irene how Uncle Roy even had his wife Pearl talk to her about how she got used to going to bed with him. When Pearl's real father died, her mother was married to Uncle Roy—he was the only father Pearl ever knew. If Uncle Roy hadn't taken her as one of his brides, she might have had to marry a young boy who wasn't proven yet.

"But just because she slept with her stepfather doesn't mean I want to," Emilia went on. "I could never sleep with Daddy! And Pearl has children with her father...never!" Emilia looked at Irene. "Do you think I'm terrible, too? I still love Leonard, but I know he's no good, and I shouldn't even think about him."

Irene twisted uncomfortably. "I know I'd hate to be married to Dad. I don't know what to say. Talk to Adam again when he gets home tonight—he'll know what you should think." She looked over her shoulder and tried desperately to change the subject. "We better get the bread baked and get back to the garden. Jan'll be furious when she gets home if it isn't weed-free."

She turned to me. "Well, Deb, does the fact you're up and not dead mean you can work? We thought you might have died days ago. You can fix dinner while Emilia and I work in the garden." They sauntered ahead of me as I made my way to the kitchen to warm up some leftover potato soup. When the bread came out of the oven, we had soup and thick warm slices of brown bread.

After Jan's baby was born and the scar from her gall bladder operation was healed, she got some exciting news. "Finally, the Lord has answered my prayers and is sending someone who'll be a real help as a teacher. It's so trying to have to use people with no training or imagination at all. Laman's coming home from his work mission, and they've married him to one of Stanley Miller's talented daughters. We won't be able to pay her much as a wage, but Daddy and Adam both say not to worry about it—God will pave the way!"

Irene was a less-than-enthusiastic audience. "Yeah," she mumbled. "It'll just be terrific to have a constant musical with her prissy Miller ways around every day instead of only twice a year when they come for a visit. At least Celeste isn't one of the prettiest ones from that family, so maybe she'll be bearable."

We sure needed a new teacher at the school. This could only be a good thing, especially if Celeste could teach singing. We got to meet her at church. She sparkled and laughed like someone special, and even though this was their first Sunday here, she and Laman sang a song together. Daddy told us the brethren had decided to appoint Laman as caretaker of the school, and in return for his work and Celeste's teaching, they could have the little apartment Uncle Michael had built in the back of the school. Uncle Isaac and Daddy split the needed cash, and the new couple was given food from the ranch and milk from Uncle Isaac's dairy.

Fast-and-testimony meeting was the very next week. Celeste was sitting on Laman's lap, and when he got up to talk, she jumped up with a wiggle and a squeal. Laman's testimony was even more cocky and self-assured than it used to be before he went to Colorado City. "I am grateful the Lord is governing my life and I can be used by Him. I know I'll never have to work for the Gentiles of the world if I keep myself in tune with the prophet and with my father, Isaac Merrick. Anyone who is serious about the gospel and has a true testimony will be taken care of by the Lord in every way and will never have to expose his mind and heart to the temptations and sins that are right here in the town of Creston!" With a satisfied smile, he went back to the chair he and Celeste were sharing. She giggled proudly and wiggled back down into his lap.

With blazing eyes, Lem vaulted to the pulpit. "I guess I'm just not very good at suckholing to the right people, and everyone can't sit around living off Dad. I'm working for Gentiles, all right, but at least I can pay my tithing and help out instead of being a drag on the Work!"

I couldn't get over how much Lem hated Laman now. Most people said it was because Laman was younger and got a wife first and Uncle Isaac gave him all kinds of extra things. It was really embarrassing for everyone when they fought, but I guess it did make church more interesting.

I got my hopes up last summer when Lem came to visit us in Canyon, and we all walked to the river to look at the red fish running. He told Daddy he was going to work seven years for me like Jacob worked for Rachel in the Bible. I thought he might be joking, but he winked at me and told Daddy he wouldn't be accepting any tricks like Rachel's dad did in the Old Testament—he didn't want the ugly sister first. Daddy just laughed. I couldn't figure out what Lem was talking about because I didn't have any ugly sisters, and I thought he liked some of the older girls better anyway.

That winter Celeste taught us different songs and helped out with little things around the school. She was such a pleasant change from what we were used to—she was so soft and pretty, and her words were kind and gentle. She cried one day because Jan told her she was setting a bad example with her worldly, vain curls. Her hair was always so nice and clean and wavy—not like the other women in our group. She said she didn't know what to do about her hair since her curls were natural. I'd never thought about the problem before—it would be so hard to be born with something that worldly. Maybe she could ask Heavenly Father about it if He wasn't too busy sometime. I supposed He would even be embarrassed about the way Laman and Celeste bathed together; they splashed and giggled for hours in the tub and all the grown-ups were really disgusted.

Lots of the songs the Miller girls performed were from musicals by Rodgers and Hammerstein. Celeste had so many good things to say about their newest one called *The Sound of Music* that Daddy said Jan could take Aline, Jean, Nettie, and I to see it. The seventy-five mile trip to Cranbrook and the experience of sitting in a theater for the first time with all the fantastic music and colors was unforgettable and worth the terrifying ride home in the snowstorm afterwards. Daddy brought the record home and whenever no one was around I played it. I sang with it until I could make my voice match either Maria's or the Reverend Mother's.

If I could just find a place to learn and read and write things away from Jan I'd go to school forever...but when she came down the row behind me in class and peered over my shoulder, I would stop breathing and pray she would keep walking. I tried hard to stay out of trouble and keep from doing anything that might upset her, but at least two or three times a week I seemed to be the brunt of one of her attacks. Sometimes she only pinched me, pulled my hair, or poked me in the belly. She always waited for the nervous laughter from the rest of the kids before she went on.

One rainy day at the end of March Jan was in a foul mood from the second she got out of bed. She argued with Daddy about where the money for her next order of school books was coming from. He was trying to tell her to be sweet and have faith, that he and Uncle Isaac would take care of things. She burst into tears. "This is the last straw, Adam...you can't accuse me of not having faith. I have faith! I know you'll get the money eventually, but I need it tomorrow." Daddy patted her arms and tried to tell her he would never say such a thing. Jan left the house in a rage, jumped in her car, and tore away in a spray of gravel to her dental appointment.

The first few hours of the morning were fun, with Celeste filling in for Jan and practicing songs from *The Sound of Music*. I loved them and knew most of them off by heart, but a couple of the boys caused a fuss about having to sing such "prissy" music. We had just finished when Jan slammed through the door and took over for our math class. She scratched a long list of multiplication questions on the blackboard, pressing so hard on the chalk that it kept breaking. Each time, she threw the pieces viciously into the corner and grabbed another from the ledge.

The big boys had been rowdy all morning and had frustrated Celeste to tears a couple of times. As soon as Jan left the room, they started throwing spitballs, and three of them were scuffling at the back. But she burst back through the door and in two leaps was upon them. The boys melted into their seats, and a deathly silence fell on the room. Jan began pacing and swinging her arms with clenched fists. Her voice sent a shiver up my spine. "You bunch of useless, irresponsible ingrates…You're a shame to the priesthood, our prophet, and our file leader! You are disrespectful, no-good idiots who will never amount to anything the Lord can use in any parts of His Work, let alone the celestial kingdom. I sacrifice myself day after day, and this is the thanks I get! Celeste told me how bad you were while I was gone this morning. I can't even turn my back for a measly two hours, and you forget you're supposed to be the chosen race of Israel to build the New Jerusalem."

My pencil was frozen in my hand, and I was wishing I could disappear. I kept silently repeating, "Yea, though I walk through the valley and shadow of death."

When Jan's voice became a shriek, the hair prickled on the back of my neck. With no further warning, her closed fists pounded on my head and down my back, "You! Deborah! You're the worst of all. You would try the very patience of Job. You have the best example to follow, yet you continue to be a trial no one should have to bear. You are a slovenly ingrate!" The force of her fists knocked me out of my desk, and I curled into a ball on the floor. She grabbed the braid I had pinned around my head and yanked it. Pins flew in all directions as she jerked back and forth. I struggled to stay curled up when she began kicking me. Just as she backed up and aimed her muddy, brown Tender Tootsie shoe at my stomach, there was a blood-curdling whoop and a crash that shook the entire room. Jan's foot stopped in mid-air and she dropped my braid.

Jonah had driven his fist through the moldy pressed-cardboard wall at the front of the room. "Leave her alone! You're a cruel, hypocritical bitch, and somebody should take you to jail! You're no sister of mine. I'm sick of this. We're all sick of it. Now, just leave!" His face was dark purple, and his fourteen-year-old body trembled as he pointed to the door.

Jan looked at every stony face in the room except mine. Putting her hands on her hips, she shouted, "I demand an apology! No one talks to me like that and gets away with it. You'll be sorry—all of you—unless I get that apology by the time I count to five." She tapped her foot and counted. No one had ever defied Jan like this before.

She left the room and seconds later so did Jonah. Everyone else stayed glued to their desks in a pall of silence for at least twenty minutes. I sat with my face in my arms. Slowly, one by one, the kids filed out of the room and left the school. Several of them lightly touched my shoulder as they left. No one spoke to me, not even Jean.

For a long time I sat hunched over my desk listening to sounds from other parts of the school—muffled voices, Celeste singing in her room. Everything seemed like a dream I should wake up from. Nothing was real but the pencil smell on the old wooden desk and the horrible pain in my back and thighs.

Jan's voice kept echoing through my mind. I truly was a trial no one should have to put up with. I hobbled to the door, grabbed my coat from the lobby, and headed outside. The air was chilly and damp. I felt nauseous and stumbled along holding my stomach. When I reached the pond, I retched until there was nothing left, then continued across the pasture and into the woods. After twenty minutes, I stopped beneath the branches of a huge cedar tree and leaned against the trunk. I knew I was no longer on priesthood property, but somehow it didn't matter. I huddled there, praying for Heavenly Father to take me to Mother.

Later that afternoon I heard Jean and Nettie calling my name and listened until their voices faded in the distance. It wasn't until after dark when I heard Daddy's voice and the sound of the Whitmer boys tramping through the woods that I finally answered their call. One of the boys helped me to my feet, while the others ran for Daddy. When we got back to the house, Bettilyn met us at the door wringing her hands. She babbled to everyone about why Jan couldn't help herself when she beat me. She begged me, "You have to forgive her! She's really sorry and will try to never do it again. I don't know why it has to be this bad, but you really have to forgive her. Can you, please?"

Daddy started talking about Jan using me as an example for the other disrespectful kids. He admitted it really wasn't the best thing, but it was that way with children. "Where much is given, much is expected." He said at least ten times he knew I could forgive Jan for Mother's sake. Finally, I told him I would. He hugged me and thanked me, but somehow the comfort I usually got in his strong arms was not there that night.

After a horrible week of avoiding one another, Jan called me to her room and told me she hoped I understood she didn't want me to take it personally every time she criticized me in class. She explained it was because I was in Daddy's family, and he was the superintendent of God's private school and she was the principal. Heaving herself off her bed, she draped her arms heavily around my shoulders. She said there were some kids she couldn't discipline the way she should.

"I can get away with chastising you when I'm trying to get a point across to the rest of the class, and I won't get in trouble. The rest of the students pay attention and are much more respectful to me after—you have to admit that."

I nodded my head as if it made perfect sense. All I wanted to do was get away from her—away from her touch, away from the smell of her sweat and sour breast milk. I vowed not to let her see me cry the next time she needed to beat me as an example to the rest.

The bigger our family got, the more problems Daddy had to resolve. Having Elsa in the apartment under the kitchen had worked out pretty well, but Daddy needed space to put bedrooms for us girls. The cabin the Whitmers stayed in burned down, so that wasn't an option. He decided the solution to the dilemma would be to build a little house up on the hill. Uncle Isaac called a few "work days," and people from the ranch came to help for several Saturdays. The foundation and floor were poured and by summer's end there was a three-bedroom house for Elsa. She fluttered around the new place, thrilled to be planning curtains for her very own windows and figuring out how to finish the rooms for her children. Irene snorted about, wondering how long it would be before Elsa's new house was as big a pigsty as her apartment had been.

We girls were really happy to have our own bedrooms. Mine was Elsa's old room—the room with the grease pit under it. Daddy said it wouldn't be long before the prophet called me to be a wife in Israel, so I should have a room to myself where I could fix things up the way I liked. The other girls had beds in the big room Elsa had used for a kitchen and living room. I was a bit nervous about my new room because Elsa claimed snakes dropped from the windowsill and slithered under the cracked battleship linoleum, but everyone said she was exaggerating.

The best part about Elsa's living up on the hill was we could pretend we were going for a walk in a whole different direction, then take a detour to her house. We could visit without anyone knowing we went there and keep from getting into trouble. If she didn't come down to visit Jan or Irene for a few days, they actually seemed happy to see her most of the time. Although she had delivered a healthy little girl at last, she lost another one right after that. Now she was pregnant again and didn't seem to be having as much trouble keeping it inside her. Daddy said we should try to talk her into going back and forth to her house on the gentle trail, but she was stubborn and seemed proud to be able to hike up and down the steepest trail, even when it was icy.

I was having trouble practicing for my Royal Conservatory piano exams because my hands were all cut up from cleaning innards out of chickens. Daddy had made this great deal with two poultry farms in town. We could have the hens out of their huge barns if we moved the chickens out, cleaned the coops, and moved the new chickens in. Daddy was so proud of himself when he announced in church how the Lord had seen fit to move the hearts of the Gentiles for the good of our people.

He came up with a plan to get money to support the school out of the sale of the processed hens. We slaughtered and cleaned them as a school project and sold the meat. That got some money from the Gentiles, but also from some of the kids' fathers who didn't like to pay toward their tuition.

I sliced myself the first day of the slaughter. By the third day there were more cuts than I could count, and the first ones were infected. Daddy said since I was hurt doing the Lord's work, I'd be blessed, so I should keep on practicing piano to the best of my ability. He was truly inspired because when I took the exams, even with half my fingers in bandages and pus oozing from the end of the middle finger of my right hand, I passed with honors.

All his dedication and hard work was undoubtedly creating a great place for Daddy in God's kingdom. Jan was forever saying it was so sad that all women couldn't be married to guys as inspired and committed to the gospel as Daddy. Many times she wept and said she could never be good enough for him. But sometimes he came home from work with a great invention or an idea, and she made fun of him so much he got red in the face and went off by himself. One time that very hot summer he came home with some steaks and announced we were going to venture to Kootenay Lake for a barbecue.

Jan barely looked up from her sewing and in a sarcastic voice said, "Well, I hope you have fun. I'll not be eating more of your steak. The last one was burnt on the outside and had blood dripping from the middle—the cow was still bawling—not to mention sand blowing into everything. Besides, why would you want to expose the kids to the naked Gentiles at the lake?"

Daddy's shoulders slumped and he put his arm around her. In a sad voice he said, "Now, dear, you know we'll have a good time once we're there, and the children will enjoy the lake. Please come along...You'll see how wonderful it can be."

She grudgingly agreed to go but made sure no one had a good time. She wouldn't even let us get our feet wet, warning that the lake was too cold. She was horrified the Gentiles were exposing themselves and "trolloping around" in the sun. As if on command, the wind picked up and blew sand in our eyes and mouths. The whole time, Jan ground words bitterly through her teeth about the waste of time, the waste of good food, and the utter stupidity of some people. Over and over she said she couldn't abide stupidity. She ranted on Irene and Elsa until they were totally miserable. When Daddy finally packed us into the station wagon for the trip home, no one dared speak. The only thing we could hear over the sound of the engine were Jan's barely muffled sobs.

The radio said the summer was breaking all kinds of records for high temperatures, and there were forest fires all around the Creston Valley. Usually we heard about this sort of thing in other places, but when there were fires on all the mountains we could see, we were scared. When the apostles from the States came to see us again, they were even more serious and sober than usual. They told us the fires were signs of the times: "The final cleansing of the world will be with fire, and no man knoweth the day or the hour."

Apostle Guy Musser addressed the Saints with his usual intensity. He told us about a war the United States was waging against Vietnam. His fervor injected itself into the meeting until we could barely breathe. "Satan is conspiring with the wicked, corrupt governments of the world, and Communist China with its yellow hordes is going to sweep over the country, killing, burning, and cleansing the land. The prayer circles of our people from Canada to Mexico are the only thing that will save the world from complete destruction by the devil's communistic governments. We must learn to speak Spanish, so we can speak more easily with our fellow Saints in Mexico."

He said that some of our covenant boys in the States had been drafted to fight the evil war, but we didn't have to worry—if the boys kept the Spirit of God they would be spared. I already knew this to be true because the army sent the Williams boys from Colorado City to fight fire just south of us in Idaho instead of to Vietnam. Uncle Guy warned us the fires and the war could be the beginning of the end, and we better start putting away a supply of food and not be caught like the ten foolish virgins with empty lamps.*

Uncle Isaac's presentation at the meeting was truly magnificent. From the moment he took the pulpit he seemed ten feet tall. "It's time to listen to this direction and stop pretending all is well in Zion. A country that thinks it can govern its people without the

*The reference is to the parable in which ten virgins traveled to meet their bridegroom. Five took no oil for their lamps and so were left out of the festivities—symbolic of being refused entrance to the celestial kingdom to be with Christ.

revelation of the Lord will end like a woman who thinks she can get to the celestial kingdom without her husband. She'll go to hell cross lots!"* He rose up on the toes of his shiny black boots. His face glowed as he stretched his arms to the heavens. "Some women think they can worship a being way up here and ignore the counsel and advice of their husband. I testify to you that in the hereafter these women will be servants in their husband's kingdoms. I have a wife that I'll have dunging out the stables of my kingdom, and she'll be glad to do it."

For months Naomi hadn't been coming to church on a regular basis, and everyone was edgy that she was sitting in the back listening critically to everything being said. Everyone had been so intent on Uncle Isaac's sermon that when she let out an enraged howl, it nearly lifted us from our chairs.

I whirled around just as she sprang to her feet. Her face was a mottled red; her eyes burned with passion. "Who are you to stand in judgment like this on me? Who are you to put yourself above God and decide it will be your right to decide if I have sinned enough that God will condemn me to hell?"

The bedlam escalated as Uncle Isaac shouted repeatedly for her to "shut up and get thee behind me, Satan!" Every person in the room was embarrassed and not sure where to look as the antagonism between this uncle and his niece intensified. The situation was further inflamed by the fact that the nine children their marriage had brought into the world were all there in the room. It felt as if the flames of hell would descend upon our heads and burn us all alive.

Our file leader was quivering with such rage I was afraid he would vault the distance between them and tear Naomi limb from limb. As Daddy tried to get to her, one of Uncle Isaac's flailing arms struck him in the stomach. He struggled to keep his composure. At the sight of Daddy's dilemma, Naomi looked disgusted. He got closer to her, but she put up both her arms to block him. "Don't bother, Adam! You're such a well-meaning fool. They'll take you

---

*A colorful expression used to describe how wicked or rebellious people would be sent directly ("cross lots") to hell.

down and smile while they're doing it...and you, you'll tell them you deserved it and beg them to forgive you. I'll live to see it happen, too...and you can write that in stone!" Daddy stopped dead in his tracks at Naomi's admonition. "Not me! No more. I've had it...My cow has more priesthood than all the men in this room put together." With her pronouncement, there was a collective gasp from the group.

"And, Adam, you can just go back to your seat and live according to the dictates of Isaac. But beware you make one mistake or think for yourself just once...because if you do, you'll see yourself dunging out the celestial shit in their celestial horse barns while they stomp on your neck. I'm finished...I'll never set foot in one of your meetings again as long as I live. I'm through being treated like a leper if I don't bow and scrape to Isaac and these other evil idiots. My Savior, Jesus Christ, is the only man I'll worship and the only man I should worship!"

Many of the women were weeping openly; Bettilyn was bawling with her usual gasping sobs. Jan jumped up and ran to comfort her.

Naomi looked around the room in complete disgust as if she were seeing each person clearly for the first time. Daddy made another feeble attempt to step toward her. "Stay where you are, you sad sack. You don't want to be seen acting like you give a shit what happens to me, and I won't talk to a man who won't even stand up for his own kids." She shoved a chair out of her way, and the people sitting between her and the top of the stairs leapt from their seats like scalded cats.

With that, she was gone. Seconds later, her old truck roared to life and disappeared in a cloud of dust. Daddy was crying as he went back to his seat. Naomi's children, who had been sitting in different places, slowly got up from their seats. Sobs from the three youngest ones echoed back up the curve in the stairs as they left the building. By the time they were far enough down the road that we could see them from the windows, the dust from their mother's truck was gone.

For some time Uncle Isaac seemed rooted to the spot, and the room was quiet except for the occasional sob from Bettilyn's corner. Finally, he moved back behind the pulpit. "You see what I have to put up with," he stated flatly. "How can a good priesthood man make anything out of a woman like that? All you young girls who are waiting to become wives in Israel to further this great Work, remember this day. Let this be a lesson to you. You'll never be a jewel in your husband's crown if you follow her example! She's a curse to the Work and to her children." He paused before addressing the apostles directly. "I apologize to my prophet and the brethren…that they had to witness such a scene of rank apostasy and rebellion."

All the men sitting behind him nodded in sympathy and murmured acknowledgment of Uncle Isaac's great trial. Uncle Marion jumped up, hugged him, and clapped him on the shoulder. "Each one of us has been blessed by the Lord with such a trial. Each of us knows the feeling of a thorn beneath his saddle."

So it had really come to an end with Naomi—Uncle Isaac's worst fears had come to pass. Since she had built the house on the other side of the hill, he had occasionally gone to visit her at night. The day after her explosion in church he went by to see his bed dumped on the edge of the road. She told everyone she saw that Isaac had slept in her house for the last time, and she didn't need the crumbs from his table.

One of the crumbs Naomi left behind was the vehicle she always drove. If she could just be kinder and sweeter like Daddy was always saying, I knew Uncle Isaac would have helped her get to town to thin apples and do the other odd jobs Gentiles gave her. Jeanie said her mother walked the seven miles to town to get food for them, and as she went she sang:

> "You got to walk that lonesome valley
> You got to walk it by yourself
> For nobody else can walk it for you
> You got to walk it by yourself."

I guess it went right along with what the apostles said at the meeting—that loneliness was a tool of the devil. Daddy always told us a good man of the priesthood would never leave a woman to go it alone, if she would take direction properly. He promised me I wouldn't ever have to worry if I could be as good a wife as Mother had been. Uncle Isaac really should never have had to put up with rebellious women in his life—after all, he was the file leader of all of Canada, and any woman would be grateful to be a wife to him.

Daddy didn't stop trying to be kind to Naomi. He kept going to visit her with the mothers and watching television—she still had one of the only television sets around. Uncle Isaac had decided it was a wasting-time tool of the devil. One day he went into his house and kicked the picture tube in with his cowboy boots and told us in church that anyone who was serious about the gospel would do the same.

Chapter 12

I'd always wanted to hold the rhinestones that Mother wore in her wedding picture and touch the green silk leaves of the temple apron.* I so wanted to read the letters she wrote Daddy and the ones he wrote back. I had seen Jan give Elsa some of the special things out of my mother's hope chest, so I decided to find out just what Elsa had. In the most selfish corner of my heart I didn't want anyone but Nettie, Brent, and I to have Mother's things.

One afternoon after Jan and Elsa left for town, I sneaked up the trail and dashed across the field to Elsa's house. This time of year the field was loaded with wild orange tiger lilies and creamy velvet three dots,** and it seemed such a shame to go inside. I slipped through the front door. The smell of the diesel furnace and Elsa were rank enough to make me want to gag. I didn't understand why she had to be so dirty. After I could breathe again, I slipped into her bedroom.

---

*A green apron, which can be intricate in design, made of a layering of silk leaves. It is symbolic of the story of Eve's disobedience and shame, and the eviction of mankind from the Garden of Eden.

**Mariposa lily—a showy white flower with three petals. Each petal has a perfect black dot close to the center.

She had a picture of Mother on her dresser, but I couldn't look at it because I knew Mother would hate that I was snooping in someone else's private belongings. I moved everything off the top of Elsa's hope chest, memorizing the way she had things arranged. Opening the chest, I slowly removed the contents. I found my mother's double boiler set and some of her fine wedding linen. I also found some Harlequin Romances hidden in one corner. I knew how Jan despised them because I heard her telling Elsa how they were trite drivel and an evil waste of time and brain cells.

After flipping through a few of them, I realized that even with all the pursuing and catching, loving and hating, and happily-ever-aftering, the books were much easier to read than *The Darkness and the Dawn* or *As You Like It* or *Macbeth* or the Bible or The Book of Mormon or the myths of the Greek and Roman gods.

At the bottom of this pile of books, I found a well-read volume with its cover gone. It looked interesting and I wanted to read more than just the back and a few pages in the middle. I checked the clock and estimated I'd be safe for at least an hour. Before long I was lost in a fascinating gentile world where a woman was greeting her husband after a hard day at the office. They were getting ready to go to a party, and all of a sudden they were stripping each other naked and touching and sucking on each other. I dropped the book and felt a flush come from deep inside me and rise to the top of my head. My hands trembled as I picked the book up again. I knew that actually touching like that wasn't good unless you were married, and I would never do it...but the people in this book were married. I remembered a story about Jesus called *The Silver Chalice,* where the young girls were taught how to please a man. Was this what it was talking about?

I was almost thirteen now. When Daddy came to say goodnight the last time, he whispered that soon I'd be married to a good priesthood man. He said this man would teach me about the kind of love he and Mother had. I knew he forgot his strength when he hugged me sometimes, because I couldn't breathe and my lungs would hurt. Every time he held me and talked about Mother, he cried. "Oh Deb, the love between a man and woman is just so special...I miss your mother so much. You look more and more like her all the time."

As I read the romance book in Elsa's house, the ideas in my mind flashed like a summer lightning storm, and I suddenly felt very warm. The woman in the book touched herself all over in front of her husband, and when she was alone she did it again. The place where the stick had been started to burn until I was touching myself, and the feelings the woman talked about happened to me. I was overcome with a rhythm and explosion of feeling that scared me. After the weakness was gone, I staggered to my feet and carefully replaced everything in the trunk the way I took it out. I looked back when I left the bedroom. My body and my brain both seemed different now—just the bedroom was the same. There were words to explain the feelings that had tormented me since that awful night with "the doctor" and the day in the old car, and sometimes even when Daddy hugged me. The most important thing to me now was to learn how to please my husband in every way. I knew I could do it.

I cleared the door of Elsa's house and dashed across the field again. When I hit the trees, I stood shaking for what seemed an eternity. When I finally started down the hill, the intensity of the last hour peeled away like husks from a cob of corn. I felt the core of my existence was bared for all to see, and wondered if everyone I passed would know what had happened. I came out of the trees at the bottom of the hill and wandered onto the lawn where the kids were playing tag around the crabapple tree. Irene called me to help her with supper.

No one seemed to wonder where my husks had gone, but I knew life would never be the same. Even after I had read three chapters in the Book of Mormon and prayed for half an hour, I still had dreams about the wild woman in Elsa's book. Sometimes, the husband and wife were both holding me and kissing me. Sometimes our apostle, Guy Musser, had me alone in a room taking my clothes off, one piece at a time, until I was naked. Then he unpinned my braid, shook it, and the hair swung loose in a wave that covered my back to below the curve of my bum. He meticulously folded my clothes and wrapped the pins in a napkin. He laid everything in a gleaming cherry-wood coffin. I saw my old yellow chest beside it, with its Arborite top and chipboard sides, full of baby clothes and keepsakes. He snapped the lid of the coffin down, and both boxes burst into flames and disappeared.

The sweat rolled down Guy Musser's face just like when he was giving one of his all-consuming sermons. His hands were damp and clammy as they brushed my breasts and my naked arms. He sat me on a huge bed. His whole body was shaking now as he knelt between my naked thighs and started to pray.

Every time my dream would get to that place, I couldn't stand the horror and revulsion one second longer, and I would open my mouth to scream. No sound would come out, but Apostle Guy Musser would turn into a huge writhing cobra with red fluorescent eyes and a long flickering tongue. Just as I knew the scream was about to break through, the snake would curl back on itself until it disappeared in a ball of flame.

I would wake up with the scream still in my throat and stifle it to a silent sob, but my nightgown would be damp as if my whole body had been crying. I was terrified I was possessed of an evil spirit, because the dreams were so real. I wanted to talk to someone about them, but I didn't dare. I knew Daddy was doing his best and still missed Mother terribly. Last night he cried into my hair again. He called out Mother's name and when I got up to go to bed, he held me in his arms with such a hard hug that my breasts were crushed into his chest. I couldn't tell him it hurt—he was already hurting so much. I was so tired I started to fall asleep standing there. When he kissed me, I tasted the salty tears on his lips. I wished I could help his loneliness, but I didn't know what to do.

I went to my room and was about to get into bed when I felt eyes on me. I looked up. On the window ledge lay a garter snake that had slithered through the river rocks forming the basement walls. As I stood paralyzed, the snake uncoiled, dropped down the wall, and slipped through a hole into the grease pit. I slid into bed as far from the wall as possible, took up a book of Shakespeare's plays, and disappeared into *As You Like It*. In a while I was so tired I no longer cared about the snake and I could sleep.

As soon as Ophelia came back from Colorado City and married Sidney, she was called to teach at our school. We all loved her class; she taught us new ways to sew our own dresses and different ways to style our long hair. She started a little club just for us older girls. We met at lunch hours across the creek on the far hill past Lydia's house where we would sit and talk about our dreams for the future without being pestered by the big boys. We loved to hear Ophelia talk about girls from Colorado City and find out how different they were from us. She said even though she liked Celeste and her family when she lived with them, there weren't many other girls like her in the whole city. With tears in her eyes she told us about the Williams cousins and how much she missed them.

Since she was sixteen and all grown-up now, we wanted to know if she would have married any one of the men in the group if the prophet said it was God's will. She refused to answer us and wouldn't talk much for the rest of the noon hour. Just before the bell rang, she brightened up. "I'm going to ask Janessa if we can have a picnic with our club next Saturday. I found this great big rock halfway up to the shale last time I climbed the mountain. It's the best rock I've found yet. I'll bring the sandwiches and we can make a special day of it." We raced down the hill with our dresses and hair flying, excited that we had something to talk about besides who was supposed to marry who.

Much to my surprise, Jan let me go. We had a grand time hiking up the mountain, and when we arrived at the rock we were famished. We devoured the chicken sandwiches and sat around sucking pickles and talking about future plans for our club and our upcoming graduation. When the two quarts of pickles were gone, we christened our special meeting place Pickle Rock. Aline, Jean, and I talked a lot about marriage, trying to guess who the prophet would place us with. Aline said she would absolutely refuse to marry almost anyone we knew. I tried to reason with her.

"I know I could marry anyone the Lord chose for me. Daddy said the Lord would never ask us to do anything save He prepared a way. The only sacrifice required of us is the sacrifice of a broken heart and a contrite spirit."

Aline turned on me angrily. "Just shut up, Deb...Sometimes

you're really annoying. Anyone I would even think of marrying I'm already related to." She shuddered. "I would never marry a Whitmer…and you can have Wilhelm Mueller or Dolan Barnley if you think you could stomach it." I was about to open my mouth when she cut me off. "No, I would never marry your dad. He makes me sick. He used to make me come with him and Irene when he would take her into the top of the school and sit with her in the dark and kiss her before they were married. I think he's a horny creep." Her harsh criticism of Daddy filled me with horror, and then I couldn't talk because I was crying. Jean put her arm through mine.

Aline kept talking as if she hadn't noticed the tears. "This is supposed to be a secret. Uncle Michael's Gilby is coming for the graduation. He loves Emilia and is coming to take her back to the States with him. Aunt Pauline and Aunt Loren wrote Mom and told her. Mom says she doesn't care if Dad or your dad says that Uncle Michael has gone to hell because he wouldn't go along with the crooks in the States. Emilia would be better off with Gilby than stuck with some horny old man." Aline's nostrils flared and she accented her words with sharp hand motions.

I knew Emilia didn't want anyone to know, but she had been secretly married to her own dad, Uncle Isaac. I bit my lip. As the anxiety built up, I got a terrible pain in my stomach. I decided I better make sure I got to talk to Daddy tonight. He would know what to do. I couldn't understand why Aline seemed so happy and pleasant when she was with Laman and Celeste and so unhappy when she was with us. Celeste was helping her make her graduation dress and would be doing her hair for her. The poor girl would just die if she knew the way Aline really felt about the apostles. Her calling our leaders crooks was the very worst thing I could imagine. What would ever become of anyone for speaking so terribly about God's own messengers?

When I talked to Daddy he said Uncle Michael was a silly old man, and the Lord would never permit him to hurt His Work. He said the devil always tried to defile the Lord's anointed by lying about them, and that Aline's mother was the girl's biggest problem. His face was sad. "Naomi will have to pay the price for the terrible lies she's telling her children. Her daughters will be nothing more than common harlots." I was only a little relieved by Daddy's message. It sounded as if there was little hope for Naomi's children and for my only friend, Jeanie.

The prophet decided we would call our school Hope Private and our colors would be white and blue. The whole community was excited about our first graduation and the visit from our special guest, Uncle Roy. Jan had worked night and day for years to finish her grade twelve, and it seemed fitting that she receive her diploma with Martin, Aline, and Emilia. We all swooped from home to home cleaning and painting, and everyone cooperated to get the school painted and the yards cleaned up.

In the middle of the schoolyard, Laman created a huge fountain with colored lights around the base that lit up the entire yard. The flowers in his gardens were in full bloom, and the vines covering the front of the school were a vivid green. At night with the lights on and the music Celeste played on the piano or a tape going, this spot truly felt like paradise.

The prophet was bringing several of his apostles to the graduation. Jan told us we were more honored than if the Prime Minister of Canada or the President of the United States were coming. Janessa's floor-length graduation dress was made of white Fortrel. She claimed it was the wedding dress she never had and her grad dress all in one. She cried when she told us it had taken her ten years to finish her grade twelve, teach all of us, and give birth to five children at the same time. She was right—it was really quite an accomplishment. When she got her graduation certificate from the B.C. Correspondence Branch, she had passed with high honors in all of her courses.

Gilby arrived. You could tell with just a glance at him that the evil influences of the world were already ruining his life. He had long sideburns like a hippie or a rock singer, and he stood with slumped shoulders. He wore tight pants. Emilia went out with him one night, and she must have told him the truth about her being married. Daddy said Lemuel took Gilby for a walk, too, and told him "where the skunk ate the cabbage." Gilby went over to Naomi's to lick his wounds. Daddy said that was a good place for him. He said misery loved company, and that Gilby wasn't very bright if he thought people wouldn't know he was complaining against the apostles.

We couldn't have asked for better weather for the graduation. The sun was hot, the skies were blue, and a gentle breeze blew down from the mountain and across the pond to add to the magical feeling of the evening. This ceremony would have been perfect if Gilby had just left. Daddy and Uncle Isaac told us to try to pray him away, but he was hanging around like he was still waiting for something even after Emilia told him she couldn't marry him.

The afternoon was a wild flurry of curling all of the girls' long thick hair, waving the boys' short hair, and setting last-minute tucks in the white dresses and the blue shirts. It was hard to believe everyone looked so grown-up.

Before we knew it, we were in front of everyone, and Daddy was praising the efforts of our community and crying as he said, "This is truly a land flowing with milk and honey. We are blessed above all other people. Nowhere in the entire world are there such beautiful children as these born under the covenant of plural marriage. From here to Mexico, wherever our people are, you find the Lord is blessing us beyond our comprehension, and we must be willing to do our part. Our children are being prepared and will be turned over to the Lord's prophet when the boys turn twelve and the girls turn fifteen. These children no longer belong to me. They belong to the Lord. If I can take my daughter to the Lord's servant and put her hand in his and say here is a vessel ready to be a mother in Israel, this is the sole purpose of my life. When my sons turn twelve and are given the priesthood of the living God, then I no longer have any right trying to control their lives unless I present them to the prophet and tell him we are as clay in the hands of the Potter. Then, and only then, if the prophet turns my sons back over to me for a while, do I have a right to go any further in my training of them...And I do it in fear and trembling at the awesome responsibility of it. In the words of one of our early leaders, 'I would rather see my daughter in the grave than to see her marry outside of the purview of the leaders of our Holy Work.' "

During Daddy's whole talk, the leaders sat in the front row and solemnly nodded their heads. By the time Daddy was finished, I was trembling and weeping—grateful he was so in tune with the will of Heavenly Father. I knew of a certainty all I would ever need to worry about was taking Daddy's direction.

Aline and Jean and Nettie and I changed into our new crinolines and dresses. They were made of cloth with a Hawaiian print and looked so exotic with our flower leis. The lights were dimmed and the ingenious moon that Laman had made framed our faces with colored light. We began to sway with the music—it became us and we were the music. We all sang a song about the haunting islands of Hawaii, stardust, and enchanting midnight skies. The trance deepened. Uncle Isaac was just on the outside rim of the light. His eyes were as dark blue and mysterious as the bottom of the Sea of Galilee, and his gaze was locked on mine.

He asked me to dance with him. Being with him was heavenly; I felt as if I were floating across the floor. His eyes twinkled and it seemed we were the same age instead of his being forty years older. In Uncle Isaac's arms I felt so safe—like a woman grown like a sheaf of wheat to fulfill the law of Sarah and be a mother in Israel. He whispered the Song of Solomon while we whirled around the room:

"Thy two breasts are like two young roes that are twins, which feed among the lilies...My dove, my undefiled is but one; she is the only one of her mother, she is the choice one of her that bear her. The daughters saw her, and blessed her; yea, the queens and the concubines, and they praised her. Who is she that looketh forth as the morning, fair as the moon, clear as the sun, and terrible as an army with banners?"*

The rest of the words blended with the music, filling my bosom with the joy I knew I would feel being a queen and a goddess for the eternities with Uncle Isaac. It was easy for me to see why the apostles said we were so blessed with the opportunity to marry the older men. Compared to Jonah or Martin, Uncle Isaac was like

*Verses from the Bible, Song of Solomon, chapter 4: 5 and chapter 6: 9–10.

majesty in the presence of his silly subjects. In Uncle Isaac's arms, I could even forget Jan's beatings. When, for a moment, I did remember, I suddenly realized she would never beat me again if I were married to her father. I would then be one of her mothers.

At Uncle Isaac's attention, my thirteen-year-old breasts tingled with an energy that invaded my whole body. I swayed to the music and imagined myself gazing into the eternities. When the song was over, the other girls turned to sit, but I couldn't move until Jean tugged on my arm. With a terrible effort, I pulled my heart and my body back out of Uncle Isaac's eyes and sat down beside my friend. The congratulations, the music, and the dancing were all dreamlike after that. I managed to shake Uncle Isaac's hand at least twice. The way he touched my hand left me feeling as if he had worshiped my whole body.

When everyone else was in the school eating and dancing, I went out onto the lawn. The music filtered softly through the door and windows, and it filled me like a glass of bubbly yarrow beer. I started to twirl and leap and float like the ballerina I dreamed of being. I leapt higher and faster until I felt almost weightless. I was the Little Mermaid, whose humble wish was to be a sea breeze if she could only kiss the prince this once. On one pirouette, when my feet touched the earth, I was facing the door of the school. Standing in the shadows was Gilby.

I wanted to pretend I hadn't seen him; he would destroy the sacred mission of our Work if he could. I whirled away and when I looked again he was gone, and Jean and Nettie were standing there. I tried to stop then, but my legs turned to jelly and I sank into the grass. They asked me what I was possessed of. Nettie's petite form was indignant. "Deb, you know we could see your underpants. What if we were someone else? You're always doing some crazy thing. Too bad if you're hungry, the best food's all gone." She looked at her plate. "Here, you can finish the rest of mine if you want."

The next week Nettie, Jean, Aline, Ophelia, Emilia, and I went down to the Creston flats to rogue. How I hated those early morning rides when I would much rather have been sleeping. All my companions shared my feelings. Not one of us would be here by choice pulling mustard weeds out of clover fields for the gentile farmers Daddy knew from his work. Anyone who had ever rogued before knew the best time of day to pull the weeds was in the early morning so the millions of honeybees that pollinated the crops would still be sleeping. When the day was hot, the bees became very angry at the long skirts and the disturbing human smell.

At first we all worked in silence. Aline stomped along yanking at the yellow heads of the mustard weed. "Soon I'll never have to do this rotten kind of work again...Gilby says he'll take me home with him, and I'm going." Her dark eyes flashed fire, literally daring a negative response. "Dad doesn't want me to go. He said the apostles would let me take my pick of anyone I wanted to marry in the whole group if I would just stay. I told him no!"

Emilia cried and sullenly picked at the mustard. Ophelia was silent. Jean was silent. The blue sky and the sun became an oppressive, evil thing. I didn't realize it was going to happen until it did. All the passion and devout belief in my body burst from me at once as if the crumbling walls of a mighty dam suddenly released a great flood of water. I turned on Aline. "You have come under the influence of the evil spirit that Gilby has with him! Uncle Michael has been lying about the prophet, and now Gilby's trying to steal you away from the Lord. Heavenly Father will never send his chosen spirits to be your children, and you'll die like the woman who ran away from her husband in that booklet your dad reads to us."

The horror and pain in *To the Buffetings,* where a young plural wife ran away from her husband's home to be with a swindler and con man, was real to each one of us in the clover field. None of us could picture leaving a beautiful baby born under the covenant of the Lord sleeping all alone in its bed. Uncle Isaac read the story to us in our Sunday school class, and his own daughters had heard it many times. The contempt he had for the adulterous girl reached into this field and wrapped us like the tentacles of a deadly giant squid. The girl's fate was ugly and befitted the unthinkable evil of her breaking her covenants with a righteous man who was on a mission for God. Short years later, this woman, haggard and dying of a gross venereal disease, was found by a missionary to whom she told the story. Her five children were pale and sickly—suffering horribly from the result of her wretched choice. Her testimony reached though all the years and came spilling out of my mouth in a torrent of fear.

"Please, Aline...please pray about it. I know Heavenly Father will change your mind. Your dad is the file leader. How could you think of doing anything so terrible when he's promised you can choose anyone you want in our whole Work?"

Aline attacked me with fire in her voice. "I will never marry anyone in the Work! Irene isn't happy with your dad. Lydia is crazy, and you can't show me one other woman who's really happy."

With despair in my heart, I tried again. "Your mother doesn't even try to come under the direction of your dad. If she did, she would be happy and so would you. I could marry any good priest-hood man. Your life will be hell if you leave, Aline, and then it will be too late."

The image of her living her life with the son of an apostate and ending up with sin eating the very flesh off her bones was more than I could stand. I wept into the bouquets of mustard I held in each hand. When a bee stung me on the face, I screeched and wailed even louder.

Aline looked at me with contempt. "Deb, you give me the creeps."

CHAPTER 13

"We must be physically fit! We must be physically fit! I am youth...I am health...I am strength." Uncle Isaac's dark blue eyes blazed. His body vibrated as he paced back and forth on the stage. Swinging his arms vigorously, he did several jumping jacks, then firmly grabbed the sides of the plywood pulpit and preached about our health being too important to be taken for granted. Finally in a fit of passion, he left the stage and maneuvered up and down the aisles as he orated. Like the captain of a pirate ship, he ordered his crew to man the battle stations and load their cannons.

He ranted about how the good old mother church had fallen into the rankest apostasy—Uncle Isaac was in true form for another lecture. Every session ended with the pressing message: "We are the heart's core that has been led by the hand of our leaders out of the mother church, the whore of all the earth, into these mountains to usher in the millennium."

Uncle Isaac taught the teenage classes, while Daddy and Uncle Kelvin went to a different room to teach the adults about the Doctrine and Covenants or The Book of Mormon and to discuss the secrets of the kingdom. I was relieved I was the right age to stay in Uncle Isaac's class, because I would have hated to miss it. Although I was ashamed to admit it, I wished Daddy were not so friendly to Uncle Kelvin. Everyone muttered about his strange parables and his worldly support of the town in his job as a street sweeper. Association with him hurt Daddy's image.

The decay of their classes began gradually. One by one the adults stayed in Uncle Isaac's class until finally Daddy and Uncle Kelvin only had one or two people to teach. They encouraged others to attend their scripture study, saying everyone should be in his proper place after sacrament meeting. All of Uncle Isaac's faithful fans were furious that their place in his class would be questioned. For weeks the vicious name-calling and bickering went on. The tone of suspicion and dissension reminded me of the horrible infighting before Uncle Michael moved to the States. Everyone found a way to tell Uncle Isaac about the insinuations that they were being babied in his class and needed to graduate to the "meat of the gospel." They all told him the other classes were horribly boring compared to his—that he had special ways of making the gospel understandable and fun instead of tedious.

Uncle Isaac settled the matter once and for all in a sacrament meeting. "When we are given an assignment and think we have a little authority, we can let it go to our heads. When this happens, know this: we are immediately out of order with our file leader and are in danger of the deadly sin of criticism. The pure in heart will be in harmony with their file leader and want to be near him. They will not be comfortable being taught by any other voice; just as water seeks its own level, so will the chosen of the people be drawn to the pure words of their leaders. Christ said, 'My sheep hear my voice and a stranger they will not follow.' "

Daddy and Uncle Kelvin left the meeting shaking their heads. "Well, Kelvin," Daddy said wryly, "I'm not sure what we've just been told, but I take it there will be no more adult classes."

Uncle Isaac spent more and more time in his classes talking about health and the evil schemes of the devil working with industry to poison the unsuspecting people of the earth with preservatives and chemicals in their food. He challenged us all to go to the exercise classes he had instructed Lemuel to teach in one of the sheds that Uncle Michael built before this land was United Effort property.

Uncle Isaac seemed seven feet tall when he straightened up and stabbed more words at us. My body and my soul responded to his challenges, and I was devoured by his energy.

"I have been to see more doctors the last six months than in all my life put together. The Spirit of God cannot dwell in an unclean tabernacle, and all the devils in hell conspire to tempt us to eat chocolate bars and white sugar and white flour." Uncle Isaac spat out the words like they were boiling lye on his tongue. "The doctors suspect cancer—leukemia. They say I will be a dead man. We must cleanse our bodies of all the impurities of the world. How can we have the unmitigated gall to suppose we can live the laws of Abraham and Sarah, the highest law of the celestial kingdom, plurality of wives, if we cannot control our earthly appetites and passions?"

My heart flopped heavily in my chest as the reality of his statements sunk home. Uncle Isaac couldn't die. I had to be his wife. I knew it was the eternal reason I was born.

Faithful to the direction of the file leader, Daddy took us to Lem's exercise classes. We ran one way, then the other. We did sit-ups on the cold cement until our stomachs screamed. We did every military exercise Lem had ever heard of, as well as the ones he was learning from his gentile judo instructor. We practiced the judo horse, advancing on our imaginary opponents with wild screams of defiance. Sometimes Uncle Isaac was there, and he showed us how his fifty-five-year-old body could stretch taut between two chairs, and how two children or a grown woman could sit on his stomach, his muscles supporting their weight. I wanted to feel his body so badly my fingers ached…but I stayed behind Jean.

Sometimes he overdid it and didn't come to exercise class for a while, but I still thought about him. I could be so tired I was sure I couldn't jog another step, then his image flashed into my mind and my body kept on past the fatigue and pain. Sometimes I chanted "The Lord is My Shepherd" over and over. My body was not strong, though, and Jeanie and James did many repetitions beyond when I had to quit. I became obsessed with the fitness Uncle Isaac worshiped and the youth he wanted back. Part of my late-night routine became sit-ups over a chair until my stomach ached deep inside. Other nights I ran in the moonlight, imagining Uncle Isaac with me. In my mind we leapt through the stars and the moonbeams, and our feet never touched the ground.

Every morning on the way to school I begged Jan to let me off at the gate to the ranch when she stopped to pick her mother up. I ran up the hill to help Bettilyn carry her homework box to the van. I would wait at the door for the box, hoping to see Uncle Isaac. Then I'd run back down the hill and push the box into the van before heading down the long road toward the school. Sometimes I got to run with Jean and James; other times, I followed lengths behind them as they ran ahead like deer. Each time my feet hit the smooth hard dirt, I prayed for the strength of my body to infuse and extend life for Uncle Isaac.

Bettilyn and Jan often sat together at noon and cried about him. Jeanie and James were downcast as we did our lessons together. Sometimes we were able to take our minds off the terrible reality by playing basketball in the yard.

I memorized "O My Father" on the piano. Whenever I played it, Jeanie would stand beside me and tell me she knew I was thinking about her dad again. Every opportunity I had to talk to Mother, I would plead with her, "Uncle Isaac is dying of leukemia, Mother. Heavenly Father already has you. Please tell Him He should wait at least thirty or forty years for Uncle Isaac."

I was always anxious and filled with the feeling that if I prayed hard enough, Heavenly Father would tell me how to heal Uncle Isaac. His sister, Elizabeth Russell, had a book called *Joseph Smith and Herbal Medicine*. We knew God had inspired the book because of all the miraculous stories of the healing of faithful Saints obeying Joseph Smith's words.

I kept thinking Elizabeth would be my sister-in-law if the Lord said I could marry Uncle Isaac. I could tell she would like the idea, because she told me what herbs to gather and brew so he could be healed. She was glad to find someone who would search for the plants and brew them with the needed faith—someone to do this labor of love for her brother. Bettilyn and Jan both thought the herb cures were strange, but as I walked the fields gathering sour dock*

---

*Sour dock, also called curly dock or yellow dock, can be used for tea or in salads. The root has had medicinal purposes from ancient times.

and crawled through the underbrush pulling violet roots, I felt the power of the earth was in my fingers. When I passed the gallon of strong tea to Uncle Isaac and his hand brushed mine, my fingers tingled for the rest of the day. It made me feel so important when I knew he drank my tea.

It was a bit of a mystery when Uncle Isaac started his treatment. There was a lot of talk about the horrors of chemotherapy. His whole body became swollen and puffy; his nose bled frequently and apparently without provocation. When he was away in Vancouver for his sessions of radiation, I had a strange feeling of unease and loneliness. I realized if the Lord gave the prophet the word that I was to become Uncle Isaac's wife for eternity, much of my time would be spent with Bettilyn. I watched and listened to her, trying to imagine myself as her sister wife. The knowledge that Emilia, Lydia, and Naomi would be my sister wives, too, was challenging. I felt sorry for Emilia since she was still not a wife in anything but name. For some reason, she was having difficulty with the transition from being Uncle Isaac's daughter to being his wife. She could not force herself to lie with him. She just hadn't realized yet that she was one of the luckiest girls in the entire world.

Whenever I thought about her situation, I knew I wouldn't question God's will about how life was happening. I often wished I had been the older one. When Emilia was married to Uncle Isaac, his body was still strong and hard, and he could work most of his sons into the ground. Since this cursed disease had gripped him, his stomach and face had swollen, and he had sores that never seemed to heal. If I had been Emilia, I would have tried to conceive a child every year. When I thought about Uncle Isaac, all I could remember was the strong, passionate man who had danced me around the stars at the graduation ceremony. It didn't matter how sick he was or how different his body had become. If Heavenly Father told the prophet Uncle Isaac was the man I had covenanted to marry, I'd be the happiest girl in our Work.

Every chance I got I'd hang out at the big house, waiting to see him. I'd sit on the top of the basement stairs at the time he was likely to come in from doing chores. I lived for those private special looks he saved just for those moments when we were alone.

One day Jan gave us permission to walk to Uncle Isaac's and wait there for her while she finished preparing assignments. It was a mild day and the long dirt road was treacherously slippery, with melting ice in the middle and deep puddles in the ruts on either side. Nettie and I struggled to keep our long dresses out of the water, but by the time we got to the ranch, they were soaking wet and soiled with mud. We got to go into the house and watch Uncle Isaac's television. He had changed his mind about the evils of watching TV when someone found him a perfectly good one at the dump.

After a few minutes of watching *Dialing for Dollars*, I left the other kids and went down the basement stairs in hopes of finding him. The huge cast-iron wood stove was belting out heat, and I was soaking it up in an attempt to dry out my wet feet and dress. The lights were off but I was content to sit and bask in the glow from the stove. The television paused for a moment over my head, and I heard the muffled sounds of sobbing from a dark corner of the basement. Just as I was about to turn the light on to see who it was, the heavy door to the cool room used for storing canned goods swung open. The light from the bare bulb inside illuminated Emilia and Sidney. The skin of her breasts glowed ivory. Her head rested on Sidney's shoulder. They moved as if in a dream, slow dancing out into the main part of the basement. Emilia's fingers absently fumbled at the buttons of her dress in a half-hearted attempt to cover her nakedness.

I ran up the stairs and turned on the light for fear they would stumble upon me in the dark. They both blinked at the sudden brightness. Their faces betrayed their shock and embarrassment. Emilia's lips and cheeks were a blush of scarlet, and Sidney's big ears turned red. Quickly, he stepped away from her.

He started blathering. "Deb…Emilia needs a friend. She needs hugs and a friendly shoulder. When I'm home, it's the least I can do to help my favorite sister-in-law out." He hugged Emilia awkwardly with one arm. The red flush of the girl's face faded to a ghostly white. The tears she'd been struggling to hold back broke free, and she spun out of Sidney's arm to flee out the bottom door.

Sidney looked dismayed. After a few steps in her direction, he stopped and came back. "You know, Emilia really needs a friend," he stammered. "And Uncle Isaac has asked me to help her out...He says he trusts me more than anyone else." He came up the stairs and extended his arms to me. "You know what it's like to need someone, Deb." When I ducked his hug, he charged out the door after Emilia. I sat looking into the empty basement. My mind was whirling. I knew that Sidney wasn't just hugging Emilia and touching her hands...I was sure he was touching her breasts, too.

Daddy and Uncle Isaac had both started teaching us that when we were with the opposite sex, the only body part we should touch was the hands. They insisted the Lord would make the decision and tell the prophet whom we should touch in a different way when we were assigned to marry. Only the prophet would know for sure who was promised to us in the spirit world. How often had I seen Daddy cry when he talked in church about the immoral men in the LDS church who pawed and handled his sisters before they were married? He always went on at great length how fortunate we were that the inspiration of our leaders saved us from the terrible evil of courting. If Sidney and Emilia got too close and couldn't help themselves, they might end up having intercourse. Then both Ophelia and Uncle Isaac would have to be told, and the sin would be adultery.

In school one day Janessa read a sermon Brigham Young had given in the Salt Lake City Tabernacle. It was about adultery and how the only way to repent from the sin was to offer yourself up to be blood-atoned. He said if he ever caught one of his wives in bed with another man, he would kill them both on the spot. Worlds without end, they would thank him for it because they could then be forgiven. I was anxious, imagining the dreadful consequences for Emilia and Sidney. Somehow they must be stopped from committing a terrible eternal sin. I knew that Daddy would know what to do. When I was in his arms telling him of my fears—telling him I knew that Sidney and Emilia had been touching more than each other's hands—I was sure I'd done the right thing. Daddy asked me to describe in careful detail everything I saw and exactly what was said.

He broke down and wept, his shoulders bowed in sorrow. "I'm

so sorry you had to witness such a thing, Daughter. They'll have to be dealt with. The forces of procreation and the desire for love between a man and a woman are two of the most powerful feelings created by God. Sidney and Emilia were abusing the beauty of it." Daddy held me close and hard against his chest, and all my fears drained away.

In my nightly prayers I beseeched the Lord to bless me that I may be worthy to be a wife and mother in Israel—clay in the hands of my husband and an example to all good women. Above all else, I prayed for the health of Uncle Isaac. After all, my body was but a fertile field awaiting the planting of his seed. If he died before we were able to accomplish this great task, the spirits of the children in heaven who were waiting to be born to us would be left stranded. If he were to die, I, too, must sacrifice my life like the noble women in India who threw themselves on funeral pyres to be burnt alive beside the bodies of their husbands.

I found myself poring over the scriptures more and more often. The Truth books became my constant source of inspiration. Daddy often read from those same volumes in church when he was in the pulpit. He quoted them to us at home all the time and challenged the whole family to compete to see who could memorize the most scriptures. Aside from Jan and Elsa, and Daddy of course, Nettie and Brent seemed to remember the most. Elsa could read faster than anyone, and Irene swore she had a memory like a steel trap.

Hearing the prophet himself speak about the stories in the Truth books really brought them home to me, and made it obvious that Satan had inspired the worldly governments and the Mormon Church to persecute our people and destroy the Work. We read the complete history of the 1953 Short Creek raid and studied the pictures of the women, men, and children persecuted by the States of Utah and Arizona. The state troopers doing the work of the devil had ripped the women and children away from the priesthood men who were their husbands and fathers. The devil stirred up all kinds of difficulties for our people, but the power of God on behalf of our prophet put him to shame. Uncle Roy saved all the women and children from the evil-designing men and brought them home where they belonged. The Lord even inspired Uncle Roy as to where to have geologists dig for uranium to help pay off the debt created by our defense lawyers.

We were truly blessed that our prophet and his apostles visited Canada every three months now so they could update us on what God had in mind for his people. They arrived shortly after the gentile media made a big fuss about the United States being the first world power to build a spaceship and send a man to walk on the moon. Newspapers, radio, and television were talking non-stop about beating Russia in the race for space. We were all excited, and most everyone managed to find a television to watch "the moonwalk" over and over again. Uncle Isaac reminded us that our prophet had said, "God would never, worlds without end, allow a man to walk on the moon. The moon and all the celestial bodies in the heavens were protected from man by God, and He would never allow man to reach any of His creations off this earth."

That certainly dampened the excitement in our group, and some of the kids were even wondering if the prophet had been wrong. We all stopped talking about it until he arrived to explain to us why the newspapers and television were contradicting what he'd told us. We were relieved to find out how Satan had inspired the government of the United States to create fake pictures of the moonwalk in order to further trick and confuse people on Earth. After the meeting, everyone was distraught to discover the lengths the devil would go to to make people "believe a lie and be damned." Jan immediately included the prophet's teachings about the treachery of the gentile nations in our classes at school so we wouldn't be tempted to believe what we heard on television or happened to read. We just needed to be very sure to remember that Satan's number-one tool to deceive and destroy people through temptation was television.

For weeks now I had been restless and filled with fear that Uncle Isaac would die before I could become his wife. I'd been reading about Short Creek and became enthralled with the story of Vera Johnson. She had been the most faithful of the women, and her steadfastness had made her famous among our people. The State tried to make an example of her, figuring if they could win the right in court to take her children away, then they could proceed to disband the entire polygamous community. They talked about the success of the program to Americanize the Indians and felt it would work equally well with the polygamists. Vera stood her ground with her children, and the Lord fought the battle. Hand in hand, the faithful men declared the troopers would have to drench the sand with their blood before they would give up their right to live plural marriage. With this solid front of support for Vera, the result was that all of her children were returned to her, and she went back to her home in Short Creek.

She was a heroine like Joan of Arc. We had learned about Joan of Arc on the *Dialing for Dollars* show, and I dreamed of sacrificing like her someday. With each re-reading of the story in the Truth book, my heart swelled with the splendor of Vera Johnson's faith. The victory of Uncle Roy in saving her proved beyond a doubt that he was a prophet and the Lord was with his Work.

I put down my book, overcome with the desire to be about my calling and to become a strong woman in Zion. From my big velvet chair in the corner of the living room, I realized Daddy and I were alone. He was still reading The Book of Mormon. Everyone else was either already asleep or nursing a baby to sleep for the night. I flew to his side on the sofa.

"Daddy! I must see Uncle Roy Johnson...I've been fasting and praying, and I know the Lord wants me to marry Uncle Isaac."

Daddy looked at me in surprise and dismay. "Oh Daughter, you know we need to keep our feelings in order so the Lord can let Uncle Roy know what we are supposed to do. Marriage is the most important part of our life to take direction in. I never believed you would get your heart set on anyone."

He slipped his arms around me and squeezed tightly. I tried not to notice the tears in his eyes or the look of disappointment on his face...My calling was urgent and I just had to be true to it, even if Daddy was temporarily disappointed. Wringing my hands together, I answered, "I'm certain Uncle Isaac and I made covenants to be together in this life when we were still in the spirit world—you told me that sometimes the Lord will reveal this to the woman. I know I'm only fourteen years old, but I feel much older than that...and you know Uncle Isaac could die."

I was rattling through my words without breathing. I took a couple of quick gasps, stared into Daddy's eyes, and pleaded, "I can't wait...Please present me to Uncle Roy." I didn't dare mention to Daddy that the other reason I needed to marry Uncle Isaac was to ensure I wouldn't be beaten by Jan even one more time.

I thought back to one of the worst episodes with her and her flailing fists. It happened as Jan was preparing for visits from both Grandmother and the prophet. She was going to town for groceries so she'd be ready to entertain. Her intense blue eyes burned through black horn-rimmed glasses, instilling a sense of terror deep within me. She produced her list of jobs for me to do and shoved it into my hand. "Make sure you clean the bathroom, the porch, and the patio. I want all the potatoes in the pan peeled so we are ready for the Sabbath...And make sure you beat all the rugs from the living room and get started cleaning and waxing the lino."

She opened the door, then stopped short and glared down at the floor where I sat polishing shoes. "If you expect to get done, you better take those cookstoves off your feet and get moving!"

I cringed. Irene looked exhausted just listening to Jan. Her cheeks were red and puffy from the heat, and her legs were half again their normal size. She was in advanced pregnancy and had been feeling poorly for weeks. During a prenatal checkup, the doctor discovered she had diabetes as a complication of her pregnancy. He recommended bedrest.

Now Irene stood stoically over the ironing board, processing one item of clothing after the other. Carefully folding a flowing white temple garment, she glanced over her shoulder as the door slammed behind Jan. She grabbed a white shirt from the heaping basket at her feet, and we continued the conversation we'd started before Jan's interruption. Aggressively scrubbing the iron back and forth over the shirt, Irene repeated how much she hated Elsa.

I grabbed one of Daddy's shoes and daubed it with black polish. After his pair, I had sixteen more to go. Polishing shoes was an art form, and every time I did it, I thought about Mother's teaching me how to shine my first pair of patent leather loafers.

I looked up at Irene and answered with Daddy's best logic, "How can you really love Daddy and not Elsa, when she's part of Daddy and he must love her, too?" I was sure that when I was married, loving my sister wives would come naturally, especially if we as wives were all in tune with our husband. "You know the law of Sarah is the highest law a women can be called to live." I brushed aggressively at the toe of Daddy's shoe, took a deep breath, and looked up at Irene. "What would you think if I was meant to marry Uncle Isaac? Just think, I would sort of be one of your mothers. Jan would never be able to beat one of her mothers, would she?"

Irene looked at me as if I had suddenly sprouted horns. She snorted derisively. "You've lost your mind. Why would you ever want to marry Dad? Anyway, being married isn't a guarantee that you won't get beat. My mom beat Lydia more than once after she married Dad—one time was when Lydia screamed and cursed at me. Mom gave her a bloody nose and she had an epileptic fit. Dad had to move her into town with her mother again." Irene rolled her eyes and shrugged. "I guess my dad would be as good a person as anybody since you can't marry your dad, which would be the best thing you could do."

I dreamily poked along with the shoes, cleaned the bathroom, and finished beating the first throw rug out on the patio. Standing in the fresh air, I dreamed about fulfilling my mandate for the Work. Irene doggedly stood at her post and was ironing the last basket of white garments.

"You know, you'd best hurry up," she called. "Jan'll be home soon and all this daydreaming hasn't helped get your work finished. I don't know about you, but I can't handle any more of her fits this week."

The words had scarcely left her mouth when we heard the sound of tires crunching gravel on the roadway.

"Jan wouldn't beat me this close to Grandmother being here." My words were confident, but the blood left my face and my whole body suddenly felt weak.

The door burst open and Jan appeared. She looked harried, with beads of sweat on her forehead; hair escaped from the bun on her head and hung in tendrils about her face. The packages in her arms shook as she surveyed the living room. Her eyes narrowed. Without so much as a word, she took the bags into the kitchen and deposited them on the cupboard. I swept the area around the throw rug before I carefully knelt to position it. My hands were trembling, and I refused to look in Jan's direction. Every cell of my body was electric with the vibrations of the floor as she moved deliberately toward me. I forced myself to look into her blazing eyes. The hatred was tangible. She clenched and unclenched her hands and hissed through gritted teeth.

"You haven't finished even one job, and you think you're grown-up. You're the most lame-brained, lazy person I've ever seen. I pity the poor man who'll have to marry you! I'll never be able to hold up my head to anyone who knows I did such a poor job of raising you. Your mother would never forgive me, and the poor family you go into will suffer dearly."

In one cat-like motion she cleared the door to the library, snatched up the nearest copy of the Richards Encyclopedia, and leapt back. Before I could raise my hands to defend myself, she began beating me on the head and back. The blows rained down mercilessly. I tried to get up, but she beat me down again. I screamed in terror. Irene had been standing frozen. When my screams turned to sobs, she wrenched the book from Janessa's hands.

"You have to stop. Isaiah and Selma will be here before long. They'll be able to tell you've been beating on her again...You don't want to kill her!"

Jan relinquished the book and wheeled into the kitchen. Slamming the cupboard doors, she started slashing with a long-bladed kitchen knife at a head of lettuce. Her bawling was occasionally interrupted by huge gasping sounds. Later she went into her bedroom and locked the door.

By the time I finished my jobs, my sobs had turned into a hard pain in my throat that no sound or feeling could get past. As I peeled the last of the potatoes, my mind was lost in a book I'd been reading the night before by Thomas B. Costain called *The Black*

Rose. I was Maryam, the beautiful Chinese woman. I was wandering the streets of medieval England with my little son crying, "Walter and England!"—they were the only words of English I knew.

Suddenly, Nettie appeared in front of me. Very softly she said, "Mother wants you in her room." The expression on her delicate face begged me: Please make up with her. You know you can never win—just tell her you're sorry and get it over with. She left quietly; her long thick braids seemed almost too much of a burden for her tiny body to carry. My back and arms ached; I flinched as my fingertips probed a huge bruise on my head.

I knocked on the hollow mahogany door of Jan's bedroom, the same room in which Mother spent her last few months in this house. Jan told me to come in. The room was noticeably cooler than the living room, as it was shaded from the afternoon sun by the huge cedar trees on the north side. On stiffly wooden legs, I marched to the side of the bed where she lay nursing her baby.

She patted the heavy white cotton of the chenille bedspread. "Sit here." Her expression softened. "You realize why I lost my temper, don't you? If you weren't so difficult, I could make better sense out of our relationship. I'm ashamed of beating you, though." She sighed. I couldn't force myself to sit beside her. She heaved herself off the bed and unlatched her baby. I fought a gagging spasm when she draped her arms around me; Janessa seemed totally unconcerned that a constant flow of her milk soaked into her clothing. Her breasts were fully exposed as she crushed me to them. Her lips were right next to my ear when she wept into my hair and begged me to forgive her and give her another chance. I was smothering in revulsion; I wanted to push her away and run outside. The Lord is my shepherd. He maketh me to lie down in green pastures. He preparest a table before me in the midst of my enemies. His rod and His staff will protect me. I fought to calm myself and hear her words.

"You know I've tried my best to make up for your mother being gone. We can't disappoint your grandmother with problems when she comes so seldom. I know I can make this up to you…Just don't worry your grandmother with this." Her grip tightened. "Promise me!" she demanded. I nodded.

She needn't have worried. Grandmother and Grandpa arrived

late. Sweet greetings and loving words filled the house. I knew Daddy and Grandpa would be going to the men's secret meeting, and Grandmother would be doing the women's ordinances. While I set the napkins around the table in the kitchen, I overheard Grandmother speaking with enthusiasm to Jan.

"I feel so humble and grateful to be called to do washings and anointings. Won't it be marvelous when the temples are restored, so this women's work can be carried on within the sacred walls designed for it?"

Jan's voice sounded melancholic. "One of the things I love most about being pregnant is receiving my washings and anointings from you and Mother. It's reminiscent of the temple work done in the Old and New Testaments by the priests and priestesses—the holy robes, each layer with a special significance. It would be the ultimate privilege to have these garments sealed onto my body." She looked at the wall clock. "Well, we best be about our business or we'll make you all late. Adam does not suffer tardiness gladly, as you well know."

Grandmother smiled at her. "Bless you…you sound like your dad when you speak of these things. He's such an inspiration and understands the gospel in a divine way."

Jan announced to Daddy that the meal was ready, and we all gathered and knelt in prayer. After Daddy told the Lord how grateful we were that He saw fit to bring the brethren to Canada again, he asked for a blessing on the food. I said an extra thank you for Grandmother and Grandpa's safe arrival and begged Heavenly Father for Uncle Roy to be inspired that I should marry soon. That way, I could bear covenant children and receive the sacred washings and anointings. To be washed from the crown of my head to the soles of my feet and then anointed with oil so every limb and organ would be healthy and protected while elect spirits of the last days formed their earthly bodies within mine would be a glorious, beautiful thing. At that moment the beating of only three hours before seemed insignificant.

To his spellbound audience, Uncle Isaac read about Unc' Billy Possum and Reddy Fox from Thornton W. Burgess, then taught us a lesson about the story. He likened his stories to Christ's parables and seemed in his glory when children gathered at his feet the way they did for Christ in the Bible. We all loved listening to him teach the gospel because his stories made it all so much more interesting.

He explained, "If you understand animals, you'll understand people. Why, I know a lot of people that are sneaky and sly like Reddy and Granny Fox, and others like Sammy Blue Jay, just waiting to get their brethren and the priesthood in trouble with their spying and screeching. The rest of the animals, like thoughtless people, flock to hear the gossip. These useless, dangerous people are like a gaggle of silly geese. They are a stench in the Lord's nostrils, and He will not be mocked."

Whenever Uncle Isaac said the words "gossip" and "stench" together, he ground out the words through clenched teeth and his eyes looked ferocious. I ached to smooth the fierceness from his bristling brow, but once I understood where he was going, I knew there was no hope.

I looked around the room at all Uncle Michael's handiwork as Uncle Isaac thundered on about the world growing dark as a result of betrayal by the apostates. Uncle Michael's trademark was stamped upon the walls of the huge home he had built. Uncle Isaac and Laman had already started to renovate to get rid of the hated colors, the boards, and even the smell.

The other apostate who brought pain to Uncle Isaac's eyes the most often was still among us. She was none other than his own niece and wife, Naomi. The prophet had instructed us all to "pray away" the apostates so they would leave and join the other dogs of the world. With all the praying away we'd been doing, the spirit didn't move Naomi very far. She sold the first home she built to Uncle Isaac for five thousand dollars. He was anxious to get her off his land and away from the group before she polluted any more of the people.

But she did the most amazing thing. She went to the government and put a bid on a tract of land not far from the ranch that Uncle Isaac told her she would never in this world or the next be accepted for. The government gave her homesteading rights and a contract, and she started building another house. Uncle Isaac's pain only grew then, because whenever he went to stay the night with Lydia, he had to walk right past Naomi's new house. It hurt Isaac that it was on land he someday hoped to have for the Work. One day after he and Naomi had had another screaming, cursing fight, he took Jonah away from her and brought him to Bettilyn's. Isaac had moved her into the house he bought from Naomi, so for Jonah it was just like going home.

I was waiting for the lunch box the morning after Jonah went to live with Uncle Isaac and Bettilyn. Uncle Isaac was pacing the kitchen, swinging his arms and stabbing the air with his fingers. His limp was so much worse today that he was walking on his toes. His agitation was palpable.

He swung on me. "You mark my words and write them in stone somewhere. A woman may curse her husband and leave the priesthood and make whores out of her daughters, but she will never get her sons! The sons will go to the father every time, and the woman will go to hell cross lots!" He was shaking violently. Bettilyn seemed mesmerized by his performance. Weeping, she took his arm and led him to his chair.

"There now, Daddy, you've got to calm down. I know you do the best you can. No one could ever ask anyone to do better—not even Christ. We don't know how anyone could ever treat you this way...You know what happens when evil spirits take over. It has happened time and again with both Lydia and Naomi. If they don't explode together, they go off separately, just like Old Faithful. You'd think we'd be used to it by now." She started to giggle crazily through her tears.

During lunch at school, once they were sure that Naomi's children had gone home, Jan and Bettilyn discussed the problem. Jan spoke in an uncharacteristically low tone. "You know, Mother, I'm everlastingly grateful for the kind of example you've been to me as a wife and mother. Naomi has been a workhorse, but she has no idea of the proper order of things, so her daughters don't have the same chances I've had. It's such a pity and such a waste of special covenant spirits."

Bettilyn wrung her hands as she spilled out her anguish to her daughter. "I get so angry when Isaac suffers like he does. Even with all his pain from the chemotherapy, he declares that the rebelliousness within his family causes him more misery. He's hardly spoken for days, and finally this morning he told me he had another visit from the devil. Remember when Lemuel was so sick in the hospital, the devil appeared at the foot of the bed and told Daddy from then on he was waging all-out war on his family? Daddy told me what he recognizes first is the smell of brimstone. He won't tell me what the devil had to say this time. He just goes for long walks alone and talks as if someone is by his side."

The moment Bettilyn saw Naomi's children coming through the trees she patted Jan on the arm and changed the topic of conversation to the school money problems. Commencement was almost upon them again, and she was wondering where the money for material for school clothes was to come from...and then there were plans for the school trip to Cardston in June.

Daddy had brought back hopeful messages from Uncle Roy on two separate occasions, and I was sure in my heart I would soon be Uncle Isaac's bride. I prayed constantly to Heavenly Father that Uncle Roy would make the announcement at the Cardston meeting. One night after everyone else was in bed, Daddy spoke to me with urgency in his voice. "Oh Deb, how I pray you'll be the jewel in some man's crown that I know you could be in mine." With that pronouncement, he drew me close and wept into my hair.

My breasts had grown, and Daddy's massive hugs were becoming increasingly painful. The style of bra that I wore molded my breasts into points that were further emphasized by the bodice of my clothing. The higher the bra straps were pulled, the higher the darts could be. When I was being fitted for the last set of school clothes, Jan forced me to let the straps down before the bodices were fitted because my breasts were indecently high. She and Irene both told me Emilia pulled the straps of her bra so tight that she had a permanent ridge in the bone of her shoulder. They agreed it was indecent and certainly not fitting for a woman of the priesthood, whose body was a sacred vessel to bear children, not a constant source of arousal for men.

I was sure the Cardston trip was going to change my life forever, and I wanted to look special for both the prophet and Uncle

Isaac. I was delighted when Daddy gave me thirty dollars to buy material for new dresses. I bought a piece of fabric with blue cornflowers and a heavy bright pink piece covered with wild flowers and geometric designs. Out of the blue material I made a plain princess-line shift with a hidden zipper, and of the pink cloth, long gores with a high breast and ruffles to set it off.

I got Jean to help me with the fitting, and contrary to Jan's advice, pulled my straps as high as I could stand to wear them. The yards of hand hemming became a labor of love. When I was finished the sewing, Jean and I linked arms and walked around the school past Laman and Celeste's apartment, modeling one of my creations. We strolled out to the main gate past all the little kids playing ball and around the pond toward the peace of the trees.

"Just think, Jean, after this meeting maybe I'll be your mother. Uncle Roy told Daddy for me to get my feelings in order to marry anyone the Lord dictates, and I think I can. Like Daddy says, any good man or woman under the direction of the priesthood can be easily loved. Daddy says he could love any man or woman he was asked to…and if Daddy can, then so can I."

Jean turned on me with a dumbfounded look. "Do you really think so?" She looked away and mumbled, "I guess anything can be done if you have enough faith. Sometimes I know I can make up for Aline's leaving. I don't think I could ever marry Dolan Barnley or Wilhelm Mueller, though."

I shuddered. Since Dolan Barnley had come to visit the ranch five years before, the thought of marrying him had given all of us girls nightmares. And then there was his daughter, Blythe. She'd been left at the ranch with her sister to live with Uncle Isaac while her dad worked out of the area. The two of them survived in a horrible little holiday trailer that was parked down by the barn. She was the same age as Jean and I, and for some reason she'd decided she liked me. She combed her hair like mine and followed me around both during school and after. When she spoke to me, she held her face just inches from mine. All the kids laughed at me for being nice to her. Lately, whenever she was with me, the boys made rude faces and taunted me for being a "Blythe-lover." They kicked her whenever they had a chance; her legs were always black and blue from bruises.

I felt sorry for her but at the same time wished she would stop hanging around me. I didn't want to admit it, but sometimes I felt a morbid sense of satisfaction when the boys hurt her. I begged her to stop copying my hairstyle, but that only made her cry and me feel guilty. I could never understand why the boys hated her so much. She told me the only time they didn't treat her mean was when they invited her to play in the hay tunnels in the big barn. She said the boys had built special rooms in the tunnels where she got to crawl and stay on her hands and knees while they came up behind her in the dark and bred her. I knew I should talk to Daddy about this, but Blythe wasn't married to Uncle Isaac like Emilia was, and the boys weren't married like Sidney. Besides, Daddy said all the children in our Work were protected from the really bad things, but sometimes I wondered. I told Blythe that being almost fourteen, maybe she shouldn't play in the tunnels anymore.

I didn't like thinking about her. I pulled my mind back to Jean and our exciting plans. She suddenly looked very serious. "Dad and Mom always pick on Uncle Freddie. No one seems to like him. Maybe I could change that…What do you think?"

I wasn't sure what she meant at first, and then I saw the inspiration in her plan. Suddenly I burst into a smile and hugged her excitedly. "Jeanie, that's absolutely brilliant! Of course it'll work. It'll be hard, but you and I'll be queens in the end. Freddie and Uncle Isaac are already kings in their kingdoms—it will be just like an alliance between kingdoms. Of course, they'll have to forgive each other and be kinder to each other." I became calmer and a shiver ran through me. "Your calling will be much harder than mine, though. I've seen Erica cry for days and days after Freddie visits. But Daddy always says the Lord will fight our battles if we are in the line of duty."

There were just two weeks of school left. My theory exam for the piano conservatory was a few days before we were to leave on our trip to Cardston, and I was determined to pass my level one. I got up to practice my pieces every morning at five o'clock. I studied my music and finished sewing my outfits at lunch break. The whole time my mind was focused upon Uncle Isaac; my heart was in his hands. I couldn't concentrate on the music theory and failed by two marks. Although I was terribly disappointed, I realized my future was in being a mother in Israel, not in being a pianist.

The days before the trip were hectic with activity. Uncle Isaac had the boys scrape all the manure out of the back of his huge three-ton truck. With the scrubbing done and the stock racks loaded, it was ready for the boys to travel in. Daddy would be driving the extended van loaded with all of us girls.

The night before we left, I carefully pressed my new dresses again. Laying them next to my new bra, panties, garter belt, and stockings in the new suitcase Daddy bought for the occasion felt almost spiritual. I was preparing for the bridegroom. I knew my life here in this dark basement bedroom was a thing of the past. My spirit quivered with the possibilities, half in fear, half in anticipation.

The drive to Cardston was a blur except for the stop beside a field in Waterton. The entire pasture was the heavy purple of the shooting stars that grew there. The moment the vehicles stopped, the meadow came alive with girls sporting long dresses of every color of the rainbow and restless boys racing for the top of a bluff.

When we reluctantly got back into our confined space in the van, we almost choked on the smell of the shooting stars we all clutched in thick bouquets. Clenched in my fist were three perfect flowers that Uncle Isaac had picked for me. I brushed them against my lips and held them gently the rest of the way to Cardston.

Chapter 14

The Cardston meeting was held at Wilhelm Mueller's squat little house in the center of town. As Daddy parked the van, I walked into the meeting with Jeanie, Nettie, and the Whitmer girls. It was a hot day and the living room was full to overflowing. People were seated in the hall, the kitchen, and even some bedrooms. We found a spot close to the back of the room where the open door allowed for a nice breeze. As we settled into our cramped quarters, I was thankful for the incessant wind that blew in this peculiar prairie town.

This was the first time I had ever been to a meeting at the Muellers. Wilhelm was a strange little man in almost every respect. All of us girls called him Brother Mueller because we couldn't imagine calling him Uncle Wilhelm. For any of us to be told by the prophet to marry him would be the supreme test of faith—in the prophet and in placement marriage. Brother Mueller was barely five feet tall. He wore his hair cropped so close to the skin that every knob on his bony head was prominently displayed. According to gossip in the group, all but one of his collection of wives had been stolen from other men in the Cardston area. He had a son with Down's syndrome and a stepdaughter with eleven toes. All of us girls joked that if these women actually chose Wilhelm, we would hate to see the men they ran away from.

Brother Mueller claimed he had been commissioned by Christ to guard the Cardston Temple for the Lamanites,* and he was sure he was expected to be on guard until the new millennium. I heard Jan talking about his being worse than Kelvin Whitmer at severing himself from the mother church, but that had been solved when he was recently excommunicated by the old LDS for practicing polygamy. Daddy said Brother Mueller still pined for the trappings of the temple. He often arrived at meetings with a wild look in his eyes. At the last meeting in Creston he hinted he'd been given a mysterious communication from space creatures who provided him with secret and confidential information. Although he made his living by fashioning false plates for teeth, he was sure God had called him to make miniature violins. The women from the ranch all talked about his being like a cocky little rooster. Whenever he left the room, everyone made fun of him. Uncle Isaac did, too, but he said that his tithing money was good, so we would all have to put up with him.

The prophet was here already with the apostles, and I was absolutely certain this was the day my life as an eternal wife would begin. Although I was braced for the supreme sacrifices that becoming Uncle Isaac's wife would mean, I was ready for the challenge. The way his otherwise fierce eyes softened every time he looked at me reassured me I had made the right choice.

Last night when Jean and I were still girls, the warm prairie wind blew in a magical way, as if angels were in and around us. When the men were at their secret meeting, all the girls gathered in groups outside the motel and ran up the hill toward the lights of the holy temple. Jean and I talked about the very top room of the beautiful structure and how Heavenly Father must visit there sometimes. We were enthralled with the possibility He was there that very moment. In absolute awe, we gazed up at the white stone walls. The magnificent stories we'd heard about this place overwhelmed us, and we turned and ran over the carefully kept grass, through the trees back to the motel. We didn't talk even once about marriage.

---

*In The Book of Mormon, the Lamanites were the descendants of Laman. They rejected the gospel and God cursed them with red skin because of their crimes.

We discussed how we hoped the prophet wouldn't call on Uncle Freddie at the meeting. Last time he had harangued us about "the unnatural natural man" being his enemy. I didn't understand that, but it had something to do with "being born of the flesh of the fallen woman, Eve, out of the Garden of Eden. When the serpent bit her heel, he affected all men's heels, forever." I watched wise men like Daddy and the priesthood men from the States shaking their heads, trying to decide if the natural man was the problem or the unnatural man. It seemed to me they should just go back to Eve and blame it all on her.

I took extra care with my hair before the meeting. Grandmother said she liked the way the soft waves curled around my face with the rest pulled to the side in a braid and pinned around my head like a crown. My blue shift dress was truly beautiful. I looked at myself in the mirror at the hotel before we left for the meeting, and I was so proud of my sewing. The fabric was the color of the cornflowers that lined the sides of the road going down to our house in Canyon. I shivered when I realized this might be my wedding dress. Daddy told me the prophet would tell me soon. I prayed fervently that I could do whatsoever the Lord desired; this was what I knew I was born to do. I tried to gather my wandering mind and listen so I wouldn't miss the words the Lord was sending for my guidance. I wanted all the help I could get to make things special for Uncle Isaac over the next few months.

I felt Mother's presence. If only she could talk to me from where God sat, she'd put everything into perspective. I knew she'd be proud of me. I was so happy to be here, listening to the sermons from the Lord's anointed. With an effort, I collected myself and looked back to the front where the prophet was seated. I felt strangely humbled with the powerful inspiration coming from him as he looked straight into my heart.

I dragged my eyes away from Uncle Roy to look at Apostle Uncle Guy Musser. He was speaking about Apostle Richard Jessop, one of the oldest of the Council of Seven,* who had been an active

*One group of Mormon Fundamentalists believes the Council of Seven is of the highest order of the priesthood, of a higher authority than that of the Quorum of Twelve Apostles in the mainstream church. Joseph Smith taught about the Council of Seven in his School of the Prophets.

member of our polygamist work since the early 1920s. He had known John W. Woolley, Lorin C. Woolley, Leslie J. Broadbent, John Y. Barlow, Joseph W. Musser, and LeRoy Sunderland Johnson, all of the presidents of the council, all apostles and prophets who walked and talked with God. Uncle Rich had a sprinkling of gray hair and the stooped shoulders of a man who had wrestled a living for his family from the desert. Uncle Guy went on and on about Uncle Richard—about all the work he did for the Lord's storehouse in Colorado City and about how ready he was to travel to Canada or Mexico to visit the Saints.

Uncle Guy's voice was measured and quiet as he went on with his sermon, but his body was vibrating with an intense inner fury, as if an electric current were passing through it. "We have the example of a man of God who has stood up to the rack, hay or no hay. It is the responsibility of every elder to completely surrender and sacrifice himself to the principles of the priesthood, the United Order, and celestial marriage. We have to always be prepared to do the right thing…I am not foolish enough to suppose that you and I have not been given attributes and characteristics in our bodies that insist on being gratified. Those of us who will surrender and bring our earthly passions under total subjugation will not be held accountable, but those who won't will have to pay the price. The Spirit of God will not stay with anyone who is not willing to surrender themselves in all things. We *must* have the Spirit of God. We have no license. We have no authority…and we have no right to lose the Spirit of the Lord. We cannot accumulate more than we can use or sanctify, in clothing, foods, lands, families, or anything else..."

He paused and surveyed the congregation. "Saint Joseph White Musser, my father, told me, 'Son, I'll tell you what not to do easier than anything else. You should never, no never, go anywhere, taste anything, look at anything, or do anything that will cause you to lose the Spirit of God. My boy, if you accomplish this, it will be because you have surrendered yourself and made the sacrifice.' So there is the key. We have no right in the covenant to go anywhere, taste anything, look at anything, or do anything that will cause us to lose the Spirit of the Lord. This man, Apostle Richard Jessop, completely surrendered himself financially, politically, and spiritually to the kingdom of God, and his character is saturated with the elements of the kingdom of God. He lived through the raid on Colorado City and came back to an empty home for the first time in twenty-five years. His wives had been taken into the custody of a gentile army financed by the Church of Jesus Christ of Latter-day Saints.

"The social affairs of the patriarchal law have caused more wars than any other principle since the beginning of time. Women and children unwilling to make the sacrifice of their feelings under the direction of their husband make a mockery out of this sacred and holy Work. When financial jealousies take hold of a patriarchal order and families, the Spirit of God is destroyed, and hell comes rolling in on wheels. This is not a bad dream; we are not going to wake up and find ourselves in the beautiful and free state of monogamy!" He shuddered at the awful thought. "Let us follow after this good and humble man who has come under this covenant and law so we can be called to go into the temples and give each other our endowments. These men with me, and the ones before, have been called to be high priest apostles and will lead us to a glorious victory in the millennium, the final great day of the Lord."

Even the most stubborn, fussy baby was hypnotized into only occasional whimpering by the intense mechanical tone of Uncle Guy's voice. My bosom was kindled with the realization I was soon to take my place as an adult member of this great celestial order Uncle Guy was talking about. The meeting drew to a close and everyone stirred, hoping to get out of the stifling heat. My legs gave out from under me as I tried to stand, and I fell back to my chair. By the time my head cleared and I found my feet again, Jean and Nettie were eight people ahead of me in the line shaking hands.

I shuffled along behind other members of the congregation for my turn with the apostles. When Uncle Isaac took my hand, he covered it gently with his other hand, and our eyes disappeared into one another's. Next, Uncle Guy took my hand and stared into my eyes until the warnings of his teachings were branded into my brain. Then Uncle Roy took my hand and everything stopped. When he spoke, the room started moving again. "Sister Nilsson, I want you to step into the hall over there and wait for me." Like a wooden puppet, I did as I was told.

Daddy came along. "I've been looking all over for you, Daughter. What are you doing here?"

"Uncle Roy told me to wait." I looked at him nervously. "I'm shaking but I'm so happy, Daddy."

He held me and rocked me gently, whispering, "Are you sure about this, Daughter? It isn't too late."

In a heartbeat the prophet guided me into the bedroom that had been appointed as the secret, sacred sealing place for this conference. Uncle Roy spoke quietly to Daddy for a moment in the hall, then entered the room and closed the door behind him. I had never been alone with this man before...He was the prophet. His hooked nose and crippled fingers added a mystical air to the moment. He circled me as I stood timidly shaking.

"Your father tells me you feel you belong in Brother Isaac's house." His voice was accusing, and I winced as if stabbed by a knife.

"Uncle Roy, I'll never marry anyone the Lord has not revealed to be the right one. I'll marry anyone you instruct me to." I wept penitent tears, feeling ashamed that I'd be telling God's own voice what I thought. He took me in his arms.

"What you have asked *is* the Lord's will...and it shall be done. Brother Musser is just outside, and you will be taken care of." He opened the door to Uncle Guy, Uncle Isaac and Bettilyn, and Daddy and Jan.

In Salt Lake Uncle Guy was a marriage counselor who even had gentile couples seeing him for help. He was the one who performed most of the marriage ceremonies for us. He stepped forward, took Bettilyn's hand, and placed my hand in hers. He looked intently into her eyes.

"It is your great privilege today to perform the law of Sarah by placing the hand of this sister in the hand of your husband, fulfilling the commandment of the Lord to Joseph Smith, helping restore the law of celestial and plural marriage. Your husband's descendants will be as numerous as the sands of the seashore, just as the Lord promised Jacob. When you obey the law of

Abraham, Isaac, and Jacob, you receive the blessings thereof. Blessed is that woman who can add jewels to the crown of her husband and multiply the blessings on his head. She will share his glory as a goddess in the realms of her husband. Bless you, Sister Bettilyn. I want all of you in this room to take careful heed—a final warning on this great day. When the Lord pours out His blessings, the devil and all his angels writhe in hell and double their efforts to destroy us and possess us. Take care, for we have seen it happen again and again."

Uncle Guy directed our hands reverently and gently into the outstretched hand of Uncle Isaac, into what he said was the patriarchal grip. Bettilyn turned my hand just so, and Uncle Isaac guided my fumbling fingers until the middle finger of my left hand was pressing the center of his wrist and his was pressing mine. Our thumbs were overlapping and enveloping. A powerful jolt passed through me from Uncle Isaac's hand, and I became weak. Uncle Guy read the marriage covenant.

Oh Mother, I thought, I'm all Uncle Isaac's, his wife for time and eternity. Uncle Roy affirmed he was of royal blood from the line of kings of Joseph who was sold into Egypt. And now, at fifteen, I was his bride—Deborah Ann Merrick.

Uncle Guy bade Uncle Isaac kiss the bride. His lips on mine were tender, and I wished we could just be alone. I looked to Daddy. His eyes brimmed with tears. Jan pulled me close to her and whispered in my ear as if to tell me more secrets of the kingdom. "Stay close to Mother...You'll be the happiest if you stay close to her. She'll never steer you wrong. She understands Daddy better than anyone."

In a few moments I found myself outside the house, standing beside a high fence in the shade of some shrubs, trying to catch my breath. I wasn't sure if I was supposed to get my suitcase and put it in my husband's truck or wait to be told what to do. I was fighting off a heavy dark feeling that had suddenly descended upon me. Remembering Uncle Guy's warning, I concentrated on telling the evil spirit to go hence and not darken this blessed day. I looked up to see my friend Jean, now my stepdaughter, standing awkwardly on one foot, not sure what to say. We hugged but I could feel her tension, the trembling of her body. Her breathing was rapid. Her normal ivory skin tone was now scarlet in some places and dead white in others.

I shook her. "Jean, are you all right? What is it?" The dark feeling intensified, and now an overwhelming fear gripped me.

"I've done it," she said. "I talked to Uncle Roy and told him about Uncle Freddie. Uncle Guy was with him, and neither of them seemed the least bit surprised. They told me I had faith like the ancients, and that my request was a miracle." Her arms were prickly with goosebumps. "What'll Mom say?"

"You know you won't be able to tell her…not until it's over. She'll ruin everything! Oh Jean, you're so good and strong. I'd even be kind of afraid to marry Uncle Freddie after seeing the way he was with Erica. They're right about your faith." I gave her a big hug and then held her at arm's length. "When are they going to do the marrying? I wish we could travel together so we could talk about this…but now my place is with your dad."

As I looked into her face, I realized she was frozen like one of the Greek marble statues I loved to look at. It was as if she were in a trance. She hadn't heard a word I said. I thought maybe she was thinking about her mother and about Uncle Freddie being fifty-one. Suddenly, she shuddered, told me she needed to find something to eat, and returned to the house.

Nettie and one of Bettilyn's daughters, Babette, were sitting on chairs on the lawn and eating from paper plates. The Whitmer girls, Lucia, Rose, and Lorena, were standing in their perpetual circle, laughing, talking, and tossing their heads in the way that always caused Jan to suck in her breath. After the talks about eternity and Christ and the law of Sarah, the realization that Jean and I were on the threshold of being mothers in Israel made me feel light-years older than my sister and the other girls.

The call to load up came and I was still waiting for instructions. The facts that Uncle Isaac had Bettilyn with him, Laman was driving the three-ton truck, and the boys and Celeste were there also made me uncertain about what I was supposed to do. Bettilyn had ridden in the front with Uncle Isaac the whole way to Cardston, and there obviously wasn't room for all of us.

Uncle Isaac came to me. "Well, what are you waiting for? Where are your things?"

I blushed and stammered, "I'm...I...I'm sorry. I didn't know what you wanted me to do. I can ride in the van with Daddy and the girls if you need me to...if there isn't room, that is. You know...where will Bettilyn ride if I'm with you?" I suddenly felt as exhausted as if I'd run a very difficult race.

His eyebrows seemed to jump from his head and he looked absolutely fierce. "That's not your concern, unless you don't want to be with me!"

"Oh, I do! I do." I was devastated. Married only an hour and already I was blundering. I ran to the van and asked Daddy to help me find my things. The girls in the back sighed dramatically and they all teased me. How much easier it would have been to just crawl in with them. Instead, I flew away with my suitcase.

Uncle Isaac was supervising the loading of the truck, energetically encouraging the boys to hurry and get settled. Bettilyn stood arguing with Celeste and Laman.

"No, Mom, I don't want you riding in the back," insisted Laman. "Celeste will take the first shift, and then Dad can drive while I ride back there. It isn't right for you to do this."

"No, Son...you know that Daddy gets rattled driving. I'd love to ride in the back with the kids. Now quit your fussin'." Her eyes were fixed in a hard stare—the kind that had tears behind it. Celeste took up the cause.

"Come on, Mother, this is an exciting time, and you want to be in the front of the truck to share it with your new sister wife...You know you do. I'm not going to enjoy myself at all with you in the back the whole time." She shook her curls and pouted.

Bettilyn's stare grew harder and so did the tone of her voice. "Don't be ridiculous! I won't stop you from having a good time. I'm going to ride in the back!" With those final words, she proceeded to get in. Uncle Isaac tried to help boost her the four feet onto the deck with the boys, but she shrugged his hand off and scrambled up the ladder.

The sacred feeling of the ceremony faded into one of painful embarrassment as I felt the stares of the twenty-some boys on me.

It was hard to believe that one short hour ago many of them became my stepsons—James, Martin, Nephi, Ward, even Laman. From the back of the truck came catcalls and whistles as I climbed into the front beside Celeste, and Uncle Isaac climbed in beside me. We followed Daddy as he led the way out of Cardston with the van. I looked into the prominent rear-view mirror that stuck out from the side of the truck. The disappearing temple that sparkled in the sun seemed to wink at me. Our mini-caravan traveled north, and the temple was left behind in gentile hands. If only Christ had returned before my marriage, my wedding could have taken place in one of the sacred sealing rooms.

Celeste broke the silence with wonderful stories of the love her father Stanley Miller had for his wives and the love her mothers had for each other. She told us how the mothers, most of them sisters, walked arm in arm and held family counsel meetings. She rattled on about the incredible passion Uncle Stanley had for excellent music and his insistence that his children be prepared to perform well, and gladly, at a moment's notice. Anytime I had seen Uncle Stanley and his family perform at the ranch, he usually arranged to be the star in the grand finales. I could still see him standing there with outstretched hands like Mario Lanza. The way Uncle Stanley performed, his songs were powerful, humble prayers that struck your heart and stopped your breath.

Celeste told us of a special assembly in Colorado City that he and his boys practiced for until Oscar Hammerstein's song "Stouthearted Men" flowed like a heavenly choir. Uncle Stanley started singing, and with each stirring stanza more of his sons marched out of the audience to join him on the stage. Grown sons with large plural families of their own marched up, and younger sons with only one wife yet, and still younger sons working to prove themselves as men to the priesthood council. The ranks grew to thirty and then the boys in Colorado City on work missions marched shoulder to shoulder, inspiring the audience until every man was singing.

Uncle Isaac remembered the performance with a glint in his eye. "Stanley is a masterful man and a credit to this Work. We'll see the millennium ushered in with men like him. The Lord uses men of the world to give us inspirational messages in their songs. They don't even know they're doing it. The real matter of fact is the world, and the good old mother church will be set in order by the very men who marched with your father. Mark my words...when the Lord has seventy thousand stalwart men who have answered the call of the priesthood and proven unquestioning faith in all things, the earth will be renewed and receive its paradisiacal glory, and Christ will reign supreme. The governments of the world will be done away with, and the earth will be ruled by the theocracy of the priesthood."

After a lull in the conversation, Uncle Isaac told us we were stopping at the Hutterite colony because Daddy wanted to, and we could visit Jack Merrick, who was the teacher there. "You know Adam. He's a sociable guy and he figures the kids'll learn something from it. A lesson could really be taken from these Hutterites. Nobody knows how to live the United Order like they do."

When we got to the big communal farm south of Calgary, the kids spewed out of the vehicles. James and Martin helped Bettilyn down from the truck deck. Remembering Jan's words, I tried hard to figure how Mother would have handled this situation. It didn't seem fair for me to be the one to ride in the front the whole way.

I approached Bettilyn awkwardly. "You know, if you want to, I would like to take a turn riding in the back."

She looked at me as if I'd grown wings. In a terse voice she said, "Daddy isn't into this turn thing...I like the back anyway. I'm fine."

I cringed at her tone and slipped back to stand by Uncle Isaac. The fascination of being shown through a Hutterite colony soon overtook us all. I wanted to follow the girls, but instead I tagged along with the grown-ups, who visited with Jack and sang songs in the teacherage—cowboy songs, love songs, goofy songs, and a couple of gospel songs. When they sang a frightening song about snakes, war, betrayal, adultery, and murder, Jan declared it was a song unfit for the lips of a Saint.

Uncle Isaac was lying on the carpet enjoying the performance; whenever he thought no one else was looking, he stared at me lovingly. I felt uncomfortable being with the older people and was most grateful when Daddy finally said, "Let's get this show on the road. We thought we'd take this crew to Heritage Park in Calgary, and then go through Banff and let them see the caves." He extended his hand to everyone and after several hearty shakes got into the van. "It's been great seeing you—keep on keeping on."

Once we settled into steady travel, Uncle Isaac asked Laman and Celeste to sing for him. They sang duet after duet—"Blue Canadian Rockies," "Red Sails in the Sunset," and even "My Blue Heaven." I wasn't sure why they didn't leave that one out, because Jan hated it as much as she hated songs by Elvis. She insisted this one was especially bad, because it promoted the gentile monogamous idea of one man, one woman. She said anyone who would sing it was against the spirit of celestial marriage and was "living at a slow dying rate." She had spoken out against the gentile spirit of this song at home, in school, and at church. She loved comparing Winston Churchill's battle against Hitler and Communism with her fight to keep all gentile connotations out of the speech, books, and songs of our covenant people: "...we shall fight in the fields and in the streets, we shall fight in the hills; we shall never surrender."*

I struggled to chase Jan's orating image from my mind and bring myself back to the front of the humming truck and my eternal husband. With the setting of the sun, the cab became as cozy as a cave. In this twilight, Uncle Isaac's hand stole to mine and covered it. As warm and comforting as that felt, I kept thinking of snakes and of Bettilyn rattling down the highway in the back of the truck. I began a mental chant of the 23rd Psalm the way Jan had taught us to purify our minds. I tried to start out again and again, but each time got stuck on "the valley and the shadow of death."

It was late evening when we arrived at Uncle Nick's house in Calgary. I wished I knew Mother's brother better, but I'd only seen him twice before and just couldn't worry myself about it. I was tired and numb and very much afraid of what this night would bring. I tried to ask Daddy what I should know or do because it occurred to me that the books I had read to learn all I could about

---

*From a speech by Winston Churchill to the House of Commons on June 4, 1940.

pleasing a man might not have included some of the important priesthood rules about lovemaking.

Daddy answered with a catch in his throat, "Oh, my Daughter, Uncle Isaac is your husband, and he'll teach you everything he thinks you should know. Because of who he is, I can't be the one who teaches you." I didn't understand what Daddy meant. Feeling awkward and out of place, I wandered into the basement of Uncle Nick's house where the thirty-five children who used to be my classmates were settling into sleeping bags for the night. Daddy found me and took me to the van where Jan, Bettilyn, and Uncle Isaac were waiting. I kept thinking if this was to be my honeymoon night and my first night alone with Uncle Isaac, why was Bettilyn here? Surely, she would stay with Daddy and Jan. Daddy pulled up at a motel and went into the office to book our rooms. Jan was chattering busily away to her mother. My mouth was dry and I was so uncomfortable. Uncle Isaac wasn't holding my hand anymore, and it had been a long time since he'd even looked at me. We got out of the van and unloaded our suitcases. Bettilyn grabbed her little bag and followed Uncle Isaac into the motel. When I hesitated, Daddy gave me a gentle push.

"Everything will be fine, Daughter...Go on in."

I followed them and cringed when Bettilyn closed the door behind me. Uncle Isaac had us kneel and he prayed before he told me to go into the bedroom and prepare myself. I wasn't sure what he meant, so I stood around waiting with the hope he would soon come in and give me direction. He stayed with Bettilyn in the little sitting room for a very long time. I undressed, keeping my bra and panties on because I was afraid he would think I wasn't modest enough if I slept only with my nightgown, as I normally did. I slowly put on my nightie. I took the heavy crown of hair off my head, let it loose, and brushed it with hundreds of idle strokes.

I sat on the edge of the bed until my eyes drooped shut, and still he didn't come. His and Bettilyn's voices droned on and on. Finally, he came. I stood up and he reached for me as if in slow motion. His hands were shaking as he lifted my hair gently and asked me to turn around so he could see. He ran his fingers through it and encircled my throat. Pulling me toward him, he kissed me. His voice was slow and heavy when he put his arms around me and held me close.

"Naomi dreamed a few years back that she died and went to a huge hall where there were lots of women. They were all naked and someone announced that Christ was coming and the women should cover their shame. There was nothing in the hall to cover even one naked body with, but Naomi realized if she undid her braids, her hair would cover her nakedness. Christ came and gave her a personal commendation for the beauty of her covering." Uncle Isaac shuddered and held me even tighter. His voice faded to a whisper in my ear.

"The first thing she did when she let the spirit of rebellion take over her soul was cut her hair off. I love your hair. You must never, ever cut it." He sent me to the far side of the bed and then turned the light off. I could hear him undressing. His holy garments glowed white in the reflection from the streetlights. The image of the sacred robes of the priests in the temples where John the Baptist's father lived played in my head. I longed for the time when I could come to him dressed in nothing but these sacred, flowing garments.

Hypnotized, I gazed at my husband of eight hours. His silver-gray hair was shining like a halo in the reflected light. I took a deep breath when I realized that under his baggy garments was a naked primeval man. I looked at his face and the hair curling through the ties on his chest.

Uncle Isaac knelt and stretched his arms across the bed. "Give me your hands and we'll pray again—just you and I." I knelt and reached across to him. He thanked the righteous and eternal Heavenly Father that we had come to this. He whispered his prayer for thirty minutes. I almost fell asleep a few times, and my knees were aching when he finally stopped. We crawled into bed. He pulled me into his arms, cupped my face with trembling hands, and kissed me gently. Although my mind seemed removed from my body, I really liked everything he was doing, and I was disappointed when he stopped. I was ashamed of my body, and I hoped he didn't notice. I couldn't shake the image of Christ complimenting Naomi on the beauty of her hair. I kept picturing Uncle Isaac holding her like this as they conceived the children they covenanted to bring to this earth. I was thankful they had, or I wouldn't have had a friend like Jeanie. I said a little prayer for her and for her wayward mother.

Uncle Isaac kissed me again, and his quivering hands slowly unfastened the buttons of my high-necked flannel gown and slipped inside. When he felt the cloth of my bra, he drew in a sharp breath and slipped his fingers inside the cup. His hands on my breasts were frightening and magical at the same time. His kisses became quick and breathless; my body was responding and beginning to writhe without my conscious effort.

Uncle Isaac froze the instant the sound of heavy sobbing began to filter through the wall from the other room. He stopped caressing me and sighed deeply. He lay motionless for several minutes before he apologized and got out of bed. "I better go to her. This isn't likely to stop if I don't." Long hours later I drifted off to sleep. Uncle Isaac didn't come back.

Before we left for Heritage Park the next morning, I tried to insist that Bettilyn ride in the front. Celeste argued with her again as well, but she flatly refused us both.

Heritage Park was having its first opening on completion. As we walked through the park in our long colorful dresses, many people thought we were part of the exhibit. Daddy, Uncle Isaac, and Laman were delighted with this. Uncle Isaac whispered to me several times that he could hardly wait until we could be alone. I ached to tell him I felt the same way, but I couldn't force the words out. I was afraid he'd be shocked.

Once, Nephi and Brent came up to me, laughing, and Nephi said, "Well, Mama Deb, how does it feel to be married to the best man on earth?"

My blush was huge. "I love it, I really do," I gushed.

We headed for Banff and home. Uncle Isaac made a point of taking my hand this time in front of everyone. Celeste took a picture of us coming down the steps of the stalagmite caves. I didn't even ask Bettilyn to take her turn in the front this time—I was too tired. On the last lap of the trip, Uncle Isaac told me to make sure I didn't have false hopes of his being a romantic husband.

"I don't go in for all that mushy I-love-you stuff. In my book, people just prove it, they don't talk about it. Just ask anyone, it goes against my character."

Celeste laughed at him. "Oh, Uncle Isaac, your bark is much worse than your bite, and I know better." She turned to me. "Don't listen to him. He needs more hugs and kisses than most people, and you're the one to see to it. Don't ever give up. When he's the most grouchy is when you get the closest. He'll always be tender and love you the more for it." I thanked her for the advice.

We didn't arrive at my new home until after ten. Grumpy, sleepy kids limped out of the vehicles. The thought of finding a place to sleep was overwhelming, and before I could ask Uncle Isaac what to do, he gave me a quick kiss and hug and said he guessed he better spend what was left of the night over at Lydia's. The couch in the living room was made into a bed where my new teenage stepdaughters, Babette and Phoebe, were already sleeping. I couldn't find Bettilyn, so I just crawled in and slept with them on the couch.

Morning came early, and the confusion of this new home made my head ache. When I asked where I could help, Babette gave me a job setting the table for breakfast. Emilia wouldn't even say hello, but rushed out of the house as if the devil were on her tail. I needed her to tell me how I could help best—after all, she was my sister wife now. I had prayed every mile of the way home that she'd be my friend. Since she didn't want to be Uncle Isaac's wife in a sexual way, I could think of no reason she'd be jealous of me.

Just before lunch, Bettilyn planted herself in front of me and disclosed, "I might as well tell you. Daddy instructed me to give you the end bedroom...So, we might as well make it up for you." I spent the rest of the day fixing the room. Uncle Isaac came and went. Remembering Celeste's instruction, I tried to make sure that when he was around, I was in quiet private corners so he could hug me if he wanted to, without our being in Bettilyn's face. I called Jean to come over, but when she did she spent most of the day with Ophelia and Emilia. Uncle Isaac decided they should take Jean shopping for cloth so Ophelia could make her some new clothes. He said given the things that were important to Naomi, Jean wouldn't likely have any decent clothes to take with her to her new life.

Every man, woman, and child in the order was made to understand they were to take special care to keep Naomi from finding out that Jean was to marry Uncle Freddie. If Naomi could persecute her husband, the file leader for all of Canada, she would stop at nothing to stand in the way of the Lord's Work. For the next two weeks we lived as if we expected the sky to fall at any second.

Uncle Isaac stayed away again the second night home, but the third night he came to me in my new room, bringing me one of the black- and gold-bound volumes of *Truth* open to "The Law of Chastity." I read the passage he indicated, words of doctrine written by Saint Joseph White Musser. "Inasmuch as we have embarked on a holy mission to live this patriarchal order of marriage, the restoration of all things, we can expect the Lord to require further sacrifice at our hands. This restoration was brought about in these last days that covenant children, the Lord's chosen race, prophets and prophetesses, could be born through the loins of the faithful."

Joseph White Musser decreed the Lord required us to bring our earthly needs and desires under subjugation "every whit" before we'd be allowed to parent these choice spirits. When a woman was married to a man for all eternity, she shouldn't think she could let her passions run loose in the way of the gentile world. He said the Lord's commandment to multiply and replenish the earth has an order.

"We watch the animals of the earth and see that they follow the natural order the Lord has designed for them. Therefore we must counsel together as husbands and wives and find out the time when we may conceive, and otherwise bring the passions of the flesh under control so our energy will be used in serving the Lord." This commandment weighed heavily on the woman; if she deceived her husband and did not inform him of the proper times, she would be guilty of adulterating the birth canal, and the consequences would be "dire and severe." There was a short verse at the end of the passage: "Sow in the morn thy seed, In the eve hold not thy hand."

I read the passage several times before Uncle Isaac finally returned. He reread the whole thing to me and then told me that living this law was of utmost importance. I said I didn't know how to tell the time of month I could get pregnant. He admitted he didn't, either, but said I should ask Ophelia, because she and Sidney had done very well conceiving their children in the way of the Lord.

"Until you find out the procedure, it's important for us to be diligent in fulfilling our covenants." As he was speaking, he rose from the bed and in one smooth motion slipped a knife between the door and the casing. He came back and immediately unfastened the buttons on my nightgown. He slipped his hands around my back.

"You don't need this stiff old bra on. Take it off for me." I was embarrassed to be seen and looked toward the light switch. "All I want to do is look at you. You're beautiful—your eyes, your hair, the blush in your cheeks."

I must have looked pained, for he got up and turned the light off. In the safety and privacy of the dark we slipped under the blankets.

"I want to feel your beautiful body…For three days now, I haven't gotten to touch you. I can't stand it anymore." Uncle Isaac's whisper was husky as he pulled the voluminous folds of my new cotton plissé gown over my head and sent it flying in a ghostly cloud to the floor. Now, all that kept our bodies apart was my underwear and his holy garments. He pulled most of the cotton ties on his robe, and then placed my hands on the remaining one. "Undo it for me, please," he pleaded.

With that request, I caught a glimpse of the passion and power that mortal women have had over the gods since the beginning of time. I thought of Uncle Isaac's zealous description of God the Father visiting the Virgin Mary, and in His resurrected flesh covenanting with her and making her one of the goddesses of His universe. And then the consummation and the beginning of the most important baby to be born on this earth—the one true king that through His example was to save the earth, without an earthly army, and without force.

I understood better in that moment Uncle Isaac's passionate determination. His words echoed within me as he removed my underclothes and began kissing and stroking my body. He opened the front of his garment, pulled me to him, and wrapped the flowing cotton fabric around me. My arms were around his nakedness inside his holy garment, and he was over me and under me.

To conceive a child with Uncle Isaac would be the ultimate gift. All the images of passion I had ever been exposed to flashed through my mind—Mary and God, the women in *The Silver Chalice* practicing from childhood the ancient art of pleasing a man, the unbidden images of the couple in the book from Elsa's hope chest. They were all inside me and outside me until Uncle Isaac was lying exhausted on my breast.

He left my arms and bed early in the morning. Moments after he was gone, I heard him in the bedroom below hollering at the six boys to get up. They groaned and the room erupted with noise as they tussled with one another, then the doors banged and the house was quiet. Before I dropped off to sleep again, it occurred to me if I could hear the boys so well, could they hear their father and me as clearly? Did they hear the iron bedsprings creaking with our timeless dance the night before?

I woke to the smells of breakfast and dressed quickly, feeling guilty because I hadn't helped again. I said good morning, but Bettilyn couldn't hear me, or at least she didn't reply. Bettilyn and Emilia were sister wives like Bettilyn and I were, but they were also mother and daughter. I wondered if that was why they always talked to each other and to me only when it was unavoidable.

The household swung into excited preparation for the coming of the priesthood brethren, being careful to contain it around Naomi's two youngest daughters, Rhoda and Pamela. We had decided they couldn't know yet, because they were too little to keep a secret. The day before Uncle Roy and Uncle Guy were due to arrive, Rhoda overheard that Jean was being married the next day. She knew her mother didn't know, and her little nine-year-old body trembled with furies. She bawled and cussed and said she was going to go home to tell her mother. Everyone panicked and spent a long time convincing her not to go home until the next night after everything was over. She was promised anything she wanted if she would just stay over.

Uncle Roy brought a wife with him from Salt Lake City this time; Uncle Guy came alone. On this, Jean's special day, Uncle Isaac and I were downstairs stealing a few moments from the constant hubbub when she came in search of us. We were in the fruit room behind the big heavy door, hugging. Jean's face was so white that even her freckles were gone. From Uncle Isaac's arms I wanted to somehow communicate to her how beautiful this eternal marriage could be. She was trying to talk to me, but we were telling her about all the wonderful things she was soon to experience.

In exasperation she said, "Will you two just shut up and quit hugging and kissing. I feel so strange when you do that." Suddenly, there was no more time for talk. One of Uncle Isaac's boys ran down to report that Uncle Frederick had arrived.

Uncle Isaac gave Jean a hug. "You'll be just fine, Daughter. You wait and see."

The rest of the early evening was a blur. Uncle Roy said the wedding should happen right away so Uncle Freddie could get Jean into Alberta as quickly as possible. Daddy came with Irene. The prophets felt Irene must be a witness so she could tell her mother that Jean had entered into this marriage of her own free will. In fact, everyone must stress that she asked for it, and her wishes were just being fulfilled. And one more girl would have been saved from a rebellious mother.

The ceremony was performed in Bettilyn's bedroom. Jean was wearing a beautiful mint green dress Ophelia had made especially for her. I watched them usher my friend in and close the door. When they came out, Uncle Freddie's face was almost as white as Jean's. He tucked her hand under his arm and walked her to his car. With an abrupt wave, he disappeared down the gravel road with my best friend, his fourth wife. Uncle Guy and Uncle Roy repeated over and over that Jean was the most shining example of faith exhibited by any of the young women who were part of the great priesthood Work. They sat down for a quick supper and then left. They were adamant they had to be across the border in case the devils in hell cut loose and tried to get the police after the Lord's apostles.

Tensions were high at the ranch as Rhoda and Pamela were

allowed to go home. After bedding down the animals for the night, Uncle Isaac stretched out in his favorite chair with his feet up under the long narrow window that looked out onto the west meadow. As far as we could see, the land was Uncle Isaac's, and now I truly shared it with him, his other wives, and his children. My new husband had a volume of the Truth books on his lap and was reading, when, about eight o'clock, a messenger from hell descended upon this scene of reverence and peace. She didn't knock—she burst into the house and spewed wrath all over us. I had seen Naomi flush with fiery anger before, but tonight her face was a dark purple.

She was cursing and screaming. "If that horny old bastard doesn't get Jean home by morning, every RCMP officer from here to Cardston will be all over this place! And *then* you'll know the meaning of persecution!"

Uncle Isaac looked her up and down with his lip curled. "I've always known it would come to this! Do you have any idea what you're doing, woman? This kind of interference in the Lord's Work will guarantee you a home in the eternities with the other persecutors of the Lord's prophets. Are you prepared for that? It's my duty as your husband and file leader to tell you this!"

I was terrified Naomi was going to attack him. She advanced at him, then backed off a step. Her expression was menacing.

"You're just not worth it," she growled. "Your threats don't scare me…I'll take my chances at my judgment day, and I doubt you'll have any say in the matter. You and your brethren wouldn't know truth or honesty if they jumped up and bit you in the face…Just mark my words, Jean better be back here tomorrow!" She waved her fist at Uncle Isaac and then faced me. "I hope to the God you all profess is guiding you that you know what you're doing. This is the kind of family you're married into." She seemed to expect me to answer her, but I was frozen in fear. She shook her head. "How could you know, anyway…You're still a child and your dad is a bloody fool!" She turned on her heel and left.

Being called a child when the Lord's own servant had touched me with his hand and called me to the highest calling a woman could have was a horrible insult. I flew into the bedroom, undressed, and disappeared under my blankets. My sobbing eventually took me into a dark cocoon of semi-conscious sleep. Then, as if in a dream, Uncle Isaac was in bed with me, holding me passionately. I held onto him frantically and with total abandon. The incredible tension of the day peaked with the rhythm of his body and with a groan that spoke of more than the earthly act of sex. After he was spent, he refused to touch me. I lay there alone, mere inches from him, trying to figure out what had happened and what I should do to reach out to my husband. Just as quietly as he came to me, Uncle Isaac left.

Chapter 15

Naomi's fury reached over the Rocky Mountains to Cardston. As soon as she left our house, she called Uncle Freddie to tell him an RCMP officer would be knocking on his door to arrest him for statutory rape if Jean was not home before noon the next day. He had her back the following morning. Standing by his side, Jean told her mother she had chosen to obey the Lord's will in being married to Uncle Freddie. She begged Naomi to let her go so she could be a mother in Israel.

The fierce aggression in Naomi's attitude dissolved like a block of ice in the sunshine. In a subdued tone, she agreed. "As long as you're sure this is what you want." She turned to the man she so despised. "But I'll be watching you, Freddie." She shook her work-twisted finger in his face. "I know the misery you're putting Erica through...It better not happen to Jean!" He nodded at her, mumbled something about a sacred trust and covenants, and retreated with Jean to Cardston.

The thrilling news that the spirit of repentance had touched Naomi and there might be hope for her after all spread through the community like wildfire. We all felt a lot better about her for a while. Jan arranged a wedding shower for Jean. Quilting bees were organized, and everyone was determined to send Jean to the Russell family with fine things for her new life.

Stepping through the front door of Daddy's house as a shower guest was a strange experience for me. It was the first time I'd been back since my marriage, and although it felt odd, it felt safe, too. Jan would never again be able to pound on my body or ridicule me with her cruel words.

Uncle Freddie arrived with Jean and Selena, his third wife, shortly after I did. With his arm over his bride's shoulder, he kept looking around as if afraid he'd be attacked from behind. Selena wore a pleasant smile that never left her face. She didn't say a word; when asked a direct question she merely nodded. Freddie sat with Jean to open the gifts, and the moment they were finished, the threesome gathered up the parcels and drove off to Cardston.

A few minutes after they left, Erica phoned wondering if anyone had seen Freddie yet. She was waiting for him to pick her up for the party. Daddy was dumbfounded; it was obvious he didn't want to be the one to tell her the festivities were already over. But he did tell her, and Erica hung up crying. She said it had been weeks since Frederick had even stopped by her house to say hello. Immediately, the excitement of lavishing Jean with all her beautiful gifts was dimmed by the vision of Erica sitting home alone with her children. Everyone in our group was unhappy about the way Freddie treated her. The property he bought in secret had become her prison. Frederick kept her tucked away in the stark farmhouse, concerned only that the hay be cut and that she and the children cause him no trouble. Unless Daddy or Naomi sent someone to drive her to town to see the doctor or help her with things that broke down, she was totally isolated. She bought what little food she didn't grow herself at the Lister store with the family allowance money she got from the government.

Erica was still struggling to get over the terrible loss of her baby, Amy, who had been injured in a tragic fall. By the time Erica called for help and got Amy to the hospital, the doctors could do nothing. The baby died.

Daddy and Uncle Isaac organized the funeral and talked to Uncle Freddie on the phone to find out if he had any special wishes. He was quiet about everything. We had the funeral director from town come to the meeting room at the top of the school. Baby

Amy was laid out in a beautiful little casket wearing the dress with the embroidered bluebirds I had made for her. Uncle Isaac held up the funeral for almost an hour waiting for Freddie to arrive. Erica was sobbing in the front row with her two children, refusing to be comforted by anyone. We finally found out Uncle Freddie hadn't even left Cardston.

Most people in our group had trouble understanding and liking Uncle Freddie to start with. When he wouldn't be there for Erica at a time like this, they asked Uncle Isaac to please not have him speak at meetings because they all wanted to smack him. A couple of weeks later, Uncle Freddie decided he was taking Erica to stay with his other two wives and children in his house in Cardston. We worried about her more than ever, because no one had faith he would be any kinder to her there than he was here. He let Erica come back to the farm when she was pregnant with another child, and she wouldn't talk to a soul about what happened to her while she was at his house. Her baby Heidi was just two months old by the time Jeanie was married to Uncle Freddie, so we felt even worse he didn't want to show off his new daughter at the shower.

Daddy told Jan that Frederick thought he was fooling his friends and neighbors in Alberta by pretending Elizabeth was his only wife. He said the man would be a lot smarter to appreciate Erica and keep her beside him, because there wasn't a kinder, harder working woman anywhere.

Daddy's next sermon in church was about that very thing. "My wives will be the jewels in my crown. I will keep them close to me, where I can love them. I want to live proudly in the company of other believers, not in a hostile town where I have to lie about who I am and be afraid to claim my wonderful children in the daylight. Any man who tries to ride two horses or serve two masters will have nothing but confusion and pain until he decides to repent. You can't try to preserve your membership in the LDS church and deny the existence of the most important people in your life. We've all seen the pain women live through because of it." Everyone nodded in agreement and gratitude. I marveled at the wisdom and goodness of my father.

Shortly after Jean moved to Cardston, Uncle Isaac asked me to go for a walk with him. He said he needed to check the fence line. I was thrilled to be asked. We walked hand in hand in silence beside the long stretch of barbed wire and up the rocky knoll. When he started to talk, I wasn't even sure he was talking to me, as his voice was agitated and anger dripped from every word.

"I try to get your father and Freddie to understand that every time they give that wicked woman a job and pay her, they're enabling her to make it on her own. Naomi already has an inflated idea of her own importance. She needs to be taken down a peg or two, not encouraged in her rebellion. This wouldn't have happened if they'd just listened to me."

We topped the hill and sauntered across a grassy clearing. All around us, bushes hung heavy with honeysuckle flowers, and wild roses bloomed in profusion. With one arm around me, Uncle Isaac reached for a perfect bright pink rosebud. He picked it and brushed it to his lips. His whole body softened, as he became my lover instead of an angry, bitter man. "We will have a beautiful little daughter, as perfect as this rosebud. Her hair will be black, and she will have skin as soft as these petals...Should we create her now?"

I didn't know how to respond to his offer of intimacy when his words of pain and fury about Naomi were still echoing in my mind. As I accepted the rose, he pulled me toward him. I felt his warmth, and my body melded to his. He found my breasts as I helped him undo the buttons of my dress. We sank onto the thick bed of grass surrounded by wild roses, Indian paintbrush, and honeysuckle. We made love. This must have been what Daddy meant when he talked about the sacred closeness between him and Mother.

I needed Mother's help now more than ever before. I tried to remember the special way she was with Jan, in hopes of putting it into practice with Bettilyn, Emilia, and Lydia. Daddy was always saying if every woman could follow her example and sacrifice her feelings, then the earth would be restored much more quickly, and everyone would gain a testimony of the beauty of the Work. Since I was Mother's daughter, and she was held up as a perfect sister wife so often, I knew I must be an example to all.

The trouble was not knowing where to start. Emilia pretty

much had her way around the house and went out with the haying crews while Bettilyn and I did the cooking for them. When Emilia said jump, all of her brothers and sisters didn't even look around—they jumped. Sometimes they complained she was working them to death, but then she took them to the drive-in movie or to Bonners Ferry just across the border in Idaho to buy goodies, and they worked harder than ever the next time.

Daddy bought a gas station in Creston and hired Emilia as his secretary. Now she had her own money and was able to buy a little car called a Gremlin. She also bought herself very nice pantsuits. That got tongues wagging about the rules: Was it now acceptable for women to wear pants? Uncle Isaac said maybe it was all right if the tops came to four or five inches above the knee. Daddy was not at all happy about women wearing anything like men's apparel. I didn't have to worry myself about such things as new pantsuits and consoled myself by saying Emilia could have her car, her money, her beautiful hair decorations, and the new carpet in her remodeled bedroom if I could just have one of Uncle Isaac's covenant babies. I knew she was still unwilling to fulfill her covenants with him and hated to be reminded that we were not just friends, but sister wives.

I was learning sad and painful lessons with all my sister wives. Bettilyn got really angry when she caught Uncle Isaac and me kissing. I tried to be discreet and careful, but one night when I was sure that Bettilyn was in the basement, I slipped into the living room where Uncle Isaac was watching *Bearcats!* and gave him a kiss. Just as our lips met, Bettilyn came around the corner. She glared at me venomously, turned on her heel, and started making as much noise as possible—banging pots and pans around and scrubbing the already spotless kitchen. I was full of guilt and fear; I longed to take the kiss back. I went into the kitchen, ready to do penitence.

"Is there anything I can do to help? Have I done something to upset you? Can we talk about it?" My attempts were lame, and Bettilyn sneered at my insecurity.

"No! There's nothing wrong. Talk, talk, talk...talking never changed a thing. You just go on back to what you were doing." Her voice resonated with rage, and her false teeth clicked with each word. She wheeled, slammed the door in my face, and charged out into the night. When I went back to the living room, Uncle Isaac was watching television as if nothing had happened. I was worried he would be sad like Daddy always was when the sister wives fought, but Uncle Isaac was seemingly oblivious to what had been going on.

He turned to me with an incredulous stare. "So what are you doing, letting her problems smoke you out of your tree? This is none of my affair. You just set yourself up."

I asked him if I should try to find her in the night, but he only snorted. I went to my bed in frustration. A dull pain had crept into my head, and it was now all I could feel. I was almost asleep when Uncle Isaac lay down beside me and put his arms around me. Running his fingers through my hair, he kissed the back of my neck.

Just then the door in the kitchen slammed mightily, and the same terrible sobbing that derailed our wedding night filled the house. Without a word, Uncle Isaac rose from the bed and was gone for the night. When he came in to say good morning, he told me he had followed Bettilyn into the trees across from the house where Lena was buried. She was on her knees, sobbing onto the wooden fence that surrounded the grave, lamenting in a tortured prayer that the only sister wife who really understood her had died so young and left her at the mercy of these other impossible women. The rest of the day was strained. Bettilyn wouldn't look at me or let me help.

Quietly, a few days later, Uncle Isaac told me Lydia wanted to welcome me into the family; he said she would come over to see me. And sure enough, Lydia walked with her eight children from where she lived over at Uncle Michael's old place. Approaching the house, she sent one of the children in to get me; she was not comfortable coming into Bettilyn's home. As I walked toward her, I remembered the day so many years before when she had come to Mother, weeping in fear and frustration, amazed that Mother would dare be kind to her. I knew all of Bettilyn's children were watching my every move, and their animosity was burning holes in my back. I had to be careful how friendly I acted toward Lydia, but we were sister wives and were supposed to love and support one another. I lifted my head and stepped firmly into her open arms.

She hugged me. "Welcome to the family. I want you to come over and visit me sometime, if you dare be seen with me. I don't want you to go through what I did, so welcome…Welcome." She looked to her feet. "You know, your mother was kinder to me than any other woman ever has been…To this day, I love her for that."

I nodded and smiled nervously, trying to picture the Lydia of those years. She was thinner then, but the sky-blue eyes were the same. I could still see her weeping in my mother's arms, with all that wild pain and hate toward Naomi and Bettilyn. Her battles with those two women and the antics she used to get back at them were still talked about by our people from Canada to Mexico. Even Apostle Guy Musser said we really needed to just accept the fact that Lydia was possessed of evil spirits. Especially at meeting times when the spirit of the priesthood grew more powerful, the devils came raging out of Lydia, and Bettilyn paid the price.

It seemed strange that nine years after Mother left me, I would be standing here with Lydia, woman to woman, sister wives sharing the same husband, feeling I must continue the compassion and charity Mother showed to her. The eternal scope and importance of the principle of plural and celestial marriage was as real with us on that hillside as were the Canada thistles. To sacrifice our earthly passions, selfish feelings, and jealousies was the only way we could live forever with our brother, Christ. Uncle Isaac kept repeating how we must sacrifice all things the way Christ did in order to be entitled to eternal glory.

All of the images of happy sister wives and the highest degree of glory faded rapidly when Lydia spoke again. With a twisted smile she said, "You really are beautiful, you know…Isaac tells me he thinks so, too. He likes the high, firm curve of your breasts and buttocks, and he loves your hair. Isaac raves about your hair. He says it's so thick and long…Mine is scruffy." She twisted a strand of hair that had escaped the high wave twist pinned to the top of her head. I was speechless. I felt naked and had no idea how to respond to her.

I was stumbling over my words, trying to tell her I was sure

Uncle Isaac must love her hair, too, when she interrupted me. "Isaac can be a very jealous man, you know. He's even jealous of the children. If any of the kids rests his head on my breasts and Isaac is around, he says my breasts are his mountains, and he quotes the Song of Solomon." She shuddered and grasped my arms. King Solomon's words echoed in my mind as I remembered the graduation dance.

Just then Bettilyn came out on the small porch and hollered up the hill to the children gathered around us. The trance of sisterhood was shattered, and I mumbled I had to get back to work. I fled into the house past Emilia and Bettilyn, who both glared at me. Later Emilia came to me and warned me to be careful, because Lydia was a liar and caused so much trouble for Bettilyn that if I ever took sides with her, I would be frozen out of trust and friendship. The dull pain in the back of my head returned with a vengeance.

Sundays brought a flood of families as all of Bettilyn's older children came home for dinner. Sidney's truck-driving job kept him away from home a lot, so Ophelia was at her mother's more than she was at home. She and Lem's wife Holly did their laundry at the big house most of the time. Sometimes Ophelia was very kind to me; at other times, I sensed hostility that would only make sense if I were married to her husband and not her father.

Laman and Celeste and their children, Lem and Holly and their children, Ophelia and Sidney and their children descended on the house after church—it was always thirty to forty people. Bettilyn would have baked all Saturday night, setting out sixteen pies, eighty cinnamon buns, and other goodies to cool. Huge pots of potatoes had to be peeled, and we washed dishes for most of Sunday.

I was overtaken with continual fatigue and a loneliness that was impossible to quantify. I longed for quiet, private time with Uncle Isaac. Every day I fantasized he and I alone on the top of the mountain or anywhere without sister wives and children. I was ashamed of myself. Mother would never have felt such selfish emotions. I watched Ophelia and Celeste getting into their trucks with their husbands and children to go to the peace of their homes. The boys swooping by on their motor scooters or horses, whooping and yelling long into the night, and the continual arrival of more people—it all made me tense. This should have been part of the glory of my calling. These people were my husband's children and wives. They were all part of his kingdom, and I would be one of his queens. I prayed intensely for a broken heart and a contrite spirit and for the ability to keep sweet like my mother.

My body hurt, especially my feet, and my mind hurt unless Uncle Isaac was holding me in his arms and we were making love. I felt anxious from the moment he left until he came to me again; I longed to talk to him, only talk. But I didn't know how. When he did come to me, my mouth seemed to freeze shut, and sex happened. Even then I didn't really communicate with him. I didn't dare touch his body anywhere except his face and hands. He never asked me to.

Uncle Isaac called the whole family to evening meetings and firesides. He would read from a book called *Jonathan Livingston Seagull* by Richard Bach. Over and over he told us, "When it is my time to die, which could be anytime, none of you will ever see my face again, let alone the face of Christ, if you are not prepared to suffer as Christ suffered. You people cannot expect to slide into the celestial kingdom on someone else's coattails. You've got to suffer and sacrifice and be maligned and hated. Do you think the world will love you if you're doing the Lord's will? We can be dull, stupid, and common like all the other seagulls on the shore fighting for the rotten, stinking fish, or we can soar like Jonathan Livingston Seagull into the next life with a celestial vision." Uncle Isaac was fierce and bold and we loved it. I became determined I would be a high-flying seagull, no matter what the pain or sacrifice.

After he was finished speaking, Uncle Isaac would often lean back in his chair, put his crippled foot up, close his eyes, and say, "Sing some songs for me, girls, sing some songs." Usually, it was Babette and Phoebe who sang for their father. Their first song was always "My Daddy Is the Best Man in the World," which they composed themselves. His son Martin had written both words and music for another favorite, "No Man Wants to Die." Other times,

Celeste and Laman sang. If Celeste got Uncle Isaac talking, she'd sit at his feet for hours listening to him and asking him questions.

Later on that summer the prophet came to Canada and assigned Laman and Celeste a second wife—she was Grace Barnley. Grace was as grateful as a rescued puppy to be part of the Merrick family and worked long, hard hours to earn a place in Laman's life. Her sister Blythe had gone with her father to Trail where he was working. For some reason Blythe decided she didn't want to be in our Work anymore. Daddy said he heard she had mixed up with a gentile man and was no longer worthy. I struggled with the guilt of not treating her in a kind, Christ-like way—the way I would have liked to be treated. They still came to meetings sometimes, and whenever I saw Dolan Barnley, I was thankful I was married to Uncle Isaac. When he finally stopped coming to meetings altogether, the unmarried girls heaved a sigh of relief. They all felt God had protected them, especially when Dolan sent out letters announcing to everyone he knew, the Mormon Church, and the world that he was the Prophet Onias.*

Just when life found some kind of pattern, and all I was waiting for was to become pregnant and have Uncle Isaac's baby, Uncle Freddie knocked on our door. I opened it to find him standing there white as a ghost and looking as if he'd bolt if anyone made the wrong move. He asked for Uncle Isaac, who immediately went out to sit with Freddie in his car. They talked for an hour before Uncle Freddie departed down the gravel road in a cloud of dust. When Uncle Isaac came into the house, he seemed weary, and his limp was worse than it had been for weeks. My heart ached for him as he disappeared into Bettilyn's room.

It wasn't until a few days later that I realized Jean was home. Uncle Isaac took me aside and warned me not to visit her. The look in his eyes left little doubt that he meant it. The grief and pain over Naomi started all over again. Uncle Isaac's sermons in church were all about rebellious, wicked women who didn't have a clue about

---

*According to Jewish history, Onias was a high priest in Jerusalem who protected the temple for the Jews.

"the measure of their creation." As he preached he marched, swinging up high on his crippled foot, first in front of the pulpit and then in back of it. We were a captive audience and had no wish to be set free.

"Some of you women think you'll be able to bypass your husband to get to Christ...Wrong! I have a rebellious wife who thinks she can thumb her nose at me and take her daughters down forbidden paths. She will pay! In this life or the next, I'll have her dunging out my stables. You people mark my words. The sons of these rebellious women will always go back to their fathers, and the daughters will reap the results of the wilful disobedience of a wicked mother. They think they are going to get an *education!*" He spat out the word as if it were a foul, rotten carcass. "And have money! Their money will be a curse and they will die the second death. If they had never heard the fullness of the gospel or had a chance to participate in this order of the priesthood gospel, they could be excused because of ignorance. The worst sin, which is the sin against the Holy Ghost, makes you a son of perdition. It is the result of wilful disobedience to your file leader. You will pray for these mountains to fall on your head and pray for the eternal destruction of your body. There is no forgiveness in this world or the next for a son of perdition, and the blessing you can all pray for is to be cast into outer darkness, ground into native element, and purified. Then and only then will you find peace. Then the Lord can make use of you in the creation of other spirits. But you will cease to exist, worlds without end!"

I kept myself busy so I couldn't think about Jean. I knew if I did, I'd want to see her. I had so hoped she would be safe from the terrible fate that Daddy told us happened to all of the girls and women who had forsaken their covenants. I put Jean out of my mind—I just couldn't think about her.

In August Sidney took holidays from his work and decided to take a truckload of kids to Colorado City to see our people there. Ophelia told Bettilyn she wanted her to go with them. I would have to keep up with cooking for the chore crews, the hayers, and the fruit pickers. The day Bettilyn left, I panicked until Uncle Isaac told me he was bringing Lydia over to stay the week. I had fantasized about living with a sister wife I could joke and laugh with, and Lydia had told me she wanted the same thing. She hoped to share our husband in a loving way like Mother used to with Jan and Daddy. Uncle Isaac brought Lydia over with her children and her favorite aluminium pot, and we started to cook. Although she moved into Bettilyn's room, she refused to sleep in her bed.

We spent hours talking as we worked in the kitchen. I heard her side of the days and nights of pain she had suffered when Mother was alive. I heard about how Uncle Isaac bought a set of dishes for Bettilyn, and Lydia was given some of the discarded ones. She took them back to the ranch house at suppertime, opened the kitchen door, and flung them to the floor, breaking them all like a bride at a Greek wedding party. She punctuated her performance by screaming at Bettilyn that she refused to accept the crumbs from her table. As Lydia told me the story, I could almost hear the wailing of frightened babies and the disgust and horror of Bettilyn and her older daughters.

When they came from her own lips, Lydia's narratives about howling through the foothills like a wounded coyote were tortured tales of agonizing loneliness. Weeping into the night, she begged a merciful God for a reprieve from the harsh reasoning of the Merrick mind.

I cringed at Lydia's stories. Her words echoed the feelings I'd been living with…but if I was lonely, it could only mean I was defective in some way. How could anyone be lonely floating in such a sea of priesthood spirits? To be a success in the principle of plural marriage, I had to be best friends to both Bettilyn and Lydia, but I had twinges of fear at what Emilia would say if she could hear Lydia talking. She'd already warned me that friendship with Lydia was traitorous, and I would suffer the consequences. As we canned hundreds of quarts of cherries, I tried to put all of these contradictory, painful stories into a box in the back of my mind.

Lydia made her savory chicken noodle soup and we served it with fluffy white buns. Bettilyn's boys loved Lydia's soup, but they would never tell their mother that. Nephi came to me indignant, making sure I knew what Emilia had already said. His mother would be furious with me for letting Lydia into her kitchen. I explained to him there was no reason to be mad at me when Uncle Isaac had brought her over. How wrong I turned out to be. Bettilyn was furious for weeks and refused to believe my stuttering attempts to explain that I hadn't asked Uncle Isaac to bring Lydia into her house.

My first conference as the wife of the file leader finally arrived. There was something almost sacred about being able to rush to the car to greet the apostles as they pulled up from their long trip. After they retired to their carefully prepared rooms to rest, Bettilyn and I finished peeling the potatoes for supper. Her son Martin came in, his heavy brows knitted together tightly.

"How can you tell a lie to beat the devil?" he asked. Bettilyn and I both knew he was referring to what Uncle Guy Musser had told us about how he'd lied to the Canada Customs officers about bringing something across the border.

"He brought holy garments and sets of the Truth volumes," Bettilyn responded.

Martin shook his head in defiance and looked fiercely at his mother. "How can you tell a lie to beat the devil? Is everything justified if you're doing it in the name of God?"

"Oh Martin, you're just eighteen and feeling the spirit of rebellion." In a fury, Bettilyn washed the last of the potatoes and slammed a pot onto the stove. "You know God doesn't recognize the borders between countries. God's laws are more important and necessary than man's laws, and the Lord prepares the way for His will to be done at all costs."

Martin leaned back against the doorjamb, seemingly satisfied he had flustered his mother. "What's good for one is good for all."

Water splashed from the pot onto the stove as Bettilyn dumped in some potatoes. "Now don't you be fussin' about this anymore...Goodness knows, I don't have time for it!"

Martin disappeared. I thought about his argument. I knew Bettilyn was telling the truth, but what about the twelfth article of faith? Joseph Smith said, "We believe in being subject to kings, presidents, rulers, and magistrates, and in honoring and sustaining the law." We were supposed to be fundamentalist believers in Joseph Smith. Didn't that mean we were to live plural marriage, but also be kinder, more honest, and more forgiving than everyone else? My head started to hurt, so I stopped thinking and set the table with our finest dishes.

The prophet and the apostles came to eat, and then the men went to their secret meeting. I hoped Uncle Isaac would come to me when he returned that night. I needed him badly. Earlier in the week I had spoken to him only briefly and said goodnight to him, but I wanted much more.

He had kissed me and told me, "One of the commandments of the prophet is that all worthy brethren should abstain from sex for one week before the men's secret meeting. We are instructed not to talk about it other than to direct our wives. The most important thing is to be obedient, and thus the Lord can work through us. When we have been free from all carnal activity for that long, the Lord can reveal the secrets of His kingdom." I clung to him throughout the long week and was anxious for him to come to me after the meeting. He stayed at Lydia's.

That night after my bath, I stood on the heat vent near the entrance to the kitchen. I was wearing my rose-flowered plissé nightgown. It was cold both inside and outside the house, and I found the heat calming and sensual on my bare skin. My gown billowed around me like the dress of a fairy queen. I looked toward the main door, and there was Jonah staring at me. Black-haired and as fierce-looking as his mother, he whirled and slammed the door.

Emilia came out of the kitchen and saw me standing there. She rushed over, stopped only inches from my face, and hissed, "Don't you know that anyone coming through that door can see right through your nightgown? Are you some kind of whore that you want to show off your nipples and legs and all the hair in your crotch? You make me sick!" After that I never left the bathroom without wrapping Mother's rose chenille robe tightly around me.

In the weeks following that episode, when Jonah joined the rest of the boys on their way to do morning chores, he would linger under my bedroom window and sing "Devil Woman" at the top of his lungs. I pulled the covers over my ears to shut out the words.

Even then, I couldn't shake the memory of Jean and Aline and I walking and talking about the clay heart Jonah had made for me. It was five years since Jean had given it to me because he couldn't get up the courage to do it himself. The girls told me they had it all planned—I was going to marry Jonah and live in the house their mother built with his help. How could we have known then that I, three years his junior, would one day be his stepmother and sleeping in the very same house? Since he hadn't crawled over "fool's hill" yet, I guess it was really much better to be married to his dad.

During the first two weeks after I missed my period, I was afraid to tell Uncle Isaac I was pregnant. What would I do if he wouldn't hold me and make love to me anymore? He certainly never had anything to do with me otherwise. I hated the thought of telling him, but I knew I had to. I couldn't be found guilty of adulterating the birth canal by disobeying the law of chastity. This child would be a covenant child.

When I told him, he was pleased. He suggested I go to the doctor to confirm it. I was terrified at the thought of actually having a gentile doctor put his hands on my body. I got an appointment with Dr. Morgan, who had been Mother's doctor at the medical clinic in Creston. He was kind with his questions, but I blushed scarlet when he asked me if I was married. For Uncle Isaac's sake, I had to say no. The doctor took my little bottle of urine. When he came back, he said I was pregnant and told me he would do a full prenatal checkup. I was so nervous when the nurse told me to take off my clothes and put on the skimpy cotton gown. With gloves on his hands, the doctor put his fingers deep inside me. In a flash I was back in the playhouse. I was tempted to ask him if he could see anything wrong. Sometimes my vagina still hurt, and when it did, all I could think about was that stick.

The doctor kept saying, "Uh-huh, that looks good. Yes, this is fine." He wiped his hands and said everything seemed to be all right. He asked me gently if I needed to talk about anything—anything at all. I thought he was wondering if I was happy about being pregnant. I was offended. How dare he think I would ever talk to a Gentile about anything like that? If I did, I'd be a worse traitor than if I talked to Lydia. Jan said any woman who spoke against the sacred principle was but a hiss and a byword. She continually brought up the women's shelter in Salt Lake City that was built back in 1876 for unhappy polygamous women to escape their husbands. That was when the Church of Jesus Christ of Latter-day Saints still lived plural marriage. As Jan told the story, only twelve women had ever used the shelter, and it was auctioned off for a quarter of its market value. I wouldn't think of complaining or giving anyone a hint I might be sad or worried. I squared my shoulders and looked the doctor in the eyes. "Thank you, I'm fine."

When Uncle Isaac told me the law of chastity was officially in effect between us, I felt a chill settle over me that deepened with the fall weather. He didn't even come to my bed to hold me in his arms anymore, and the loneliness was painful. I knew he still stayed the night at Lydia's. Partway into the winter, he decided television was a waste of time; he said the boys should be out getting physically fit. He took the cord off the TV set in our house but left Lydia's alone. Lydia told me how much he loved to watch *The Sonny and Cher Comedy Hour*. I babysat her children while she went into Creston to clean house and stay with an older woman who paid her to help her sometimes. Uncle Isaac came over one night while she was gone. He watched Sonny and Cher and *Bearcats!* and then was gone.

I bathed in Lydia's claw-foot bathtub, the whole time hearing her voice in my mind: "You know how much Isaac loves to have his back washed. I always get the kids to bed and then he says, 'Get in here, woman,' so I do. Almost every time he ends up pullin' me into the tub with him and then..." She nudged me and winked. "You know what happens."

I bit my tongue to keep from saying, I can't say I do, having never had the pleasure.

"Sometime when he's here we should push him into the tub together—that would be such a good time." I nodded numbly, mortified at the vivid picture I now had of Lydia and Uncle Isaac's intimate moments. I wished him back but he didn't come, and I managed to sleep.

He invited me to go to Rosemary to conference to see Grandmother and Grandpa. I could scarcely believe my ears when he asked me, and I begged him for money to make a dress. I wheedled Ophelia into making it. It was princess-style, bright yellow, and the baby in my belly could hardly be seen. My first trip alone with him was heaven. Uncle Kelvin Whitmer drove us, and I spent the whole trip hugging myself for joy. Grandmother asked Uncle Isaac for permission to take me to say hello to Grandmother and Grandfather Norton. Instead of coming straight back after our visit, Grandmother drove around Rosemary and told me how proud she was of me—now we were truly sisters in the Work.

When we got home, Grandmother ended up crying in my arms. I felt helpless as she sobbed, "Oh, Deb, you are at the beginning of this sacred calling and have so much opportunity. I'm heartsick about your Uncle Nick. He's left the wife he married for time and all eternity in the Cardston Temple. He's with another woman and I'm scared for him. He has the knowledge—and still he committed adultery. He knows better and will be judged so harshly because he does." Grandmother was wringing her hands. We hugged and got out of the car.

She showed me the bed I was to share with Uncle Isaac. I hesitated, worried he'd think that sleeping with me would be out of place because of the law of chastity—especially considering his week-long sexual fast would be over after the men's secret meeting. He should have brought someone along who wasn't pregnant. Uncertain as to what to do, I just went to bed. I was in the middle of a sound sleep and dreaming about Uncle Isaac when he slipped into bed and became part of my dream. I turned to kiss him and soon our bodies were intertwined.

His voice was a pleading sob. "Tell me you want it...Tell me you need it...Tell me. You don't know what you're doing to me." Even though my mind was racing now, I couldn't answer him...not when we were making love. Not when I was finally getting the affection I so badly needed. I lay in his arms for several minutes after he was spent. He was subdued and repentant as he whispered, "I'm sorry. I shouldn't have done that...Why do you have to be so damned beautiful, anyway?" He turned his back on me and spoke no more.

I was fully awake now and more lonely than I was before—only now I was afraid, too. I had allowed the law of chastity to be broken.

Just a couple of days after we returned home from the conference, Jean came to see me unannounced. We both turned sixteen the same week in October. The last three months had been very long, and I was sick at the thought we could never really be friends again. Only if her mother were to repent and come crawling back to her husband on bended knees could that happen. She rested her hand on my bedroom door. "This used to be Grandma's room."

I nodded uncomfortably. "I know." We felt so awkward with each other; neither of us knew what to say. At that moment I felt years older than she was. I longed to tell her my body was experiencing the most beautiful changes, making it part of creation. I hadn't told anyone except Uncle Isaac, and I was dying to tell Jean she would soon have another half-brother or sister.

"I hear you're going to school at the Prince Charles high school…I remember when Irene went there. Is it hard?"

Jean shook her head. "The school part isn't. I have one friend from church—Mom is taking us all to the Mormon Church in town. I'm in 4-H, too." She paused. "You know, some of the kids from here walk by our place on the way to school and throw rocks and call us harlots and bitches. Such righteous brothers and sisters!" Her cheeks were white when she said this, and her eyes were bright and hard like her mother's.

I had no idea what to say to her. Suddenly, I just had to know if there was any chance of her coming back—if not to Uncle Freddie, then to some other good priesthood man. "What happened, Jean? Why did you leave Uncle Freddie? Was he unkind?"

She shuddered and shook her head. "I went to a wedding with Aunt Elizabeth for one of our relatives in Cardston—the ones who belong to the Latter-day Saints church. They had so much fun. The bride and groom were happier than I had ever seen anyone. That wasn't how I felt being married. Do you feel that way?" Her voice suddenly became quiet. "I told him to bring me home for a while. I thought maybe I could go back, but when he came to see me, I didn't want to see him. I hid in the bedroom even though Mom said I should talk to him. I crawled under the bed and Rhoda sat on top and told him to leave...I'm going to have a beautiful wedding like that some day. It won't be anything like what happened here."

I easily conjured up the image of the twelve-year-old Rhoda with her fierce eyes, coal-black hair, and folded arms facing down a fifty-one-year-old man. I vaguely wished God could have softened her heart.

Jean looked at me expectantly. "Well, say something."

But again I had no idea what to say to her, and she left without another word.

For several weeks after the conference in Rosemary I was plagued with morning sickness and consumed with guilt. The first week in December was the Creston conference. Lately, Emilia had been living down at Daddy's. Soon after she started working for him at the gas station doing the bookkeeping and ordering parts, she became more and more unhappy. Uncle Isaac and Daddy decided she should live with her sisters at Daddy's house for a while. Uncle Roy had even given her a release from Uncle Isaac, which would be something like a divorce in the gentile world. The prophet would decide at this coming meeting if Emilia should be married to Daddy for a time, so he could take care of her for Uncle Isaac. After she died, her spiritual understanding would be perfect, and the worldly limits on love would be different. She'd be able to love Uncle Isaac the way she should and get over the kind of love she had for him as an adopted father.

The last few weeks had been very tense with all the preparation for the conference. Ophelia had been here every day cleaning and sewing to help get things ready. My bedroom was prepared for company, so I was to sleep on a cot. I heard Uncle Isaac come in from chores and because the house was quiet, I decided to slip into his bedroom where he was resting. He'd scarcely look me in the face when we were in the company of his family, and I had a hard time ever catching him alone. I bent down to kiss him. He rolled over on his elbow and reached out to me. At that moment a warm, sticky fluid gushed from inside me, and I ran for the bathroom.

When I found blood on my legs and panties, I started shaking so badly I was afraid I might never stop. The house was busy with people, and there was soon a knock on the bathroom door. I cleaned myself up the best I could and went in search of Bettilyn. She instructed me to go right back to bed on the living room cot and lie down as much as possible.

The day dragged on until it seemed like a week since the morning. I kept listening for Uncle Isaac's voice in the hopes he'd come and comfort me, but he never showed up. Once, I heard his voice in the kitchen, and I was sure he was coming, but he didn't even look around the corner. I pretended to sleep, and by lunchtime I thought I might be all right. In the late afternoon, waves of pain attacked me every twenty minutes. I was still bleeding. Bettilyn sent Babette in with a bowl of soup and even came by herself with a few kind words. I longed for a quiet corner I could curl up in, but the conference guests arrived when I was in the middle of the worst of my anguish. I felt so out of place. The wives of the prophet and his apostles glowed with the peace and joy of all things celestial. I tried to smile and greet them but the pains were increasing in both intensity and frequency, and it was hard to keep sweet. Bettilyn was embarrassed by my performance; she rushed to set up my cot in the laundry room where I could be out of sight. I was grateful to be away from the festivities, to be able to hide my shame from the rest of the world. I was afraid the prophet or one of his wives would guess my baby was dying because I'd had sex with Uncle Isaac.

The pain was constant and merciless now. The men returned from their secret meeting, and Daddy came to see how I was doing. He promised me the Lord loved me as much as he did and that all things happened for a reason. Through the thin walls of the room I could hear Uncle Roy talking to Emilia. He told her the Lord would bless her always and she would be crowned with the queens in the celestial kingdom if she made the proper choice. She did. Emilia was resealed to Uncle Isaac for time and all eternity. She and I were sister wives once again.

Daddy went home, and Uncle Isaac and the prophet came in to see me. They talked to me for a minute, then stepped outside the door. I couldn't make out what Uncle Isaac said, but I could hear the prophet's reply. "I think you should take her to the hospital. When I was in Mexico under the direction of President Barlow, Martha took sick and by the time we got her to the doctor, gangrene had nearly killed her because the baby she was carrying had been dead for over a month...We'll go in my car."

Uncle Isaac helped me off the cot and into the car. On the drive to the hospital, Bettilyn and the prophet's wife sat in the back while I sat up front between my husband and Uncle Roy. I prayed for this nightmare to end and for our baby to live. Ever-present was the fear and guilt that I had killed my own flesh and blood because I had tempted Uncle Isaac. I was certain the prophet knew I had committed this transgression, and the spirit who was this child had been offended enough to want to leave.

Bettilyn was determined to play the role of a devoted sister wife in front of the prophet. To show she really cared about me, she helped me out of the car and down the hallway to the emergency room. Uncle Isaac was nowhere to be seen. He wanted nothing to do with me in public, never mind being registered as my husband. No gentile nurse or doctor would understand how the Lord wanted a fifteen-year-old girl to be married to a fifty-seven-year-old man. The prophet had warned him he must be wary of the possibility that he could be charged with statutory rape.

It was after midnight; the hospital was quiet and dark. The nurse shooed Bettilyn away and helped strip off my blood-soaked clothing. She stroked my hands until they relaxed, then gave me a hug and began rubbing my shoulders. I knew I should resist this strange gentile woman's handling of me, but I was too tired and suffering too much to be afraid of her. She gave me an injection after a doctor had seen me. In the early morning hours, I pushed out the baby. How fitting that a blessed spirit would choose to be discarded into a gentile toilet rather than live on in my defiled body.

The nurse got me back into bed and scooped up the tiny baby. I could hear the murmur of her voice in the hallway as she spoke with Bettilyn. When she came back, she told me it was a boy about six inches long. Bettilyn left to give the news to the others while the nurse filled a basin with warm water and bathed me. I was shaking violently and begged for more blankets. She brought them and asked if I wanted my back rubbed. I didn't know what to tell her—no one had ever rubbed my back before, not even Mother. Finally, I mumbled that she could if she wanted to. The touch of her hands in the smooth, cool lotion was almost painful, because I had to accept that the body she was touching was really mine. She gave me another pill and I drifted into a fitful sleep. My childhood nightmare about Mother's nameless baby becoming my doll with no name jolted me awake. I lay thinking about just one more nameless entity that had drifted through my life. Where did all these spirits go? Would I ever have a chance to tell my baby boy just how sorry I was to steal his chance for life?

No one knew how to talk to me when I got home, and because I was still hiding the horrible secret of my transgression, I preferred avoiding them as well. Bettilyn seemed content for me to stay by myself, and much of my time was spent alone in my room. It seemed appropriate when Uncle Isaac declared that Christmas was a gentile tradition to be done away with. Celebrating the birth of a baby, even if it was the Christ child, was so unfair. Bettilyn wasn't ready to totally dispense with the tradition of giving gifts, so she decided we would open them on the 28th instead of the 25th and just call it "gift day."

As we all gathered that morning to open presents, I started to bleed. Blood and clots gushed out every time I moved. I tried to explain the situation to Bettilyn, but she said she'd been having periods like that for years, and so had her daughters.

I called Lydia and told her I was terrified because the bleeding wouldn't stop. She said to drink onion-skin tea; one of the apostles had told her to drink it, and it had saved her life. I dug through my books to find the one on the healing power of herbal medicine. It said the same about onion skins as it said about hops: both herbs would cause a woman to bleed when she lost her menstrual cycle for an unhealthy reason. After reading that, I lost my faith, then chastised myself the way Mother used to. If the apostle told Lydia it would save her, I had to believe it to be true. She sent some skins over with Uncle Isaac, and I drank several quarts of the tea. I felt tired. Every time I moved, the blood still gushed. The toilet bowl looked as if it were brewing red Jell-O soup. Just when I was beginning to fear I would flush away the last of my life's blood and collapse white on the floor, Grandmother called from Rosemary. She instructed me to phone the doctor immediately. He said he'd send me some tiny pills called ergot, and I thought he said a D. and C. might be necessary. He made me promise to call him if the bleeding hadn't stopped completely in three days. After three days of hard cramping, the bleeding did stop, and I didn't have to find out what a D. and C. was.

I was terribly discouraged with the course of events. My guilt hung over me like a thick black cloud. I was certain Uncle Isaac was blaming me for the death of our child and afraid he'd never want to hold me again. I wanted so much to be in his arms; I wanted him to want me again. I slept most of the time, and when I wasn't sleeping I was crying. The few waking moments I had, I daydreamed about Uncle Isaac making love to me—of his holding me and touching me. I knew if he'd come, I'd hold onto him with all my strength, because when we were separated my body felt dead and I was afraid.

With the coming of the New Year, I had to get out of bed and struggle through seemingly endless days. The school session had started again and Uncle Isaac announced I would be babysitting Laman and Celeste's little boys. I dragged myself around, determined I wouldn't let Bettilyn catch me crying. She told anyone who would listen that I was "busy enjoying poor health." I cringed with embarrassment as she told the boys and girls in her class that it was time for girls who thought they were old enough to be married to be much more responsible. Her condemning sarcasm was echoed by Jan, who enjoyed being proven right by my failure as her father's wife. When everyone was out of sight and I was alone with the little boys, the tears never stopped.

One day in February Celeste was with her children and everyone else was at school. The house was empty except for me. The fire had gone out and I was in the basement struggling to chip some pieces from a knurled block of spruce to get enough kindling to start it again. Uncle Isaac had brought us a few blocks of wet wood he'd cut to "tide us over" until he could replenish the dry stacks. Every time I swung the axe, it settled with a dull thud into the punky wood. The harder I tried, the more the block defied me. When the head of the axe became embedded so deeply that I couldn't pry it free, I sagged onto the log pile. Praying to Heavenly Father, I begged Him to forgive me and to see fit to still let me be a mother in Israel. Uncle Isaac's words came back to me. "The wages of sin are death." I had proven his words and killed my baby. "Oh Heavenly Father, please give me a second chance," I sobbed.

The sound of the kitchen door closing stopped my prayer. Uncle Isaac crouched at the top of the stairs looking straight down on me. Impatiently and without a word, he took me by the shoulders and sat me on the chair beside the stove. He pried the axe from the block, split some wood, and made the fire.

Later, when he came in from doing chores, the house was warm and I had strings of wet, clean laundry hanging downstairs. I was supposed to be making bread but was still in the basement warming my bones and soaking up the smell of the lye soap and drying spruce. The moment I heard his footsteps above me, I wanted to fly up into his arms. The possibility that he wouldn't want me kept me glued to the chair. A few minutes later, he came down, took my hand, and led me through the strings of laundry and up the stairs to his room. Without uttering a word, he took the clothes from my body one piece at a time. Wrapping me in his flowing underwear, he carried me to his bed.

The house seemed full of secrets, and Uncle Isaac resolved to rearrange his family. One morning Babette came up to my room and said in a singsong fashion, "We're moving to Lydia's and Lydia is moving here."

"How do you know that? I haven't heard anything yet. I wonder why Uncle Isaac didn't tell me." I struggled to keep from showing her my confusion. I had learned that in this family, showing any sign of weakness was a guarantee for further attack. "I don't see how we could move there anyway...Lydia's house is half the size of this house. There are only three bedrooms."

Babette sneered at my questions. "You'll never get anywhere if you think you can question Daddy like this. He tells us everything. If you'd get up before five and help with the cows like we do, you'd know. Besides, it doesn't matter what the size of the house is. If Daddy says we can do it, then we can."

As the time for the move approached, everyone was busy sorting things and packing. I helped with meals and wondered when Uncle Isaac would tell me what he wanted me to do. Every time I saw him, I asked him. He only chuckled and told me he would not stand to be questioned. "You'll see," he said. "You'll see."

When the big day rolled around, I confronted him. "What do you have in mind for me? I haven't packed anything yet…I don't know what to do." I burst into tears.

He just stood there with the smug half-smile he so often wore when he knew he was in control of a situation. Finally, he laughed. "You told me you were willing to do what I said without question. I want you to stay here…I think you and Lydia will be good for each other."

My face dropped as he turned his back on me and walked from the room. I was not much comforted. My faith was terribly weak, and the feelings of loneliness only intensified as all the rooms but mine emptied one by one. I watched as the hundreds of jars of fruit and vegetables I had helped can were cleared from the fruit-room shelves and put into boxes. I ran from the house and climbed the hill above the ranch to where Uncle Isaac had picked the rosebud and told me we would make a beautiful baby together. I stomped down the snow and lay back on that very same piece of earth. I wandered for hours in the cold. When I got home, Lydia had been delivered with her eight children. They were emptying boxes and sorting things into the cupboards. I asked her when the rest of her stuff was coming, and she said it was all here. Her cooking supplies scarcely filled one cupboard, and her jars of preserves covered only half of one of the twelve shelves that had been heavy-laden earlier in the day. The difference in the amount of food frightened me; I asked her if she was sure we wouldn't starve.

"Don't think I haven't been scared of that before," she retorted. "I've taken a safety pin, string, and a stick and gone out to the pond in the night and prayed I could catch enough fish for breakfast because the kids went to bed hungry." Lydia's bright blue eyes glistened with angry tears.

I heard again the words of Bettilyn, Jan, and Emilia. "Lydia is the most wasteful woman on earth. Some women can throw out the window with a teaspoon more than their husband can bring in the front with a scoop shovel. She's just the trial of Daddy's life, and all we can do is support him. If they don't have food over there, it's their own fault. They get the same family allowance we all get." I looked around at the few things on the floor and the shelves and wondered.

As the days crept by, I wasn't sure I'd be able to go on. Sometimes Lydia was fun and exciting to be with, but the stark reality of getting by from one day to the next was numbing. Uncle Isaac rarely came around. We often saw him drive by with a truckload of his other kids or with a load of grain he was hauling to the dairy barn. One day he drove by with Bettilyn on his way to the bunkhouse, where some of the boys now had to sleep due to the lack of room in Lydia's old house.

Lydia became enraged at the sight of the two of them together. She dragged up all her old resentments and went over and over the humiliation she'd been handed in her life. When the food got really scarce, she ranted about Uncle Isaac's neglect and her helplessness. If only my baby had lived, I could have helped her with money from family allowance. Now, I had nothing to offer. I didn't know how to encourage her. Sometimes I told her about the hard times and the pain I received at the hands of Bettilyn and Emilia and Jan. When we heard they were on a trip to Colorado City with Uncle Isaac, we were both angry and I got sick to my stomach. I just wanted to die.

When Uncle Isaac finally showed up at the house, Lydia was full of love for him and flaunted her knowledge of the scriptural reasons for the beauty of plural marriage. I had a much harder time than she did switching passionate feelings off and on. For me, turning rejection into love and condemnation into compassion was difficult—like changing a rock into a gold brick. All I knew was that I wanted Uncle Isaac to make love to me and give me a baby to hold.

My head hurt almost every moment of the waking day, and more and more I was having difficulty sleeping. After weeks of being alone in the house with Lydia, her children, and her bitterness, I had to talk to someone else. I needed someone to help me decide what was wrong with what Lydia was saying. I walked to the school. The road I used to run down just a short year before thrilled with my holy mission to be a mother in Israel seemed very long. I felt heavy and sluggish.

As I entered the door at the bottom of the school, Emilia was coming out. I was excited to see her and hoped we could talk. She hesitated for just a second as she passed me by. There was a look of total disgust in her eyes. "How could you choose to live with Lydia?" she hissed. She was still growling as she turned her back on me. "You wait and see—you'll get exactly what you deserve."

Chapter 16

Emilia stomped from the building, slamming the door in my face. The shock of my sister wife's attack left me numb. I stood in a daze as children ran past me in their rush to get to the schoolyard. Emilia's contempt made no sense at all. How had she gotten the notion that I preferred to live with Lydia?

In desperation, I searched the school for Bettilyn. I found her in her classroom marking papers. The moment she saw me, her eyes snapped downward to focus on her work. When I begged her to talk to me, she continued with a flurry of red marks on someone's scribbler. She was cool and unreachable until I managed to blubber that I didn't understand why Uncle Isaac wanted me to live with Lydia in the first place—it had all been a terrible mistake.

Even as I wept, I was disgusted with myself. I felt I was not only betraying Lydia, but also Mother. "I can't live with Lydia. She's crazy—just like you said. I never know when she's going to be really happy or really angry. If I'm friends with her, I don't get to be friends with you, and everyone else hates me, too. Please talk to Uncle Isaac and tell him I have to come back to live with you."

As I spoke, Bettilyn's demeanor changed. She was gloating. "Well, if you're really sure you want to leave the wonderful environment over there, I guess I could. Daddy said Lydia told him the two of you were living in celestial bliss. He said you chose to stay with Lydia. That's why everyone is so furious. No one can possibly imagine what possessed you to want to live with her." I shook my head vigorously. With a smug smile, she resumed her marking, promising to fix things at home before she sent me on my way.

The very next morning, Uncle Isaac arrived at Lydia's house unannounced. With Laman at his side, he simply walked into the house and threw open the door to my room. I looked up in shock, not knowing what to expect. "Well, don't stand there like a dolt!" he said in a harsh voice. "Get your things."

I looked into his cold hard eyes like a deer staring into the headlights of an oncoming vehicle. "I don't have all day!" he shouted. I immediately grabbed my suitcase and started throwing things in while the pair of them stood there with their hands on their hips. As Uncle Isaac and Laman loaded my stuff into the truck, Lydia watched from the kitchen. I couldn't bear to look her in the eyes. The pain and betrayal etched on her face left me hollow to the depths of my soul. I didn't know how to tell her I longed to love her, understand her, and be her friend. The loneliness being with her had brought upon me was unbearable. I had lived on this planet for just two years longer than she had been married to Uncle Isaac—how could I possibly understand how fear and pain and isolation had become the total focus of her life?

I was surprised when Uncle Isaac brought the truck to a stop outside the school. I thought maybe they were going to pick something up at Laman's before dropping me off at Bettilyn's, but instead they grabbed my hope chest off the truck. Uncle Isaac said, "Well, what're you waiting for?"

I followed them upstairs to a little box of a room directly over Laman's apartment. It was empty other than a couple of wooden desks with broken seats that had been shoved to one corner. This was not at all what I'd been expecting. Rather than ingratiating myself to Emilia and Bettilyn and getting back into their lives, it seemed all I had done was alienate myself from Lydia and everyone else. I looked out the multi-paned windows that covered most of the west wall, feeling like I had jumped from the frying pan directly into the flames. How was I ever going to see more of Uncle Isaac now?

I was jolted from my daydreaming when he yelled at me. "Damn it, woman, you'll have lots of time to stand around when we get done with this…so unless you want to drag this bloody bed up here yourself, give us a hand!"

I rushed downstairs to help him with a rusty set of springs. He was sweating profusely and looked to be all but done in. We maneuvered it up the narrow stairwell and dropped it in the center of the room. Laman and I made another trip to lug up the mattress while Uncle Isaac rested on top of a broken desk. Leaving me to carry up the metal end boards and put them together, they disappeared. Uncle Isaac hollered back up the stairs that I could go to Bettilyn's house for meals or eat with Laman, Celeste, and Grace. It was up to me.

I sat on my hope chest in frustration and surveyed the room that was to be my home. Uncle Michael had constructed everything from one-by-four lumber—the shelves, the walls, the ceiling, the doors, everything. There were no curtains for the windows, and although it was nice to look out over the yard now, it would be like being in a goldfish bowl at night.

The flowers Laman and Celeste had planted, together with the graceful willows, gave the place the aura of a southern plantation. I couldn't help but think about the contrast between this and Lydia's. At her house we had worked diligently to dig up the rocky earth and plant a few flowers and a small garden with a shovel, a hoe, and a rake. Remembering the few pennies we had to buy food, let alone seeds, left me feeling sad and ashamed that I was so grateful to be gone.

To brighten my room, I arranged flowers, hung a picture of the prophet on the wall, and used bits of lace to cover my hope chest and lampshade. I hoped that Uncle Isaac would come to me in the moonlight and hold me until the empty place inside me was full again. I waited night after night for him to come. I spent hours pleading with Heavenly Father to bring him to me, and equally as much time reproaching myself for my selfish attitude. Uncle Isaac was an important man, and like Christ, he "must be about His Father's business." Who was I to question his motivation or complain about his lack of attention?

Laman had made up plaques and signs so every household could display them on their walls. They were all simple, practical messages. *Uncle Roy says: Whatever we do we must never complain; Uncle Roy says: We must keep sweet*; *Uncle Roy says: The Spirit of God is the Spirit of Peace.* I helped him sell the messages at the school bazaar and had a difficult time deciding which one to display on my own wall. Heavenly Father knew how hard it was for me to keep sweet, but after thinking about the trials I had endured over the last few months, I decided on *Uncle Roy says: We must come before the Lord with a broken heart and a contrite spirit.* I knew I needed to be reminded constantly that the only way I would ever get to be with Mother and with Christ was to suffer.

Almost every night I cried until I fell into an uneasy sleep, and then the dreams came to me. Sometimes I saw my tiny six-inch baby with no name drifting just out of my reach. I would follow him and as I got near, the earth would give way, my bare feet would sink into a swamp, and a cold mist would descend upon me. That was when Mother would come to take my baby. The swamp was all that remained...but the muddy water became warm and welcoming and soon my gauzy white gown was mired in mud and I sank away into the black peace. Invariably, when I woke, I was sweating and nauseated.

Sometimes in my dreams I was in an orphanage. Rows and rows of babies were lined up in metal cribs in huge white wards, and almost all of them were crying. I floated down the rows until I saw a girl baby who was not crying, just gazing curiously at my white lace and footless body. She was dressed in a white flannel gown with smocking and a finely embroidered kitten on the yoke. I knew the gown to be one Mother had made. This baby had round blue eyes and lots of thick black hair. As she smiled and gurgled at me, I told the nurses I'd take her. And then the dream changed and I was in the bottom of this building—the one Uncle Michael built for his family—but it was transformed into a type of bomb shelter camouflaged with vines. The roots of the vines formed the beds, the cupboards, and even a waterfall. Into this comfortable green cave I brought babies—hundreds of babies who lived with me, all happy and safe.

Being a mother in Israel and having a healthy second child with Uncle Isaac became the focus of my existence. He'd been doing well of late, but I was concerned that illness could befall him before we brought the spirits we had promised to earth. More worrisome even was the fact I hadn't had a period since I had miscarried. I wasn't certain my body was working properly or if it ever would again, but I knew that women who stopped having periods stopped having babies, too.

I'd been thinking about calling Grandmother to ask her advice, but I didn't have access to a phone. In desperation I sneaked over to Bettilyn's when she was at school and used her phone to call Dr. Morgan's office. The receptionist gave me an appointment, and I begged Emilia to give me a ride to town so I could get some sanitary pads. When she dropped me off at the drugstore, I watched her little car disappear from sight before I headed up the street to the clinic.

The doctor asked me how I'd been doing since my abortion. The moment he said "abortion," my face burned as if on fire and I squirmed uncomfortably. How could he have known I'd killed my own baby? Was he able to talk to God like Uncle Isaac? He realized my reaction was in response to his choice of words and explained that the word "abortion" was a generic term that could be used in the same connotation as miscarriage. After he told me that, he sat for a long time just looking at me.

"Have you had sex again since you lost your child?"

I flushed, looked at my feet, and nodded. "But only once," I mumbled.

He smiled and grabbed a container from the shelf. "First things first," he said softly. "Can you just step down the hall and give me a sample?"

When I came back, he handed the bottle to the nurse and put me on his exam table. He told me he had worried about not seeing me after my miscarriage and just wanted to make sure all was well. By the time he'd finished doing a pelvic exam, the nurse had returned with a slip of paper from the lab.

I felt giddy the moment he told me I was pregnant. I couldn't believe Heavenly Father had forgiven me and answered my prayers so quickly. I'd been given a second chance. After I left the doctor's office, I was overcome with guilt. I felt terrible about wanting Uncle Isaac to come to me when I was already carrying his covenant child. Now I knew why we hadn't been together since that moment of passion. I marveled at my husband's inspiration, because surely the Lord must have told him I was with child, and he had prevented us from committing the same grievous adultery that caused our first baby to die. I realized my husband's abstinence and the lonely nights had been purposeful, and my baby had been protected by God's mercy and my husband's obedience to His law.

Late one Saturday night, Laman and Celeste came upstairs into the school where Celeste was practicing her piano. I had changed into the fuchsia silk pajamas she had made me for a wedding present and brushed out my hair so it was long and loose. I sat in the corner where I wouldn't bother them and just listened as they sang. All of a sudden, Uncle Isaac was there watching me. My heart skipped a beat when he settled beside me. He sat in silence for a while, then spoke to Celeste. "Sing for me, Daughter."

I had rehearsed an imaginary conversation with him hundreds of times, but now I felt tongue-tied. Why was that? Mother and Daddy had discussions about everything...Why couldn't I find one thing to talk to my husband about? I kept thinking if Celeste and Laman would just leave before Uncle Isaac disappeared, maybe we could communicate. Finally, they went downstairs.

With his arm around me, Uncle Isaac walked me to my bedroom. This was the first time he'd been in this room since he'd dumped the bedsprings in the middle of the floor and abandoned me. I made a feeble attempt to talk to him. I explained I wanted to get to know him better, that I needed more familiarity. I told him he was right—the doctor had confirmed I was pregnant. I told him I was impressed at the way Heavenly Father revealed all to him so he knew things about my body that even I didn't know.

I asked him to hug me. He put his arms awkwardly around me, and we sat in stiff silence. Before long, we were lying stretched out on the bed, and he was touching me all over. My pajama top was lying on the bed when I froze and sat up. I couldn't do this and risk killing another baby!

Caressing my cheeks with his lips, Uncle Isaac whispered in my ear, "You want me to stay, don't you? Just say the word and I'll stay...It's up to you."

I wanted him to stay...He had to stay. I didn't know how to tell him yes, and yet not make love. My confusion was obvious. My head was hurting worse than usual. Uncle Isaac's kisses got more passionate, and although my lips were responding, my mind was screaming *No!*

He explained it all to me: "The brethren tell us some women need to be made love to more often than others. They say refusing that love is more damaging to the baby than intercourse would be, so it's the responsibility of the husband to see to his wife's needs. I think you're like that. All you have to do is say the word."

I forced the words from my mouth one at a time. "I really want you to stay, but we can't make love. I love you, but I love our baby, too." I started to cry because I couldn't see how to separate his staying with me from making love to me. I would have given anything for him to just hold me in his arms all night long—no sex, only touching.

"I know what you need," he said. "Let me give it to you."

I grabbed his hand as he tore at my pajama bottom. "Please, just hold me."

His whole body went rigid. He turned away from me, and then he was gone. I wandered around the schoolrooms, wondering vaguely if he'd go to Lydia for the sex I had denied him. Finally, exhausted, I turned off the lights and curled myself around the floor vent that provided for the transfer of heat, light, and happy family sounds from the apartment below. I thought if I could freeze myself in the moment, I would hide forever in this dark cocoon.

Uncle Isaac renovated the house that Bettilyn was living in. With a crew headed by Laman, they raised the roof, added a special room upstairs, built new cupboards, and put down new lino. Not a hundred feet from this house was the rambling structure that Celia Whitmer lived in. It was a dark barn of a building which had never had proper plumbing, lighting, or heating. There were not even doors on the bedrooms. All winter, after the above-ground pipes froze solid, Celia carried water for laundry and cooking up a treacherous hill from the creek. In a thrilling, grand ceremony, Celia Manning Whitmer, Lydia's sister, was taken from her dreadful house through a crowd that had gathered to watch. Bettilyn led her into the renovated house and told her it was hers—complete with furniture since Celia's filthy old stuff was hardly fit for the dump. As soon as she'd moved her personal belongings over, an enthusiastic crew loaded all her junk on Uncle Isaac's truck and hauled it to the nuisance ground without giving Celia time to even think about it. Uncle Kelvin was there for the presentation, but he didn't seem very happy that one of his wives and her children had been given such a fine house. Like Uncle Isaac said later, some people would go into the next life guilty of the sin of ingratitude.

Jan and Bettilyn went on about this being just one more example of how "Daddy's godly generosity is misunderstood by people who are out of touch with the true meaning of the priesthood and the United Order. When some poor men don't take proper care of their wives, someone has to."

Uncle Isaac's plan was clear. He had decided from the beginning to give that house to Celia, and then move Bettilyn into the school with me. So I was once again living with Bettilyn. Uncle Isaac's symptoms returned, and he made several more trips to a cancer clinic in Vancouver. The doctors were worried that the leukemia was out of remission; I was afraid for him and for the spirits we had promised in the pre-existence.

One day when I was sitting on the cupboard visiting with Emilia and Ophelia, I felt the baby move. It was just a weak flutter—like having a goldfish swimming around in my stomach—but it was evidence the baby was real. I prayed it was all right and that nothing would go wrong. I was sure I had visited with its spirit before it had quickened in my body. Ophelia was pregnant, too. From our calculations, the babies would be born within two or three weeks of each other. It was amazing that mine would be the sister of the mother of the other one. I couldn't wait for the next conference to arrive because Grandmother would be here, and I'd be able to receive my washings and anointings. Once this sacred ordinance was done, I knew my baby would be safe and alive when it was born.

Uncle Isaac was spending thousands of dollars, and Laman was busily renovating this huge home/school. They were determined to erase everything to do with Uncle Michael's architecture. The massive cupboards were ripped out and replaced, and modern paneling was used to cover the hand-planed wooden panels. We had such an overabundance of kettles and other utensils that with those spacious old cupboards gone, we had no room to put our things.

Life in our community took on a sense of urgency after Uncle Isaac's turn for the worse. He talked all the time about Jonathan the seagull and flying—about being an outcast from family and friends. "I have family outside this sacred Work who point the finger of scorn at anyone who would be different. I'd rather be an outcast like Jonathan and spit on and reviled by fools than be a hail-fellow-well-met. I testify to you that in order for anyone to think they are going to sit on the right hand of Christ, they must give up all popularity with the world." He held up the little blue book with the seagull flying across the cover. "This book has more truth in it than you know."

Conference was here again, and it was exciting beyond words. I'd be able to wear maternity clothes and show the Lord's servants I was an important part of building up the kingdom. Uncle Isaac had taken to wandering around shaking his head and talking to himself. Celeste spent a lot of time with him trying to comfort him. She had been beside herself lately with enthusiasm, and it swept like a contagion throughout the whole group. I heard the whispers that her sister Lily was coming, and she would be married to Laman so he'd have three wives. He was a very young man to have three wives. Bettilyn certainly had special sons in the eyes of the prophet.

When the special guests arrived, Celeste was one of the first to reach their big silver Cadillacs. She rushed up and hugged her sister. Just sixteen years old, Lily was known even in Canada to be talented and kind. As I watched her, I was thinking she presented herself with the grace and dignity of a queen. She was standing right next to Apostle Rich Jessop. Well into his seventies, Uncle Rich was the Saint that Guy Musser said "knew how to stand at the rack, hay or no hay."

The joyful greetings were interrupted by a shriek from Celeste. Covering her face with her hands, she ran crying into the building with Lily following close behind her. Everyone stood frozen in shock that Celeste had been out of control in front of the prophet. She had just discovered that Lily had been married to Uncle Rich a few hours before they left Colorado City.

Uncle Isaac whispered to me that tonight I would receive my woman's ordinances. Grandmother was already here and had been hustled away with Bettilyn to prepare for the ceremonies. The afternoon sped by with Celeste lamenting loudly the whole time. I was sorting my clothes to make sure they were ready for the meeting. On my way downstairs I stopped abruptly. Celeste was talking with our prophet, wringing her hands and weeping desperately. "There must be some mistake, Uncle Roy…I know that Lily belongs with us. Can't you do something about it?" One of Uncle Roy's ever-present wives was looking on with a frown.

Uncle Roy's answer was patient and deliberate. "What good are we if we can't accept the hand of the Lord in all things? You are letting the spirit of Satan take over your body. The spirit of fault-finding and the spirit of criticism are nothing more than Satan in disguise. You must repent or these spirits will win the day. Your father has been the example of sacrifice of physical and spiritual things, and you have been faithful until now. You can take yourself in hand if you put forth the effort." He placed his hands on her shoulders and immediately her attitude calmed. They moved away, and I hurried to help with the meal in anticipation of seeing Grandmother.

Soon the men all disappeared into the white-curtained room prepared for their secret meeting. Those of us who were pregnant and had come to receive our ordinances were waiting patiently in the kitchen. Grandmother and Bettilyn had prepared the bathroom as their sacred site. Irene and Ophelia had already been blessed; I was the last to be called. Grandmother and Bettilyn showed me a folded sheet I was to use for a covering after removing my garments. They left me and I slowly took my clothes off.

Waves of memories washed over me in this little room. When I went to church in this building while Mother was still alive and Uncle Michael lived here, this was the first indoor bathroom his wives ever had. I smiled when I remembered how Daddy moved us here to live that winter the school was first in session. And after a particularly inspiring sermon that Uncle Isaac had given about being "white and delightsome," I had bathed in this very tub with bleach and Ajax, trying to wash off the olive color so I could have the same creamy skin as Uncle Isaac's daughters. Then, two years ago when I was still a child and a student, right in the middle of the day when all the classes were in session, my monthly flow started. I came to this bathroom in a panic, passed out, and hit my head on the toilet. I had awakened to the stench of the urine-soaked wallboard.

For this special occasion, the bathroom was draped in white sheets, and none of the scars of years of use could be seen. The dim light from a single naked bulb cast halo-like reflections. On the cupboard sat a silver bowl of water with a white cloth; beside it was a vial of olive oil. I was now as naked as Eve was before she stole the apple. I draped the sheet around the swell of my bare stomach and clenched it tightly around my neck. There was a gentle tap on the door and I told them to enter. Bettilyn instructed me to sit in the chair in the middle of the room.

After a few seconds of awkward silence she turned to Grandmother and said, "I will put the consecrated oil on her head and you can pray over her. I think that's the way for us to do this. Viv would like that, don't you agree, Selma?"

Grandmother nodded. I felt oil dribbling into my hair, then Grandmother's trembling hands rubbing it gently into my scalp. Her voice was full of tears as she started to pray. "Our righteous and eternal Heavenly Father, we want to thank you for the privilege and opportunity to participate in this sacred ordinance. We have been called and set apart to bless the vessels of the Lord's spirits in this way. We will pray together and then we will do the ordinances."

The chair was hard and I lost track of the words of the prayer. They decided that Bettilyn would do the washings and Grandmother the anointings. I clutched at the sheet as Bettilyn washed and dried first one arm, then the other. She repeated the procedure with my breasts and then my stomach. I had to stand as her hands reached further toward my darkest private places. I tensed. She washed my hips and thighs and started washing my pubic area. I heard her take a deep breath when she started. My throat swelled. I clamped my mouth shut, resisting the urge to scream. What was wrong with me? Grandmother and Bettilyn were blessing my baby.

I was afraid Bettilyn would be even angrier with me in the light of day when she thought of this again. She had to know Uncle Isaac touched me there. I closed my eyes tightly as she continued. She relaxed and took a breath when she moved on to my legs and feet. There was a special prayer for every part of my body, and I had to concentrate on the words with every ounce of my energy.

Grandmother took the oil and anointed my body from the crown of my head to the soles of my feet. The prayers were dedicated to the strength of my body so it would be able to serve the Lord in all holiness, and the baby would be born well and strong to do the same. They left the room remarking that they didn't understand why some women, especially Lydia, had never received these ordinances even once.

Outside, the men had emerged from their secret meeting. Daddy came straight to me. "How are you doing, Daughter? I understand you had the washings and anointings done tonight. I can be here with you to help seal the Work if Isaac would like."

I ran to ask Bettilyn what I should do. She told me she thought Uncle Isaac was in bed, and I should go and get him. In the darkened room he was lying with his back to the door. Slipping in, I sat on the bed and shook him gently. As my fingertips touched his arm through the silky white of his shirt, the baby in my body danced. The surge of knowledge that my baby could recognize its covenant father filled me with joy. Delighted, and wanting to share it with my husband, I shook him again with more fervor. He leapt from the bed with a bloodcurdling Maori yell. His face was white, his eyes wild.

When he managed to focus on me, he relaxed only slightly. "What do you need? Don't ever come up on me like that again! You remind me of a pesky fly."

My face burned. "I'm sorry. Bettilyn and Daddy said I should get you. The ordinance work is finished and the sealing needs to be done."

"I don't need anyone to tell me my duty. I'll do what needs to be done in my own time…Everyone can just mind their own business and leave me in peace." He crawled back onto the bed and turned away. Dismissed and shattered, I told Daddy and Bettilyn that Uncle Isaac didn't want to be disturbed.

Later on that week after the brethren had gone, Uncle Isaac slipped up the stairs to my room. In moonlight that filtered through the ivy-covered window, he laid his hands on my head and sealed the blessings. He kissed me and left. I lay awake for a long time, trying to assure myself that he had actually been there.

I was right to worry about how Bettilyn would feel about me after the ceremony. Ever since I was allowed to live with her again, I wasn't sure what my jobs were. The days were agonizing because she wouldn't speak to me at all. When I asked what I should do, she pretended she couldn't hear or see me, but she'd send one of her daughters off to do a job. I became grateful for any task, even if it was assigned to me by one of the girls.

With the advance of summer came more changes. For some reason, Uncle Isaac decided we needed to move back into the house Lydia was in…but before that could happen, he had to find a home for her. He went to Sidney with a plan. He told him the place he'd built wasn't large enough to house any more than one wife. Besides that, the property wouldn't support any kind of garden. He pointed to the spot where the septic tank spewed its foul-smelling effluent in the back yard, then took Sidney to a plot of ground on what used to be Uncle Michael's place and was now United Effort Plan property.

The priesthood Work was going very well. The whole town of Colorado City in Arizona was built on land donated to the United Effort Plan by good priesthood men forty years earlier, and it was strictly dedicated to building up the kingdom of God. As in the days of Joseph Smith, when obedient men answered the call to live the United Order, everyone worked for the Lord and divided the surplus. Living under the direction of the prophet and the rules of the UEP should guarantee no one would ever be poor. The UEP owned the land and gave people lots to build homes; the apostles acted as trustees to decide what should happen to that land. Daddy and Uncle Isaac said the lots the UEP divvied out were like part of men's inheritance of the kingdom of God. They said no one on earth actually owned anything anyway, so the fullness was always the Lord's.

Sidney was grateful to be given such a direct calling, and before the week was out he had donated his home to the Work and moved a trailer onto the other property. Within a short time, he was building his second new home with the idea that it be big enough for another wife.

As soon as Lydia was moved into Sidney's, we all moved back home. I was grateful to be given a different bedroom this time, because the other one reminded me of my failure to live with Lydia and her pain. As soon as we moved in, Bettilyn began crying. She swore that the evil spirits had been bad enough in this house after Naomi moved out. Now that Lydia had lived here, too, the evil spirits had taken over completely. She said if the place was fixed up a little and then rededicated, the Spirit of the Lord would be able to live in the house, and that would allow her to be happy again.

One day after trying to convince Uncle Isaac of her plan for change, the talking stopped and wild sobbing started. Grabbing a hammer, she went into one of the bathrooms that she really hated and started bashing at a wall. Uncle Isaac got up from reading his Truth book and wearily went into the living room where his boys were stretched out after the morning chores. "Here you, Martin...James...get on in there and take that hammer away from your mother before she hurts herself. I'll be right back."

He slammed the door, jumped in the pickup, and drove off. When he came back, Laman was with him. They both sat down with Bettilyn to find out exactly what she wanted done. For weeks the house echoed with the sounds of saws and hammers. Walls were torn down and new ones put up. By the time the renovations were finished, it looked like a completely different house. Bettilyn stopped her sobbing, but there must have been a few evil spirits left, because she was still not happy.

Uncle Isaac was getting more and more worried that the growing boys would be tempted to search out worldly entertainment if something wasn't done to distract them. There were fifteen boys between the ages of twelve and eighteen, and Uncle Isaac was adamant they couldn't be running off to the drive-in movie or the lake or the recreation center in Creston without supervision. He and Lem decided to start a hockey team. Their team would be called I. Merrick and Sons, and all the jerseys would be red and white—the colors of fire and light. The boys looked magnificent! They resolved to play harder and meaner than any other team in the Kootenays, and they took Creston by storm. After every game they came home bursting with the excitement of the win.

Uncle Isaac was thrilled with the victories. "We sure showed them! Those pantywaist town boys don't know what hit 'em. I'm proud of you …You've proven again that Merricks can't be beaten. This should prove to you all, if you stand shoulder to shoulder no one will ever prevail against us, worlds without end."

The big downside of the hockey team was the cold of the rink—it caused Uncle Isaac's limp to get worse. He had pain from his crippled leg all the time, but now he also had what he called "a raging fire in my bones" from the leukemia. The other problem was the terrible fighting that seemed to go along with the Merrick attitude on ice. It was bad enough when the resulting animosity was toward the Gentiles. When there was fighting among the boys, things at home took a rapid downturn. After a night like that, the boys would file in grimly, and Uncle Isaac would go silently into his room and close his door with a heavy thud. No one dared speak to him until he left the room of his own accord.

One night about halfway into the season, Lem burst through the front door boiling with rage. "Where's Nephi? I'm going to kill him! He doesn't need to think he can get away with this." He looked from one to the other of the boys. "You all think you're really smart...I'll show you." The line of boys wouldn't even look at him. "You're all in it together, aren't you, trying to make me look like a fool! I had a clear shot at the goal and you all froze me out—left me standing there and you all snickering. We lost the game because of it, I hope you know that." He lowered his voice in disgust. "You can all act as his spies and lackeys if you want, but if he was the man he wants you all to think he is, he'd be here to face me instead of hiding like a sniveling coward...Well, I know where to find him. Nobody treats me like this." He thundered out into the dark, and seconds later his truck roared up the hill spitting gravel. Martin quietly got up and left the house.

After the sound of the vehicle died, the remaining brothers joked, "I guess we showed him. He doesn't need any help looking like a fool—he does a good enough job himself. And we got the chance to put him in his place for Nephi." They slowly drifted off to bed, and I was left trying to go back to sleep.

Some time later, the door crashed open again, and I heard Martin's calming voice and moans from Nephi. Bettilyn was sleeping in the living room on the couch beside Uncle Isaac's bedroom door. She had cried herself to sleep when Lem left the first time. Now she was quickly rousted by the call of her sons. I heard her horrified gasp, then, "Nephi! What's wrong? Oh good Lord, how can this be happening? Martin, tell me what happened!" Nephi was sobbing and I could hear water running. I got up to see what was going on. Bettilyn retrieved the first aid kit from one of the high cupboards and began wiping blood from Nephi's face.

Martin's voice was solemn. "It's the story of Cain and Abel, Mom. Lem found Nephi in the very top of the barn, and if I hadn't come along when I did, he would've killed him."

Bettilyn talked the whole time she doctored Nephi's face. "I've known from the time Nephi was conceived he was a special chosen spirit. I fasted and drank only water and honey for two weeks before Daddy and I were together."

She paused for a moment and Nephi let out a holler. "That hurts, Mom!"

Bettilyn continued as if she hadn't heard him. "I received a powerful witness. After we were together only once, I knew I had conceived and the Lord had sent one of his most special spirits to be

Nephi. When anyone is that special, you have to know Satan will be more determined to destroy him and the mission the Lord has for him...We won't let that happen." She went about cleaning up the kitchen. "You go on to bed now, and everything will work out...You'll see. Thanks for being there, Martin. You were right to go after Lem. Nephi has a great Work to perform."

Uncle Isaac withdrew somewhere inside himself after Lem beat up Nephi. He took Nephi everywhere with him, and soon the favored son was talking about being on the right-hand side of his dad, "the good father." He told all his supportive brothers that their father shared stuff with him he wouldn't think of telling anyone else. "All I have to do is stand up to the mark he's set for me." One day I heard him telling his mother, "Dad says I'll be like Joseph who was sold into Egypt."

As my body grew heavier, I obsessed that something might still go wrong with this pregnancy. When I discussed my worries with Dr. Morgan, he told me to count the number of times the baby moved in a day—if it was over ten, then the baby was probably all right. I had a terrible time concentrating on everything else going on around me until I reached the daily count.

I was used to pretending I was pregnant out of wedlock whenever I went to town, and it even got so it didn't bother me much when the Gentiles stared. On the last day of October, one of the neighbors we used to stick-pick for knocked on the door. Gentiles never came to the ranch, so I was surprised. I went to answer wearing my wine and white maternity dress. My belly was huge—I had only two weeks left before the baby was due. Emilia and Ophelia, who were standing by the kitchen table, leapt toward me with angry hisses. "What do you think you're doing? Are you trying to get Daddy thrown in jail? How can you be so stupid? Get away from there now!" They pulled me quickly around the corner into the living room where I couldn't be seen from the door. "If Daddy invites him into the kitchen, you must go into your room or down to the basement. You're lucky Mom isn't home...You can bet she won't be happy when she hears about this."

Uncle Isaac opened the door, and the neighbor gave him a box of oranges and some Halloween candy for the kids. Everyone crowded into the kitchen to thank him. I was standing dumbly in the living room not knowing what to think or feel. How would this man know I wasn't one of Uncle Isaac's pregnant daughters or daughters-in-law? Prime Minister Trudeau had made it legal for common-law marriages, and all the men and the prophet celebrated how the immoral ways of the earth could be turned into blessings for God's sacred Work. Ever since then, Daddy had signed paternity forms for all of his polygamous children, and he bragged about his kids and took his wives everywhere with him. The wicked, adulterous, stubborn woman they called a whore in *The Scarlet Letter* was never more humiliated than I felt then. I couldn't think about it. My head was hot and numb. I could have a broken heart and a contrite spirit…I would!

I wanted to ask Uncle Isaac what we should name our baby. When everyone was gone, I slipped into his bedroom while he was having his afternoon nap. I fantasized his holding me close and listening with his ear on my stomach the way Ophelia told us Sidney did with her baby. Ophelia said that every time Sidney spoke, her baby jumped for him and even kicked him in the ear one day. Everyone laughed. They said Sidney's ears were so big they'd be hard to miss.

Uncle Isaac heard me come in. His eyelids were heavy and his eyes were black-rimmed. "Well? What do you want?" His voice was impatient; immediately I felt confused, and I stumbled over my tongue. "Please…I wonder what we should name our baby…I think it would be fun to talk about it."

He dismissed me. "I need to think about it."

Several days later he came up to me and said just one word: "Selma." I asked Bettilyn what he meant by "Selma," and she said he must have had some inspiration that the baby would be a girl and Selma would be her name. I was amazed that he knew such wondrous things and felt grateful to be the wife of a man who was so in tune with the mind of God.

Early on Sunday morning, November 12, 1972, I felt the same warm trickle that had so alarmed me eleven months earlier. For a few hours I had mild contractions that were far apart. Uncle Isaac decided to take me to Daddy's house where Jan could watch me. We stayed home from church, cooked dinner, and timed contractions. The realization that this baby was really on its way had yet to hit me—it all still seemed like a dream. By evening the contractions were ten minutes apart, and the dream had become reality. Uncle Isaac came to the house for a while. Sitting with my father, he rested his hands on my head and gave me a blessing. In that prayerful moment, I felt closer to my husband than I had in months. Around ten o'clock it was decided Jan would take me to the hospital. Uncle Isaac squeezed both my hands in his and left without saying a word.

As I walked down the hall of the Creston hospital, I wondered which room Mother had died in and whether I could contact her spirit more easily here. When I had donned the hospital gown and was lying on the bed, the contractions were suddenly more intense. The nurse examined me and said I still had a long way to go. I was exhausted and fought back tears. She and Jan talked about pain relief, and they decided to give me Demerol. They explained the painkiller would let me sleep, so I'd be more rested when the baby was born.

A few moments after the shot, I noticed the hospital smells were more prominent, and I jerked every time Jan or the nurse touched me. The nurse said I'd likely sleep and not have the baby until morning, so Jan went home. I was sorry to see her go; she had never been kinder to me. It was so nice that she spoke to me in gentle tones and brought me ice water and washed my face with a cool cloth. When she left, I stared at the ceiling. My lips and throat were parched. I reached for the cup of water on the bed table. My lips were pursed in anticipation before I realized that my hand was still beside me on the bed and the water was still on the table—I couldn't move.

The contractions came in waves that I couldn't seem to prepare for. My mournful wail brought the nurse running, and she immediately called a doctor and moved me onto a stretcher. With the help of another nurse, she wheeled me into a cold, white, frightening room. My legs were shaking uncontrollably as she placed them in an apparatus she referred to as the stirrups and put on some white stockings to hold them in place. I could tell from her actions and the sound of her voice that she was worried. I was writhing from the pain. She calmed her voice and told me to work with the pain, not try to get away from it. She told me she could see the baby, and I was to push. I tried but was still holding my breath. Suddenly, I was overcome with a tremendous feeling of urgency. I pushed with all my might and screamed. There was intense pain as the nurse cut me. She shouted, "Push...you've got to push!"

This time my body took over and pushed on its own. Immediately, the pain stopped. In a daze I turned to the big clock in the delivery room. It was 2:30. I heard my baby cry. The nurse told me it was a girl, but I couldn't see her beyond the stirrups.

The double doors to the delivery room flew open and a gray-haired man in a green gown rushed in. I looked around. I wanted Dr. Morgan, but I was told that this doctor would finish the delivery. He mused, "Hmm, I see...Good. Good...I see you did an episiotomy. We'll take care of that with some good old catgut." He poked and prodded, then started to stitch. "You'll be better than new when I'm done with you...This'll hurt a bit, but it won't take long." He gave me a pat on my exposed buttock and chuckled to no one in particular. The nurse clucked at him and gave him a stern look, but he just laughed.

Soon I was cleaned up, and the nurse pushed me into a different room. When another nurse brought me the baby, I was horrified. Her head was squished in the front, and her forehead was bruised. I took the baby and held her to my breast. As soon as the nurse left the room, I pulled the blanket over my head and wept—I was so ashamed. In spite of her battered look, the baby sucked madly when I got a nipple into her mouth. I kept staring at this little mite of a person, trying to convince myself she was really mine, but my eyes were blurred, my hands heavy, and my mind in some far-off place where "hospital" was only a bad word.

On the third morning, my milk came in with a vengeance. My breasts were swollen so large I couldn't put my hands to my sides, and my bra wouldn't close. The baby nursed until she threw up, and then she sucked some more. I worried she wasn't getting enough to eat, so the nurse weighed her before and after feeding.

After the second weigh-in the nurse came running. "That little pup just drank eight ounces of milk! No wonder she screams so much between feedings...She's getting too much."

Bettilyn came the following morning to see the baby. Speaking just above a whisper, she said, "She certainly is a fine baby. Isaac's out in the truck but he's worried about what the nurses'll think if he comes in to see you...You know we have to be careful. Gentiles wouldn't understand." My sister wife cuddled the baby for a moment, then handed her back to me. "Your dad brought Jan, Irene, and Elsa over with the babies the other day to see Isaac. Isn't that the cutest thing, to have three babies so close in age, and all named with the same letter...Natalia, Nakita, and Nanette. Jan said it would be great if you named your baby Janessa, then Isaac's oldest and youngest would both be Janessas." She smiled at the baby and then at me. "So I guess this baby will be Janessa...You do understand about Isaac, don't you? With the possibility of being charged and all..."

I found myself not wanting to listen to her any longer and pushed every word she said to the back of my mind. I focused on the pain in my nipple as the baby latched on and began nursing.

The next day Jan came in. Repeating the same story Bettilyn told me, she stressed how much Uncle Isaac liked the idea that his oldest and youngest daughters bear the same name. I wanted so badly for this baby to be named Vivien after my mother, but if Uncle Isaac wanted her to be Janessa, then it had to be so.

Long after the hospital was dark, I lay awake tossing and turning. I propped my head against the wall and watched the reflection from the nurse's flashlight as she made her rounds. Why couldn't Uncle Isaac have just pretended I was his daughter or his granddaughter? Jan's daughter, Tabitha, wasn't much younger than I was, and he would have come to visit her. I was desperate for some sign from him that he was pleased with our child. Nothing in all the years I had spent in the group had prepared me for admitting to the Gentiles that my baby was a little bastard. The nurses were kind and they never questioned me, but I knew what they were thinking. Why couldn't Isaac have come for a few minutes to look at his daughter?

I couldn't stop myself from crying. Every time the nurse left me, I started to cry. Every time the baby was brought to me, I cried. If I loved this baby so much, why was I so sad? The nurse who had delivered her caught me crying in the middle of the night. Resting her hand on my shoulder, she sat by my bed and talked to me about Mother. She told me she had nursed her before she died. She said the day Mother died, everyone in the hospital cried, and even though she didn't get to know her really well, this gentile nurse said she loved her. I drifted off to sleep with the thought that this nurse liked me, too.

After a week I still wasn't in a hurry to leave. I felt a sense of paralysis. Every time the nurses or the doctors asked me if I was ready to go home, I would say yes and start to cry. They immediately suspected some sinister reason for my reaction and didn't send me. Finally, I convinced myself I must get back into the spirit of the Work and all would be well. When my nurse asked again if I was ready, I told her I felt fine. This time my eyes remained dry—I knew I needed to get on with my calling.

The moment I arrived home, all the kids from school came to visit the baby. I wanted my brothers and sisters to see their first little niece, but she slept lightly and was easily startled. I hated it when she cried—it made me so afraid. I kept her in my room in a crib that Bettilyn had produced. Uncle Isaac seemed glad to see her and for the first few days came to my room to hold her when no one else was home. Much to Bettilyn's chagrin, he wasn't at home much. He was spending more time than ever on his chores, and when he wasn't working, he camped at the little house where Lydia lived. Lydia called me from time to time to fill me in on how much Uncle Isaac loved coming to visit her. She said he loved how she had decorated the place. He called it his sanctuary.

"Isaac just loves to read the scriptures to me," she gushed. "He looks at me when we're studying together and says, 'Oh woman, you give me goosebumps. You have a special gift and discernment about the gospel and spiritual things.' " She stopped, savoring the moment. "You know, Deb, I have never been so close to Isaac. He won't have me get those women's ordinances done. I worry that your grandmother won't understand, but Isaac gives me his own private blessing. He's always inspired as to what the baby will be, and tells me the name at the same time. This one will be Velma after his sister." She paused for emphasis. "I surely hope your relationship with Isaac is as wonderful as mine."

I tried to be happy for her—and most of the time I was—but sometimes while I was dragging baskets of heavy blue jeans or towels out to the clothesline where they froze solid as fast as I could hang them, I longed for a small moment like the ones Lydia described. I guess I was just being selfish. Mother certainly wouldn't have had these thoughts, and she'd have worked fast enough to get all the work done. Supper was always late; Bettilyn and the girls would get home from school and have to fly at the work I hadn't finished. That made me feel as useless as Jan said I was. It seemed unless I was feeding Janessa or holding her, she was crying. When I got real tired, I wanted to scream at her, shake her, clamp my hand over her mouth, or lock her away behind a door where I didn't have to listen to her. This made me feel absolutely evil. How could a mother yell at her precious child?

Jean came over to see the baby. The last time she was here was on my birthday. She stared at me in horror when I told her the baby's name was Janessa Dawn. With a strange twist to her lips, she said in a hollow voice, "When you married Dad, I wondered if you might just be crazy, but now I know you are. Jan was always so horrible to you…She acted as if she hated you all the time at school. I was secretly glad when she treated you like that, because when she was angry with you, I knew she wouldn't be talking about Mom or calling down Aline. How could you possibly name your baby after her?" She looked critically at the disarray in the room, and I found myself wishing I'd had a few moments' notice that she was coming. "Look at your bedroom—it looks as if a cyclone hit it. You've been here for months and don't even have pictures on your walls. If you were happy you would at least make your room look settled."

I felt so uncomfortable with my old friend; I didn't know what to say to her and didn't want her criticism. I asked her about school and tried to think of something else that wouldn't cause friction between us. I should have felt sorry for her, because she didn't understand that the promise of the Lord to those of us living this law of plural marriage was worth any sacrifice.

I searched for some way of justifying Janessa's name, but no matter what twisted explanations I came up with, I couldn't put them into words. Jeanie picked the baby up and held her for a few minutes. Suddenly, in the middle of a sentence she stopped talking and passed Janessa to me. Her voice was distant. "I should apologize for being glad when Jan was mean to you, and for saying stuff about you behind your back. I feel guilty about that sometimes when I think about it. You really are so gullible, though—we could get you to believe anything." With a shrug she disappeared out the door before I could even thank her for coming.

I tried to shake the feeling of despair that hung over me after Jean left. I dug out some pictures to hang on the walls but couldn't find any nails and didn't want to ask Laman for his hammer. Finally, I just sat nursing Janessa and allowed the exhaustion to keep me there.

Ophelia delivered a twelve-pound girl they named Denise. She was a contented baby who slept most of the time. From the second week, she was quiet the whole night through. The family was impressed with her, and everyone kept asking me what I was doing wrong with Janessa. When we were working together as a family, Denise was much more pleasant to hold and play with, so Janessa ended up in her crib, where she cried incessantly.

In early February I was doing laundry and couldn't get the wringer to work properly. All the clothes from the sixteen batches of laundry were soaking wet and heavy as I trudged out to the line. My dress front got drenched and frozen several times. By that night I was feeling sick. One moment I was chilled and couldn't feel warm no matter how many blankets I piled on; the next, I was on fire and stripped everything off. In the morning, the fever was in my breasts. They became rock-hard and red, with the veins standing blue on the surface. Nursing Janessa was agony and made the struggle to love the little creature harder than ever. I begged Uncle Isaac to take me to the doctor.

When I tried to show him my swollen breasts, he waved me

away and growled, "Oh ye of little faith!" On his way out the door, he told me to pray for guidance and chucked me a vial with large white pills his doctor had given him for his leukemia. He had Lydia call me. She told me to alternate hot and cold packs on my breasts, so I sat in the tub while Janessa screamed from her baby seat on the floor. Eventually the hardness left, but breastfeeding was always painful after that.

On the heels of this small relief came a terrible hacking cough. My lungs seemed to be on fire. I gagged up red-streaked gobs of greenish phlegm until I vomited. I was exhausted right down to the ends of my fingers. Again I begged Uncle Isaac to take me to the doctor, but instead, he gave me Dodd's kidney pills, saying they were a blood purifier and would make me well. Lydia and Bettilyn both gave testimonials as to how well they worked for them. My cough persisted for months, and everyone told me my faith must be really weak.

I ended up babysitting Denise on a regular basis. If Ophelia wasn't busy doing her laundry, she was driving Bettilyn to town or to Bonners Ferry to shop or to Cranbrook to sell chickens. Daddy's deal with local poultry farms to slaughter and dress more than a thousand chickens when they replaced their laying hens kept the kids from the school busy. I was glad to help the work along by tending Denise. The trouble was she refused to take a bottle, and Ophelia was often gone for seven or eight hours. Inevitably, Denise wailed her dissatisfaction. Sometimes I got so desperate to shut her up that I nursed her myself. I didn't think it was such a big deal—Irene sometimes nursed Jan's babies when needed, and so did Elsa. When Babette figured out what I was doing to pacify her, she told Ophelia, and they were all as furious with me as if I'd fed the baby dollops of poison. Once again, I received the silent treatment.

I had started out with five dozen cloth diapers after getting home from the hospital. Now after six months, I was down to two. My only source of spending money was the baby allowance check I got from the government. I wanted to use that money for other things I needed, so I started watching the diapers closely, wondering what could possibly be happening to them. I realized that

Babette and Phoebe were using Janessa's diapers for Denise, and she often wore them home. I nervously phoned Ophelia and asked if she would check Denise's diapers to see if there were any marked with a small D.M. in the corner. Everyone was still mad at me, and I was hoping to avoid a showdown.

Ophelia was furious. "You suspicious little witch…You'll never survive as a part of our family, as selfish as you are. If you think you can win friends by keeping things to yourself, then you're crazy. We all know you hide your comb and brush away, and you never let anyone borrow your pillow. Mother has never had a comb or a brush of her own—she shares everything she has. You can't accuse me of stealing and get away with it! I feel really sorry for you, Deb…I'm not going to keep encouraging Babette and Phoebe to be nice to you if you don't change."

I stammered that I just thought the diapers might have gotten mixed up by accident, since the girls changed Denise in my room. Ophelia hollered, "I'd give anything to be able to be in Daddy's family like you are!" She slammed the phone down.

A few days later, when Babette and Phoebe were doing Ophelia's laundry, they left clean wet diapers over the backs of the kitchen chairs. Desperate to reclaim Janessa's diapers, I sorted through them and took the ones I knew to be mine. The entire family was furious—Uncle Isaac, Bettilyn, and all her children. It seemed I was nothing but trouble.

The only consolation was that some other women in the group had trouble keeping sweet. Uncle Isaac and Daddy had talked to the prophet about the problem the women were having with the long sacred undergarments that were visible under their bulky stockings. They didn't like the Gentiles staring at the women's legs when they were out in the devil's world selling chickens or working at the shop. Uncle Isaac found a pattern designed by Brigham Young that looked like a Chinese coolie suit. He decided if the early prophet of the church had wanted the women to wear such clothing, there would be no problem with our wearing pantsuits if the tops covered our hips and thighs. Uncle Isaac and Daddy were horrified that even back then the rebellious, worldly minded women in the church had started to say no to their priesthood heads. They told us reluctantly that Brigham Young's own wives refused to wear his style of clothing. Uncle Isaac delighted in informing us this was when the church started getting into trouble, and the tail had wagged the dog ever since.

Bettilyn had some colorful suits made up. Emilia was already wearing pants; she was still working for Daddy and always dressed immaculately. Babette and Phoebe whispered to one another about her. They were sure she was buying suits out of the Sears Catalogue. They even suspected she wore light makeup and shaved her legs. They were horrified about this, but when they were with Emilia, they told her how beautiful they thought she was. They were also more than happy to tag along with her when she offered to take them on trips or to the movies.

I asked Uncle Isaac to allow me to buy fabric to make some pantsuits, too, but he looked at me as if I'd lost my mind. "What in thunder is wrong with your dresses? You don't go anywhere you'll be needing a suit like that, so why be concerned? Don't bother me with such triviality!"

He was right. He had to be. He was my priesthood head, and I would be his wife for eternity…How could I not do as he wished? I'd hate to work at the shop or sell chickens all over the Kootenays, anyway.

Several weeks later, Bettilyn took Emilia and me into the storage room. She addressed us sternly. "With your being resealed to Daddy now, Emilia, and with us all back in the same house, we must set some things straight." She stared directly at me. "I'm disgusted with the rotation that Adam does with his wives, and that Daddy did before your baby was born." Her lips curled in derision. "It's just as bad as sending a bull in with cows. When Naomi, Lydia, Lena, and I all lived together, Isaac had his own room and we went to him when we had to. We can set up a schedule as to when each of us will spend time with him…then there won't be any confusion."

I wondered what difference it would make. Most of the time, when I tried to talk to Uncle Isaac, he was too impatient to carry on a conversation anyway. The few times I'd given thought to going to his room, Bettilyn was asleep on the floor or the cot in the living room, and I would never have been able to open his door without her knowing. It was just how Lydia said it always was. I knew I would never ask Bettilyn if I could spend the night in Uncle Isaac's room.

Besides, when he finished his chores in the mornings, and he came here instead of to Lydia's, he could hardly walk. He'd put on his record of Eddy Arnold singing "What's He Doing in My World" and sink into his favorite chair. He'd play the song again and again. My brain buzzed with it, and the words echoed over and over. For just a moment I closed my eyes and imagined that Uncle Isaac was the one singing to me. It sent a chill up my spine.

That night while he sat in his chair with the record on, I put Janessa in his lap. He held her until she started to fuss and Ophelia picked her up and brought her back to me. Ophelia and Emilia took me into the kitchen to inform me I shouldn't ever just take the baby to their dad again—I should wait until he asked for her. The trouble was he never asked for her, although he did spend time with Denise, especially after she burned her mouth sucking on an electrical cord that was strung across the sewing room floor of Ophelia and Sidney's new home.

I couldn't shake the horrible fatigue that had haunted me since Janessa's birth. I had a hard time starting my chores in the morning, and when I stopped to nurse the baby, I fell asleep almost every time. I remained in a dense fog and found myself accomplishing less and less. Lydia had her baby, Velma, and invited me to visit with Janessa Dawn. I decided to make hers a place to look forward to going so I could make a schedule and get myself on track. When Lydia and I were together visiting and the babies were playing, I imagined the love and sharing that might be possible in celestial marriage. She had a record player and a big stack of records. The one I loved the most and played over and over was "My Special Angel." I wrote down the words to the entire song and memorized them. After the pain from nursing Janessa subsided, I sang it to her.

Lydia had an opportunity to get a job working with mentally handicapped people in Creston. The moment she found out, she told me she'd pay me a wage if I'd come to her house and babysit

Velma. I was embarrassed to take money for looking after my husband's children, but she insisted. Twice Uncle Isaac came over to eat lunch with me and the girls while I was babysitting. He sat there quietly while I made him grilled cheese sandwiches and soup. It was strange to be with him when no one else was around, and I didn't know what to say to him. He said nothing to me, ate his lunch, and left.

I was ashamed to tell anyone how tired I was. I was still having bad dreams even when I read the Book of Mormon or the Truth books. I would read until the wee hours, hoping if I stayed awake another second longer, the dreams wouldn't come. They did anyway, and then the mornings were a horror. One morning I thought I'd just lie on the cot for a minute so I could get more rest. If someone came, I'd be able to jump up fast enough that they'd never know I was sleeping. Janessa started to cry, but in my exhausted state she was just another baby in my nightmare. I was jolted awake when Uncle Isaac came in and sat my cranky baby with her urine-soaked diaper on my head. He left the room without uttering a single word. As I changed my daughter's diaper, I was weeping as bitterly as she was.

Uncle Isaac got word that his brother in Cardston had died. Uncle Daniel was well known in his area as a schoolteacher and a good dairy farmer. Uncle Isaac had talked for years about his brother's teaching techniques and how well he was respected by the Natives. They had even appointed him an honorary chief of the Blood tribe. Uncle Isaac, Bettilyn, and some of the kids were going to the funeral, and I would substitute for Bettilyn at the school. It was laundry day but I was confident I could do it. I fixed breakfast for all the kids, then wrapped Janessa up in her snowsuit and went to school. A lot of the students were my brothers and sisters, so although it was strange to teach them, it was also fun. After school I told Babette and Phoebe to hurry home so we could surprise Bettilyn with having the laundry done and the house looking its very best.

I struggled home over the icy road with Janessa and started the laundry and supper at the same time, expecting the girls to be home any minute. When they didn't come and the boys were waiting for their food and Janessa was screaming in her walker, I called Ophelia and asked her for the girls. She told me I was a lost cause: that the girls would not be coming to help now or ever, and it was not my right to think I could have them as my slaves. If I had an organized bone in my body, she said, I'd have done the laundry before breakfast, so it was my own fault I'd be working late. She also pointed out, in case I hadn't noticed, that most of her brothers never ate at home unless Bettilyn was there, because they couldn't stand me and hated the food I cooked.

I couldn't respond, but the moment I hung up the phone, I turned on my five-year-old stepdaughter and screamed at her. I called her mean names and told her to go and tend to Janessa. Nora started crying. Just as I prepared to yell at her again, Martin, who was sitting in the armchair waiting for supper, glared at me and told me in a stern tone I must never speak to his sister like that again. I burst into tears in my frustration. I was so far from the special Christ-like mother in Israel Daddy wanted me to be that I prayed the mountain would crumble and fall on me.

The morning after Uncle Isaac got home, I told him I wanted him to take me up on the offer he made when we were first married—to let me live in the cabin on my own. I imagined I could create a special little haven for him. He turned away from me in frustration.

That evening when I went to the storage room for a jar of tomatoes, he and Bettilyn were in the basement. I listened from the darkness. "Now, Daddy, why is it, do you suppose, that we've had nothing but trouble? If it's not Lydia, it's Naomi, if it's not Naomi, it's Emilia, and now Deb…and I've tried so hard. If only Lena were still alive. We had special good times, and we really understood each other. I suppose there's no changing her mind. I guess I'm being blamed for it again. That's Lydia's favorite thing to do." I felt sick to realize they were talking about me—there was no doubt that now I was classed with the troublesome wives.

Isaac sounded tired. "No, Mother, I know you try. We can't think about it too much…there's nothing we can do but give into the demands. When people realize that the problem is the inability to follow gospel principles, maybe we'll make some headway, but the way it is now, we're living at a poor dying rate…a poor dying rate." I peeked around the corner of the door. Uncle Isaac sadly shook his head while Bettilyn rubbed his shoulders.

For the next three days he didn't talk to me. When I finally asked what I was supposed to do, he spun around on me and responded angrily, "Oh, hell, you're still on that kick…I hoped you might have forgotten." He went away and returned a little later with Laman. "Well, we're here for your things," Uncle Isaac said. "What are you waiting for?" I was shocked.

As I dragged clothing from my drawers and shoved it into garbage bags, they grabbed them, carried them outside, and tossed everything haphazardly into the back of Uncle Isaac's pickup. I was seated next to Laman in the truck with Janessa Dawn on my lap, not sure where we were going. When we stopped in front of the school, I sat in the truck waiting when they both got out. Uncle Isaac grumbled impatiently, "Well?" I scrambled out and followed their lead. With my hope chest between them, they hurried up the stairs to the very room where we had all the big meetings when Mother was still alive. In mere minutes, my things were stacked in a huge pile on the floor. Uncle Isaac told me Laman would be putting up a wall and a door to partition me and Janessa from the school classes that were in session—this would be my new home. I asked him about eating and where I would get food for my baby. He said maybe I should have thought of that before I stirred up such a fuss. He supposed I could work for food from Laman again.

Chapter 17

I stood amidst all the clutter: cardboard boxes stacked in the corner, hangers with Janessa's baby things piled on the bed, garbage bags with my own clothes scattered everywhere. I stared at the blackboards listening to echoes of the memories of the four other times I had lived in this house during my eighteen years—this was the second time I had been dumped here in disgrace.

Babette sauntered up the stairs. No longer the saucy little girl I remembered, she had transformed into a thirteen-year-old miniature of Bettilyn. She smirked. "Well, now I guess you know what happens when you think you can boss us around. Nobody treats us like you did and gets away with it. Look what happened to Naomi and Lydia—they didn't fit in either."

She laughed mockingly, and Janessa Dawn started to cry. I picked her up and turned on Babette. "Someday, somehow, Babette, you're going to know the pain I feel right now, and you'll remember this. When that time comes, I pray that God will help you, because you'll need it!" She blanched and her laugh trailed into a nervous gulp. Without another word, she turned and fled down the stairs.

By the time I managed to set up the bed and pull necessary clothes for the baby out of the tangled heap, it was long after midnight. I fed Janessa some applesauce from a jar and went to bed. I tossed and turned for hours trying to settle down enough to sleep. Every time I opened my eyes, I stared into the darkness of the enormous room, trying to figure out how I had ended up here. How had I managed to become such a failure in less than two years?

I was awakened promptly at eight when school kids started arriving for class. Circling the bed and my things, they gawked as if they'd happened upon a garage sale. I had become the main attraction in my own freak show: See What Happens When a Sister Wife Fails to Keep Sweet. To my brothers and sisters and stepchildren, I was Lydia, Naomi, Celia, Enid, and every other woman who was ever a trial for her husband and his faithful wife, all rolled into one. I was still too confused about what had happened to feel as humiliated as I knew I should. I was in worse trouble than Aline or Jean who had run away from the priesthood direction, because I was still a daily trial to everyone. Was my life over at eighteen? How would my daughter ever be happy growing up with sisters and brothers who despised her because of her mother?

After the first classes started, Laman came with his tools and began throwing up a partition wall. I was praying he'd have the door hung before the kids were out for lunch, but he didn't. The final screws for the hinges were driven with Brent holding the door in the middle of a horde of curious onlookers. The older kids, including Nettie, shook their heads at me and ran to class buzzing with whispers and snickers.

Just as the kids were beginning to thin out, Nephi arrived and surveyed my things. When I asked what he wanted, he answered in a patronizing tone, "You'll know soon enough. No one messes with my father's family and gets away with it. I have a mission to be about my father's business. You'll see!"

"You act like you're Christ teaching the priests in the temple, and Uncle Isaac is some kind of god I've sinned against. What are you talking about?"

For a brief second his eyes registered surprise that I would know the story of Christ in the temple in Jerusalem. He turned away from me. At the top of the stairs he looked back. "You watch yourself."

Laman put the last screw in the doorknob. "Well, Dad says you're to work for your keep by helping organize the storehouse." His cheeks were flushed, and when I tried to talk to him he looked everywhere but at me. He said he had enough to do remodeling Celia's old place for a new church. The storehouse was to be in the basement of that building. "I know you're good at painting, so I'll keep you busy." Before he left he said, "If you need anything for little sis Jan there, ask Grace or Celeste...I'm sure they'll help you."

I didn't know where to start; in my frustration I phoned Daddy to come talk to me. When he walked into my two rooms, he nodded his approval. "Well, Daughter, there are lots of ways a woman can serve the Lord and further the Work. It looks like things weren't going too well over at the other house...this should be fine. You know how much you like to paint and fix things, and you're good at it. As long as you're doing the very best you can do, then you'll be found pleasing in the eyes of the Lord, and you can hold your head high no matter what. You know you can be a big help around here to Jan and the kids...and the school needs a janitor."

I burst into tears. Daddy stroked my hair until I settled down, and, after giving Janessa Dawn a hug, went back home to my mothers and brothers and sisters.

At first I was wondering how we were supposed to feed ourselves, but after a few days I realized we might be able to survive. Bettilyn brought us a few bottles of applesauce so I could feed Janessa snacks, and I got to have some of the leftover food from the school lunches.

I was aware that Celeste and Bettilyn were the best of friends. Celeste called Bettilyn "Mother" and fixed her special treats and had Laman take her for drives with them. I was worried about asking Celeste for anything and putting her in an uncomfortable situation when I was in disgrace with Bettilyn and her children. When I asked Grace if I could have a few slices of bread and some milk for Janessa Dawn's bottle, she flushed. "I can't say yes until you've talked to Celeste. It's not my place to help with anything unless I know for sure it's what they want."

I spent the rest of the day pacifying Janessa with tidbits I scrounged from the lunchroom. When I was sweeping up the school, I managed to catch Celeste alone in her classroom. Still at her desk preparing for the next day, she became flustered when I entered the room. I apologized for disturbing her, then asked about the milk and bread.

She frowned. "Yes, I'll tell Grace she can help you with food, but you can't expect her to babysit when you're painting on the church house or sorting the storage. She's busy enough with our kids and our needs." Her voice took on a sharp edge and she tapped her foot under the desk. "I can't begin to imagine what's wrong with you that you just can't live with Mother Bettilyn. She's the sweetest, kindest person I've ever known, and you've certainly been taught right. All I can say is *shame on you!* You didn't need to cause all this heartache for Uncle Isaac, either. You know, Uncle Roy prophesied that Uncle Isaac would be completely healed if his family would cooperate and get along. Now, look at what you've done! I could be a wife in that family with no problem. You better figure out how to repent and beg for forgiveness." I couldn't speak without bursting into tears, so I fled from the room.

Janessa hated following me around while I moved desks and dragged the mop through the filthy classrooms—she wailed the entire time. It was long past nightfall when Celia appeared with a broom in one hand and a loaf of fluffy white bread in the other. We stared at each other for a moment, then I dissolved into tears and sank into the desk nearest me. Celia had her arms around me in seconds and held me quietly.

She took my hands in hers. "I don't think we really have to say anything about why you're here. I guess I'm the same age as your mother, and I watched how things went while you were growing up without her. None of us ever knew what to do about how Jan treated you. I'm sorry." Her grip on my hands tightened. I looked into her eyes to let her know I understood. Tears were soaking the front of my dress, and Celia passed me a clean cloth.

She talked through her own tears. "When you were married to Isaac, I was hoping things might be better for you than for the others...Your mother was so good to me. I didn't get to see her near as much as I wanted, but the times we talked and the times she helped me will be with me my whole life. Deb, I'll help you…I'm here for you now."

There was nothing more to say; she knew what was in my heart. She called to two of her daughters and instructed them to take Janessa home with them until we finished cleaning the school. They gathered my distraught baby in their arms and disappeared, being careful not to look at me. Later, Celia brought Janessa back with a belly full of her homemade soup.

Laman presented me with a long list of the tasks I was to accomplish to earn my keep. He told me it was a high honor to be allowed to organize the supplies purchased for the Lord's storehouse. According to him, there were enough dried foods, honey, beans, lentils, thread, candles, lamps, kerosene, old clothes, and shoes to see every man, woman, and child in God's Holy Work in Canada through two years of famine and destruction while Christ cleansed the wicked gentile earth with fire. The trouble was that Uncle Isaac, Daddy, and Uncle Kelvin had dumped barrels and boxes full of supplies into the basement of the old building, and there was no sense of order.

Laman described to me, with excitement and intricate detail, the amazing storehouses organized by the prophet's workers for our people in Colorado City. He said the tunnels the supplies were stored in went far back into the red cliffs behind the city. Although the grand storehouses were fortified with heavy iron gates and padlocks, they were probably pretty safe without them, because few people who grew up there would dream of defying the prophet's orders to stay away from the canyons. They stretched hundreds of miles behind the sacred city like a maze built by God for a race of giants, and were all the more terrifying because they were guarded by Gadianton Robbers. These mysterious beings were the worst of the wicked, slothful servants of the Lord and the prophets; they were cursed with dark skins and doomed to roam the canyons and surrounding desert until the Second Coming of Christ ushered in a thousand years of peace in the celestial kingdom.

There were stories of rebellious, wicked people, born and raised in the Work, who were a problem to the priesthood and strayed into the canyons never to be seen or heard from again. All the kids in our group there called them "poofers" and were terrified to be out after the curfew set by the police officers who were controlled by our prophet. Whenever Laman spoke about Colorado City, he got so excited one would think Christ already lived. He often mentioned he'd give anything to receive the word to move his family there, too.

When I had a good start on the storehouse, Laman said he'd be ready for me to start painting the church room on the main floor. He gutted all the walls to make one cavernous room with a vaulted ceiling. He was enthusiastic about the project, because Uncle Isaac told him to make it look like a room in the celestial kingdom. That meant we would be painting gold filigree scrolls on the finished trim. Bettilyn was always bragging that she had two sons who had been touched by the finger of God. Nephi was foreordained by God in the pre-existence to be an apostle and maybe even a prophet, and Laman was going to be called to build the temples in the New Jerusalem in Jackson County, Missouri, when we all walked there after Christ came in the new millennium. Laman told me excitedly that this work of saving a monstrous building built by an apostate was practice for his calling in the New Jerusalem.

I started my first day of work full of hope. I was eager to redeem myself by making shelves and carefully organizing all the goods. When I swung open the heavy wooden door and clicked on the light, I couldn't believe my eyes.

Laman laughed at my gasp. "Oh yeah! I forgot to tell you Dad and Mom were called on the weekend and given the leftovers from some church rummage sales in town. I guess you'll be needing to sort through all the clothes and bag 'em up or hang 'em so the moths don't get to them. And one more thing—Dad says he wants you to strip all these old white shirts and sheets into bandages and sterilize them. He figures we'll need them when we're walking to Jackson County." Laman gave me a crooked smile. "Good luck, eh! I gotta run in to the builders to pick up some supplies."

I rearranged some boxes of clothing so Janessa had a place to play and wouldn't get hurt while I worked. She hated it there and complained no matter what I gave her to play with. Soon, I was crying with her. When I couldn't stand to listen to her any longer, I gathered her in my arms and walked the same path we once ran with Mother—only now it meandered through a huge garbage dump. The Gentiles had taken over the hill covered with brush and trees and polluted it just like Uncle Isaac said they would. They desecrated a beautiful piece of land with the evil of their garbage and proved that whatever they touched was "a stench in the nostrils of the Lord." How odd that Heavenly Father would allow the Gentiles to put a dump between two pieces of land dedicated for his chosen people. I began to run the moment I entered the dump property. Not until I was safely back on Uncle Isaac's land and down the steep hill to Lydia's house did I dare take a full breath of air.

When he was getting sicker, Uncle Isaac asked Lydia to quit her job with the Gentiles. She wasn't at all surprised to see me. She invited me in and showed me the renovations she had just finished on her little house with the money she made in town. She fed us, and then as I sobbed my story to her, she agreed to let Janessa stay with her. She would care for her and Velma together. I stayed until it was dark outside, and she let me bathe Janessa and put her to bed. As I was leaving, she stopped me. "I've always wanted to hear from you why you didn't want to live with me at the other house. Can you tell me…or is it the usual crap about Bettilyn? I'll help you with Janessa and worry about you because you're still basically a kid…but I know you agree with them sometimes about me, and you talk behind my back."

My heart sank as I tried to figure out what to say. "Lydia, I'll forever be sorry I didn't try harder to live with you longer. I know you know why I couldn't…Thanks so much for helping me with Janessa." I gave her a quick hug, flew out the door, and tore up the hill over the rough trail as fast as I could run. I was glad there was a moon high in the sky because I couldn't stop running, and the trail was strewn with stumps, rocks, and fallen logs. I ran to the school and up the stairs into my room, fighting to catch my breath.

I wondered if I'd done the right thing leaving Janessa at Lydia's. I knew there was no way of accomplishing my calling if she was constantly screaming, but when she was here demanding my attention, it gave me something other than myself to focus on.

I was badly in need of sleep, but when I lay down and shut off the light, my mind shifted into high gear. Image after image popped into my head, like a ghostly procession. I was here in this very room for a Sunday meeting, and Uncle Isaac and Uncle Michael were both haranguing the congregation about why they should be file leader. One angry son after the other testified from the pulpit...Suddenly I was sewing on my wedding dress, so excited at the thought of being the wife of a great man and a mother in Israel. Then Grandmother and my sister wife Bettilyn were standing over me washing my pregnant sixteen-year-old body and anointing it with olive oil. I panicked when I saw Uncle Isaac doing sex to me, knowing I was allowing him to kill my unborn son by defiling the law. I sat bolt upright in bed. The ghosts were taunting me now as if they could sense the aching of my body and feel a need that was wild and hot—a need I had no idea how to communicate to my husband. It was only when I was in this exhausted state, unable to sleep, that I dared own that craving and touch myself where experience had taught me I needed it. After losing myself in those moments of release, I found the closest state to peace my body ever experienced.

I wondered if I was any better than the young sister wives from Colorado City who had created such a commotion. We were horrified when we heard how Satan was trying to tear our Work apart in a way we could never have imagined. Some apostles had thirty or more young wives they were too busy to spend time with, and the worst spirit of perversion had taken over a few of them—some the same age as I was. Together they stripped naked and took pictures like the ones in the *Penthouse* magazines I found at the dump. Even worse, they sold the pictures to young men in our group, which gave the boys the idea they could help their father's wives have babies.

Initially, when we heard some of the new wives of our apostles had started to bear children, we rejoiced because we thought the prophecies about these older men becoming fertile again had come true. The prophet's older wives blamed the whole scandal on the young women for their immoral ways. Now as I battled the urges of my lonely body, I wondered if I could have been tempted to take part in the picture-taking had I been one of those girls.

I shunned the thought. Was I allowing evil spirits to possess me the way Bettilyn said they did with her other sister wives? I left my bed and rummaged through my boxes for the little tape recorder Daddy had given me. Putting on a tape of hymns, I sat cross-legged in the corner and tore strips from the first batch of shirts and sheets. Daddy said scriptures and hymns were supposed to stop the terrifying nightmares and the urges of my wayward body. He once told me if thousands of nuns who believed they were married to Christ could deal with having no man to hold them, then I should be fine. How often had I been told that idle hands were the devil's workshop? I knew I had to keep busy and control my mind as Uncle Isaac said, or I'd "be cast into outer darkness and ground into native element, never to be redeemed, worlds without end."

Mornings were awful because of the sleepless nights, and the school kids were poking around my door a few minutes before eight. My favorite time of day was late afternoon when the classrooms were mostly empty. That was when I organized the desks, picked up the garbage, and did battle with the never-ending dirt that got tracked in from the muddy schoolyard. Celia came to help most afternoons. Sometimes we worked in the same room; other times, one swept while the other mopped. When she found out Janessa Dawn was at Lydia's, she sadly told me a child should be with her mother, no matter what. I knew she was right, but trying to find a solution to the problem only made my head hurt.

I told her about the horrible nights and days after Janessa was born—how I hated myself for not wanting to care for my own child. Celia shared with me some of her darkest moments about how she tried to live the way Uncle Kelvin's legal wife wanted. She told me how she and her older sister were married to him at the same ceremony, and about what it was like for them to go home to his first wife in the two-room shack and sleep on the floor with the five children. When it was her turn to sleep with Uncle Kelvin, she was expected to lie with him in the same bed as the first wife. Celia recounted her humiliation at having to perform under the critical eye of another woman while her sister and all the children listened. She said the only slight joy she derived from the physical relationship with her husband was when they finally decided to sneak away and find a private place. That usually meant having sex in the straw barn or under the pine trees in the forest.

I told her I was glad she could talk about her intimate needs to Uncle Kelvin, because I was too tongue-tied around Uncle Isaac to ever tell him what I needed. Celia burst into tears when she told me about her refusal to live in town. Months and even years passed before Uncle Kelvin would come to her. It was his form of punishment, his way of trying to get her to give in to his edicts. I vowed to find some way to seek Uncle Isaac's forgiveness—to be a blessing instead of a trial to his family.

I spent long days in the Lord's storage house, working to protect the goods from the cold, damp basement environment. I ran to Lydia's several times a week to see Janessa. She was glad to see me, but was usually more interested in playing with her little sister. Lydia went on in great detail about the romantic moments she was spending with our husband and how he was teaching her the secrets of the kingdom. When she'd exhausted that subject, she expounded on her favorite topic—how much she hated Bettilyn and what the evil woman had done to undermine her and Isaac's other wives. She told me again what I already knew, that the only sister wife Bettilyn had a good word for was Aunt Lena, who'd had "the good sense to die." Lydia repeatedly made the point that no one could ever be as good as a dead sister wife.

I'd always end up taking the shortcut through the dump in the dark to get home. Several times I heard motorbikes that seemed to be right on my heels. I could never see any lights and kept thinking they had to be crazy to drive at night through all the rocks and debris. On one of my midnight runs, I stopped above the dump to catch my breath and found a stack of paperback books—it was as if they were waiting for me. Their pages weren't saturated with the overwhelming stench of the dump, so I carried them home.

One night all was quiet downstairs, so I decided to run a bath. With the tub full to the top, I added a few drops of the rose-scented bubble bath Celeste had forgotten to take back to their apartment. As I lowered my body into the water, I imagined Uncle Isaac at the door begging me to open it for him. I pictured our sensual play in the tub—just like Lydia had described. My longing for Uncle Isaac was so vivid that I realized I was holding my breath in anticipation of the knock that never came. I finally dried my hands, picked up my new book, and started to read. This book was just like the one I'd found in Elsa's hope chest; it was probably worse, because most of the people in it weren't married and they did sex in ways I'd never heard of. I was mesmerized by the story, the characters, the sex, and my feelings. I was perplexed—if people could make love that often and with so many others, something must be amiss with me that Uncle Isaac didn't want me at all. What was I doing wrong? Lydia had told me that very night he still enjoyed her body, and sex was better for them now than ever in their whole married life. Maybe his illness wasn't all that serious.

My body tingled as the author described the bodies of aroused men; I couldn't believe the way he wrote about women loving their own bodies and each other. I kept reading until I fell asleep. When I woke up, I was cold and shaking so hard I had to force my fingers to bend. My nose was not a quarter of an inch above the water. I had just pulled the plug when I heard car doors slamming and kids hollering. I pulled my flannel gown over my head and wrapped the evil book in my towel just as the first person banged on the door. I hurried up the stairs to lock myself in my room. No one seemed to pay much attention, even though the kids and several of the teachers saw me.

I woke up late in the afternoon, feeling guilty about wasting valuable daylight hours. After I dressed and put up my hair, I went to look at the storage room. I was proud of myself. Where there had been chaos, there were now shelves with all the supplies neatly categorized. Anyone could find matches, candles, thread, needles, kerosene, boots, and hundreds of other items just by looking in a card index. I had managed to build long racks to hang clothes and coats on.

Laman appeared moments after I did. Shifting his weight from side to side, he cleared his throat. "Well, it looks like you've done okay down here. It's been a pretty big job, but I think we need to leave it for a bit. Dad thinks I need your help upstairs in the meeting room now. Mom and him ordered some of those fine drapes from Uncle Miller's factory in Salt Lake, and I'm just not getting the painting and carpenter work done fast enough. There's no reason you can't get right at it, is there?"

I followed him upstairs. I was aching to ask if Uncle Isaac had mentioned me while he was going over the work that still needed to be done. I was anxious for him to tell me what a good job I was doing and what his plans were for me. Several times I thought of phoning him at Bettilyn's, but just thinking about it scared the daylights out of me.

Being on the main floor of this huge building gave me a very different feeling from shuffling around in the cold basement. As I gazed up at the ceiling pieces and the trim I was to paint, I asked Laman how I'd get up there—was there scaffolding for me to stand on to do the painting? He shifted uneasily. "We rented some from Creston Builders, but Dad said they were too expensive to keep long enough to finish the whole job. You'll have to stand on the piano and do the best you can—unless you've figured out how to fly with a bucket of paint in your hands!" He chuckled at his joke.

I couldn't bring myself to tell him how afraid of heights I was. And I kept thinking that Uncle Isaac might actually have asked for me to do this job. Besides, complaining was a sin, and like Daddy told me again just the other day: "The Lord asks no man to do a job save He prepares a way."

Laman's comments about flying made me think about my dreams. Sometimes they were beautiful and I was happy, but other times I was flying through a black fog that reeked of coal dust—at times I almost had to swim. I vaguely pictured myself floating around the room, reaching the highest points with ease. I snapped back to reality when Laman showed me the stack of supplies—the paint cans, the brushes, the rollers, the paint thinner. I didn't dare tell him the industrial oil-based paint made me dizzy. With great deliberation he gave me instructions on what the finished meeting hall was to look like. Although the sun was beginning to fade, the lighting was good and I got started. I was splattered with paint by the time I heard a scuffling at the door. Celia appeared. "Someone told me the light I could see was you over here painting, but I didn't believe them. Do you know what time it is?" She stared at the mass of space I had covered.

"I've sort of lost track of time, Celia. I'm hungry, though, so it must be around nine."

"Well, you're off by four hours—it's one in the morning. If I didn't have to get up with the baby, I wouldn't have known you were still here. Just stop and clean up! I know your nights and days are all mixed up, but unless you start taking better care of yourself, you'll be getting sick before you know it." She shook her finger at me, advising I'd better get some air circulating in the room or I'd be passing out. She shooed me on my way after telling me to stop at her house in the morning for a loaf of fresh bread.

When I saw her the next day, she told me she'd been praying about me and was sure she'd been given a message for me. She told me to call Uncle Isaac and invite him to Sunday dinner after church. She said since I didn't have an oven, she'd help make it nice by baking some special bread and a dessert—I'd have to figure out the rest myself. I decided if I was going to go through with this, I should bring Janessa home for the weekend. Maybe seeing her with me would remind Uncle Isaac I was not only his wife but his daughter's mother, too. Maybe he'd even agree to come back after chores and stay the night; the closest I'd been to him over the last few weeks was at church. My imagination caught fire at the possibilities of what might happen if he liked what he saw.

I painted the walls in a frenzy for the rest of the week so I could start the highest trim and the ceiling. Early Saturday morning I plucked up the courage to call Bettilyn's house. I was praying that one of the kids would answer, but it was Bettilyn. From the sound of her voice when she called Uncle Isaac to the phone, it was clear she'd rather have gone to the hangman than tell him it was me. I was startled when he actually came on the line. As hard as I had been practicing my speech, I was terrified he'd say no. When he said he guessed it wouldn't hurt him to stop over after church, I thanked him and hung up the phone quickly, afraid if I kept talking, I'd manage to stick my foot in my mouth. I ran to get Janessa from Lydia's and spent the rest of the day cleaning and arranging things so they'd be perfect for the next day. I was excited. This would be my very first meal alone with Uncle Isaac and our daughter.

I got up early to prepare the canned chicken Irene had given me when she was afraid Janessa Dawn and I might starve. I boiled potatoes and made a milk sauce for the canned corn before church. Dressing us both in our very best clothes, I did my hair the way Uncle Isaac liked it. I agonized after the meeting about whether I should stay and go through the lineup to shake hands and to ask him if he was still coming, or if I should bolt back to my rooms and make sure everything was ready. I couldn't stand waiting to find out. I lined up, making sure I wasn't close to any of Bettilyn's kids in case someone heard me talking to him. When I finally reached him, I tried to smile my most beautiful smile. I was quaking inside, thinking how desperately we needed to recapture some of the mystical emotion we had when I was thirteen and he danced with me and quoted the verse from the Song of Solomon.

"We're ready for you up at the school, Uncle Isaac…we're glad you're coming to eat with us!" The words all jumbled together in one breath as I tried to hold Janessa forward and remind him that his beautiful little daughter needed him, too.

He nodded with a quizzical look and said, "Who's we? Do you have worms?"

I flushed. When I looked up, Lem was standing off to the side, smirking. I fled the building and managed to get inside the school before I broke into tears. I chastised myself bitterly for reminding him. Everything would be a disaster if he came, I knew it, and all I could do was cry. The moment I almost had myself under control, I remembered he had made fun of me in front of Lem, and I started crying again.

All the vehicles had left the grounds, and Uncle Isaac had still not come up. I told myself he was likely just enjoying the flowers in Laman and Celeste's garden. I brought up the food I had warmed in the oven downstairs and set my little table. Things were already getting cold by the time I heard his voice through the heat vent in the floor. Celeste was speaking in her best wheedling voice. "Oh, Uncle, you really don't need to go up there. I'm not going to let you. We have a wonderful meal here, and we're going to keep you!" I imagined the cute pout on her face as she clung to his arm and stamped her tiny foot.

"There are some things a man just has to do," he replied. "Tell you what, Daughter. You and Laman come up and sing for me in a bit—how would that be?"

"It's just not fair!" she whined.

When I heard his footsteps, the sound of my heart beating in my ears drowned out everything else. I had already fed Janessa because she was fussing so much and wouldn't have been the cute little daughter I needed to help plead my case. Now she was sleeping. I opened the door before he got to it, then cursed myself for seeming too eager. Lydia would have locked the door and told him to go away for being late or at least made him wait.

I apologized profusely for not being able to keep the food warm. He said he wasn't really hungry anyway and didn't touch a thing. Instead, he sat in silence in the rocking chair. I wasn't sure what to do with myself—the other chairs would have put me too high, and I couldn't just keep standing. Finally, I sat cross-legged on the rug. When I looked up at him, he was leaning back with his eyes closed. I started a sentence three different times, three different ways, stuttering with every attempt.

"What are you babbling about, woman?" he shouted. "Spit it out!"

His harsh command made me forget all the ways I had rehearsed my speech. I also forgot about the romance I hoped might happen later on. I blurted, "I don't know what to do anymore. I thought when you brought me here you'd come see me sometimes so we could get to know each other—so I could figure out how to be your wife and maybe be your friend, too. Please tell me!" I was begging, and the tears refused to stay hidden. He leaned back in the chair again with the tip of his thumb in his mouth and his eyes closed. "Please say something. Anything! There has to be a way I can redeem myself—some way you'll forgive me." I wanted to scream.

He leaned forward. "You knew you were where I wanted you—why couldn't you just get along over there with the kids? You couldn't live with Lydia! You can't live with Bettilyn! I always say every tub has to sit on its own bottom—well, your tub is leaking. You don't know how to take proper direction, and you ask too many questions…you are always going to find yourself on the wrong side of the priesthood. The priesthood can't use a leaky tub. I don't know what in tarnation to do with you. Besides, this isn't my house." He settled back in his chair again and became a stone statue.

I struggled to keep my voice calm. I knew if I didn't, Celeste would be up the stairs like a shot, and my opportunity would be lost. "Uncle Isaac, please tell me what you mean? Do you want me to go back to Bettilyn's place? What?"

"If you can't tell from what I just said, you're a lost cause…Can't a man have a little peace?"

As if on cue, Celeste and Laman came up the stairs. When I heard them, I quickly wiped my tears and jumped up mumbling about checking on Janessa. Uncle Isaac turned to Celeste. "Play some tunes for me, Daughter."

For over an hour Celeste played the piano. Sometimes Laman sang, sometimes they both did. Then they all left together. I sat like a frozen lump on my bed as Uncle Isaac said goodbye to them and walked out onto the road. I listened to the gravel crunch beneath his boots, then there was silence. I cried until I drifted into a fitful sleep. When Janessa began rattling the sides of her crib, I gathered her things and began the long trek back to Lydia's. I tried to convince myself that Janessa was better off there than she was with me—at least she could see her father once in a while.

Lydia anxiously grabbed my arm and pumped me for details about my meal with our husband. On the way I had argued with myself about whether or not to tell her the truth. I still hadn't made up my mind by the time we started talking, but within moments I was battling tears, and there was little sense in trying to lie.

When she heard what had happened, she was livid. "That sneaky Bettilyn…she set up interference with Celeste and Laman to keep Isaac from you. I'd bet you anything—that's just the way she works!" Lydia rocked furiously. "Even if Bettilyn hadn't deliberately instructed them to keep you from having private time with Isaac, that sneaky Laman knows how to protect his mother's territory. You mark my words!" She was shaking her head as if it were unhinged. "No one will ever know the truth, this side of heaven or hell, about what that woman and her children have put me through. But there'll be a judgment day when all this is recorded. The innocent who've suffered will have their day. You can mark my words, Deborah! I wish that woman were here right now. I'd tell her...she'd know how possessed of the devil she was to want her sister wives to suffer this way!"

I hadn't given any thought to the possibility of Bettilyn's involvement in this until Lydia suggested the idea. Then, in a horrible way, it made perfect sense. Lydia stormed on and paced the floor. I wanted to get back to my room to think, but before I could excuse myself, she grabbed the phone and dialed. I felt sick to my stomach as she began to holler.

"Bettilyn!" Lydia's voice was harsh. "I see you're as good at destroying Deborah's life as you ever were at destroying mine! I hope you're proud of yourself. I'm calling to tell you I'm not a stupid, naïve little girl anymore, and I intend on protecting Deborah's interests if you won't. You think you can keep Isaac all to yourself and destroy anyone else's chances with him. You're so far from living celestial marriage—believe me, God is taking note!"

Lydia had lost total control and started shrieking and swearing. I forced myself out of my chair and took hold of her arm. "I have to go back to the school and work there, Lydia...please stop. It'll be so much worse if you don't stop...I don't have anywhere else to go, and Bettilyn's kids will just be worse. They'll all know by morning."

Even through her rage, my desperation must have registered in some corner of her mind because she bellowed, "If anyone torments Deborah about this, they'll have to answer to me...and believe me, they won't like it!" She slammed down the receiver. "You tell me if any of them treat you that way again. Isaac talks to me now, and you better believe I'll give him a piece of my mind."

I felt like I was teetering once again on the brink. As Lydia wound down, I glanced at her brightly lit apple clock—it was one-thirty in the morning. Promising to tell her if I needed help, I raced up the trail as if the devil were tearing at my skirts. My mind was numb and my body bone-weary. It wasn't until I saw the cold

Sunday dinner still sitting on the table that I realized I hadn't eaten anything all day. I fell into bed and curled up in the fetal position. I slept fitfully, with Lydia yelling and Bettilyn drifting around me with a pinched smile on her face.

When the vehicles and kids started to arrive the next morning, I was still in my clothes and consumed with anxiety about getting on with the painting. I just knew I could get this job right and redeem myself. I pulled all the pins out of the long braid still curled around my head. When I reached for my hairbrush, I stood to look in the little mirror nailed to the wall. At first I just stared at the letter that was taped to it. Who had put it there? I was sure it hadn't been there when I went to bed, but would someone have come into my bedroom when I was asleep? I stared dumbly at the note as if expecting it to speak to me. A cold shiver ran up my spine as I read.

To this wife of the Good Father:

You don't realize you are being watched and records are being made of every action you make and every word you say—night and day. It is my sacred responsibility to tell you that you have been tried and found guilty of betraying the Good Father. You are a murderer, and innocent blood will be on your hands forever because of it. We were all told by the prophet that the Good Father would be healed and restored to full health if his wives and children would keep sweet and be obedient.

You are guilty of the sin of gossip and stirring up wicked and vile spirits to destroy the peace and healing power in the Good Father's family. You will pay before the judgment bar of God for the sins you have committed. You will know the pain of the damned in this life for destroying the prophecy of our prophet, LeRoy Sunderland Johnson—the prophecy that our Good Father would be healed and live forever without ever tasting death.

Watch yourself, because I am watching you. From this day forward, someone will always be watching and recording every act you commit, so beware! You will know me. Never forget this day.

Protector of the Faith and the Good Father

I was rooted where I stood, not sure if I was awake or in one of my nightmares. I reached shakily for the note. It had been taped in a dozen places, and I could hardly peel it off without tearing the paper. I had to show this letter to someone.

With my hair a terrible mess around my face and shoulders, I stumbled down the stairs. My brothers, sisters, cousins, and stepchildren ran past me—laughing, talking, quarreling—all heading to classes as if this were a normal day. Brent stopped abruptly on the bottom step staring at me. "Deb! What's the matter? You look terrible—you have to fix your hair. Don't tell me you're in some kind of trouble again?"

I mumbled to him and continued into the old kitchen. The first person I found was Bettilyn. When she ignored me, I clutched her shoulder and thrust the note under her nose. "What's this? Who came into my room in the middle of the night? It wasn't there when I went to bed, and this morning it was taped to the mirror." I looked directly into her eyes and implored her. "I didn't wreck the family—Lydia hated everyone ever since I was little. I'm trying to paint the church house and make it like a temple. I just took Janessa Dawn back to Lydia last night. What did I do that was so wrong? What did I do?"

I continued babbling and shaking my head wildly until my hair was a whirl of brown choking me and sticking to my wet face. "It can't be just my fault the family is wrecked, can it? Help me!"

Jan charged out of the bathroom, grabbed my shoulders, and slapped me hard. "Quit your bawling—you're making a fool out of yourself! None of this would have happened if you could just work and mind your own business. Instead, you have to go gossiping with Lydia."

I pushed the note at her, and she took it. She and her mother read it at the same time. Bettilyn said, "Well...I guess this might be a bit much...really."

Jan read the note again. "I dare say someone is very passionate about hating gossipers. The Lord does say he hates liars, whoremongers, and feet that are quick to run into mischief. You, Deb...you are certainly right there when there's a chance to stir up trouble. I told you to mark my words—that something like this would happen—and here you are. Good grief!"

Celeste stopped to see what the fuss was about. When she read the note, her face turned bright red and she thrust it back into Jan's hand. "Ooh, for awful! Who could do such a thing? Oh goodness, Deb, what are you going to do? It's probably not a good idea for you to live here if stuff like this is going to happen. Really!" She ran up the stairs.

Jan declared she'd be talking to Adam about this and stomped off. Bettilyn made a big fuss about being late for her class and disappeared into the side room. I was alone in the old kitchen holding the cursed note.

I went back upstairs, determined to follow Jan's advice and get on with my painting. Stuffing the note in the bottom of my hope chest next to my doll with no name, I did up my hair and got ready to go. I was still shaking, but if I could finish covering the ugly old wood with beautiful white paint and turn that room into the celestial kingdom, then I'd be on my way to redemption—even if, with the curse on me now, I might never qualify to be a goddess there. The white and gold drapes were coming from Salt Lake City, and when they arrived I was going to make sure we were ready for them.

When I got back to the job, it became painfully obvious it wasn't going to be easy. I had painted as far as I could using the roller and extension, and even when I stood on the piano, I couldn't begin to reach the highest places. Balancing a chair on top of the piano got me closer, but only when I placed a five-gallon bucket on top of the chair could I manage to paint the final trim with a brush. At the end of two hours, my clothes were sweaty from the effort of stretching from my precarious tower while balancing a can of paint. Getting up and down to move the piano was the part I dreaded the most. It was a heavy beast to budge, and each time I maneuvered it into place, the effort left me exhausted. The fumes from the oil-based paint were really beginning to get to me. I was thinking about going out for a breath of fresh air when the door swung open; I shifted my weight in an attempt to see who it was. Nephi's stocky body and square shoulders came into view. I was glad to see him until I saw the look on his face. My heart pounded as I made my way down from my makeshift scaffold to sit on the piano. He tapped his foot impatiently.

"Hi, Nephi, nice of you to come visit me. Hope you brought a sandwich with you—I'm starving!" One look into his hostile eyes brought my babbling up short.

"I know you've seen my words already today—I want you to know you're on notice. Do you think I'd allow you to be part of the destruction of the Good Father's family without trying to stop it?" He glared at me with an intensity that made me wilt. "Do you? Don't pretend you don't know why I'm here. I know you better than you know yourself, and I'm keeping records of everything you do, everything you say, who you're with, and where you go." I gripped the edge of the piano to keep from falling to the floor. I felt a horrible weight of guilt crushing me. How could he insinuate I would be the sole cause of the destruction of Isaac Merrick?

"I don't know what you're talking about, Nephi. You left that note on my mirror? Why? If you know everything else, you must know why Lydia was so angry." My mind was spinning, trying to make sense of all this. "What are you up to? How could you sneak into my bedroom and put that note there? You act as if I'm killing Uncle Isaac! There was fighting and hate in this family long before I married your dad...I remember how terrified we all were when I was a little girl, and I'm sure you remember, too. After all these years, how can you come along and say it's my fault?" I was crying and angry with myself for letting him see my weakness.

"I have my ways of seeing and hearing things. I have a faithful crew of boys who'll do *anything* I tell 'em, and I'm writing records. You know you can accuse anyone in a court of law with records like I have and a judge will find the offender guilty...Don't forget that. I have records on more people than anyone knows!" His small round body was menacing and stiff. "No amount of tears will ever get you forgiveness for the sins you've committed against this family and the Good Father—just think on it. I don't have any more time for your pitiful attempts to explain yourself. You'll have to explain to the Good Father and God when they judge you. You can bet I'll stand at the bar to testify against you and make sure you meet the judgment." He turned to leave. "Just remember—I'll always be watching you! You won't know when or how, but I'll know what you're doing...and I'll be recording it."

As the door slammed, I lost my grip. The last thing I remembered was the painted yellow floor coming up to meet me. When I regained consciousness, I tried to prop myself up with my right arm, but it buckled and was almost useless. I carefully picked my way home, slumped onto the bed, and disappeared again into a black void.

In the morning I woke with a start to see Daddy at the door of my room. "I've been hearing some disturbing stories about goings-on over here. I had a talk with Isaac, and he agrees it would be best if I took you home for a bit. You can have your daughter with you there, and Irene can use your help. The thistles and burdock have just about taken over the strawberry patch, so there's lots to do. Just gather up Janessa Dawn and a few of your things. Jan'll take you home after school this afternoon." He gave me a quick hug, then disappeared.

Nettie came to me at the noon break and shook me awake. "Deb, you better start getting ready—you're supposed to be coming home. Don't start out with Mother being mad at you from the very first minute." I dragged myself to a sitting position. "What's wrong with you—you're acting like you're drunk!" She grabbed my arm to help me; I winced and pulled back in pain. "My word, Deb, what on earth happened? You better get yourself straightened out in a hurry. You know Jan has no patience for sickness."

I mumbled something about falling off the piano. Without asking for details, Nettie helped me to my feet. She offered me a piece of her egg sandwich, but the sight of it made me want to retch. She helped me throw a few things together, then urged me to hurry and pick up Janessa Dawn. I walked over to Lydia's, and after a brief explanation, thanked her for helping. I arrived back at the school just in time to get into the rickety old bus with my brothers and sisters. All the way home they stared at me and whispered back and forth. I looked straight ahead, concentrated with all my strength on sitting upright, and contemplated these new instructions from the Good Father.

Chapter 18

The transition from the enforced solitude of the meeting house to the noise and confusion at Daddy's unnerved me. Although within a matter of days my daughter was swallowed up in the routines of my twenty-five siblings, I was in a perpetual state of panic about her well-being.

Irene blasted me. "What makes you think we have time to worry about just one brat—if she can't play, eat, and sleep when the rest of them do, she won't fit in. No one has time for that here. Get to your job and quit worrying about her." Irene was already on the fly with her morning chores. "Adam's forever bringing home the stray dogs of our community. At least you're not one of those 'weakling' Whitmer girls! I do get sick of them...but if you don't get busy, you won't be any more use to me than they were."

When she wound down, I begged her to let me fold laundry and polish the shoes for church. She thought it was crazy for someone my age to care about Sunday shoes but told me to go ahead. There was something about polishing Daddy's shoes that relaxed me—maybe it was because in my mind I was doing it for Mother.

It was difficult to sleep with Janessa Dawn in the crib-sized cubbyhole in Nettie's room. When it was my room, I had a single bed and some privacy, but now that the house was literally bursting at the seams, it had a double and a single bed and slept three girls. To get to our corner we had to maneuver through a maze of beds in the main dorm room, where twelve more girls slept.

After a few days I was introduced to my primary task—weeding and pruning two acres of strawberries and raspberries. While I dug up the burdock or yanked out shriveled brown Canada thistles and matted dandelions, I remembered when I was a little girl and could keep going by telling myself I was wrestling with the devil. Now, as an eighteen-year-old wife-in-exile, I had more reason than ever to do battle with him. If the tasks of hoeing, pruning, and burning didn't subdue him, then at least they kept him from occupying my mind.

Dressed in gumboots and my oldest dress, I was pulling on a pair of work gloves when Daddy stopped me. He was wearing his suit and newly shined shoes. I was vaguely pleased to see how nice his shoes looked, until I saw a bit of mud on one of them. I knelt before him to wipe it off with a clean bit of my glove. He pulled me up.

"Come now, Daughter. I must say I'm worried about you—you're acting rather oddly. It's Sunday, and here you are heading out to the raspberries. You know that no daughter of mine is going to miss church. I let it slide last Sunday because you were just settling in, but you have to know you'll not be missing church again...now run, get ready!" He spoke as if the thinking was done.

I had lost all track of days and time. I didn't know it was Sunday, but the thought of getting back on the bus, driving to the ranch, and walking into the meeting hall I'd been painting made me physically ill. I couldn't face my husband and sister wives. I sagged into the corner of the porch and begged him not to make me go.

"Now, Deb, I've never seen you like this...You've got to get hold of yourself. You're scaring the little ones, and I'm not about to stand for your theatrics—it could be Jan's right about all that. Things are a bit rough at the moment, I'll grant that...but staying away from church is only a downhill ride to worse things, and I won't have it."

"I'll try, Daddy, I really will...but I can't today. Please don't make me!"

He opened his mouth to speak just as I tried to get past him to the patio. I didn't make it. My stomach heaved and I threw up my oatmeal porridge all over his shiny shoes. I was too miserable to care if I had angered him further. He looked pained and handed me his handkerchief. "Well, I guess you're off the hook this time, but I'll be talking to you about this before next week. It never did anyone any good to hide away like they were ashamed of something. I won't allow it."

Nettie refused to look at me as she passed through the porch to the waiting bus. The other kids either ran past holding their noses or went out the back door. After cleaning up my mess, I spent the rest of the morning in my corner. I blocked Janessa Dawn in with my boxes so she couldn't crawl off the mattress and escape to the danger of the basement stairs. Although with all of Daddy's own children, she wasn't much of an added bother, I still had to keep her away from Jan. The first weekend after we arrived, when I left the baby playing with one of my little brothers, Jan got angry. Waiting until all my siblings were crowding around for supper, she said, "Some people think they can be *married*, and then do nothing but be a trial to everyone they come in contact with. It behooves every girl here to learn they have to pull their own weight...I'm going to add that reality to my lessons at school!" Every time she preached about my shortcomings, Nettie and the other kids glared at me because it was guaranteed they'd be listening to lectures about the topic for weeks to come.

I never knew what to expect from Jan. On weekends when she was finished reading scriptures to the assembled household, she would talk about some new sermon she was studying in the Journals of Discourses or the Bible or the Doctrine and Covenants. At these times she consulted me as if she really wanted my opinion. She knew I studied all these books and could quote chapters and verses and discuss doctrine principles on her level. I took her interest as a compliment, because she bemoaned the fact there were so few people in the priesthood who cared about the gospel enough to be able to discuss it. Whenever I debated with her, though, I was cautious, every sense alert.

Daddy lived up to his promise to search me out whenever he had a spare moment. He repeatedly admonished me to beware the sin of false pride. He was adamant that if I had a proper offering of a broken heart and a contrite spirit, it wouldn't bother me to sit on a bed of hot coals in the presence of my enemies. The important thing was to do the Lord's will. "All the Lord expects of us is our best," he said, "so hold your head up and make sure you're offering your all on the altar of the Lord for the Work. You know that's why I work as hard as I do every day, Daughter. I give my all, and I expect you to do the same. It'll come out all right."

By the end of a month I had survived three church meetings and had managed to develop a routine in my new surroundings. I was either outside working in the gardens or helping Irene with the kids. I couldn't shake the feeling of nausea I'd had since the morning I made a mess of Daddy's shoes. I threw up so often that Irene asked me if I was pregnant. I would've told her it could only be the result of an immaculate conception, but I didn't want to admit to anyone that Uncle Isaac hadn't touched me for almost two years. I assured her that pregnancy was probably not the cause of the vomiting because I was running a fever, too.

Early one Friday morning, I was stuck in the only bathroom in the house, vomiting. I threw up green, slimy liquid, then was hit with a terrible attack of diarrhea. Children soon started pounding on the door. Sharp pains stabbed my right side, and a flush of fever left me sweating and weak. I crumpled in a ball onto the floor, unconcerned that I was lying in my own mess. A stern command from Daddy brought me to my feet, and I unlocked the door.

Jan was up by this time. After a quick feel of my forehead and a look around the bathroom, she pronounced, "She can't be in the house in this condition. Irene already has too much to do. You'll have to take her to the hospital, Adam—unless you expect me to."

My heart sank as Daddy explained he had an important client coming to the station. He had no time to drive me, since the fate of his new machinery dealership was dependent on the meeting. Jan heaved a sigh and gave me a look of disgust. By this time, all my brothers and sisters were scurrying around to check out the trouble Deb had managed to get herself into once again.

Jan slammed into her room, and after several minutes of banging drawers and doors, she was ready to go. When she ordered someone to get me out to the van, Brent put his shoulder under my arm and encouraged me to keep walking. He whispered that he knew I'd be okay. After warning me not to say anything to bug Jan, he tucked me into the van. Jan finished giving instructions to the kids so they'd be ready when she got back.

At the hospital she hurried me through admitting into the emergency room, telling the nurses in one breath I was a Nilsson with one child and that she had to leave. After she stormed out, the emergency nurse asked me in an irritated voice, "Just who is that person to you? It's as if she couldn't get rid of you fast enough. She treated me like some kind of witless fool—no one treats me that way!"

I was apologizing for Jan when another bout of pain doubled me up on the narrow mat. I begged the nurse to help me to the bathroom before I soiled the bed and myself. She scurried around cleaning me up, pumping me for more information about my home life. "Must have been just great having her for a mother. I thought all your people out there were supposed to care for one another." She shook her head. "Doesn't make sense to me."

I sat on the edge of the bed, hoping someone would find a way to stop the agony. Just as another wave of pain hit, the same doctor who had delivered Janessa Dawn pulled back the curtain. Even through my suffering I was dismayed to see him; the moment I laid eyes on him, I just knew he'd say something that would leave me speechless.

He spoke quietly to the nurse for a few minutes, then gently prodded my abdomen. He checked the chart and put on a latex glove. No experience in my life had prepared me for what he did next. He rolled me on my side and proceeded to examine me rectally. I was horrified and my groan graduated to a scream.

"Enough with the fuss…I'm sorry, but this wasn't meant to feel good." I looked at him, wondering how to respond. He said to the nurse, "We have a red hot appendix. With her temperature, there's no doubt it has to come out. We can reorganize things in surgery and get her right in." He turned to me. "Who do you want to operate? Dr. Morgan's away…there's myself and a new doctor from England. We're your choices."

I squirmed uncomfortably, wishing someone else were here to make the decision for me. "If it's all right...I'll have the doctor from England."

I woke up retching into a stainless steel bowl being held by a very patient nurse. She kept wiping my face and offering me chips of ice to chew on. The surges of pain that had plagued me were gone, and I couldn't feel anything until I puked again; then the incision across the lower part of my abdomen burned as if on fire.

I found myself in a room with two other women who looked as old as God. One of them was singing a strange soft song in a language I couldn't understand; the only time she ever stopped was when the nurses forced her to eat her lunch. The other one lay flat on her bed chanting "Hu! Hu! Hu!" I begged for a sleeping pill and something to dull the pain. The nurse brought me a pain pill but said the doctor wanted to check me before I could have anything for sleeping.

When I was more alert, I found myself looking forward to meeting him. I was convinced that a doctor straight from England would have to look more exotic than the doctors I knew. I was disappointed when I met him—he was quite ordinary. He introduced himself, and after checking my abdomen, gave me his verdict.

"We were just in time getting that appendix out. It hadn't burst yet, but there was certainly no time to waste. As for your general health, I'd encourage you to get rid of your extra weight. I had to cut through several thick layers of fat even to get into your abdomen. Healing will take more time because of it." With a warm smile, he added, "You'll find life much easier if you keep within the recommended weight for your height. I'll have a nurse get you a copy of a diet you may find helpful. Also, I'll be ordering something to help your pain and make you sleep—it isn't exactly peaceful in here." He frowned at the old lady who'd been singing the entire time he was talking.

In moments the nurse returned with two pills that I swallowed without question. I mulled over the doctor's comments about my weight. Daddy's wives were always competing with one another to see who could lose weight the fastest after a baby was born, and the ritual of measuring and recording waist sizes was equally important. I was five foot seven. When I married Uncle Isaac, Jeanie and I were around one hundred and twenty-five pounds and forever racing to the scale to see if we were up or down. I gained fifteen pounds when pregnant with the baby boy who died, and I couldn't lose the weight no matter how hard I tried. After Janessa was delivered, I lost ten pounds but had stayed at one hundred and sixty-five ever since. I didn't have any huge bulges and wasn't sure what the doctor was worried about, yet I couldn't stop obsessing about his comments. Maybe that was the reason Uncle Isaac wouldn't stay with me. The prophet had instructed his wives to tell us women in Canada that the Lord took it to be a sign of rebellion and the evil spirit of dissatisfaction in a woman to let her body become repulsive to her husband. He said they couldn't keep sweet properly with a cumbersome body, and stressed that women who were obese must know better than to complain if their husbands found it a trial fulfilling their procreating duties.

I'd convinced myself my weight gain had something to do with Uncle Isaac's attitude, when the drugs started to take effect. As with the Demerol shot when Janessa was being born, I lost control of my functions. I panicked when I tried to reach for the buzzer and my hands lay trapped beneath the blankets where the nurse had tucked them. That moment of terror was replaced by a strange sense of peace as part of me lifted off the blankets and floated toward the ceiling. All around me were flowers. They were all there—every tame and wild flower I had ever seen or read about. The droning from the two women was amplified as if through a microphone, but I found when I concentrated fiercely on the flowers, I could almost drown it out. I began counting how many blooms I could name; however, my brain was so fuzzy I kept losing track and had to start over. How silly it was of that doctor to think I was fat when I could float this well.

When the nurse came in and shone her flashlight in my direction, I rolled in the air until I was staring down at my bed. I was terrified to realize the ragged body in the bed was mine, and wondered if I might be dead. Panic struck me as I struggled to swim down to grab the buzzer and get the nurse's attention. She left the room so I went back to counting flowers. A myriad of blossoms rippled and flowed like a river, cascading into a waterfall at the corner of my cubicle.

Sometime during the night I lost my power to float and rejoined the wretched body on the bed. The next thing I knew, a nurse bustled into the room, threw open the curtains, and announced breakfast would arrive soon. She glanced at my chart. "You won't be having breakfast—we'll see how liquids settle on your stomach first."

I was sipping at my broth when a different nurse hurried in, briskly pushed a bedside table closer, and set down a vase with flowers. "There's a card. You can read it when you're up to it."

I stared at the bright yellow flowers in the tall, thin-necked ceramic vase, trying to imagine who they could be from. I had convinced myself Uncle Isaac had sent them, when someone broke my line of vision. I was worried I was still hallucinating when I realized it was Jean. She had been at nursing school in Lethbridge, and I wondered vaguely how she found out I was here. She set down a second vase of flowers and looked at me with genuine concern. I was grateful to see her, but I felt uncomfortable she had to find me in such a mess when she was so trim and tidy. I thanked her for the bouquet.

She looked at the other flowers, the blankets, and my roommates—everywhere but at me. She talked to the wall. "My nurse friend called me and told me you were here, so I thought I'd come by. The nurses are really uncomfortable with you." I wasn't sure how to react to this information. How would they normally deal with nauseated girls and uncooperative old ladies? Jean continued to enlighten me while staring at the curtain. "You realize they know you're married to Dad, and they don't know how to treat you...I guess I'm not sure myself. Do you want me to read this card for you?" She glanced directly at me and laughed. "You really do look like something the cat dragged in. You must have had a hard night." She picked the oversized card from the bouquet, opened it, and scanned it. Her lips curled the way they always did when she was particularly disgusted with something. "It looks like your grandmother was here again doing the *women's work* with Bettilyn...Oh, gag! You mean she didn't come see you? Brother, I'm glad she's your grandmother."

For a second I saw pity in her look. I hated that, more than anything she could have said or done. I didn't want her pity. I was the one living the sacred principle of celestial marriage, and she was the one who had followed her mother to the apostate church.

She began to read. "Dear Granddaughter, I'm so sorry to hear of your time of distress and especially your operation. I know the Lord will take care of you in His own way and time. You know He sends special spirits to this earth to be tried and tested in all manner of ways we don't understand. We can't question Him or the prophet. I was glad to hear your operation was a success, and Jan tells me you're healing well—so, as time was scant (I had to come on the bus at short notice to do the special women's work with Bettilyn) I have to get back to the farm. I know you'll understand at this busy time of year. I was able to order these flowers and have them sent just before the bus left. I love you. Remember! The Lord chasteneth those whom He loves, and He sends us special trials so He can tell if we are a diamond or a stone. If we are a diamond, we will be polished and shine bright as a star; if we are a stone, we will grind away into dust. I know you are a diamond, my darling granddaughter. I know you can make your mother, my beautiful Vivien, proud of you! Please understand why I was not able to visit you at the hospital. Never give up. Love, Grandmother."

Jean stuffed the card into the envelope and stabbed it back into the flowers as if it were burning her fingers. I thanked her again for the bouquet and for coming to see me. Her eyes met mine for a split second and she mumbled a goodbye before she turned on her heel and fled the room. The longer I thought about Grandmother not coming to see me, the more my head hurt. I listened to the chorus from my two roommates and stared at the flat yellow paint surrounding me. The longer I stared, the easier it was to look at—and to be one with the walls.

The remainder of the day passed in a blur. In the evening I begged for more medication—something different that wouldn't have such a strange effect on me. That night there were no more flowers, no more chanting old ladies, nothing but blissful, black nothingness.

During the ten days I was in hospital Jean didn't visit me again.

Jan came for a few minutes one day. Daddy came to see me every other day. Nettie and Brent visited once, and Bettilyn came several times. Whenever she was there, she fidgeted and moved from chair to chair, struggling to think of something to say.

The doctor cursed under his breath when he removed the bandages. "Damn! I had a feeling I should have put a drain in there, but thought we'd caught it in time." He talked to the nurse as if I weren't there. "She's going to have a rough go of healing now, for sure." He swore again. "Well, there's nothing for it but a course of antibiotics…Start them now." He looked sadly in my direction. "This is just what this one needs." There was a hint of pity in his voice. Before he left, he glanced at my roommates and ordered that I be moved to a different room in the morning. He thought I might appreciate some peace and a different view.

By nine the next morning, I was resettled but exhausted. Although the room had two beds, I was the only occupant. It was great to be free of the annoyances of the old ladies, but I was vomiting again and had a hard time enjoying the peace. On the morning of the ninth day, a nurse I'd never seen before hustled into the room and threw open the curtains.

"I've been reading your charts…I must say in all my years as a nurse I've never seen anyone take this long to get over a simple appendectomy. You'd think you were looking for an excuse not to leave…We'll just have to do something about that." She threw back my covers. "Now up you get, and after you've eaten breakfast…into the shower with you."

I told her the doctor didn't want my bandages wet because the incision was still leaking. She frowned and hurried out, returning with two clean gowns, a washcloth, and a robe. "I assume you'll be able to shower without assistance?" I was beginning to feel I would as soon be cared for by Jan as this nurse, but managed to follow her instructions. When the doctor arrived, she hurried him along and told him I was so much better that she was recommending I be sent home the next day. He seemed concerned, but didn't contradict her.

In the afternoon I was startled awake from a heavy sleep. Bettilyn was sitting in the chair by the window looking at me. In my drowsy state I couldn't read the expression on her face, but I felt uneasy.

"The nurses tell me you'll be released tomorrow morning. That's good news, isn't it?" Her voice was strained. "You know that Daddy's been really busy selling the cows and quota. He thought one day he'd come see you for a minute, then we realized how stupid that would be—I mean, what would people think? You can't expect him to be put in that position, can you?" She paused as if I were supposed to say something.

For the first time in weeks, I felt like laughing hysterically. And what position would that be, I wondered—the position that he's my husband and yours, and the nurses have all guessed that? He would have come to visit a daughter, a granddaughter, someone else's sick daughter. I could have been any or all of those—in fact, I was his step-granddaughter because two of his daughters were my mothers. So, of course, he couldn't be put in *that* position! I managed to stop my racing thoughts and realized that laughter of any kind would really hurt. Instead, I turned to look at the wall. "No, of course not."

"Daddy and I have really been worried about the right place for you. Jan must have told you he had us go down to Adam's and bring Janessa Dawn home. She has her crib back there and is doing fairly well. She certainly seems to love Phoebe—they're practically inseparable. We talked about you coming back home to live, but I don't know if having both of you there is the answer. We're not sure Babette's ready to have you back. It's really a conundrum." She sounded mournful, as though burdened with a life-and-death decision.

I couldn't stand the thought of being an object of pity in my dad's home or hers. I wondered about the word "home." What did it mean, anyway? Had Bettilyn's house ever been my home?

"Do you know where Jan Dawn and I sleep at Daddy's?" I wanted her to ask me and really act as if she wanted to know. I wanted her to be my true sister wife like Mother always said sister wives should be. I wanted her to know how scared I was of trying to take care of my baby when I was still so sick, but she refused to look at me and went on as if she hadn't heard my question.

"Jan says there really isn't room for either of you to sleep there, but we have problems about Babette. You know what I mean."

"No, Bettilyn, I don't want to bother Babette. What did you and Uncle Isaac decide I should do, then? Does he want me to call him?" Bettilyn looked as shocked as if I'd caught her in a lie.

"Oh, no...Daddy will come for you in the morning. I imagine he'll tell you then. Just be out front at eleven and he'll be there—he's coming in to get feed for the calves." She left without once making eye contact.

The evening passed quietly and morning came too soon. The nurse who had looked after me since the surgery shook her head and pursed her lips as she removed the pus-soaked dressing and put a fresh bandage over my incision. She made sure I had enough antibiotics for two days and the prescription from the doctor for an additional two weeks. She gave me a small bottle of the painkillers and an envelope containing three sleeping pills. I nervously watched the clock and told her I didn't want to miss my ride. After telling me she wasn't supposed to allow patients to check out on their own, she walked me to the front door and left me there with my bag.

I kept looking at the big black clock in the foyer. By ten past eleven I was distraught. Uncle Isaac was never late, and I didn't know what to do. I was wishing I had phoned him, after all. I flashed to the times Bettilyn had told Lydia that Uncle Isaac wanted her to do one thing, when he really wanted her to do something completely different. Sometimes he wouldn't forgive Lydia for months. I suddenly felt as if a giant spider were tangling me in her web as a feast for her children. I realized I'd better check the parking lot. My overnight bag felt heavier with each step I took down the hill. There in the lot was the big blue three-ton truck with Uncle Isaac at the wheel. I knocked on the door.

He jumped and rolled down his window. "What on earth did you do that for? Can't you see I'm waiting here! And you're still dawdling. Get on it!" He watched as I struggled to climb in, and started backing the truck up before I got the door shut. "It's a good thing I picked up what I needed before I came for you, or I'd really be running late...So what do you have to say for yourself?"

I didn't have a clue what he was asking—whether he wanted to know how I was feeling, to explain why I was late, or to apologize for my sins and ask for forgiveness.

"I'm sorry I was late. Bettilyn said you'd pick me up out front. I didn't realize I was to come to the parking lot." When he said nothing, I babbled nervously, "She told me you were trying to decide where I'm supposed to live now. She says Babette isn't happy to have me come back. Did you decide this morning what I'm to do?"

He turned on me. "Not this old crap again! What on earth are you talking about? I didn't say anything about Babette. You've got a wild imagination, girl, and you better learn how to curb it. Look at the trouble it's gotten you into already…great saints alive!"

For the remainder of the silent drive to Lister, I pulled further into my corner of the cab. I was completely unsure about what he wanted now. He stopped on the hill by Bettilyn's house, waited wordlessly while I got out, then drove off. I entered the house to the sound of Phoebe singing a beautiful little song to Janessa, who was trying to copy her. I noticed that Bettilyn had redecorated the walls and changed doorways since I had lived here. Phoebe looked up, brought Janessa to me, and hugged me with a glad hello. When I told her I couldn't lift the baby, she offered to play with her while I rested. I forced myself to ask about Babette. A shadow flickered in Phoebe's eyes, but she didn't answer. I never asked again.

I forgot the prophet was coming for spring conference and was suddenly even more worried about being in Bettilyn's house. The next day was Saturday, and I made a concerted effort to stay out of the way of the preparations. I still had a fever and was running low on bandages. Each time I changed one, it was soaked with slimy fluid. I managed to corner Uncle Isaac with the antibiotic prescription. "Please get these for me…the doctor says I have to take them for two weeks. He says the incision isn't healing."

He was furious. He knew I'd been trying to get his attention, but he'd managed to avoid being in the same room with me. As I looked on in horror, he grabbed the prescription slip and crumpled it. "You're always whining about something. I don't think you need these at all. Just get some fresh air and exercise, and you'll be fine!"

I tried to stop him from leaving, but he batted my hand out of the way and was gone. I needed to ask him if we could talk about the misunderstanding—if that's what it was—but then the priesthood men arrived and nothing else mattered. I had my cot in the narrow laundry room again and chose to stay there most of the time. Babette avoided me; when we did meet eye to eye, her face was an inscrutable mask. Except for Phoebe and Emilia, everyone in the family treated me as if I were invisible. Emilia actually asked me how I was feeling a couple of times and told me I wasn't looking good.

I was lying on my cot in the dark when I heard Uncle Isaac and the prophet talking. As I gingerly hoisted myself up to go to the bathroom, I could see into the afternoon light of the living room. Uncle Isaac handed a huge roll of bills to the prophet.

"I've decided to do it this way," Uncle Isaac was saying. "I got a lot more than I expected for the dairy quota and figured you could use this a lot more than that bunch of bickering family. I've named Adam the executor of my will, and I wish him luck." Uncle Isaac chuckled as the prophet took the wad of money and stuffed it in his jacket pocket. "Adam prides himself on his peacemaking abilities. I think that'll be the legacy I'll end up giving him—lots of feuds to settle. He's already got two of my daughters. Let's see what fun he'll have with the rest of the family—boys and all. I know he always thought he could have done a better job than I did with Naomi." He chuckled again.

The prophet nodded and said, "We'll see...We'll see."

I couldn't go to church, so Phoebe took Janessa Dawn with her. I looked for clean rags to cover my weeping incision, then went to bed. When I woke up, I was shocked to see it was the middle of the night. Somehow I had slept through the entire meal, the afternoon activities, and the goodbyes—now everyone was sleeping. I wandered the house and almost stumbled over Bettilyn asleep on one of her hooked rugs on the floor. She didn't wake up, and I slipped back to my cot. About ten o'clock in the morning, Uncle Isaac shuffled into the house. He looked startled at the sight of me. I begged him to tell me if it was really his final word I was to stay here. I told him I didn't know how to deal with the hostile family, and I was afraid I still needed antibiotics.

His face turned crimson and he threw up his hands. "You know, I really don't give a damn! You don't have a clue, do you? You people need to grow up. Just do what you want...I don't care what it is. I told Bettilyn what to tell you, and you can't seem to get it into your thick skull. Don't talk to me again!"

Before I could manage one more word, he was gone. Shaking violently, I made up my mind to go back to my rooms in the school. Most of my things were still there, and with a bit of food we could survive until I could talk to Daddy and figure out what to do. Laman, Celeste, Grace, and their children had all gone to Colorado City to stay with Celeste's family for the summer, so the telephone had been disconnected. I'd have a hard time getting hold of Daddy, but I knew I couldn't stay in this unfriendly house, no matter what.

I loaded Janessa, some bread, milk, and a few jars of fruit into an old baby buggy and started out. I felt heavy, the way Mother must have felt before she died when she took hours to get from one place to another. I stopped twice, took Janessa out of the buggy, and waited in the bushes until I got my strength back. I moved the food inside, thankful to see the fridge in the school kitchen was still working. After I fed Janessa, I crawled up the stairs and put her to bed. I dozed through snippets of a nightmare with the far-off cry of a baby, thinking someone should come to help it. Then I woke up and it was quiet. I drifted off until the sun was shining through the vines on the window and I could hear Janessa Dawn sobbing.

I cried out, knowing I had to find my daughter. She crawled to the side of the bed. Shrieking now, she dragged herself up. The moment she came near, I could smell her dirty diaper. I wondered why I felt sticky and pulled myself up enough to see that my nightgown and the sheets were soaked with pus. This time it was streaked with blood.

I heard voices and tried to call. Two of Celia's girls, the same ones who saw angels during the baptism at the river, came into the room. Their faces filled with contempt when they saw Jan Dawn in her wretched state. Noticing the mess on my bed, they gasped in horror. They gathered the baby up and took her to the bathroom. When I saw her again, she was clean, hungrily sucking a bottle and gripping a crust of hard brown bread.

Lucia and Leora talked quietly to each other, then disappeared. When they came back, they said Irene was coming to get me. They asked me why I was crazy enough to come to an empty building with no phone, especially when I was sick as a dog and had a baby I couldn't look after. When I tried to find an answer, all I could do was cry.

The girls helped me out of my soiled nightgown and into some clothes. I couldn't decide what to do about the weeping wound, because as fast as I put in a clean rag to cover it, it soaked through. I finally stuffed a flannelette diaper into my underpants and held it in place. Lucia and Leora said they were going with Uncle Isaac to watch the Blossom Festival parade in Creston. Before they left, they moved me to the rocking chair. I gathered my dignity and thanked them but really wanted to beg them to stay; I was so afraid of being alone. Tears trickled down my face as I heard the school door bang shut. Janessa munched on her piece of dry bread and played happily at my feet.

Soon, one of Daddy's battered trucks roared up to the school, and Irene bounded up the stairs. "All right, Deb, I'm here to gather you up again! We thought you were staying at Dad's, then I find you here in a moldy heap. What'll it be next? I suppose you have some stuff to bring...where is it?"

Mortified, I motioned to the pile of wet, bloody blankets, the soiled diapers, and the nightgown.

She shrugged. "Well, it's not the grossest mess I've ever had to clean up—let's get on with it." She tied the clothes in a bundle, tucked the baby under her arm, and headed down the stairs. I leaned heavily on the walls until I got outside. The distance between me and the truck seemed impossible. My little sister Rebecca jumped out, gave me her shoulder to lean on, then helped me get in.

When Irene brought me up to date on the latest battles between her and Elsa, and Jan's newest proclamations for the family, I tried to respond appropriately but wasn't sure I made sense.

"You look like something the dog's been worrying," Irene said. "Adam will have to decide if you should go back to the doctor...I can't have you kicking the bucket right in front of me. Who on earth would be Jan Dawn's mother? She's just as ornery as the rest of us, and goodness knows with all the work I've got, you need to be her mother."

The doctor was furious when he saw the mess I was in. He removed the few stitches that hadn't torn through. "Well, you'll never enter a bikini contest after this heals." He shook his head. "I'm not sure I understand you people. If you'd filled that prescription I left at the hospital for you, you'd be fully recovered by now." I didn't have an answer for him.

For the next week I didn't get far from my little corner of Nettie's room. I was slowly getting stronger, but still had trouble chasing after Jan Dawn and getting myself upstairs at mealtimes.

Late one night after Daddy had been at the ranch, he visited me. He was very serious. He spoke in a whisper because fourteen of my sisters were asleep in other beds. "Isaac has taken a turn for the worse, Daughter, and they don't think he's going to last much longer. He was out to Vancouver to be checked by the doctors. They think the leukemia has advanced and the chemotherapy would just cause him more misery." He settled onto the floor with his back to the closet, worrying his thick mop of graying hair. He held my hand. "Uh, I know you might be feeling like you should be over there…to try to see him…he is your husband and all…But with all the recent trouble and misunderstandings, it's probably best for you to just stay here and get better." He looked at me for a long time. "Wouldn't you say?"

I struggled to ward off tears. "I guess I don't know what I'd do over there. I'd kind of like to have Janessa see him…would it be possible?"

Daddy shifted. "Well, Mother Jan is going to be there a lot helping Bettilyn. I suppose she could take Janessa Dawn to see him sometime if they think he's up to it. He's not in the hospital yet, but I expect he will be by the end of the week. The pain has come on awful fast—worse than it's been before—and he's really weak." When he spoke again, his voice was trembling. "I can't help thinking about your mother, Deb. I try my best, but she'd be a great comfort to you." I couldn't look at him.

"You can't tell anyone right now, but I'm the executor of Isaac's will. We'll take care of you. A woman's supposed to go back under the direction of her father when something happens to her husband. We'll just keep you here until the prophet decides what to do with you. The priesthood always takes care of its widows and orphans." Daddy tried to smile. "You remember Uncle Marion Hammond's favorite saying—there's no such thing as a dog or a single woman in the celestial kingdom. I can promise you everything will be all right." I thanked him and he mumbled he had to make the rounds to say goodnight to the mothers.

My incision finally stopped weeping. Within a couple of days, I felt well enough to help with the breakfast. I buttered five dozen pieces of toast as they came out of the oven, while Irene served up three big pots of porridge and six platters of scrambled eggs. After Daddy organized a crew of kids to pull weeds in the potato patch and took the rest to the shop with him, I got an opportunity to talk to Jan. She was in such a hurry to be on her way that it took all my nerve to approach her. When I asked if she would take Jan Dawn over to see Uncle Isaac, she turned on me. "You really expect a lot from people, don't you? You never cease to dumbfound me. After the trouble you've caused in Daddy's family, it takes unmitigated gall to ask for anything!" She rushed away without a backward glance.

Irene was kneading a jumbo-sized stainless steel bowl of bread dough. She shook her head. "I've never seen anyone such a beggar for punishment. What do you want the little brat to see Dad for? He didn't pay attention to her when you were right there in the same house. I know how it goes." Even though her words were harsh, her tone was so kind I wasn't prepared for it. "Just let her play with all the raunchy kids here. She's too young to remember him, anyway. She's just as lucky—some of us who are older don't have too many fond memories."

The next few days went by in a blur. Daddy told me that Uncle Isaac had been taken to the hospital and visitors were restricted. Since there was still a lot of concern about the townspeople knowing I was his wife, Daddy thought it best that I not go to see him. I was surprised because it was 1974 and he'd been bragging about his plural wives for a long time. I wished he could see I needed a few minutes alone with Uncle Isaac. I was desperate to reach some understanding with the man I was bound to before he went into the next life. Would he want me by his side in his kingdom when I died, or would I be in his horse barns with Naomi dunging them out for eternity?

Two days later Jan searched me out after breakfast. She said Daddy wanted me to help her with baby Denise when she took her to Trail to see the plastic surgeon about the terrible scar she got from sucking on the extension cord. Jan said Ophelia was about to deliver so she couldn't make the trip. "We'll be leaving in ten minutes." I was surprised Jan would agree to take me with her.

I rushed to ask Irene if she'd watch Jan Dawn. She brushed me away with her backward humor. "No, of course not. I'll throw her in the pond and get rid of her for good…Why do you ask stupid questions all the time?"

The trip over the Creston Salmo Summit was uneventful. Jan didn't say a word to me on the way over, but on the way back it became clear why I'd been singled out to go with her. She started in about what a good man Daddy was. I didn't dare interrupt to ask which daddy she was talking about—hers or mine. She said Daddy would be taking care of everyone once her daddy was dead. She said there was a will, and Daddy was the executor. They expected trouble from Lydia and Naomi since they weren't named in it. She said her daddy had told my daddy he wanted all the wives and children to have ten acres of land, even though for simplicity and the sake of the government, everything was being willed to Bettilyn. She said I wasn't to worry about my or Janessa Dawn's inheritance, because the prophet and Daddy would take care of us.

As Jan talked on, I stared over the sheer cliffs, admiring the colors of the rocks. For a flash, I saw myself standing on a knoll on my very own ten acres of land, the wind blowing through my hair. It was replaced by the image of Uncle Roy stuffing the hefty roll of bills into his jacket pocket.

We were back in Creston by mid-afternoon. Daddy had instructed Jan to drop me off at the hospital. He promised he'd see if I could visit Uncle Isaac—even if it had to be with other people.

Daddy's truck was there in the parking lot, but my heart sank when I saw that Lem's was, too. I had no idea which way to go to find Uncle Isaac's room. In the main hall I heard a hiss, and Celeste darted out from the little chapel room. She pulled me back in with her and informed me that Bettilyn and Lem were with Uncle Isaac now in the intensive care room near the nurses' station, and I shouldn't bother them. I pulled away, peeling her hands off as she clutched at me.

When I found the room where Bettilyn, Lem, and Daddy were hovering over Uncle Isaac, I peered through the windows, then went around to stand in the doorway. Uncle Isaac was breathing with a deep rattle in his throat. There was blood coming from his nose and ears and dribbling from the side of his mouth. The irregular beep, beep of the heart monitor penetrated the unsettling silence; the smell of blood and something else I couldn't identify permeated everything. Bettilyn looked straight at me but gave no indication that she saw me.

A commotion at the nurses' station distracted my attention. It was Lydia informing the nurses in no uncertain terms that she should have been called sooner. She grabbed my arm and turned me around. "You need to go to that room down the hall. There are things I must do here…Isaac made me promise…he's just about gone. You'll be all right, Deb. I'm sorry." She swept into the room and ordered everyone to get out and leave her alone with Isaac. Lem and Bettilyn protested, but their words quickly died under Lydia's insistence. She closed the curtains all the way around the room. I stifled a laugh when I visualized the look Lydia must have given my sister wife and her son to shut them up. They almost beat me down the hall, and Lem kept walking right out the front door.

When I got to the chapel, Celeste was sputtering indignantly that Lydia had kicked Bettilyn out of the room. Bettilyn's face was white except for splotchy red spots on her cheeks; her lips were drawn. Emilia and some of Daddy's boys sat quietly in the corner. Daddy was across from them sitting with his head in his hands. Emilia asked me if I wanted to go to the shop, and Daddy nodded at me to go with her and the others.

His rambling machinery building on the hill overlooking the

Creston flats had been in operation for only a few weeks, and this was the first time I had been there. As we drove up, fierce thunderclouds rolled in with a wild wind that had the trees bending frightfully. We got safely inside and moved upstairs to the office windows that looked out over the valley. For twenty minutes we watched wild bolts of lightning streak from the heavens and listened to the deafening claps of thunder that shook the walls. The heavy rain flooded potholes and washed down the road like a river. From a dark corner, someone said flatly, "Boy, if this has anything to do with Dad's dying, his spirit is having one devil of a time leaving his body."

As suddenly as the storm blew in it dispersed, and the wind died to leave an eerie calm. It was four-thirty when the telephone rang. Emilia answered it. As she hung up, her voice was trembling. "It's over. He's gone." After a short silence, another voice echoed from across the room. "It's just like him to pick this time of day. It's chore time—he'd be rounding us up to milk the cows if we still had the dairy."

Everyone cried for the rest of the day, but by the next morning we all had to get busy just to meet the demands of nine children under six, the garden, and Daddy's shop. The fifteen older kids had left for their jobs, and Jan was with her mother, planning a funeral that would be fraught with challenges. We wondered what kind of service would accommodate everyone—our people with the prophet and apostles, relatives from the church, and the gentile farmers and neighbors from the Creston Valley.

I spent the morning washing dishes and churning butter. After lunch it was naptime for everyone under five. I was lying with Jan Dawn in our little corner when I heard the basement door open. It was Brent. Standing awkwardly with his hand on the doorknob, he stared at me. "I've been trying to catch up with you. I've been staying at the ranch most of the time and...I was worried how you were doing." He sat on a bed and stared at his feet. "I work at the shop a lot—I think I'll be a good mechanic like Daddy—but I can't live with Jan anymore. Are you sure you'll be all right living here with Uncle Isaac gone?"

The tears I had been battling won, and I melted in a heap on the opposite bed. "Oh, Brent, I don't know! I'm afraid I'm not much good for anything but trouble. I thought I wouldn't have to be afraid of Jan anymore when I married Uncle Isaac, but boy, was I wrong."

Brent moved next to me and put his arms around me. It felt good, but strange. I couldn't remember having a conversation with him since we were little, just after Mother died. We never talked about how we felt about anything. Over the years I had made up conversations in my head and tried to figure out how to tell him stories about Mother because I was afraid he'd forget her. Now, he was shaking with a rage I'd never seen in him before. When he spoke, I realized the depth of his anger.

"I hate her so bad sometimes, Deb! I hate her for the times she beat you and I couldn't help you, and I hate her for beating me until I thought I'd die. I never knew for sure what I did wrong, but I was afraid all the time. It's like she could smell the fear, and even knowing we were afraid of her made her want to beat us more." His grip tightened on my shoulders.

I thought back to that horrible day years ago, the day I ran away over gentile land to Jeanie's house. "How can you call her Mother, then? I still can't…and I hoped it was easier for you and Nettie because you could."

At fifteen, Brent was strong, nearly a grown man, but he was crying now. "I hated calling her Mother, but the word doesn't mean anything to me anymore. All these years I've kept my mouth shut when she got mad, and I keep my mouth shut now, but you have to promise me, Deb, if she does anything to hurt you or Jan Dawn, you let me know. Somehow I'll help you. I'll find a way, and you won't have to stay with her. Dad always says he can stop her, but it never works…Just promise me!"

We held one another with our tears mixing on our cheeks and in our hair. I wondered what Mother would think of us now: her little Brent, unable to live at home, and me barely eighteen, a widow living with the disgrace of a failed calling. We would see what the prophet and Daddy needed us to do next. God had to have a plan for us.

"Brent, I promise...but I want you to be all right, too. Are you okay over there? Every time I try to think about what's right and what's wrong and try to make sense of things, I'm afraid I'll go crazy. I just have to keep doing simple things and making sure Jan Dawn's all right. I've been a terrible mother, and she's not even two years old. I can't seem to come close to being like our own good mother."

Our tears stopped at the same time—as if there was only so much time for crying. Brent wiped his face on a blanket, and I wiped mine on my skirt. "It's weird at the ranch," he said. "I can be one of the big boys there and have a good time, but everyone thinks you're crazy, and it's like they don't remember I'm your brother. I love you, Deb. I always will. I'm sorry it's been so hard to show you."

He hugged me one last time, and then he was gone. I stared mindlessly at the patchwork quilt on the other bed until Jan Dawn staggered out of our corner whimpering and rubbing her eyes. At half-past three Irene declared she wasn't going to make anyone go back to their work crews; if the big girls would take the little kids and disappear, they could play till supper time. I asked her if it would be all right for me to go outside for a while.

She stared at me. "Do what you want—you don't have to ask me. You have to know how irritating that can be...just get!" Her voice was kind, but I found it so unsettling. Right now, I wanted to be told what to do. I wanted direction. I found myself fighting tears.

I went out the back door to sit on the cement steps until I could regain control of myself. With my eyes closed, I tried to picture sitting on these very steps waiting for Mother to make her way up from the river. The shouts of children filtered into my consciousness. I glanced at the top of the sloped cement walls that led into the basement entry where three little brothers stared wide-eyed at me. Jan Dawn was at the bottom of the other slope trying to crawl up to sit with the sisters already clustered on top. There was an eight-foot drop—one side to grass and the other side to cement.

I heard soft voices in conversation just below me in the pit between the stairs and the wall. One of the aged lilac bushes that had once been my favorite place to watch swallowtail butterflies had grown so tall it had created a cool cave in its shadow. I slid over so I could see where the voices were coming from and saw Rebecca and Rena sitting on either side of a huge toad. I used to find toads around the damp mossy corners of the house and down the bank in the swamps, and even tried to kiss one like in the fairy tales. This creature was at least a foot square. Rebecca and Rena were stroking it and trying to decide if they would really get warts like the big boys said. When they saw me, they told me they were keeping their pet safe because the boys were going to squish him with a rock if they caught him alone. They assured me they had a safe place to hide him when they weren't with him, and that he wouldn't run away because he was so big. They were probably right. When he tried to move, he could barely drag his heavy belly along the ground.

I snapped out of my trance when I realized two more of my sisters were coaxing Jan Dawn to climb the wall. By the time I got to her, she was halfway up, her little fingers grasping at the crevices in the coarse cement. When I pulled her off, she kicked and screamed until I took her hand and walked with her down the little road to the bottom of the pond where she could splash in the waterfall that flowed into the creek. We were followed by all fifteen of the little people who'd been playing on the cement walls. Before long, the children were showing me how they could sneak over the waterfall to the cliffs above or reach across the pond to gather frog eggs and water spiders. For a brief moment, I realized I hardly knew these brothers and sisters who were trying to impress me.

I was watching Jan Dawn puddle in the water when I heard someone call my name. I squinted into sunlight that filtered through the dense cover and tensed the moment I saw it was Nephi. I took Janessa by the hand. All week long, his accusing voice had played like a stuck record in my mind—I'd be the one held accountable for the death of the Good Father. He looked at the children and our surroundings, then nodded as if his approval kept the sun shining and the water flowing.

He stared coldly at me. "Well, I guess you're here for now—I'll allow it. But you must know I'm watching you. It looks like your dad will be taking care of things for a while and will be the one working with our prophet." He focused on Jan Dawn. "I want you to remember that she's my father's daughter, and one day I'll be in a position to determine what happens to her." He smiled. "I mean that." He paused, waiting for a reply. When I didn't answer him, he scooped up a clod of dirt and crushed it in his hand. He turned and retreated up the trail.

I watched him disappear from sight, telling myself I must concentrate on what I'd been taught all my life. Heavenly Father had a plan for me and this had to be part of it. Daddy had assured me that the prophet was going to be using him to carry on the Lord's work in Canada, and I only had to prepare myself to be as sweet as possible.

I returned my attention to what was real right now—this pond, the forest, and the sunlight filtering through the trees. It all held echoes of our early days here, when access was forbidden unless Mother had us by the hand. I sat on a moss-covered stump and lost myself in the smells of the leaves, the mud, and the watercress. As I watched my siblings play in this place God had created for His chosen spirits, I could believe all would be well. I knelt at the edge of the creek and picked a handful of flowers—forget-me-nots, baby's breath, and starflowers. In the middle of my bouquet were five large dandelions. A group of my brothers and sisters stared at me as I ate the heads off the bold yellow plants. One of my sisters asked me if she could taste one, too, seeing as I liked them so much.

Debbie Palmer was born in Brooks, Alberta, and taken at an early age into the polygamous community (now called Bountiful) near Creston, British Columbia. At fifteen she was assigned as sixth wife to the group's leader, who was fifty-five years old. After his death in 1974 she was assigned consecutively to two other men in the group.

She is the mother of eight children and the oldest of forty-seven brothers and sisters. She escaped the cult in 1988—one of the first women to leave any of the polygamous groups with all her children. The first few years on the outside were spent accessing counseling and supports for herself and the children.

From 1991 when she presented a paper to the "First National Conference on Women in a Violent Society" to the present, Debbie has worked as a researcher and consultant. The subject of several documentaries and news articles, she has been a speaker at conferences such as the American Family Federation and West Coast LEAF Organization. She has worked to educate and lobby government on interventions and education inside polygamous communities and has met internationally with human rights activists on this topic. Her main areas of expertise and research are fundamentalist Mormon polygamous communities, relationship violence prevention, community crime prevention, and issues of poverty and education in closed communities. She is the author of short stories and poems.

Photo by Geri Buchanan

Dave Perrin was raised in Casino, a small community nestled in the hills near Trail, British Columbia. He attended Selkirk College in Castlegar, the University of British Columbia, and the Western College of Veterinary Medicine at Saskatoon, Saskatchewan.

He graduated as a veterinarian in 1973 and practiced in the Creston Valley until 1998. After a year in Hawaii, where he began writing his first book about the profession he loved, he returned to his farm in Lister, B.C. He established Dave's Press and has published three books of veterinary adventures: *Don't Turn Your Back in the Barn* (2000), *Dr. Dave's Stallside Manner* (2001), and *Where Does It Hurt?* (2003).

In 1982 he married a woman who, as a teenager, had broken away from the Mormon fundamentalist community in Lister with members of her family. He met Debbie Palmer shortly after his marriage and followed her tribulations over the ensuing years. During his career, Dr. Perrin worked with and provided veterinary services for individuals from the community, which came to be known as Bountiful.

For more information, for comments, or to order autographed copies of this book or any of Dave Perrin's Adventures of a Country Vet series visit our Web site at:

davespress.com

Phone: 250-428-0701
E-mail: dave@davespress.com
or write to:
Dave's Press Inc.
Box 616, Lister
British Columbia
Canada V0B 1Y0

Dave Perrin's books are distributed by Sandhill Book Marketing Ltd. of Kelowna, B.C.